Anonymous

Eminent Arbroathians

Sketches Historical, Genealogical, And Biographical - 1178-1894

Anonymous

Eminent Arbroathians

Sketches Historical, Genealogical, And Biographical - 1178-1894

ISBN/EAN: 9783744725354

Printed in Europe, USA, Canada, Australia, Japan

Cover: Foto ©ninafisch / pixelio.de

More available books at **www.hansebooks.com**

EMINENT ARBROATHIANS:

BEING

SKETCHES HISTORICAL, GENEALOGICAL,
AND BIOGRAPHICAL,

1178—1894.

BY J. M. M'BAIN,

F. S. A., SCOT.,

Author of "Arbroath: Past and Present," "Arbroath Poets,"
"Bibliography of Arbroath Periodical Literature,"
&c., &c.

Arbroath:
BRODIE & SALMOND, PRINTERS AND PUBLISHERS.

1897.

PREFACE.

NOTWITHSTANDING the title of this volume, it claims to possess a good deal more than merely local interest. The sketches of "Eminent Arbroathians" aim at telling the life-stories of some of the sons and citizens of Arbroath who have taken a prominent part in the direction of the nation's and the world's affairs, who have become "Eminent Arbroathians" through being eminent Scotsmen or distinguished British subjects. To fulfil this purpose, the author has had to deal with a vast amount of historical material beyond that which concerns the chronicler of merely local history.

In dealing with the family history of the representative men who are the subjects of the sketches in the volume, full advantage has, of course, been taken of all available local records. Through the courtesy of the Officers of the various Guilds and Incorporations, the author has been enabled to gather from their chronicles a great body of information which is at once interesting and important. It throws light not only upon the careers of the men immediately associated with it, but upon the social history of the community. In this connection, the author desires to thank very specially Mr W. K. Macdonald, the Town Clerk of Arbroath, for valuable aid rendered in examination of the Records and Registers of the Burgh. He has also to acknowledge the kindness of many friends—descendants and other relatives of the subjects of several of the sketches—for many interesting items of information, and for liberty to consult family papers and other documents. To several of these friends, too, he is indebted for copies of portraits included in the volume.

In his consultation of historical volumes, &c., the author has been indebted to the courtesy of Dr Richard Garnett and other officials of the British Museum. To Dr Joseph Anderson, of the Society of Antiquaries of Scotland, he has also been indebted for valuable information.

PREFACE—Continued.

He has also to express his gratitude to Mr J. B. Salmond for most valuable assistance in the preparation of the historical introduction, and to Mr Norman M'Bain for painstaking labour in the compilation of the index.

The author takes this opportunity of correcting a mistake—an unimportant one—into which he has been led. In the sketch of Sir Peter Young, he says (page 78, line 20) that "Sir Peter predeceased Dr Philip by about a month." In making this statement, he was following Dr Scott's "Fasti," where it is stated that Dr Philip died in February, 1628. In searching the Burgh Registers for material for his sketch of the Philips of Almerieclose, the author discovered that Dr Philip died in September, 1627. As the sheets containing the article on Sir Peter Young had then been printed, he was unable to correct this mistake in the text. There is also an error on page 206, line 11—for "eldest," read "second."

J. M. M'BAIN.

BRITISH LINEN COMPANY BANK HOUSE,
   ARBROATH, *May, 1897.*

CONTENTS.

	PAGE
ARBROATH IN HISTORY,	11
DAVID BEATON, Abbot of Arbroath,	33
WALTER MYLN of Lunan,	45
JAMES MELVILLE, Protestant Reformer,	53
SIR PETER YOUNG of Seaton,	63
THE PHILIPS of Almericlose—	
HENRIE PHILPE,	81
JAMES PHILIP (1),	88
JAMES PHILIP (2),	90
JAMES PHILIP (3),	93
JAMES PHILIP (4),	100
JOHN PHILIP (5),	101
JOHN OUCHTERLONY of the Guynd,	103
HARRY MAULE of Kelly ("Earl Harie" of Panmure),	113
DAVID PIERSON of Lochlands (Author of "The Varieties"),	155
WILLIAM AIKMAN of Lordburn and Cairnie,	171
Provost JOHN WALLACE, Pioneer of Local Enterprise,	183
WILLIAM FULLERTON LINDSAY CARNEGIE of Spynie and Boysack,	201
The ARROTT FAMILY of Dumbarrow and Almericlose,	223
WILLIAM ARROTT, M.A., M.D.,	228
DAVID ARROTT, M.D.,	232
JAMES ARROTT, M.D.,	239
Professor WILLIAM SHARPEY, M.D., LL.D., F.R.S.	244

CONTENTS—Continued.

NEIL ARNOTT, M.D., LL.D., F.R.S., &c. (Physician Extraordinary to the Queen), 251
ALEXANDER BALFOUR, Poet and Novelist, - - - - 265
JAMES CHALMERS, Inventor of the Adhesive Postage Stamp, - - 275
Rev. THOMAS GUTHRIE of Arbirlot, - - - - - 285
Rev. ROBERT LEE of Inverbrothock, - - - - - 303
Rev. JAMES M'COSH of the Abbey Church, - - - - 317
Rev. JAMES LUMSDEN of Inverbrothock and of Barry, - - - 333
Rev. WILLIAM WILSON of Carmyllie, - - - - 345
JAMES BOWMAN LINDSAY of Carmyllie (Electrician and Linguist), - 359
Rev. PATRICK BELL, LL.D., of Carmyllie (Inventor of the Reaping Machine), 363
DAVID MILLER, Author of "Arbroath and its Abbey," - - - 379
FRANCIS ORMOND, M.L.C. of Victoria, - - - - - 385
PATRICK ALLAN FRASER of Hospitalfield. - - - - 393
ALEXANDER CARNEGIE KIRK, LL.D., F.R.S.E., Naval Engineer, - 407
ALEXANDER BROWN, LL.D., the Arbroath Astronomer, - - - 415

LIST OF PORTRAITS.

	FACING PAGE
DAVID BEATON, Abbot of Arbroath,	33
SIR PETER YOUNG of Seaton,	63
HARRY MAULE of Kelly,	113
WILLIAM AIKMAN of Lordburn and Cairnie,	171
WILLIAM FULLERTON LINDSAY CARNEGIE,	201
WILLIAM ARROTT, M.A., M.D.,	228
DAVID ARROTT, M.D.,	232
JAMES ARROTT, M.D.,	239
Professor WILLIAM SHARPEY, M.D., LL.D., F.R.S.,	244
NEIL ARNOTT, M.D, LL.D, F.R.S., &c,	251
JAMES CHALMERS,	275
Rev. THOMAS GUTHRIE,	285
Rev. ROBERT LEE,	303
Rev. JAMES M'COSH,	317
Rev. JAMES LUMSDEN,	333
Rev WILLIAM WILSON,	345
Rev. PATRICK BELL, LL.D.,	363
DAVID MILLER,	379
FRANCIS ORMOND, M.L.C. of Victoria,	385
PATRICK ALLAN FRASER, H.R.S.A,	393
ALEXANDER CARNEGIE KIRK, LL.D, F.R.S.E.,	407
ALEXANDER BROWN, LL.D.,	415

EMINENT ARBROATHIANS.

ARBROATH IN HISTORY.

THE common possession of a rich heritage of memories, it has been well said, is one of the two things essential to the principle of nationality. "A nation, like the individual," says Ernest Renan, "is the outcome of a long past of efforts, and sacrifices, and devotion. A heroic past, great men, glory—these form the social capital upon which the national idea may be founded. To have common glories in the past, a common will in the present; to have done great things together, to will to do the like again—such are the essential conditions for the making of a people." To this necessary "social capital" Arbroath, through prominent citizens who had found their birthplace or home within her borders, contributed in most creditable measure in the days when the foundations of Scottish nationality were permanently fixed.

It has been the glory and strength of Scotland that, throughout her history, as has been specially demonstrated at many critical moments in her career as a nation, she has been able to draw, not only the rank and file of her fighting forces, but the statesmen and kirkmen needed to control and direct, patriotically and resolutely, movements of extreme importance, from all clans, communities, and classes in the country. The ancient burgh of Aberbrothock, and the neighbourhood immediately associated with it in political, ecclesiastical, and industrial life, have contributed honourably to the ranks of the history-makers of the nation. The burgh itself has been the home of leaders in kirk and state whose names are household words in Scottish history; its boundaries encircle the theatre of more than one event in the nation's career which stands as a red-letter day in the calendar of every leal-hearted Scot. It was the Apostle Paul's boast that he was "a citizen of no mean city." A man does not choose the place of his birth; and it is better that he should be an honour to it, than that it should be a subject of boast to him. But no native of Arbroath need hesitate to regard and speak with honour of the place of his nativity. The distinguished sons—native-born and adopted—whom she has reared, and who have gone out from her borders to share in the upbuilding of national strength and influence, and in the promotion of the manifold progress of the world, have done good service for their country and their kind, and have made their native place, and what has really been, in many cases, their *alma mater*, honourable in the records of Scotland. In the roll of countrymen, gathered both from castle and cot, who have, in the course of the centuries, stood

"A wall of fire around our much-loved isle,"

the names which are intimately associated with Arbroath, taken together, represent a share in national history the record of which may well be remembered with pride by all who are connected with the ancient Abbey town.

The choice by King William the Lion of the beautiful plateau which, in the twelfth century, lay behind the fishing village at the mouth of Brothock stream in Angus, as the site of the magnificent Abbey which he founded in memory of Thomas à Becket, first brought the name of Aberbrothock into history. The foundation of the Abbey was laid in 1178; it was not completed till 1233, nearly twenty years after the remains of its royal founder—who had made its erection the chief work of his life—had been laid to rest in front of its High Altar. King William and his immediate successors, the Alexanders, gave it great wealth; the Abbacy of Aberbrothock became, and for four centuries continued to be, one of the highest and most influential offices in the kingdom. The occupation of it excited the ambition, and gave opportunity for the exercise of the talents, of ecclesiastics and statesmen who were the leading history-makers of their time. Looking at the magnificent ruins of the Abbey to-day, one is touched by a strong sense of the religious zeal, of the learning and loyalty, which must have been devoted to the upbuilding of the influence and splendour which belonged to the Abbey in the day of its power. It was this haunting sense of the shadow of departed glory which impressed Dr Johnson when he visited the Abbey. "These ruins," he says, "afford ample testimony of ancient magnificence. I should scarcely have regretted my journey had it afforded nothing more than a sight of Aberbrothock."

King William the Lion, his son Alexander II., and his grandson Alexander III., King Robert the Bruce, James III., James IV., James V., and that best-remembered Queen of all time, the beautiful but ill-starred Mary, Queen of Scots, must be named amongst the Abbey's royal visitors. Edward I. of England, too, enjoyed its princely hospitality oftener than once;

one may safely conjecture, however, that the enjoyment of his visits did not extend to his hosts. King William and the Alexanders frequently kept court at the Abbey, and there granted charters and dealt with other state business of high importance. During the reign of Alexander II. the Abbot and monks of Aberbrothock Abbey were able to help the king through a time of financial difficulty; and he pledged his kingly honour that the Abbey would not suffer for its services. This promise was faithfully kept.

In the remarkable progress which characterised the reigns of King William and the Alexanders, the Abbots and monks of the Abbey of Aberbrothock took a prominent and most creditable part. The first volume of the Abbey's Chartulary, the "Registrum Vetus de Aberbrothoc," issued by the Bannatyne Club, contains ample evidence of the enlightened views and civilising influence of the Abbacy. The learned editors of the volume—Mr Cosmo Innes and Mr Patrick Chalmers of Auldbar—bear testimony to this in their preface. "We do not know much of the intellectual state of the population in that age," they say of the reign of William and the peaceful times of the two Alexanders, "but, regarding it only in a material point of view, it may safely be affirmed that Scotland at the death of King Alexander III. was more civilized and more prosperous than at any period of her existence, down to the time when she ceased to be a separate kingdom in 1707." In originating and nourishing the national strength which withstood successfully the great dangers which followed the tragic death of Alexander III., no religious house in the kingdom laboured more wisely or zealously than Aberbrothock; and when the moment of supreme peril came, when the great power of England joined in an unholy alliance with Rome to subjugate the country and extinguish the Scottish nation, in the

ARBROATH IN HISTORY.

Abbot of Aberbrothock was found the scholar and patriot worthy to stand by the noble King Robert to bid defiance to all enemies. Robert the Bruce had conquered and driven out the English invaders; Abbot Bernard vanquished Rome.

In national interest, the sixth day of April, 1320, is the date of first importance in the history of the Abbey of Aberbrothock. Upon that date — " Apud Monasterium de Abirbrothoc ; VI. die Aprilis, A.D., M,CCC,XX.," is the superscription of the historic record—the Estates of Scotland, in Parliament assembled under the presidency of King Robert the Bruce, issued the famous Declaration of Independence, drawn up by Abbot Bernard de Linton, which asserted for all time the independent nationality of the Scottish people. The Edwards of England had wasted blood and treasure beyond measure in the effort to subjugate Scotland, and incorporate it as part of their dominions. What Edward II. failed to do by force of arms, he strove to accomplish by diplomacy. The aid of His Holiness, the Pope, who was regarded as holding in his hands the right to approve or disapprove of the independence of any sovereign or people in Christendom, was called in to undo Bannockburn. The King and nobles of Scotland had determined that the independence of the Scottish nation should be asserted in unmistakable terms, and in such a way that there could be no room for doubt regarding it either in the Vatican or in the court of the English sovereign. In 1317, two cardinals arrived at the Abbey of Aberbrothock, as envoys from the Pope, bearing letters for " Robert Bruce, governing in Scotland." " These letters are not addressed to the King of Scotland," said King Robert, in effect, to the papal nuncios. " There are many named Robert Bruce in Scotland. You must tell His Holiness that letters sent to me must be addressed to the

King of Scotland." About three years later came another message threatening Bruce, and the Scottish nation, with excommunication if Edward II. were not recognised as lord-paramount. The famous Declaration issued by the Convention of Estates at Aberbrothock was the nation's reply to the Pope's threat. It is one of the most remarkable documents in Scottish national history. It is questionable, indeed, whether in the whole history of Europe in the Middle Ages there is anything to compare with it in its stalwart assertion of national independence, and the democratic spirit which inspires it. Even Sir Walter Scott, who could hardly be accused of any strong sympathy with the democratic spirit, was so struck with the enlightened patriotism of this letter to the Pope that he declared that it ought to be engraved in letters of gold in the national records of our country.

This famous Parliament of King Robert was held in the Regality Chamber of Arbroath Abbey, and was attended by the most powerful noblemen in the country. Its letter to the Pope begins by giving the names of those present. The roll includes the Earls of Fife, Moray, March, Strathorne, Lennox, Ross, Caithness, Orkney, and Sutherland; Walter, Steward of Scotland; James, Lord Douglas; Roger de Mowbray; David, Lord Brechin; Gilbert de Hay, Constable of Scotland; Robert de Keith, Marischal of Scotland, and others, the letter being given with their authority, and that of "the rest of the Barons and Freeholders, and whole community of the Kingdom of Scotland." The Declaration sets forth clearly the story of the Scottish struggle for independence, and the establishment of the kingdom, in face of the numerous invasions of enemies, concluding with a reference to the "magnificent King Edward," whose barbarities had laid waste a great part of the country. "At length," says the document, "it pleased God, who alone can heal after wounds, to restore us to liberty from those innumerable calamities by our most serene Prince, King and Lord, Robert, who, for the delivering of his people and his own rightful inheritance from the enemies' hand, did, like another Joshua or Maccabæus, most cheerfully undergo all manner of toil, hardship, and hazard. The Divine Providence, right to succession established by laws and customs of the Kingdom (which we will defend till death), and the due and lawful consent and assent of all the people, made him our King and Prince. To him, in defence of our liberty, we are bound to adhere, both by right, and by reason of his deserts, for through him has been restored the people's safety in defence of their liberties." Then follows a democratic deliverance, which, in firmness and fervour, has hardly been surpassed even in our own century. "But," says this Declaration, "if this Prince shall leave the principles he has so nobly pursued, and consent that we, or our kingdom, be subjected to the King of England, we will instantly expel him as a public enemy, and as the subverter of his own and our rights, and will choose another King, who will defend our liberties; for so long as there shall be one hundred of us alive we will never subject us to the dominion of the English. It is not glory, it is not riches, neither is it merely honour, but, above all, it is liberty for which we fight, and that no man of honour will lose but with his life." It has been recorded that the reading of this Declaration made Pope John XXII. tremble. That need not be wondered at. The turf at Bannockburn was still red with the blood that flowed there six years before; and what was said by Umphraville of the Scots as they knelt in prayer on that memorable June day, could very well be said of the authors of the Declaration.

The Declaration is evidently from the hand of Abbot Bernard, who had fought beside King Robert at Bannockburn, and sang the glories of the victory in Latin verse. For nearly twenty years he served his country as Chancellor, and proved himself as scholar, ecclesiastic, and statesman a man of great wisdom and patriotism. The Declaration, which was, of course, written in Latin, is recorded amongst the *Acta Parliamentorum Roberti I.* in the first volume of "Acts of the Parliaments of Scotland" (pp. 474-475); a most interesting *fac-simile* of the original document, which is preserved in the Register House, Edinburgh, being included in the same volume. The Declaration breathes the spirit which never yet has been conquered, and it established for all time the nationality and independence of the Scottish kingdom, which never again was questioned, even in the darkest days of its subsequent history. To have been the meeting-place of the Parliament which issued, and the home of the Statesman-Abbot who framed, such a manifesto, gives Arbroath Abbey high national renown.

The year of the Declaration marks the acme of the Abbey's power and splendour. Fifty years later, we find Abbot John Gedy devoting himself to the erection of a harbour for the port of Arbroath; and other Abbots there were who discharged with wisdom and holiness the ordinary duties of their high office, and were strong in the management of what in modern political parlance would be called "home affairs." Of Abbot William Bonkil, we read that he was "a man come of good family, meek, quiet, and zealous for peace, loving God and the Church; humble, pious, sweet-tempered, and of good-manners." Abbot Richard Guthrie, on the other hand, was "nocht active nor gaif intendens for remeid of vrangis dwne to the haly place."

"They were not all bad, and they were not all good
Who wore the Monk's girdle, and sandal, and hood."

It is true, as the editors of the Abbey Chartulary remark, that "the Abbey of Arbroath maintained its pre-eminence as among the first, if not the greatest, of Scotch religious houses down to the Reformation." "In facultatibus opulentissimae et in aedificiis munitissimae" it continued to be; but its Abbots were no longer at the centre of things in Scotland. Great national troubles were once more experienced in Scotland, and the Abbacy of Aberbrothock became the prey of each successive faction in power. It fell into the hands of David Beaton in 1524. He brought back to the Abbacy the distinction of being in touch with the centre of governing power in the country; but he was the last Abbot who discharged the clerical duties of the office. What use he made of the wealth and power which came into his hands is described in the sketch given of him in the body of this volume.

On the dark background of history created by Cardinal Beaton's inquisitorial tyranny, appeared the figure of John Knox. The "old order," represented by the Abbey of Arbroath, had sunk into hopeless corruption and decay; the spirit of liberty in Scotland, which won Bannockburn and dictated the Declaration of 1320, called loudly for its destruction. It disappeared in blood, fire, and fury which have left many memories both bitter and sweet in the heart of the Scottish nation. There is no evidence to indicate that the iconoclastic frenzy of Knox's times had anything to do with the conversion of Arbroath Abbey into a ruin. But these ruins nevertheless tell us of the inward decay and degradation of the mediæval church of Scotland, of its unfitness to meet national needs, and of the righteousness of the popular judgment which doomed it. In spite of the luxurious and profane indulgence by which monasticism brought upon itself in Scotland popular despite and final ruin, in the day of its pristine strength and purity, it was a great power for good in the national life. We must not forget that, although monasticism became associated in the day of its destruction with infamous treachery and bloodthirsty cruelty which have made its name detested in Scotland—

> Yet was the Abbey a fruitful stage,
> In the slow growth, and the ripening age
>   Of the long history of man:
> For beaming virgin, and holy child,
> Made many a fierce heart meek and mild,
>   And the mastery there of mind began.
>
> The footsore pilgrim there found rest,
> The heartsore, too, was a welcome guest,
>   And who loved books got helpful store.
> It is God who guides the world's affairs,
> And ever it rises by winding stairs,
>   Screwing its way from the less to more.
>
> He reads the story best who reads
> Ever to find some germing seeds
>   Sprouting up to a nobler end,
> And God's long patience still
> Through all the good, and through all the ill,
>   And always something in us to mend.

Arbroath has had its battle; it has been bombarded; and the great Cromwell selected it as the port for the disembarkation of troops in the stirring times of the Commonwealth. The Battle of Arbroath comes into the family history of the Lindsays, as told in the sketch given of William Fullarton Lindsay Carnegie. It occurred in January, 1445, when, as the

ARBROATH IN HISTORY.

old record puts it, the Ogilvies and Lindsays "met at the yettis of Arbroth on ane Sunday laite and faucht." The story of the bombardment is preserved in a minute of Council, dated 26th May, 1781. Captain Fall, commanding a French privateer, named the "Fearnought," brought the American struggle for independence to the bar of Arbroath harbour. He demanded from the Provost and Town Council £30,000; if that sum were not immediately tendered he would destroy the town, he said. Lindsay of Kinblethmont and several other gentlemen skilled in war armed a number of the inhabitants. Several of the Town Councillors were for buying off the Frenchman, but the majority had more pluck. They summoned aid from neighbouring towns, while they diplomatically gained time by discussing terms with the enemy. However much the inhabitants of Arbroath may have sympathised with the Americans in the war, they had nothing but determined defiance to show to the French pirate, and many of them displayed great bravery. Musket bullets were kept rattling upon the cutter's deck, until, as a local poet puts it—

> " Shatter'd and broken again bends the sail,
> And away steers bold Fall with the tide and the gale,
> While the loud peals of musketry follow him bright,
> Till the Inchcape Rock hides the " Fearnought" from our sight.

Oliver Cromwell's attempt to land troops was made in 1651. On the approach of the belligerent forces, the inhabitants were thrown into a state of great consternation, Arbroath, in the words of a Dundonian of the period being described as "a naked town." In their extremity Patrick Wallace and other leading citizens applied to Alexander Carmichael, shipowner, Dundee, for cannon. The inhabitants of the neighbourhood were also called on to help in the defence of the coast. The minutes of the Brechin Kirk-Session bear record under date of July, 1651, that there was "no session, neither sermon, this Wednesday, by reason all within the burgh was called to go to Aberbrothock to assist there against the pursuing enemy by sea." Carmichael expressed his willingness to lend his guns on receiving a guarantee for their safe return. This pledge, in the shape of a bond for £500, Patrick Wallace and his patriotic brother councillors were not slow to give. The guns were hastily sent to Arbroath, where they were so effectively used that the troops of the Protector had to seek landing elsewhere. The Arbroath men, however, were rather hurried in returning the cannon to Dundee. They were observed by the enemy, whose ships were still on the coast. The ships at once opened fire on the Arbroath detachment, who buried the cannons in the sand between Elliot and Barry, and retired beyond the range of the ships' guns. The operation was observed, and a party from the English ships landed and carried off the artillery. This gave rise to an action in the Court of Session, in which Carmichael claimed from Patrick Wallace and his compatriots restitution of the guns, or payment of the penalty, the pursuer pleading that "albeit the town of Aberbrothock did owe to the said guns the resistance they made to Cromwell's ships in three several attacks, whereas, if they had wanted guns, their town had been burned." The Court, however, gave decree in favour of Wallace and his friends, on the ground that the cannons were used in defence of the Sovereign, and that they were captured in war.

Besides the distinguished contributors to literature and other fine arts, science, and statesmanship, whose lives are sketched in this volume, there are several whose names must be mentioned at this point. John Barbour, the eminent Scottish poet, is believed to have been born in or near Arbroath about the year 1320, an appropriate year for the birth of the author of the Scottish national epic, "The Bruce." He was certainly educated at Arbroath Abbey. In his remarkable poem—the first in Scottish literature—he has given a picture of the life, character, and times of King Robert the Bruce, which, in vigorous directness of description and artistic felicity, is worthy of his English contemporary, Chaucer, at his best. Alexander Mylne, the first president of the Court of Session, was also educated at the Abbey. David Pierson's "Varieties" associates Arbroath with mediæval literature; and in later times the burgh and neighbourhood have brought forth a numerous family of poets and other authors, who have taken honourable rank in Scottish literature. Alexander Balfour, whose life and work are dealt with in this volume, is a worthy representative of the best of these contributors to the nation's literary treasures.

But, in the world of literature, Arbroath is chiefly indebted for fame to Sir Walter Scott, who, in his great novel "The Antiquary," has made the town and its neighbourhood classic ground. "Fairport," "Musselcrag," "Monkbarns," and "Knockwinnock" are better known to the people of Scotland, and the bigger world outside, than their prototypes in Angus—Arbroath, Auchmithie, Hospitalfield, and Ethie Castle; and the great red sandstone cliffs, which stand solid against the onset of the wild North Sea between Fairport and Musselcrag, have been visited by a thousand people, interested in The Antiquary, Edie Ochiltree, and Lovel, and in the scene of their heroic rescue of Sir Arthur and Miss Wardour from the devouring fury of the waves, for every ten who have been drawn thither by the geological labours of Hugh Miller and Sir Charles Lyell, popularly interesting as these scientists have made the crags and skerries of Angus. The women of Auchmithie still sell their fish after the method so admirably pictured by Sir Walter in the famous bargaining scene between Jonathan Oldbuck and Maggie Mucklebackit at Musselcrag; and all the romantic associations of St. Ruth's Priory now belong inalienably to the ruins of the Abbey of Aberbrothock. The genius of Sir Walter has illuminated the ancient Abbey and all its surroundings.

It may be worth mentioning at this point that there is some reason for believing that Sir Walter Scott, if he did not find the prototype, had a good deal of the character of his Edie Ochiltree suggested to him by an Arbroath worthy, whose experiences provided just such material as the author of "The Antiquary" gathered with infinite industry and delight wherever he went. Andrew Gemmels, no doubt, suggested the blue-gown profession of the immortal Edie; but the experiences of Johnnie Palmer of Arbroath may have suggested many picturesque points in his character. Palmer was born in Arbroath about 1723. His grandfather was out with Dundee, and his father with Mar; and John himself joined Lord Ogilvie's second battalion in the rising of 1745. He was at Culloden, but was not brought into action. After the Rebellion was crushed, he joined the Scottish Army in Holland. On leaving the Army, he returned to Forfarshire, where he worked as a farm-servant, until old age came upon him. He then took to wandering about the country as a gaberlunzie, living on the bounty of the gentry and farmers, to whom he was always a welcome visitor, his budget of stories and his ready wit making him a great favourite. He died in Arbroath on the 13th of May, 1811, and his remains, it has been said, were followed to the grave by the "best in Arbroath." Among the many local stories which he used to tell was one relating to the celebration of Prince Charlie's birthday in Arbroath, on the 20th December, 1745 (O.S.). According to Johnnie, there was on that occasion a covered table at the Cross, on which was abundance of wine, "baith red and white; wi' sweetmeats and barrels o' beer at the corners o' the streets. But wha paid for't I dinna ken," Johnnie often said; "but it was paid for, for naebody ever said that ony pairt o't was left unsettled—Arbroath never saw sic a day, and never will mo'," was the gaberlunzie's lament over the glories of the Stuart times.

Sir Walter Scott visited Arbroath Abbey three times. The first visit is associated with that first-love experience of his which touched him so deeply. His third visit was in July, 1814, when he stopped at Arbroath during his voyage with the Commissioners of the Northern Lights. Visits are also recorded to Hospitalfield, Auchmithie, and other places in the neighbourhood; and of many of them it may be said, as Mr J. M. Barrie says of Auchmithie in his "Sentimental Tommy"—in which story, it may be remarked, Arbroath figures as "Redlintie" —"Over them the greatest of magicians once stretched his wand, so that they became famous for ever, as all the world saw except himself."

Southey has associated the name of the Abbot of Aberbrothock with the Inchcape Rock, upon which now stands the Bell Rock Lighthouse. "Every schoolboy knows" Southey's story of "The Inchcape Bell" and Ralph the Rover, which tells that—

> The pious Abbot of Aberbrothock
> Had placed that bell on the Inchcape Rock :
> On a buoy in the storm it floated and swung,
> And o'er the waves its warning rung.

> When the rock was hid by the surge's swell,
> The mariners heard the warning bell ;
> And then they knew of the perilous rock
> And blessed the Abbot of Aberbrothock.

This bell, the tradition says, Sir Ralph villainously cut from its float. Years after the pirate lost his vessel, his crew, and his own life on the very reef from which he had removed the Abbot's "warning bell." Sir Walter Scott, as mentioned above, visited the Bell Rock Lighthouse in 1814, an interesting remembrancer of his visit being the following lines which he then inscribed in the visitors' book :—

> "Far in the bosom of the deep,
> O'er these wild shelves my watch I keep—
> A ruddy gem of changeful light
> Bound on the dusky brow of night ;
> The seaman bids my lustre hail,
> And scorns to strike his tim'rous sail."

Cardinal Beaton's connection with the Abbey has already been referred to. While his name connects Arbroath with black and bloody deeds, another and truer side of the people's sympathies is represented by the martyrdom of Walter Myln of Lunan, and the association of the second Protestant minister of Arbroath, James Melville, with the immeasurably important national labours of Knox. Henry Philip, in the trying times which opened the seventeenth century ; the Rev. Andrew Arrott of Dumbarrow in the days when the Erskines and their heroic compatriots in the Secession were fighting nobly for spiritual freedom ; Thomas Guthrie, James M'Cosh, Fox Maule, and other cherished names associated with the "Ten Years' Conflict," and the Disruption, give the burgh and district a distinguished share in great struggles for Christian liberty in later times. To the remarkable progress of medical science during the present century, Professor Sharpey and Dr Neil Arnott were honourable contributors. Other sciences have been largely indebted to the labours of Dr Alexander Brown and James Bowman Lindsay; in the revolution of agricultural methods which has marked the present century, there has been no more distinguished worker than Patrick Bell, the inventor of the reaping machine. Sir Peter Young of Seaton, preceptor to King James VI., and William Aikman of Cairnie, the Court painter, kept the town in touch with Royalty after the glory of the Abbey had departed. In war and statesmanship, the Ouchterlonies of the Guynd, and Maules of Kelly and Panmure, did valiant service. Sir William Wallace did not call for aid in vain when he appealed to Ouchterlony, and the enemies of Scotland, the invading armies of the English Edwards, found in men of the Maule breed more than their match—

" The Maules struck still her foes with dread."

On that dreadful day when the flower of the Scottish nobility fell at Flodden, a Maule died fighting by his king's side, and Abbot Hepburn of Aberbrothock was also among the slain. If James Philip of Almerieclose sang the praises of "the bloody Clavers" in "The Grameid," there were not wanting Arbroath men in the ranks of those who fought and died for the Covenant. Fox Maule's (Lord Panmure) services to British statesmanship as Secretary for War, under Lord Palmerston, maintain the honourable traditions of the name and family. The Carnegies of Boysack, as well as the Maules and Ouchterlonies, took part in the wasteful warfare which attended the death of the Stuart dynasty. Carnegies also served with distinction in the Napoleonic Wars; Admiral Lord Northesk of Ethie shared with Nelson the glories of Trafalgar. The honours won by Major Rait, C.B., of Anniston in the Ashantee War carry into the present generation the honourable record of past times. The indebtedness of commerce to Alexander Carnegie Kirk for inventions in connection with marine engineering, and James Chalmers' services to civilization by the invention of the adhesive postage stamp, have to be reckoned in the category of distinguished labours in which the labourer, though eminently worthy, has not been so fortunate as to secure his fair reward. The work of Alexander Bell Middleton, artist, is not widely known. He was taken away in the early days of his promise; but there is that in the work he has left which shows that, had length of days been granted to him, he would have taken high rank in the remarkable group of artists with whom he was associated in Robert Scott Lauder's class in Edinburgh — John Pettie, Macwhirter, Orchardson, Hugh Cameron, George Paul Chalmers, and the rest of them—who gave to the world the first distinctively Scottish national art of our century. The services rendered to art by Patrick Allan-Fraser of Hospitalfield are fully described in the sketch given of his life.

Arbroath has, in the history of the party-politics of the present century, stood firmly by the progressive parties in the House of Commons. "I am proud to be the representative of Arbroath," wrote Joseph Hume in 1827, "and am anxious to see it take the lead in liberal measures." The fact that in the present year the burgh's parliamentary representative is the Right Hon. John Morley indicates that, during "the longest and most remarkable reign in British history," Arbroath has followed a consistent course, and has, through distinguished parliamentary representation, made its influence powerful in the government of the greatest empire the world has ever known.

Amongst men who are still taking a prominent part in the world's work, Arbroath has numerous sons. Only a few names can be mentioned here as representative of her contribution to the brain-power which is the propelling force of the world's civilization. Sir John Kirk, who has represented Great Britain in many important positions in her foreign service; William Wallace, F.R.G.S, now Administrator of the Royal Niger Company's territories; John Ritchie Findlay, of the *Scotsman*, founder of the Scottish National Gallery; Joseph Anderson, LL.D., the well-known archæologist and writer; and A. S. Murray, LL.D., chief of the Department of Greek and Roman Antiquities in the British Museum; Sir William A. Ogg, and Sir James L. Mackay, both well-known names in British commerce—these are all members of old Arbroath families, "Red Lichties," to use the familiar nickname given to natives of the burgh, who maintain the honourable fame of their native place among the communities of good repute in British history.

The history of Sir John Kirk's family is dealt with in the sketch given of his brother, Dr A. C. Kirk. Sir John's earlier years were spent in the companionship of David Livingstone, the most distinguished explorer of our century, and he earned distinction and the gratitude of his country through his share in the great work of opening the way to the acquisition by Great Britain of her vast and valuable East African territory. After serving during the Crimean War with the forces in Asia Minor, Sir John Kirk travelled in Syria, Palestine, and Egypt. He was afterwards sent as chief officer with the Government expedition under Dr Livingstone. This expedition was the means of discovering the Nyassa Lake and the Shire Highlands, where were established Scotch missions and a Scotch colony. When the expedition was brought to a close, Sir John (then Dr) Kirk joined the service of the Indian Government, and was stationed in East Africa at Zanzibar. There for twenty years he remained, virtually governing the country, and having under his consular jurisdiction the coast from Aden to Madagascar. When the agencies on the East African Coast were transferred by the Indian to the British Foreign Office his services were retained, and he continued at Zanzibar. There the British had a colony of about seven thousand British Indian subjects, who were exclusively under the British agent, and as all trade passed through their hands, British influence at the Sultan's Court was paramount. During the time Sir John Kirk was there, the Sultan's revenue under his guidance rose from £70,000 to £230,000. Sir John was promoted in the order of St Michael and St George by successive Governments, and received the Grand Cross, the highest grade in that Order. Since his retirement in 1887 he has been frequently employed in important diplomatic missions. At Brussels he acted as the British Plenipotentiary at the great African Conference which sat there for over a year, and for the services then rendered he received the Knighthood of the Order of the Bath.

What Sir John Kirk has done on the East Coast of Africa has been creditably repeated on the West Coast by William Wallace. Mr Wallace's heroic labours as a pioneer have raised him to the position of Administrator of the Royal Niger Company's territories, and Queen Victoria has been pleased to confer upon him the honour of Companionship of the Order of St Michael and St George. Mr Wallace has had the care of several most important missions, and in 1894 was successful in arranging treaties with the Sultan of Sokato and several other

African kings. He described his experiences before the Royal Geographical Society, and was made a Fellow of that learned body.

Of quite a different nature, but not less worthy of the gratitude of his countrymen, are the services which have been rendered to the nation by John Ritchie Findlay. Mr Findlay was born in Arbroath. From early youth he has been associated with the *Scotsman*, of which John Ritchie, his grand-uncle and name-father, was one of the founders. In building up the remarkable power of the *Scotsman* as a national newspaper, no influence has been stronger or more wisely exercised than that of John Ritchie Findlay. The *Scotsman* and the National Portrait Gallery are monuments of the energy, foresight, and patriotism of an eminently worthy son of Arbroath and of Scotland.

Interesting notes might be added regarding many other men now well-known in the world, who first saw the light of day in the burgh upon which the ancient walls of the Abbey of Aberbrothock still look down. But enough has been said to serve the end in view. An effort has been made to show that Arbroath has an honourable past ; that her sons in the present are worthily maintaining the good name of their native place. There can be no better guarantee that in days to come Arbroath shall not fail to be creditably represented in the civilising forces of the world.

DAVID BEATON,

Abbot of Arbroath.

WHILE Arbroath had an existence as a village, prior to the foundation of the Abbey, it was owing to the possession of that edifice that it became a place of note. It is befitting, therefore, that, in any series of sketches of its eminent citizens, the name of at least one of the ecclesiastics who bore sway in that great monastic institution should find a place. The head of this monastery, in the days of its ancient glory, was a man of immense influence, and the position was such as to make its possession a much-coveted prize. In the words of the author of the preface to the second volume of the Chartulary of Aberbrothock—"The Lord Abbot of such a house as Arbroath, whether bearing crosier or mitre, or buckling on more carnal armour; whether sitting in the high places of Council or Parliament, or taking homage and dispensing law among his vassals and serfs, or following his sovereign to battle, was, in virtue of his social position, his reverence, his followers and actual power, by far the greatest personage in the shire." As may be imagined, the office was held from time to time by men of considerable eminence more than one of whom might well call for special notice—men such as the celebrated Abbot Bernard, under whom the Abbey attained to its highest point of prosperity, or Abbot John Gedy, the builder of the Arbroath Harbour. But we have selected David Beaton as being the most prominent in many respects, and as one, who during his abbacy, attained not only to national but also to European fame.

The Beatons, Betons, or Bethunes—for the name is variously spelt—appear to have been a Forfarshire family. In 1290, David was Sheriff of Forfar. His estate of Ethiebeaton was confiscated by Robert the Bruce, and sometime thereafter the family appear to have quitted the county, and we next meet with them in Fife, where we find Robert of Betune, younger son of Sir Alexander Betune, marrying Janet, daughter and heiress of Sir Michael Balfour of Balfour. This couple had a son, John, who was the first Betune of Balfour. John, the fifth Bethune of Balfour, had a number of sons who occupied prominent positions in Scotland. One of these, David, who was comptroller and treasurer to James IV., was father to one of "the four Maries," the companions of Mary Queen of Scots, and of whom, with their Royal mistress, Henry Glassford Bell says:—

> And there five noble maidens sat beneath the orchard trees
> In that first budding spring of youth, when all its prospects please,
> And little recked they, when they sang, or knelt at vesper prayers,
> That Scotland knew no prouder names—held none more dear than theirs.

The name of Mary Beaton is also commemorated in the well-known beautiful Scottish ballad which relates the fate of Mary Hamilton, another of the "Maries," who, tradition says, was executed at Edinburgh:—

> Yestreen the Queen she had four Maries—
> The nicht she has but three;
> There was Marie Seaton, and Marie Beaton,
> And Marie Carmichael and me.

This Mary Beaton was cousin to David Beaton, the Abbot of Arbroath. More than one of the sons of John, the fifth laird of Balfour, were eminent churchmen. James Beaton, the youngest son of John Beaton, an able ecclesiastic, held many important appointments in Scotland, and among these the abbacy of Arbroath. On his elevation to the Archbishopric of St Andrews, his nephew, then a young man, succeeded him as Abbot of Arbroath.

David Beaton was born at Balfour in or about the year 1494. He was educated at the Universities of St Andrews and Glasgow, and afterwards at Paris. On his return to his native country about 1519, he became Rector of Campsie, near Stirling, and in 1522-23, he was appointed Abbot of Arbroath. Alluding to this appointment, Sir David Lyndsay, after the assassination of Beaton, wrote a poem entitled "The Tragedie of the Maist Reverend Father David," &c., in which he makes him say:—

> "Quhen I was ane young joly gentyll man,
>   Prencis to serve I sett my hole intent;
> First till ascende, at Arbroith I began,
>   Ane Abacie of greit ryches and rent;
>   Of that estait yet was I nocht contente;
> To get more ryches, dignitie and glore,
> My hart was set! Allace! Allace! tharfore."

But it was not his ambition alone which opened up for him the path to "dignitie and glore." He was a man possessed of great culture, splendid talents, and a fascinating manner. The possession of these qualities could not fail to attract towards him the attention of the leading dignitaries in Church and State, and it was while resident in Arbroath that he commenced that career of political influence which soon brought him into such prominence. The references to his actions in his capacity of

Abbot of Arbroath are neither so numerous, nor, of course, so important, as those connected with his greater dignity as Cardinal. In 1525, "the King, by adwisse of some good men, and his mother, calls a Parliament to be halden at Edinburgh, the 6 of Marche, to wich he comes in persone, in royall robes, and the croune on hes head and scepter in hes hand, and ther solemly takes one himselue the gouerniment." At this meeting of the Scottish Parliament, Beaton sat as Abbot of Arbroath, and took an active share in its deliberations. On the 20th of May of the same year it is recorded that he issued a presentation to the Parish Church of Lunan in favour of Sir David Cristeson, presbyter, the predecessor of Walter Myln, the last of the Scottish martyrs. Although no record can be found of a presentation by the Abbot to Walter Myln, there can be no doubt that the presentation of the curacy of that parish to Myln was the gift of the Abbot.

Beaton's hatred to Reformation principles was early exhibited Calderwood tells us that on "the last day of the moneth of February, anno 1527" (1528) among the signatories to the sentence of martyrdom on Patrick Hamilton, appears the name of "David, Abbot of Aberbrothic." In 1528, on the downfall of the Earl of Angus, David Beaton, Abbot of Arbroath, was appointed to the office of Lord Privy Seal. In the same year James V., then a young man of sixteen, came to Arbroath, attended by a large retinue, and was there entertained by Beaton in the Abbey of Arbroath. Excepting his transactions in connection with the temporalities of the Abbey, which are pretty numerous, we have little or no account of how he discharged his official duties as Abbot. If we may judge by his actions in the wider sphere which he occupied as Cardinal, we fear that his religious duties must have been performed in a very perfunctory manner.

DAVID BEATON.

In the early days of the Abbey's history, the Abbey lands were to be found in the shires of Banff, Inverness, Kincardine, Lanark, and Perth; but these were largely feued away before Beaton's time, so that the majority of the transactions of this nature, under his name, are connected with Forfarshire. From the years 1524 to 1544, his name occurs frequently in the chartulary of Arbroath. The first of these entries is on the 18th January, 1524, when he confirms Robert Scot's endowment of the altar of St. Duthacus. In 1527, he lets the croft near the Dern Yett, with the teinds, to John Barbor for nineteen years at a rent of £1 6s 8d. David Miller, in his "Arbroath and its Abbey," conjectures that this is the true origin of the term Barber's Croft, now applied to that piece of ground. The leases granted in David Beaton's time show a departure from the terms of those of his predecessors in that they were in looser and more general terms, and frequently conferred power to assign and sublet. "This," says Miller, "was the intermediate step between the former careful management of the monastic possessions, and the subsequent alienation of them in perpetual feu grant, for fixed quantities of grain, or certain amounts of Scotch money, the value of which has now fallen to very insignificant sums." Among the other estates in this quarter belonging to the Abbey was that of Ethie, which had been gifted by King William the Lion. With this land and others in the neighbourhood, Beaton made free use for his own ends.

While, as we have said, he was possessed of eminent qualities, he led, in many respects, anything but a moral life. His favourite mistress was Marion Ogilvie, daughter of Sir James, afterwards Lord, Ogilvie of Airlie, to whom he granted a life-rent lease of the lands of Burnton of Ethie, and other lands near the place, for a small sum of money *and other causes.* This was on the 22nd of May, 1528. On the 20th of July, 1530, he granted her a life-rent lease of the Kirkton of St Vigeans, with the Muirfauld and the toft of St Vigeans, and a piece of common land lying to the south of the church. On the 17th February, 1533-4, she obtained a nineteen years' lease of the eighth part of the lands of Auchmithie, with the brew-house there, and the lands belonging to it; and on 10th March, 1534, there is the record of a feu to her of a piece of land in the "Sandpots" for the construction of a toral or ustrina lying "beyond and near the red wall of the monastery commonly so called."

It is not known by whom Ethie House was built, but it was a favourite residence of David Beaton and Marion Ogilvie, his mistress. Tradition tells that long after his death his ghost haunted it. Sir William Fraser, in his "History of the Carnegies," says: "It is still reported that at a certain hour of the night a sound is heard, resembling the tramp of a foot, which is believed to be the Cardinal's, and it is popularly called his *leg*, walking very deliberately down the original stone stair which connects the ground flat with the second storey of the house." The "haunted room" is one of the attics, and when Sir William explored it, he found a veritable trace of David Beaton in the form of a large oak cabinet, exquisitely carved, which was the only article of furniture in the room. Ethie House is beautifully situated, and is supposed to be the Knockwinnock of "The Antiquary."

After Beaton's death, a natural daughter of his by Marion Ogilvie laid claim to the furniture in Ethie House, if not to the house itself. In the year succeeding her father's death, she and her husband David, Master of Crawford, summoned Lord Gray and his brother, James Gray, to appear before the Queen and Council to answer for their wrongous and masterful spoliation by themselves and their accomplices of the place of

Ethie and the house thereof. But Ethie was not the only place in this neighbourhood occupied by David Beaton and Marion Ogilvie. In 1542, he acquired the barony of Melgund, and erected the castle in which he and his mistress and their children resided. The Beaton and the Ogilvie arms are still to be seen in one of the rooms. The initials " D. B." are over one window, and " M. O." over the other ; while on the corbel of the stair leading to this room are the Ogilvie arms, and the initials " M. O." (Marion Ogilvie).

David Beaton settled the property of Melgund on his mistress in life-rent, and on his eldest son David in fee. The estate of Melgund remained in the Beaton family till about 1630, when it was acquired by the first Marquis of Huntly. From the Huntly family it passed to the Maules ; from the Maules (through marriage) to the Murrays, and from the Murrays (also through marriage) to the Minto family. There is a curious tradition in connection with Melgund Castle. It is told that in the early years of last century, while the estate was in the hands of the Murrays, the then proprietor and all his family suddenly disappeared. One winter evening, the lamps were lit, the tables spread, and every preparation made for the family sitting down to supper, but they did not appear in the dining-room, and from that night they were never more seen. The tradition is that they threw themselves, with all their silver plate—for it disappeared at the same time—into a deep pool near the Castle. The true explanation likely is that having gambled away their fortune and estate, they had made what is locally known as a " moonlicht flittin'." In addition to the many other possessions of the Church in this locality which Beaton bestowed on his mistress, were the lands of Hospitalfield, for so many years owned by the late Patrick Allan-Fraser. This property continued for years in her possession after the Abbot's death.

Hospitalfield has undoubted claims to be the "Monkbarns" of "The Antiquary." Not only is its proximity to Fairport, St Ruth's, Mussel Crag, and Knockwinnock, adduced in proof of this, but it is known that during the abbacy of Bernard de Linton, the tenants of this portion of the Abbey lands were taken bound to build barns for the use of the monks, for the storage of the produce of the lands belonging to the Monastery. Although it is long since these buildings have fallen into decay, portions of the old walls are still included in the present mansion-house of Hospitalfield, and this, no doubt, suggested to Sir Walter Scott the appropriateness of the name "Monkbarns." Among several old charters and historical documents still preserved in the mansion-house of Hospitalfield is one bearing the autograph signature of David Beaton. A *fac simile* of the Cardinal's signature will be found under his portrait.

Beaton's licentious life is one among other blots on his memory. That a professed servant of God, the head of a great religious house, should have the daring effrontery to live in open and undisguised sin, brings sharply into relief one of the phases of his character, and it earned for him the detestation of many in his own day. We know how his vices were lashed by such men as Sir David Lyndsay. Even King James V., with whom Beaton was a great favourite, could not shut his eyes to the shameless fashion of his life. It is told that Thomas Maule, younger of Panmure, who was contracted in marriage to Beaton's daughter, Margaret, was one day riding out of Arbroath with the King, when His Majesty called Maule aside, and bade him "marry never ane priest's gett." "Whereupon," it is added, that "marriage did cease." Beaton highly resented the slight, and it cost Maule 3000 merks. This same Margaret was afterwards married to the Master of Crawford. There is little else to tell about Beaton's connection with Arbroath. He was the last of the Abbots who performed any clerical duty in connection with the Arbroath Abbey. His life history and his public acts in his capacity of Cardinal are well known to readers of Scottish history, and call for but brief recapitulation here.

In 1537 he was consecrated Bishop of Mirepoix in France, and in the following year, on the recommendation of the French King, Pope Paul III. made him Cardinal. In 1539 he succeeded his uncle, James, as Archbishop of St Andrews. In 1543 he was created Lord High Chancellor of Scotland, and in 1544 he was appointed the Pope's Legate, which gave him power in Scotland second to the Pope only. Before his appointment as Abbot of Arbroath, and during his tenure of that office, he was often employed on foreign diplomatic service. He negotiated the marriage of James V. with Magdalen, daughter of Francis I. After her death he was sent to bring to Scotland the King's second wife, Mary of Guise. On the death of James V. in 1542, the Cardinal forged a will appointing himself, along with the Earls of Huntly, Argyle, and Arran joint regents. But the forgery was discovered, and for a time he was a prisoner. His imprisonment was but of short duration, and no sooner was he at liberty than he was again in the midst of intrigue, which resulted in a declaration of war from England. Hertford invaded Scotland in 1544, and the English fleet entered the Firth of Forth with the purpose of seizing the Cardinal and razing his castle of St Andrews. But both the Cardinal and the governor escaped.

While Beaton was a wily and unscrupulous politician, he was also a cruel persecutor. Many of his acts of tyranny and persecution are recorded. Lindsay of Pitscottie tells that "he caused hang four honest men for eating goose on Friday, and drowned a young woman because she refused to pray to our lady in her birth." But his crowning act of persecution was the burning of George Wishart at the stake. Pitscottie gives a very graphic account of the atrocious act of cruelty. When Wishart was brought to the stake, Beaton and his satellites sat in a window of the castle where they could enjoy the sight of the martyr's dreadful death. "Meantime," says Lindsay, "the artillery was charged and laid to the wall heads, and cushions and green cloths spread thereon for the Cardinal and bishops to sit upon, and all gentlemen commanded to stand about the scaffold in armour. During the meantime Mr George was discoursing to the captain. . . . As he was discoursing, the officers and tormentors brought him forth to the fire which was prepared without the castle gate, against the west block house, where the bishops might lie on the wall heads and see the sacrifice."

This foul deed added strength to the general hatred which his numerous acts of tyranny had brought on Beaton, and it culminated in a conspiracy to rid the country of one who was looked upon by those of the reformed faith as a monster of iniquity. The conspirators, to the number of ten or twelve persons, headed by Norman Leslie, who had formerly been one of Beaton's friends, obtained admittance to the castle early on the morning of the 29th May, 1546. The Cardinal, hearing a din, threw up his window and asked what it meant. He was informed that Norman Leslie had taken the Castle, on hearing which he attempted to make his escape, but finding this impossible he ordered his chamberlain to barricade the door of his apartment. His assailants, however, threatened to burn the door, which on hearing either the Cardinal or his chamberlain threw it open. Beaton sat down on a chair crying, "I am a priest; I am a priest; you will not slay me." But he was now in the hands of men to whom his priestly character was of no account. John Leslie struck him twice with a dagger, Peter Carmichael doing the same. James Melville, after admonishing him of his wicked life, and reminding him of his recent act towards George Wishart, struck him twice through with his sword, and as he fell he cried, "Fie, fie, I'm a priest; all's gone." The inhabitants of St Andrews, hearing of what was going on, thronged to the castle exclaiming, "What have ye done with my Lord Cardinal?" The assassins, for answer, placed his body in a sheet, and hung it out at the same window from which, shortly before, he had witnessed the burning of Wishart.

Although the deed was a foul one, its commission did not create throughout the country that feeling of detestation which it would have evoked had the victim been one whose private life had been purer. Still, there were many, even among those who detested his acts of cruelty and oppression, who disapproved of the method taken to get rid of him. This feeling is well expressed in the lines of Sir David Lyndsay—

> "But of a truth, the sooth to say,
> Although the loon be well away,
> The deed was foully done."

They did not bury the body immediately, but, having salted it, they wrapped it in lead and placed it in the ground-floor of the sea tower, where it lay unburied for nine months. Such was the miserable end to which Beaton—one of the most brilliant and talented men of his time—came at the comparatively early age of fifty-two.

While his many faults have been unsparingly commented on by most of the writers who have treated of his life and times, it must not be forgotten that he gave ample proof of his patriotism on several occasions. When the independence of Scotland was assailed, Beaton resolutely and effectively opposed the intrigues of the English Court, and for this he deserves the gratitude of his country.

As pointed out by Jervise, we are also indebted to him for the preservation of some of the most valuable remains of our monastic literature which he was the means of rescuing from the flames enkindled by infuriated zealots.

WALTER MYLN,

Of Lunan.

THE dawn of the Reformation was the harbinger of better times for Scotland, but the Church fought fiercely for the continuance of her power over the people. In the struggle for religious freedom the men of Angus played a prominent part, many suffering spoliation, banishment, and even death in the cause. The martyrdom of the gentle born and scholarly George Wishart, following as it did on the murder of Patrick Hamilton and others, instead of arresting, rather gave an impetus to the movement. But for a time Rome seemed to have the best of it. Terror reigned throughout the land, and the prospects of the reformed cause were shrouded in darkness. In the year 1556, the gentlemen of the Mearns entered into a "band" or agreement which is said to have been "the first of those religious bands or covenants by which the confederation of the Protestants in Scotland was so frequently ratified;" but of this covenant, if it ever was reduced to writing, no copy has been preserved. This was followed by the "Common or Godlie Band" drawn up, sworn to, and subscribed by a number of "the lords of the congregation" in December 1557.

This concerted action on the part of the Reformers only added intensity to the malignity of their persecutors, and led to the martyrdom of Walter Myln of Lunan—the most detestable of all the detestable acts of the period, and one, which, more than any other, hastened the downfall of the papacy in Scotland; for as Calderwood records "that blessed martyr of Christ, Walter Mill, a man of decrepit age, was putt to death most cruellie, the 28th of April. Immediatelie after his death beganne a new fervencie among the people; yea even in the town of Sanct Andrews, the people began plainlie to damne such unjust crueltie."

Of the birth-place and parentage of Walter Myln, nothing is definitely known, but that he was a native of this locality, and was educated at the monastic school of Aberbrothock there is every probability. He was born about the year 1476. For many years before Walter Myln's birth, the name of Myln was a familiar one in Arbroath and its vicinity. When David Beaton owned and occasionally resided at Ethie Castle, the Mylns were his near neighbours. As far back as 1510, John Myln, cartwright, and his son, Robert Myln, are entered as tenants of the Mill near the "Bruntone of Athy," commonly called "Raysis Myl," and frequently thereafter do the Mylns appear as tenants of lands belonging to the Church in the same locality. It is therefore not unreasonable to infer that coming into frequent contact with the monks of Aberbrothock some of the members of the family would be led to choose the Church as a profession.

It is said that Walter Myln was for some time a monk of the Abbey, and although no authentic record remains of his being so, it is not at all unlikely that he was.

In or about the year 1526, he was presented by David Beaton to the vicarage of the parish of Lunan, where he laboured diligently for twenty years. Not far from Lunan were the houses of Dysart, Baldovy, and Dun; Dysart, the residence of John Melville; Baldovy, of his brother, Richard Melville, the father of James and Andrew Melville; and Dun, that of John Erskine. Each of these houses was well known as a rendezvous of those men who had embraced

Reformation principles. Coming into contact with such men as these, as Myln had many opportunities of doing, there can be little doubt that his attention would be directed to the principles for which these men were contending. By this time also Tyndall's translation of the New Testament had found its way into this country. At the various ports along the Forfarshire coast, copies were more easily obtainable than in many other districts, the frequent intercourse between Holland and the East of Scotland giving facilities for their acquisition, of which many were not slow to avail themselves. These copies were privately circulated among Myln's parishioners, and it was no uncommon thing for several families to meet in secret at the midnight hour to listen to the reading of the Word. Probably the licentious life of Beaton, of which, as his near neighbour, Myln could not fail to be cognisant, and probably also the crafty cruelties of the Cardinal, which, with the sanction of his Church, he practised, opened the eyes of the priest of Lunan. Whichever of these means God may have used in leading Walter Myln to a knowledge of the truth, certain it is that he was found discharging his spiritual duties among his parishioners in a way to call forth the vengeance of Beaton, who condemned him and his friend, John Petrie, the priest of Inverkeilor, to be burned at the stake. Forewarned of their doom, they fled. Walter Myln, for a time, hid himself in other parts of Scotland, but Beaton's spies made it too hot for him, so he took to the sea, and after a time he found refuge in Germany. Having thus thrown off his allegiance to the Church of Rome, he entered into the married state, and became the father of a family.

He spent a number of years on the Continent, coming into contact with many professors of the reformed faith. At last he ventured to return to Scotland, having been deceived by the lull in the storm. He found a temporary asylum at Dysart in Fife, where he engaged in preaching and teaching the people. But the keen eyes of the emissaries of Archbishop Hamilton, the successor to David Beaton, were upon him, and by Hamilton's orders, the decrepit old priest was apprehended, carried to St. Andrews, and thrown into a dungeon. The story of his trial, sentence, and execution, is very graphically told both by Fox and by Lindsay of Pitscottie. When he appeared before the Court he was so weak and feeble as to be unable to mount the pulpit without assistance, and it was feared by his friends that he would not be able to conduct his defence, nor, from the weakness of his voice, would anything he had to say for himself be heard; but, to the astonishment of all present, when he began his address to his accusers, he made the church ring. He spoke, Fox tells us, with so great courage and stoutness that the Christians who were present were no less rejoiced than his adversaries were confounded and ashamed. Indeed, the vigour he displayed on this occasion is astonishing when we consider his great age and his weak frame, enfeebled, as it had been, by the many privations he had endured. His first act, on ascending the pulpit, was to bend his knees in prayer, and continuing longer in this attitude than his accusers cared for, Andrew Oliphant, one of the bishop's priests, who acted as prosecutor on the occasion, ordered him to rise and answer to the charges laid against him, saying, "Sir Walter Myln, arise, and answer to the articles, for you hold my Lords here over long." But the aged saint calmly continued his devotions, after finishing which, he replied, "We ought to obey God rather than men; I serve One more mighty, even the omnipotent Lord, and when you call me Sir Walter, they call me Walter and not Sir Walter. I have been too long one of the Pope's knights; now say what thou hast to say."

Oliphant then proceeded to put the various charges to him, asking him, with reference to his having, as his accusers held, broken his vows of celibacy "What think ye of the priest's marriage?" To him Myln stingingly replied that he held to the blessed bond, for Christ himself maintained and approved it, and made it free to all men; "but," he adds, " ye take other men's wives and daughters, and will not keep the bond that God hath made. Ye vow chastity and break the same."

As to the Sacraments, he was charged with saying that there are not seven sacraments; his answer to which was, "Give me the Lord's Supper and Baptism, and take you the rest and part them among you; if there be seven, why have you omitted one of them, to wit, marriage, and given yourselves to slanderous and ungodly whoredom." Charged with declaring the mass to be idolatry, he wittily replied, "A lord or king sendeth, and calleth many to a dinner, and when the dinner is in readiness, he causeth a bell to ring, and the men come to the hall and sit down to be partakers of the dinner, but the lord, turning his back upon them, eateth all himself and mocketh them—so do ye!"

He was next accused of denying that the sacrament of the altar is the very body of Christ really in flesh and blood; to which he answered that the mass is wrong, Christ having been once offered on the Cross for man's trespass, and will never again be offered for them; he ended all sacrifice.

Other charges were also preferred against him, which he refuted with great ability and wit. He was then asked if he would recant his erroneous opinions, and told that, if he would not, sentence would be pronounced against him.

His answer was given boldly and unhesitatingly—" I am accused of my life. I know I must die once; and therefore, as

Christ said to Judas, 'That thou doest do quickly.' Ye shall know that I will not recant the truth; for I am corn; I am not chaff. I will not be blown away with the wind, nor burst with the flail, but will abide both."

Lindsay of Pitscottie gives additional particulars of this trial. He says that Oliphant accused Myln of heresy; and of having forsaken the Mass; adding, " that thou hads't the curé of the parish of Lunan in Angus, beside Redcastle, from which thou fled'st, and one with thee called Sir John Petrie, servant to the Lord Innermeath; and you and he were condemned by my late Lord Cardinal of heresy, and ordained to be burnt wherever ye might be apprehended, so that we need no further accusation against you at this time." To which accusations Myln replied—" Indeed, I served the curé of Lunan twenty years, with the approbation, to this day, of all the parishioners, who never heard me teaching erroneous doctrine, especially my Lord Innermeath himself; but when the furious Cardinal persecuted me, and many more, for the preaching of God's Word, I was constrained to keep myself quiet, and go about, asking for God's sake, reproving vices, and instructing people in the grounds of religion, for the which I am now taken and brought to this place." Again offered his life if he would recant, he indignantly refused, declaring that he was of great age, and had not cause to fear for death; all the favour he asked was that something should be done for the relief of his wife and poor children. The Bishop then condemned him for heresy. It was, however, needful that a secular judge should be got to pronounce or ratify the sentence of death, but such was the sympathy felt for the brave old saint that no one could be found to do the foul act. After a lapse of two days spent in ineffectual attempts to get a criminal judge to pronounce sentence, the bishop sent for the

Provost of the town, but, after some temporising, the Provost left the town so as to escape the Bishop's importunity. After searching up and down for any one to act as temporal judge, the Bishop ordered Alexander Somervil, one of his own court, "a man void of all honesty, religion, or fear of God," to go through the form. So detestable did the deed appear in the eyes of the townsfolk that no one could be found willing to sell a cord to bind him to the stake, or a tar barrel to burn him; indeed, we are told that the merchants, for the love of this poor servant of God, had hid all tows and all other things which might serve for his execution.

When all was ready he was again asked, in derision, if he desired to recant. To this he boldly answered, "I marvel of your rage, O hypocrites, that so cruelly persecute God's servants; as for me, I am fourscore and two years old, and cannot live long by course of nature; but a hundred better than I shall rise out of the ashes of my bones, who shall scatter the proud pack of you, hypocrites and persecutors of God's servants; and who of you think yourself worthier shall not die so honest a death as I die now. I trust in God I shall be the last that shall suffer death in Scotland for this cause."

So incensed were the people that they erected a cairn to his memory on the spot where he was burned. This the Bishop caused to be removed, with denunciation and cursing on any man who should raise it again; but in vain were the curses, for again and yet again, as it was cast down, it was rebuilt; and it was only after the bishop's satellites had carried off the stones during the night that the cairn was finally destroyed.

But if this memorial of the venerable saint was thus demolished, his memory still lives in the hearts of the Scottish people. His martyrdom, as Spottiswoode records, was the very death of Popery. Men who before were in favour of Reformation principles, but secretly for fear of the persecution which would follow their open avowal thereof, now boldly declared their adherence to the cause, and expressed their readiness to defend themselves and their brethren against the tyrannical persecutions of the Bishops.

Although the memorial cairn was cast down the aged martyr's name has not been allowed to suffer oblivion, for near the ancient Castle of St Andrews an elegant obelisk stands recording the heroic deeds of Walter Myln, and other of the Scottish martyrs.

In the wall of the Parish Church of Lunan, in 1848, a marble tablet was inserted bearing an inscription, narrating the deed done at St Andrews. This tablet keeps green the memory of Walter Myln in the parish where he diligently laboured at so much peril to himself, and where for so many years he bore such a noble testimony to the truth.

JAMES MELVILLE,

Protestant Reformer.

JAMES MELVILLE, the second Protestant minister of Arbroath in point of time, was the first in point of importance. The first minister in the Reformation Church in "Aberbrothok Towne and Paroche" was Ninian Clement. Somewhere about 1573 Clement was translated to Forfar, and was succeeded by James Melville, who, prior to coming to Arbroath, was minister of Tannadice.

As Arbroath, through her long line of abbots, figured prominently in the civil and ecclesiastical events of Scottish history, so, in the early Reformation days, she took no mean part in the stirring incidents of that eventful period. This was largely owing to her having as parish minister a man of such acknowledged wisdom, ability, and energy as James Melville.

A scion of a distinguished family — a branch of which long held the office of hereditary Sheriff of Kincardineshire— Melville, both by birth and education, was well fitted to take a prominent part in the councils of the Reformed Church.

The Melvilles are said to have originally come from Normandy and to have settled in Scotland in the twelfth century. Towards the beginning of the sixteenth century, branches of the family were to be found in Kincardine, Angus, Fife, and the Lothians. They were allied, by inter-marriages, to the principal families in the Kingdom, and they even claimed affinity to the Royal house.

Tradition tells that one of the members of the Kincardineshire branch of the Melville family, during his sheriffship, made himself so obnoxious by his carrying tales to the King (James I.), and by his sharp practice and oppressive measures, that he incurred the bitter hatred of his brother barons. More than once they complained thereof to His Majesty. On one of these occasions the King, irritated by their continued importunity, in an unguarded moment, exclaimed—" Sorrow gin the Sheriff were sodden and supped in broo." James was taken at his word, and shortly thereafter four of the Barons—Arbuthnot, Lauriston, Mathers, and Pitarrow—decoyed the Sheriff, on pretence of inviting him to a hunting expedition, to the top of the hill of Garvock, where they had prepared a large pot or caldron of boiling water, into which they plunged the unsuspecting Sheriff. After he was thoroughly "sodden," they literally carried out the King's mandate, and actually "supped the broo." Three of them were outlawed; the fourth, Barclay of Mathers, erected the Kaim (or fortress) of Mathers, where he took refuge.

Richard Melville, the father of James Melville, was a brother of John Melville of Dysart, and a cadet of the House of Glenbervie. He was proprietor of Baldovy, near Montrose, an estate which continued in the possession of his descendants till the beginning of the eighteenth century. While his family were still young (the youngest, the celebrated Andrew Melville, being then only two years old), he fell in the battle of Pinkie, along with many of the principal gentlemen of Angus, fighting in the Scottish army under the Earl of Angus. The Baldovy family early embraced the Protestant doctrines. Richard, who succeeded to the estate on the death of his father, received a liberal education, and as became one who was expected to take his position as a county gentleman, his father had taken care to have him trained in county affairs.

When quite a young man he received the appointment of tutor to John Erskine of Dun, and he accompanied him on his Continental travels. There is no doubt that, imbued as these two young Scotsmen were in their earliest days with Reformation principles, their love for, and their knowledge of, these principles were deepened and intensified during the course of their studies abroad under such a distinguished reformer as Philip Melancthon, and the other eminent men with whom they were brought into contact. After their return home, the houses of Dun and Baldovy became the rendezvous of the leading literary and religious men of the day—John Knox and other prominent leaders of the Reformation movement being frequent visitors. So James Melville was early brought into contact, both in his father's house and afterwards in his brother Richard's, with the foremost men of his time.

Richard Melville (James's father) had by his wife, Giles Abercrombie, daughter of Thomas Abercrombie, a descendant of the house of Murthlie, nine sons, four of whom became ministers of the Reformed Church of Scotland. Andrew Melville, the youngest of these sons, is the name next to that of John Knox, best known among the great Scottish Reformers. But although not so well known as his youngest brother, nor as his nephew and namesake, James Melville occupied a distinguished position among that noble band of Scotsmen who fought the battle of religious freedom in those eventful days, and their memory deserves to be warmly cherished by all patriotic Scotsmen.

James Melville was educated first at Montrose, and afterwards at St Andrews, where in 1555, as appears from the

University records, he obtained the degree of Bachelor of Arts. The earliest mention we have of him is in 1560. Calderwood, in narrating the proceedings of the first General Assembly of the Reformed Kirk of Scotland, held at Edinburgh on the 20th December, 1560, says—"That the reader may perceave what raritie of pastors there was in the infancie of our Kirk, and what were the small beginnings of our assemblies, we will set down the names of the Commission and members of the first Assemblie," and, beginning with John Knox, he gives the names of *six* ministers and thirty-six laymen being all that made up the sederunt. At this meeting a list is drawn up of "the names of such as were thought best qualified for preaching of the Word, and ministering of the sacraments and reading of the Commoun prayers, publicklie in all kirks and congregations, given up by the ministers and Commissioners within their own bounds," and, "others thought apt and able by the ministers and Commissioners aforesaid to minister." Among these latter we find the name of James Melville. As there was a great scarcity of men qualified to perform these spiritual functions, it is quite certain—although there is no direct statement to that effect—that he was thereupon drafted into the active service of the church.

From that time, and for at least thirty-six years thereafter, his name occurs frequently in the ecclesiastical records of the period. One important service which he was instrumental in rendering to the Reformation cause was that of inducing his eldest brother Richard, to whom we have already referred, to educate his son James for the ministry. Richard Melville was determined to make his son a farmer or tradesman, notwithstanding the earnest wish of the boy to enter the ministry, and, disregarding the entreaties of the lad, he persisted in this intention. James Melville (the younger), tells that when his father sent him to the smithy for "dressing of hewkes, he begoude to weirie soar of his lyff," and "prayed God that it wald please his guidnes to offer occasion to continow me at the scholles, and inclyne my father's hart till use the saming." He then adds, "Within a few dayes thairafter Mr James Melville, my uncle, comes to Baldowy, and brings with him a godlie lernit man named Mr Wilyeam Collace, wha was that yeir to tak up the class as first Regent of St Leonards Collage within the Universitie of St Andros; after conference with whome that night, God moves my father's hart to resolve to send me that same yeir to Collage." Thus, to the opportune intervention of James Melville of Arbroath, we are indebted for the valuable services of one who is described by Calderwood, as "one of the wisest directors of church affairs of his time." His contributions to the literature of the period have been of great value to subsequent historians. Much of the information regarding the life and work of both of his uncles, James and Andrew, and of other reformers is derived from his "Diary."

Before his settlement in Arbroath, James Melville shared with other parish ministers the consequences of the avaricious conduct of Queen Mary's courtiers, having had to go without their promised stipends. His nephew tells that he remembered "the order of the fast keipit in anno 1565 — the evil handling of the ministrie be taken away of their stipends; for Mr James Melville, my uncle, and Mr James Balfour, his cusing-german, were bathe ministers and stipendles, with gude godlie and kynd Patrick Forbes of Cors."

The clergy at this period had truly a hard time of it. Crushing poverty was the lot of the most of them, so much so that in order to eke out a living many of them resorted to the expedient of tavern or ale-house keeping. That the Church was cognisant of this, and did not object to it, may be gathered from the fact that at the General Assembly, held at Edinburgh in October, 1576, of which James Melville was a member, among other questions which came up for consideration it was decided that "a minister or reader tapping ale, beer, or wine is exhorted by the Commissioners to keep decorum" or, what we would call an orderly house.

In December, 1566, he was a member of the General Assembly, and his name appears appended to an address drawn up "to their bretherin the bishops and pastors in England who have renounced the Roman Anti-christ," beseeching them to deal gently with certain of their brethren who were hindered from promoting the Kingdom of Christ, "because their consciences will not suffer them to putt on at the commandment of authority such garments as idolators in time of blindness have used in their idolatric."

At the Assembly of the following year, we find him present (as minister of "Tannados,") taking a prominent part in the business, and acting on a committee composed of some of the most learned men in the Church Councils on the consideration of difficult and delicate questions. The exact date of his translation from Tannadice to Arbroath is not known, but that it was about the year 1573 is generally supposed.

In October, 1573, and presumably after Melville's settlement here, it is recorded that the bailies and "haill neighbours" of the town resolved to establish a grammar school, and to pay the master eight shillings for "ilk bairn in the town," and twenty pounds out of "our lady's benefice, or dirigie dues with his chalmer maile free." Associating as Melville had done with John Knox and the other leading Reformers, there can be little doubt that the cause of education found in him a zealous advocate, and that it was in all probability on his recommendation that this resolution was come to. The building in which the education of the Arbroath youth of that day was conducted was situated in School Wynd, a lane which disappeared in 1890 to make room for the Kirk Square and High Street improvements then effected.

During the earlier years of Melville's Arbroath ministry, his parishioners worshipped in the Lady Chapel, then a dilapidated building at the north-west corner of what is now the Arbroath Harbour. The unsatisfactory condition of that building rendered it needful that the worshippers should have better accommodation. This was a serious undertaking for the poor burghers, but through the persevering energy of James Melville, heartily aided by the leading men of the town, assistance was got from various sources. By a precept of the Duke of Lennox, then Commendator of the Abbey, dated 25th June, 1580, addressed to "the Chalmelain captaine of the house of Arbroath" in answer to a petition by the Magistrates, the Commendator granted permission to the Bailies, Council, and community of Arbroath to "tak away all and hail ye staines, tymmer, and other pertinents of our house, ye dormitory in ye said Abbey and that ye mak yeis nay impedimen in away takyn and down casten of ye same but ye may have free passage therewith because ye haiv disponit ye sam to them for biggyn of ane kirk."

Pecuniary help came from the Convention of Royal Burghs, which, from time to time during the erection of the church, gave grants in aid of what would now be called "the building fund." These gifts of material and money, added to their own contributions, enabled the parishioners to erect a most substantial and commodious edifice, the main portion of which defied the storms of three centuries, and was only finally destroyed by the fire of 1892.

Although we do not find Melville's name appearing in any of the records of the Assembly of 1574, there is indirect evidence of his having been there. Among the articles offered for consideration of the Regent, it was asked "that his grace will tak a generall order with the poore, and especially in the abbeyes, suche as Aberbrothe and others, conforme to the act made at Leith, and in speciall to discharge the tithe—sybboes, leeks, kaill, unzeons,—by an act of secret counsell, whill a parliament be convened where they may be simply discharged." If this question was brought forward at the instance of Melville, he deserved, and no doubt got, the thanks of his poor parishioners, on whom this tithing of their garden stuffs must have borne heavily.

In the list of ministers made up this year, we find that the churches of "Aberbrothok or Sanct Vigians, Athie, and Kynnell" are assigned to "Maister James Mailvile, minister," with a stipend of £160 Scots, together with a vicar's manse and glebe. Each minister having the pastoral care of several churches or parishes, had under him a reader or readers. Melville had one reader for each of the churches named, Thomas Lindsay acting at "Aberbrothok or Sanct Vigians," David Miln at Ethie, and David Fyff at Kinnell. Lindsay's salary was £17 15s 6d Scots, with 8 bolls of bear, Miln's £16 Scots, and the Kirklands, and Fyff's £12 Scots. In June of the year following (1575), he was called on to witness the death of his elder brother Richard, the minister of Maryton. During his last illness, Richard was visited by many of "the noble and gentler men of the county," and his son records that "about the verie hour of his death he caused reid to him the 8 chapter of the Epistle to the Romans; and immediatelie after his brother, Mr James, minister of Arbrothe, asking him what he was doing? Lifting upe eyes and hands toward heaven, with reasonable might of voice, he answerit, 'I am glorifeing God for the light of His gospell,' and na mae intelligible words thairefter."

In 1581 Melville was one of the commissioners appointed to fix the bounds of the presbyteries in Angus and Mearns. In 1582 he was one of fifteen Commissioners from the General Assembly, who were deputed to present the remonstrance to the King, known as "the grievances of the Kirk." The Earl of Arran, who knew well that his conduct contributed in a large measure to the dissatisfaction which called forth the remonstrance, after the reading of the grievances, looked round the Assembly with an angry countenance, and exclaimed, "Who dares subscribe these treasonable articles?" "*We dare*," replied Andrew Melville, and advancing to the table, took the pen and adhibited his name. His brother, James Melville, and the other commissioners followed his example, at which bold conduct Arran felt surprised and awed.

The parish of St Vigeans was at that period included in the Synod of Fife, and at a meeting of that body, held in 1586, "Mr James Melville, minister of Arbrothe, and Mr James Balfour, minister of Edvie," and two others were appointed to intimate to Mr Patrick Adamson, Archbishop of St Andrews, that he was judged worthy of being excommunicated for contumacy. At the next General Assembly the Synod's excommunication was removed. For some years after this, James Melville's services were often employed on business of importance. During his Arbroath incumbency, he associated with the most learned men in the church. Writing of John Durie, then one of the ministers of Edinburgh, Melville, the younger, in his Diary says:—"He was a verie guid fallow, and tuk delyt as his special comfort to haiff his table and houss filled with the best men.

Ther ludgit in his houss at all these assemblies in Edinbruche for comoun, Mr Andro Melvill, Mr Thomas Smeaton, Mr Alexander Arbuthnot, (three of the lernedst in Europe), Mr James Melville, my uncle . . . with some zelus and godlie barons and gentilmen."

The date of James Melville's death has not been definitely ascertained. The last notices of him are given by Dr M'Crie, being quoted from the Commissary Records of St Andrews, 27th April, 1591. Thomas Ramsay in Kirkton [East Kirkton of St Vigeans] bound himself "to pay to the right worshipful, Mr James Melville, minister of Aberbrothock, four bolls beir, with one pek to the boll, and twa bolls aitmaill, with the cheritie, guid and sufficient stuff—the mail to be for the said Mr James awin eating, all guid and fyne, as ony gentillman sall eat in the countrie adjacent about him, or, failzeing deliverie, to pay for every boll 4 lib money." In March, 1596, the last notice appears, mentioning that he obtained decree against John Richardson "for the feu farme of the Kirklands of Aberbrothock assigned to him by the Lords of Council, viz.:—2 bolls wheat, 28 bolls bear, and 20 bolls aitmeal."

It is to be regretted that the local church records do not extend back to the period of James Melville's pastorate; but what we have been able to glean from different sources affords us glimpses of the life-work of one whose eminent talents and whose pure, upright, and consistent conduct exerted a beneficial influence on the character of our forefathers.

SIR PETER YOUNG.

SIR PETER YOUNG

Of Seaton.

A CONTEMPORARY of, and related through marriage to, James Melville, Sir Peter Young of Seaton was born in Dundee on the 15th of August, 1544. He was the second son of John Young, of that city, and of Margaret Scrimgeour, his wife. Both on his father's and mother's side he came of good and ancient lineage. Andrew Wynton mentions "Wylliame Yong of Ouchterlony" as being among the killed of the Ogilvie party in 1392, on "that duleful dawerk (day's work) at Gasklune." Margaret Scrimgeour, his mother, came of "the ancient and noble family of Scrimgeour."

John Young had a family of three sons and two daughters. Of the sons, Peter, as we have said, was the second. His elder brother John was a parson, and his younger brother, Alexander, is described in several deeds as "ane of the ordinar Ischearis (ushers) of our Soverane Lordis Chalmer," or, in more modern language, Keeper of the Privy Chamber Door to James VI. A sister of his mother was wife to Richard Melville of Baldovy, and mother of James Melville (the nephew of James Melville, the subject of our last sketch). His maternal uncle was Henry Scrimgeour, a celebrated Professor of Philosophy. His mother died at Dundee on the 11th of May, 1578, aged 68, and his father died, also in Dundee, on the 31st August, 1583.

Peter Young, who from his earliest years was a bright, intelligent youth, received the best training that could be obtained at home. In furtherance of his education, as was customary in those days, he was sent abroad. This was in 1562, when he was in his eighteenth year. His first destination was Geneva, where, by the advice of his maternal uncle, Henry Scrimgeour, he entered as a student under the celebrated Theodore Beza. Henry Scrimgeour was a man of great erudition. He had spent several years in Italy in various capacities and for a time had occupied the Chair of Civil Law in the University of Genoa. He had also been a teacher of philosophy in Geneva, which latter city he had left for a time. On returning thither in 1563 he was importuned by the Magistrates to resume his chair for teaching philosophy—a request to which he gave assent. This was of great consequence to the nephew, who had now the benefit of his uncle's advice and guidance in the pursuit of his studies. Here Young had also the advantage of coming into contact with the many eminent men who in those troublous times made Geneva their city of refuge.

He was fortunate in other respects. His uncle possessed one of the most valuable libraries in Europe, being remarkably rich in ancient MSS.—chiefly Greek. These treasures, collected over a long series of years, were at the student's service. This library, by the way, was bequeathed to Peter Young by his uncle, and on the death of the latter it was brought to Scotland. During Peter Young's residence in Geneva he made occasional visits of longer or shorter duration to other continental seats of learning.

Returning to Scotland, he for a time settled at home, where it was the desire of his parents that he should remain permanently. His thirst for learning, however, was too strong to permit of his acquiescing in such a proposal, so he made up his mind to leave once more his native land. In January, 1569, when he had just completed his preparations for the journey, he was offered by the Earl of Moray an appointment as one of the preceptors of King James the Sixth, then a boy of four years of age. His colleague in this office was the illustrious George Buchanan, to whose intimacy with Henry Scrimgeour no doubt Peter Young owed his appointment.

The duty assigned to these two men was a most important one; important not only to the young King, but also to the nation. How differently each of these men discharged that duty history tells. When the appointment was made, high hopes were entertained of the results which would follow, but these were soon disappointed. Buchanan, conscious of the grave nature of the charge committed to him, exercised a wholesome severity towards his pupil, while Young, on the contrary, showed a disposition to overlook his faults and flatter his vanity. Sir James Melville, in a few lines, makes this clear. He says in his Memoirs, "My Lady Mar was wyse and schairp, and held the king in gret aw; and sa did Mester George Buchwhennen. Mester Peter Young was gentiller and was laith till affend the king at any tym, and used himself wairly, *as a man that had a mind of his awen weill*, be keping of his Majestie's favour." As to the real work of teaching, however, there can be no doubt that Young is entitled to a fair share of credit for the proficiency in scholarship to which the royal pupil attained.

While Young was undoubtedly a man of erudition he was intellectually inferior to Buchanan, but in his method of dealing with his pupil he proved that he knew better how to take care of his own personal interests than did his colleague. When quite young James showed an inclination towards those vices which later in life so characterised him. While Buchanan did all in his power to check these he was not seconded in his endeavours by his colleague. On the contrary, Young encouraged instead of counteracted this tendency to evil courses. M'Crie in his life of Andrew Melville, referring to the subject, says, " It was Young's duty to have avoided everything which tended, even indirectly, to counteract the influence of such measures ; and provided he had used his endeavours to reconcile the mind of James to the restraints imposed upon him, by representing them as proceeding from the regard which his preceptor felt for his welfare, the superior mildness of his own manners might have proved highly beneficial. But he was in the prime of life ; he had the prospect of a family ; he saw the advantages to be derived from ingratiating himself with the young King ; and, with a cool and calculating prudence, which men of ordinary minds often possess in a high degree, he pursued the course which tended to advance his worldly interests by flattering the vanity of his pupil, humouring his follies, and conniving at these faults which he ought to have corrected. The consequences were such as might have been expected. The youthful vices of James were confirmed ; Buchanan incurred the rooted aversion of his pupil ; and Young had his reward in the honours and gifts that were lavished on himself and his family." Of the honours and gifts which this time-serving policy on the part of Young drew from his royal master we have ample evidence.

Besides his duty as preceptor he appears to have acted in the capacity of Royal Librarian. In the end of 1893 an interesting discovery was made by Dr Garnett, the Keeper of the Printed Books in the British Museum. This was a small quarto MS. volume of twenty paper leaves, bound in limp vellum, the bulk of which was in the handwriting of Peter Young, although it also bears specimens of the caligraphy of the boy King.

Under the editorship of Mr George F. Warner, M.A., F.S.A., the Assistant Keeper of Manuscripts in the British Museum, the Scottish History Society has printed this for the use of its members. The title of the book, as issued by the Society, is "The Library of James VI., 1573-1583, from a manuscript in the hand of Sir Peter Young, his Tutor."

The discovery of this soiled, dog-eared little volume is, for many reasons, a valuable find, and the Scottish History Society has done a good service in giving it publicity. From the description of it by Mr Warner we gather the following particulars: Both within and without it is so much soiled and worn as to render the writing in some places almost illegible. In the centre of each cover is stamped a small gilt crown between the initials I.R.

As to its contents, it not only supplies curious information as to the books forming the library of James VI., but it also includes matter of directly personal interest. In two instances the youthful King has utilised the flyleaves for a copy-book. One of these gives us a specimen of his handwriting when he was some seven or eight years of age. It consists of the letters of the alphabet, large and small, with the trilingual signature, " Jacobus.R.Scoto.R.Jaques.Roy.d'escosse. James R." In the volume of the Scottish History Society, a facsimile of this elementary effort is given. The other exercise is written in a stiff, boyish hand, showing, however, all the characteristics of James's writing in later years. Here he has written, " Si quid honestum per laborem egeris, labor abit, honestum manet ; si quid turpe per uoluptatem egeris, uoluptas abit turpe manet."

This is copied twice, and partially a third time, with the signature "Jacobus R." added. Young has scribbled on the fly-leaves and covers various remarks made by the youthful monarch, such as "Thay gar me speik Latin or I could speak Scottis," and "Cuidam dicenti ze suld neuer be angrie.' 'Than,' he says, 'I suld not waire ye lyoun in my armes, bot rather a scheip.'"

The introduction by Mr Warner is exceedingly interesting and historically valuable. When and how this MS. found its way into the British Museum collection is not definitely known, but it is believed that it came there when the Royal Library was removed to the Museum in 1759. It had thus lain neglected for more than a century.

Young's name frequently occurs both in ecclesiastical and civil records. James Melville makes repeated mention of him in his Diary. In 1574 he says—"Alexander Young cam hame from Genev from his uncle, and my near kinsman, Mr Henry Scrymgour, of honourable memoire, with some propynes to the King and letters to Mr George Bowchanan and Mr Peter Young, that ane the King's maister, that other his pœdagog." In the same year we find him "and Saunders, his brother," conversing with Mr Andrew Melville at Stirling. At the Assembly of 1574, Calderwood tells us that "Mr George Buchanan, Keeper of the Privy Seale, Mr Peter Young, Pedagogue to the King, Mr Andrew Melville, and Mr James Lowsone were appointed to revise Mr Patrick Adamson's paraphrase in Latine verse upon the Booke of Job, and if they find it consonant to the truthe to authorise the same with the testimonie of their hand writt and subscription."

On the 4th February, 1577, Young married Elizabeth Gib, by whom he had eight sons and four daughters, in the following order :—(1) Mary, born 1st June, 1579—(married to John Douglas

SIR PETER YOUNG.

of Tilquhilly); (2 and 3) James and Henry, twins, born 1st July, 1580. The first of these twins was named James at the King's special request, and, at a later period, had the honour of knighthood conferred on him by his name-father. (4) Margaret, born, as he writes, "at my house of Seton," 14th Nov., 1581 ; (5 and 6) Peter and Robert, twins, born 1st July, 1583 ; (7) Patrick, born 25th June, 1585; (8 and 9) Frederic and Joanna, twins, born 1587. Frederic died 31st Jany., 1609. (11) Michael, born 6th Nov., 1589; and (12) Anne, born 16th February, 1590. After her birth he writes, "and so God blessed me with a twelfth child, the other eleven still living." But he was destined to have more "blessings" of the same kind. His wife Elizabeth Gib died at Leith on 10th May, 1593, and on 6th May, 1596, he married his second wife, the Lady Janet Murray of Torphichen, who only survived six months after her marriage. If she left him no "blessings," she appears to have left him some "scores" to pay, for there is evidence of a summons "against Sir Peter Young for payment of debts contracted by Dame Janet Murray, Lady Torphichen, deceased, in preparation of her marriage with the said Sir Peter, her last spouse."

He remained a widower for a short time, his third wife being Marjory Nairne, who added to his already numerous family four daughters — (13) Euphemia, born 20th April, 1601 ; (14) Elizabeth, born 11th Feb., 1603 ; (15) Nicola, born 5th July, 1604 ; and (16) Arabella, born 16th Dec., 1608 — a goodly family from first to last of eight sons and eight daughters. His diary gives a considerable amount of information about his children. The following extracts therefrom, as having local references, are interesting :—" My daughter, Margaret, was born in my own house of Seton about 11 o'clock p.m., on 14th November, 1581, and baptised 5th December—James Melvin [Melville] minister of

God's Word, being sponsor." As to the twins, Peter and Robert, he tells that "the sponsors were . . . William Ouchterlony, Laird of Kelly; and also my neighbour, William, of the same surname" [William Ouchterlony of Wester Seaton]. "August 29, 1584—About midnight in the beginning of the new moon, my wife brought forth Patrick, who, indeed, was baptised next day in the Church of St Vigian; the sponsors were George Balfour of Tarry, and my neighbour, William Ouchterlony; also present, the Lady of Bonnyton, soliciting the name of the child to be that of her husband." "My sixth son, John, was born at Seaton . . . the sponsors being John Carnegie of Kinnaird," and so on. His son Patrick acquired considerable distinction on account of his scholarly attainments.

In 1579, in Lord Burleigh's list of persons worthy of being bribed to Queen Elizabeth's interests, we find in that "of persons who were not commended by the Regent (Morton) yet by others thought meet to be entertained," the names of "Mr George Buchanan, the King's tutor, a singular man, and Peter Young, another tutor to the King, especially well affected, and ready to persuade the King to be in favour of Her Majestye."

In 1580 or '81, John Carnegie of that ilk and of Seaton, sold Easter Seaton to Peter Young. The house of Easter Seaton, as occupied by Sir Peter Young from that time till his death, stood near by the site of the present farmhouse of East Seaton. A stone bearing date 1583, with the letters P. Y. and E. G. (Peter Young and E. Gib), which had originally formed a part of the old mansion-house is still visible in the north gable of East Seaton.* The avenue which led to the old mansion-house is also still to be seen.

---

* In Chambers's "Eminent Scotsmen," and other standard works, this Seaton in Forfarshire is confounded with Seaton in Haddingtonshire.

Seaton was not the only property in the neighbourhood of Arbroath which was acquired by Sir Peter. He acquired the lands of Dickmontlaw and Kinblethmont. At a later period he also, purchased half of the lands and Mill of Lunan, and the superiority of the town and lands of Arbikie, so that he was an extensive land-owner in the vicinity of the burgh ; and while, from the nature of his public duties, he was not constantly resident at Seaton, he spent a considerable portion of his life here.

The important position he held in connection with the Court led to his services being used both in civil and ecclesiastical affairs. We have already mentioned several occasions on which the members of the General Assembly of the Kirk of Scotland availed themselves of his council and aid.

He was also appointed to perform important offices in connection with the State. On 20th July, 1586, he was sent as ambassador to Denmark. In 1587, he was again sent, along with Sir Patrick Vans of Barnbarroch, to the same Court. Before the despatch of this embassy was resolved on, we find him writing thus to Barnbarroch :—

" My Lord,—I have obtained leif of his Majestie to go hame for sum few days. At my leif-taking I have recommendit te his Heines the purpos yr Lordship kenis, and has schawin that   , is ever at hand, and that wee have worne threid bair all excuses, ellis that quhither alliance be marriage be meinit or not, ambassadouris maie be send for the mater of Orkney, gif thair war na mair or less, his Majestie wald [suffer] the reproche of breaking of promis to ane prince and natioun that makis meikle of plain dealing. I have said quhat I can, and hes promis to be reddy how sune his Majestie plesis to command to cum to help to inform sic as sal be send. I pray yr L./ to go doune and hold Heines in remembrance. Alace that sa gude ane purpos hes sa feu friendis, and that his Majestie hes sa

littel care of himself. My Lord Coronnel will remember for his pairt, bot he is boune over the watter. I spak my Lord Chancellor and hes remembrit his L/ assurit of the Kingis g[racis] promis be his last writtis, as if his L/ awin. Hold matteris in frame quhill my backcuming, and I shall relief your L/ again the best I may. The Lord graunt our deir Maister and King to happen upon the worthiest Princess that is in the world for his half marrow. God bless yr L/, and send mony sic servantis to his Majestie.—From the Quenisferry the xxij. of Februar at xj. houris at nicht.—Your Lordship's awin man
"P. Young.

"As for my small particulars, gif yr L/ may help thame do it. Gif not I sall beir it the best that I may, and sall be never the less reddy for ane gude turn to his Majestie or the common weil, according to mein powar.

"To the richt honble. and my very good Lord my Lord of Barnbarracke."

The letter, which follows on the decision being come to to dispatch the Embassy, is written from Holyrood House, Edinburgh, where he had gone to consult with and receive the Royal commands. In addition to its historic value, it is interesting in other respects. It shows that Young possessed good mercantile qualifications and that he could drive a hard bargain. It is amusing to notice the careful instructions given to his retinue as to the colour and style of their dress. In consequence of the death of Queen Mary, they were to be dressed in black or "dule." His scholarly tastes can also be inferred from a passage in the letter which reads thus :—

"My Lord,—Eftir maist hertley commendation, I have gotten the arrestment subseryvit togidder with the othir letters for staying of proces, and hes delyverit thame to my Lady your bedfellow, quha has not been ydle on hir part for yr L/ departing. I have obtenit ane uther letter of arrestment to stay the schips hier presently, maid at his Majesty's awin instance, but ony mentioun of us, quhilk sal be partly put in execution this same day at Leyth, and thairafter at Montros and Dondy, St Androis and langis all the coste syde, and for that same cause I am instantly to tak over Capten Arnat with me. I have spoken his Majestie at Creichtoun sen your departing, and has his Heines promeis that na preceapts sal pass quhill we be first staikit —My Lord Secretare has hecht to hold his Majestie in remembrance and to hald band that we be not prevenit be ony. I am making hame till the first of the nixt, quhair I sall not be unmyndful of our erand, for I feir my Lord Secretare sall forget, and Mr George allsua. The Clerk Register is busy casting over all the register for sic things as I have cravit of him. The skippar was at me again to see gif we wad give the 1800 merkis. I stude still at the 1000 merkis that your Lordship offerit him. This day we be to speik farther. I sall not pass the 1200 quhill I see quhat schipping there is in uther partis. Ye will remember that the gentilmen be clad in blak but cullouris, for sa his Majestie spak unto me and my Lord Secretare baith sa, that sall represent a gravitie and half ane duell. The grat lang ruffis and meikle beliis wad be castin away. This I writ that the gentilmen may be warnit in deu tyme or they mak their claithes utherwyis, as I sall warne neyne. I shewe yr Lordship that the last Abbot Glenlusse has promesit me Hegisippas in Greek written with hand, and Commentaria Cæsaris Manuscripta siclyk. I wald pray yr L/ to inquyre quha gat his bukis that theis micht be recoverit yit war not they war ald and evil-favourit. Jhone Hume of Cumeragane had brocht thame to me, yr L/ kennis the taile. Becausse I am pressit to depart for the tyde that is at hand, I will commit yr L/ to God, be quhais grace I haist to be in this toune again the first or second of the nixt. From Halyrude house this xviii of Mairche 1586.—Your Lordship at command for ever.

"P. YOUNG OF SETOUN.

"To the richt honble. and my very special gud Lord, My Lord of Barnbarrow, Lord of his Hienes Privy Counsall and Sessioun."

Other letters of an equally interesting nature passed between Sir Peter and Barnbarroch. In one of these Young expresses a very high opinion of a Montrose vessel, for the employment of which for the conveyance of the embassy to Denmark they were on terms. "I was yesterday at Montross quhair I saw ane very proper schip and veil accouttrit—thar vantis nother ordanance, ensigne, flaggis, nor stremars. Sche is of fourscore and twelf tonne of birth or better, ane trim sailor and vierlyck ship, and sal be had as I sappose bettir schip nor any uther schip in Scotland." This letter is dated "from Setoun." In another letter written from Seaton a week later he again refers to this same ship and says :—" I know not ane schip meiter for us nor this of Montroise, she is ane trim sailer . . . and wants nathing necessare to decore hir." In this same letter he proclaims his loyalty thus—" As for my part I sal be reddy to serve, and no willing to lye ydle, and suinge [dream] with my bukis the wyffe and bairnes, gif his Majestie will permit me."

A letter of his in Latin, addressed to Beza his friend and former teacher, has been found in the Ducal Library at Gotha, a translation of which, with remarks on the portrait of John Knox by Mr P. Hume Brown, the biographer of Knox, recently appeared in the *Scotsman*. As the letter is exceedingly interesting, and, among other topics touched on, contains a vivid description of the personal appearance of the famous Reformer, we give it entire. The letter is dated Edinburgh, 13th November, 1579, and is as follows :—

"Your kind letter came to my hands last month, though shortly before I had received from a countryman of ours another letter from you commending Serranus. To the best of my ability I have endeavoured to meet the requests in both letters. The Plato of Serranus—that is, his industry in illustrating Plato—I have spoken of to His Majesty in the warmest terms at my command; and, in truth, the labours of Serranus, in their own kind, are not to be despised. According to your suggestion, I have read your letter itself to His Majesty, word for word; and you may rest assured that he is greatly touched by it. For all learned and good men he has a lively affection; but specially yourself and your city, as the port of refuge of all the good and learned, he goes out to with all his heart, as, in his letter publicly addressed to the Council of Geneva, he has shown his desire to testify.

"Mr Buchanan, whom I greeted in your name, returns your greetings with the most dutiful regard, and sends you his "Baptistes" and his dialogue "De Jure Regni." Mainly at your instance, though he is now foredone with age and disease, he has resolved to revise his "Psalms" as soon as he obtains the translation of Tremellius.

"With regard to your request that I should send you portraits of the illustrious men who have toiled for the glory of God among us, and especially that of Mr Knox, set it forever down to the negligence (not to use a stronger word) of our nation that it has never given heed to this duty. Not even of Knox, a man worthy of eternal memory, does any representation exist. However, I have approached certain of our artists, and if they stand by their promises, you will receive a portrait of him along with this letter. Meanwhile, with my own pencil I will describe his face and bearing from my own recollection of him, and from the report of such as were most intimate while he yet lived. The whole story of his life you will hear from Mr Lowson. In stature, then, he was slightly under the middle height, of well-knit and graceful figure, with shoulders somewhat broad, longish fingers, head of moderate size, hair black, complexion somewhat dark, and a general appearance not unpleasing. In his stern and severe countenance there was a natural dignity and majesty, not without a certain grace, and in anger there was an air of command on his brow. Under a somewhat narrow forehead, his brows stood out in a slight ridge over his ruddy and slightly swelling cheeks, so that his eyes seemed to retreat into his head. The colour of his eyes was bluish grey, their glance keen and animated. His face was rather long; his nose of more than ordinary length; the mouth large; the lips full, the upper a little thicker than the lower; his beard black, mingled with grey, very long and moderately thick. . . . I send you an eulogium of my revered father, Mr Buchanan, with a portrait of him done to the life.

"Just as I am signing this letter, an artist has opportunely come in, and brought in one box the likenesses of Knox and Buchanan."

In 1592, he wrote "A Short Account of the Life and Death of Mary, Queen of Scots," in which he speaks of her in the following eulogistic terms :—" A soverign lady, worthy of a better fortune, richly endowed with all natural gifts, all royal virtues, and especially clemency ; she was of matchless beauty, and her generosity was unique."

In 1594 Young was a third time ambassador to Denmark, and to the Duke of Mecklenberg and Brunswick.

By an Act of the Scottish Parliament, passed in his favour in 1587, he was appointed Royal Almoner, or, as it is expressed, "His Hienes Elimosinar," an office which he retained till his death. This honour was conferred upon him for the care he bestowed on the King in His Majesty's youth, and for his journeys to Norway and Denmark for the purpose of bringing home the King's "weill belovit spous Anna." This Act makes special reference to his Arbroath estates, as the following quotation will show :—" And, further, our said souerane lord and his saids three estaittis in parliamet of their certane knawledge ratifys and apprevis the alteration and change of the assumption of the lands of cister seytoun and half of dikmountlaw liand within the regalitie and baronie of abirbrothok and shirefdome of forfair, now pertenig heritablie to the said Mr peter, and assumit of auld in a pt. of the third of the abbacie of abirbrothock. Becaus his

Hienes has resauit als' mony als profitable landis in recompance thairof as at mair lenth is specifit in the decreit gevin thereupoun be the lords auditours of his Hienes chekker."

On James's succession to the English throne, he did not forget his old tutor. In April, 1603, Young was nominated Dean of Lichfield; but, within a month thereafter, both he and his royal patron found that the post could not so easily be conferred as they imagined, and it went elsewhere. But to make up for this disappointment, in the year following he was made tutor and chief overseer of the household to Prince Charles, a post which carried with it a pension of £200.

On the 19th Feb., 1605, he was knighted by the King at Whitehall, and at the same time his pension was raised to £300 per annum. In 1606, we find him in London as one of the Scottish Privy Council, where a conference was being held between that body and the Scottish Reformers, among the latter of whom were our neighbours, Andrew and James Melville. In November, 1616, he got the Mastership of St Cross Hospital, a license to hold it, "notwithstanding he is not a divine nor there residing," being granted to him in January following.

After this, we have not much trace of Sir Peter's public career, and, although we have no positive evidence, we have good reason to believe that he spent the greater part of his life after this in following the pursuits of a quiet country gentleman on his estate of Seaton, and that for a number of years his figure was a familiar one on the streets of Arbroath.

For some years prior to his death, he kept in his own hands and farmed a considerable portion of his lands in this neighbourhood. His foreign travels had, doubtless, enabled him to become acquainted with all the then latest improvements in implements of husbandry, for we know that *iron* harrows were in use at Seaton at a time when they were unknown, or, at least, in little use in any other part of Scotland. This is clearly brought out in the Inventory given up by his executors, where we find the following entry—" Item sevin pair of irone harrowis," &c. This Inventory, a copy of which was given in the proceedings of the Society of Antiquaries in 1889 in a paper by Mr Hugh W. Young, contains a full account of the personal estate, in this quarter, of Sir Peter Young. The document shows that he farmed extensively, and the information it conveys as to the prices of agricultural produce and live stock, as well as of servants' wages, two-and-a-half centuries ago, is both interesting and useful. On a comparison with present-day prices, it goes to show that agriculture in Scotland in the beginning of the seventeenth century was in a flourishing condition.

In the list of " Dettis awand be the dead," we find a few familiar names. The executors of Henry Philip, minister of Arbroath, figure as creditors for tiends. Sir Peter predeceased Dr Philip by about a month. Another creditor is " John Rany, cordiner in Aberbrothock." It is interesting, by the way, to know that for more than three hundred years the Renny family, of whom this John Renny was one of the forebears, has continuously occupied a prominent mercantile position in the burgh of Arbroath. The tombstone of this " John Rany, cordiner," is one of the oldest and best preserved in the Abbey Church-yard.

Sir Peter Young's death took place at his mansion house of Seaton, on 7th January, 1628. His remains were deposited in an arched sepulchral vault underneath the Kirk of St Vigeans.

At the beginning of this century there was attached to the north wall of the church the remains of two buildings, one of which was known as " Auldbar's aisle." It was underneath this aisle that Sir Peter was laid.

In the year 1803, on the removal of the ruins of this aisle, there were found a number of monumental remains, and among these a Latin inscription in memory of Sir Peter Young. This was removed from the vault, and is now seen fastened to the wall of the present Parish Church. It runs as follows :—

PETRVS YOVNG,

A SETON EQ. AVR. SERMO. AC
POTMO. IACOB. VI. BRIT. FRAN.
ET HIB. REGI A STVDIIS CONSIL.
ET ELEEMOS. PROPTER ERVDIT.
PRVDENT. ET MORVM ELEGANTIA—
EXIMIAM DOMI REGI SVO. CIVIB'
CHARVS FORIS REGIB & PRINCIPIB'
APVD QVOS VARIIS LEGAT. FVNCT'
EST CELEBRIS HIC BEATORVM RESVR-
RECT. EXPECTAT.

OBIT. IAN. VII. AN: M.DC.XXVIII
ET. SE. LXXXIII.

Of which the following is a free translation :—" Sir Peter Young of Seaton, Knight, who was ' Preceptor, Privy Councillor, and Almoner to His Most Serene Majesty James VI., King of Great Britain, France, and Ireland, and who, on account of his learning, prudence, and elegance of manners, was dear to his King and countrymen at home and abroad, to the kings and princes to whom he was ambassador, here waits the resurrection of the blessed. He died January 7th, 1628, and of his age eighty-three."

The lands of Seaton passed out of the hands of the Young family in 1670 having—by disposition, dated 14th and 25th July of that year—been made over to Henry Crawford, merchant, burgess of Dundee.

THE PHILIPS
Of Almerieclose.

WHEN James Melville died, somewhere about 1596, he was succeeded by Andrew Lamb, whose incumbency lasted only four years. Lamb, after serving the church for a time in Leith, became bishop of Brechin. Lamb's successor in Arbroath was Henry Philpe, who, prior to his transference to this parish, was minister of Creigh in Fife.

HENRIE PHILPE.

The connection with Arbroath of the Philips, afterwards known as "of Almerieclose"—so far as definite information can be obtained—carries us back to within half-a-century of the Reformation, although it is probable that that connection goes back to pre-Reformation days. Whether Henry Philpe, the progenitor of the Almerieclose Philips, was a native of Forfarshire or of Fifeshire, it is difficult, in the absence of reliable data, to determine. One authority says that he was a descendant of an old Fifeshire family, some of whom had filled important offices both in Church and State. On the other hand, we have evidence of various persons of the name owning houses and lands in Arbroath and neighbourhood long before Henry Philpe's settlement as minister of Arbroath. In one deed dated 25th

April, 1587, David Philpe and his spouse were infeft in a tenement on the north side of Lordburn, James Philpe (no designation) being a witness. It is therefore probable that Henry Philpe, whose first charge was Creigh in Fife, in looking for promotion, had naturally sought it in his native burgh.

When in 1601 he became minister of Arbroath, the civil establishment of the Church of Scotland was still Presbyterian, but James VI., notwithstanding his earlier professions of having become a convert to the Presbyterian form of church government, soon showed that his professions were anything but sincere. Presbyterianism, from its nature, could not satisfy his ambition to be regarded as head of the Church, hence his persistent efforts for the establishment of Episcopacy; and, in 1610, by dint of bribery, cajolery, and intimidation, he attained his end.

While Presbyterian minister of Arbroath, Philip was no unwilling instrument in the hands of the prelatical party in the endeavour to bring about the wishes of the King. Seeing the active part he took in furthering the object of the Monarch's ambition, and considering his undoubted fitness for the office, it is surprising that he was not rewarded with a bishopric or that some other substantial recognition of his services was not conferred upon him.

Philip was an able man and was much trusted by the party whose side he had taken. This being so, it was not to be expected that his action at the time should be looked upon by the opposite party with complacence. The following extract from Forbes' "Records touching the state of the Kirk" bears this out. "About the latter end of June, 1606, the King sent for some of the ministers to come to him against the 15th day

of September next following. The persons sent for were these :
Mr Andrew Melvill, James Melvill, James Balfour, William Scott,
William Watson, John Carmichell, Robert Wallace, Adam Colt,
and Henry Philipe, of which the first eight were known to be
of the most learned, wise, faithful, and upright in the land, and
thus most opposite to all the wickedness of the bishops and
commissioners; the last being of another disposition was purposlie
(as it was thought) sent through the policie of Mr James Nicolson, to the end that being in company with the others he might
be acquainted with their mind and give intelligence thereof to
the King and to the bishops and commissioners. But this
policie being perceived, the danger was prevented by the others
refusing to have him in their companie."

At the convention held at Linlithgow in December of the
same year (1606), out of a leet of four, James Nicolson—who,
as Calderwood tells us, had some time previously "resolved to
take the bishoprick of Dunkelden, laitlie bought to him by the
King from Mr Peter Rollock for twenty thowsand punds"—was
chosen moderator, who on taking his place assumed Henry
Philip, minister of Arbroath, as his scribe, without administering
the oath of fidelity. At this and the subsequent meetings the
proceedings are attested by "Mr Henric Philipe, scribe."

Philip was a member of the General Assemblies of 1602,
1606, 1610, 1616, and 1618. At the assembly of 1618 he was
one of those who took an active part in the promulgation of
the "Five Articles of Perth," and for his services on this occasion he was warmly commended to the King by Lord Binny.
In the official list of those present at this Perth Assembly he
is designated Doctor Philip, having two years before had the
degree of D.D. conferred on him by the University of St
Andrews.

In 1619, "Docter Henrie Philipe, minister of Aberbrothe," was appointed by the King one of his Commissioners to try those charged with certain offences, which offences were fully detailed in the Commission. If the culprit so charged was found guilty, the Commissioners were directed to bring the case before the minister of the parish where the culprit dwelt, with orders to proceed with excommunication against him. If the minister refused to obey these injunctions, the Commissioners were empowered to punish offenders by fine and imprisonment. The real intention of all this, however, seems to have been to force ministers, and other professors, to practise "the Five Articles" and to establish what these ministers, and those taking part with them, held to be the tyrannous assumption of the bishops. It will thus be seen that Philip took a very active share in the business of the Church, and especially of the prelatical party therein.

He had not settled long in Arbroath when he began to acquire property within and around the burgh, and to these possessions his descendants, for at least three or four generations, continued to add till the family of Philip became one of the most powerful and important in the locality.

It may be interesting to make a brief reference to some of these properties as they are found recorded in the Burgh Registers, not only as showing the varied acquisitions of the Philip family, but also as showing the alliances they formed with other leading families in the district, as appearing from these registers.

We have no record of the marriage of Henry Philip, but there is evidence in a document, to which we will have occasion, for another purpose, to refer further on, that his wife's family belonged to Cupar in Fife.

After his induction in Arbroath, in 1601, he and his wife, Isabella Petersone took up their abode in a house on the east side of Rotton Raw, that is the portion of the High Street between the top of Lordburn and what is now known as Kirk Square. At first they occupied this house only as tenants. It was convenient for the minister as being in close proximity to the church. For this and other reasons, they seem to have been so pleased with it that in 1605 they acquired it from Patrick Balfour, burgess of Arbroath, with the consent of Agnes Ogilvy, his spouse. This house in Rotton Raw is described as being between the lands of the said Patrick Balfour, on the south, and of Richard Watson, on the north, the Convent Gardens, without the Monastery of Aberbrothock on the east, and the common road on the west; and, together with the house, he acquired the barn and garden of the same, and a well and pump lying there. He, and his wife, Isabella Petersone, were infeft therein, but they immediately resigned the barn with the well and pump to Richard Watson, and his spouse, Catherine Lyell.

Philip afterwards acquired other tenements in the same locality, one on the west side of Rotton Raw and two on the east side of it. One of these tenements on the east side is described in a deed in 1629 as bounded by the lands of Thomas Mylne on the north; while in 1653 it is described as "betwix the school of the said burgh on the north, and the yairds of the Abbey of Arbroath on the east part."

In 1612, he acquired the lands of Guthrieshill, extending to nine acres, from James Duncanson, minister of the Church of Alloway, and Helen Livingston, his spouse. In 1614, he purchased ten and a half acres in Keptie and two acres in Dishland (for which he paid 2700 merks Scots), and one acre on the south side of Old Marketgate and one acre on the west side of Dishland. In 1615, he added four acres in Keptie (one rig being in the "dog hillocks"). In 1616, three roods of Keptie and a piece of Keptie Hill. In 1619, Robert Lyne's part of Cobis Croft and two acres of Wareslap Schcd and Loch Schede. At a later period, he acquired the remainder of Cobis Croft, and a tenement and land on the south side of Applegate. In 1622, he acquired other four acres in Keptie, and another acre in 1623.

He always signed his name "Philpe," the only one of the family who did so, all the others signing "Philip," "Philipe," or "Phillip." That he was highly respected in Arbroath, and was looked upon as a leading citizen, may be inferred from the fact that in several successive years he was chosen as a councillor of the burgh. He had probably been created a burgess some time between 1605—when he became proprietor of the house in Rotton Raw—and 1617, but during these years there are no records of the proceedings of the Council extant.

The first minute in which he appears as a councillor is dated 24th October, 1624, at which meeting Thomas Peirsone of Lochlands and John Granger are elected bailies of the burgh. The sederunt includes "John Hamilton, chalmerlan of Abirbrothok, as Commissioner for my Lord Marquis of Hamilton," besides the following "counsellares":—"Docter henrie Philp, minister; Mr Henry Peirsone, Mr Alexander Peirson, Alex. rynd, William buchan, Alex. peter, Robert Lyne, Andro eliot, Mr Patrick Carnegy, James Carnegy, John Wallace, John Mudie, John Ochterlony."

The Doctor appears in the list of councillors of 3rd October, 1625; 2nd October, 1626; and 1st October, 1627; but in the last-mentioned year the heading is "Counsellares Extraordinary,

Docter henry philp, minister, and John Hamilton, chalmerlan." To this latter, which was a higher honour than that of ordinary councillor, he was well entitled, from the position he held as a considerable landed proprietor in the burgh and one of her most intelligent and influential citizens.

Dr Philip's death took place in September, 1627. He was survived by his wife, Isabella Petersone, and by a son James and two daughters—Marjory and Isobel. We do not know if the Doctor had been in treaty for the purchase of Almerieclose, but, if he was, death had put an end to his negotiations. Whether there were such negotiations or not we find that by a charter by "David Balfoure de Guynd, heritable proprietor, and James Balfoure de north tarry for his interest," dated 11 March and 21 April, 1628, Isabella Petersone, relict of the minister, for herself in liferent, and James Philip, son of the minister, in fee, acquired the Elemosinarie Croft, Guest Meadow, a tenement of land on the east side of the Croft, another on the west side of it, and a rood of land in the Elemosinarie garden. On 26 January, 1629, James, the son of Henry Philip and Isabella Petersone, was infeft in these properties and his mother was then described as deceased, so that she survived her husband, Dr Philip, for somewhere about a year.

It will thus be seen that what was known as the property of Almerieclose, from which the Philip family afterwards took their designation, was never owned or occupied by Dr Philip as has generally been supposed, but that his son James was the first male proprietor thereof.

On the death of his widow, Dr Henry Philip's movable property fell, by bequest, to his daughters Marjory and Isobel. Marjory survived her father and mother for some years, and, so far as can be ascertained, she remained unmarried. Unlike Marjory, Isobel at her father's death was not of sufficient age to manage her own affairs. Consequently we find that on "19 February, 1629, there compeared in the Court before the Bailies, Isabell Philp, dochter lawful to vmq^{le} Doctor Henry Philp, minister of this Burgh, and being past the age of tutory and having charged David Philp in pittilly and Mr James Philp minister of Lownnan persons nearest of kin to her on her father's side, and Robert Petersone, bailly, and Peter Mortimer, merchant and burgess of Cowper, persons nearest of kin to her on her mother's side, to hear and see curators nominated; when she nominated and chose the said Mr James Philp, her uncle, and Mr James Philp, her brother german," to be her curators.

Henry Philip was succeeded as minister of Arbroath by Simon Durie, who continued to hold the office for a quarter of a century, dying somewhere about 1653. His successor was James Fraser, a scion of the house of Fraser of Philorth. On the 14th of March, 1654, James Fraser married Isobel Philip, the younger daughter of Dr Philip. Two years thereafter, he bought the lands of Hospitalfield and Kirkton, and was consequently the founder of the family of Fraser of Hospitalfield.

JAMES PHILIP (1)
Of Almericlose.

JAMES, the son of Henry Philip and Isabella Petersone, who is described in several deeds as burgess and bailie in Arbroath, was the first Philip of Almericlose. On 26th January, 1629, he was formally acknowledged by the bailies in court as nearest and lawful heir to his father, the vmq^{le} Doctor Henry Philp, minister of the burgh, and at the same time they did "creat the said Mr James Philp burges and frieman of the said burgh." On 3rd October, 1631, he was elected bailie for that year. In the year following he lost the election, but was again elected in 1633, after which his name disappears, but as he acted as a witness in a sasine on 2nd December, 1634, he must have died in that month, as from a deed in favour of his son in 1653, elsewhere referred to, he is described as having died " in the moneth of ane thousand six hundredth and threttie foure yeires."

He married Isobell Ouchterlony, daughter of Ouchterlony of Wester Seaton, by whom he had a son, also James, and a daughter, Margaret, who became the wife of James Piersone, Town-Clerk of Arbroath. James Philip (1) died, as we have seen, in 1634, and two years thereafter, his widow entered into a matrimonial alliance with James Lamb of South Tarrie. We have not come on evidence of the date of the death of Isabella Ouchterlony's second spouse, but we know that in 1653, and probably some years earlier, she was the wedded wife of Peter Young of Easter Seaton, son of Sir James Young, and grandson of Sir Peter Young of Seaton. This Peter Young signs as witness to various deeds in which members of the Philip family are interested, one of these bearing date 1650, so that he may have then been the husband of Isabella Ouchterlony if not for some years prior to that date.

In a sasine, dated 16th June, 1636, " Isabellam Ochterlony, relictam quondam Mag^r Jacobi Philip," burgess of Arbroath, is mentioned as having purchased an acre of Keptie. In less than six months afterwards she was the wife of James Lamb. In a Disposition, dated 8th October, 1653 — " me Issobell Ochterlony, relict of vmquhile Mr James Philip sumtyme Bailie and Burgess of Abirbrothok, with consent and assent of Peter

Young of ester Seatoune now my spouse" sells the acre to James Philip, her son, and in 1657, she conveys to him another acre of Keptie, a rig of it being in the "shuil breeds." In a charter of a feu "lying neire the north west port," dated 10th January, 1656, the following clause occurs—" me Mr James Philip of Almeryclosse . . . with consent and assent of Issobell Ouchterlony, my mother, and of Peter Young of Seatoune, her present husband." These extracts show conclusively that the wife of James Philip (1), of Almerieclose, was Isobell Ouchterlony, daughter of Ouchterlony of Wester Seaton, not Jane Guthrie, daughter of the minister of Arbirlot, as stated by some writers. There were Philips in Arbroath long before Henry Philip settled there. In 1614, "Mr James Philipe, schoolmaster of the said burgh" was witness to an agreement of sale to which the minister was a party, and in 1615 he was also witness to a Resignation in favour of the minister. When James Guthrie was incumbent of Arbirlot, James Philip, brother of Dr Henry Philip, and uncle of the first James Philip of Almerieclose, was minister of Lunan. Probably either of these—if indeed he was not one and the same person—first schoolmaster of Arbroath and afterwards the minister of Lunan—may have been the husband of Jane Guthrie.

JAMES PHILIP (2)

Of Almerieclose.

This James Philip, son of James Philip (1) and Isobel Ouchterlony though he succeeded, as we have seen, through the death of his father, in 1634, did not make up his titles till 1653. The Retour is dated 17th August, 1653, and narrates " that the deceist Master James Philp, sumtyme bailie of Aberbrothock, father to James Philp off Almriclose died last vest" in the Elemosinarie Croft Guest Meadow, &c., "all somtyme occupyit be the deceist Issobell Patersoun, relict of the deceist Doctor Henrie Philp, parents to the said Master James Philp and the deceist Master Johne Granger" and that the lands of Guthrieshill "have been in the handis of Issobell Ouchterlony, relict of the said deceist Master James as lady lyfrentrix thairof in sua far as concerns the lyfrent recht of the samyn, and in sua far as concernes the fie thairof they are as they have been in the handis of the said Harie Guthrie of Colistown superior foirsaid be reasoun of non entrie continwallie sen the death of the deceist Mr James who died in the moneth of   ane thousand sex hundreth and threttie foure yeires."

In thus completing his title to the proprietorship of Almerieclose he was preparing for another important event. He had for some time been courting, and he is now about to bring home as his bride, Margaret Grahame. This lady was the daughter of Walter Grahame of Duntrune and granddaughter of Sir William Grahame of Claverhouse, the cousin of and curator to the great Marquis of Montrose.

The contract matrimonial between James Philip of Almerieclose and Margaret Grahame is dated at Easter Seatoune and Duntrune 20th and 22nd August, 1653, and by it they bind themselves to get married "after the forme prescryvit be the church of this natioune," and he provides her with the life rent of all the properties then belonging to him and the annual rent of the principal sum of £1000 Scots, which he afterwards changed to an annual rent of £60 Scots. That the Philips of Arbroath occupied a good position in society may be inferred from this alliance with such a house as that of the Grahames, in whose veins flowed royal blood. The issue of this marriage was three sons—James, Walter, and Peter.

Like his father and grandfather, he continued to add to his heritable possessions. He acquired additional acres in Keptie in 1665, 1673, 1679, and 1682, and to the tenements on the west side of the Elemosinary Street he made additions in 1658, 1669, 1670, and 1672. We have failed to find out when and by whom the Mansion House still standing, and to this day known as Almerieclose House, was built. In all probability it was erected by this James Philip (2). Although we have seen that the property was first acquired by his grandmother and by his father James Philip (1), he (2) was the first to appear in any of the deeds as "of Almerieclose," our inference being that while his father owned the land there was no residence on it till this house was provided, probably against the homecoming of his bride.

Certainly the house, as it presently stands, was in existence in 1684 when John Ouchterlony wrote his "Account of the Shyre." The lands of Almerieclose had certain tenements, and amongst these was the Almshouse Chapel, the stones of which had been utilized for the erection of the Mansion House. In describing this house, Ouchterlony thus writes :—" The Almshouse Chapple, as now possessed by James Philp of Almryclose. His house is built of the stones thereof, and has all the apartments belonging thereto. The fabric was great and excellent, having many fine gardines and orchards now converted to arable ground, about which is a high stone wall, and now by the King's gift belongs to the Bishope of Brechin." Presumably it is the superiority of the property that Ouchterlony speaks of as belonging to the Bishop of Brechin. Again, he says " Almryclose is in the head of the town, ane good house and yards." In Slezer's picture of Arbroath, which was drawn in 1693, it is thought that Almerieclose House can be recognised.

Besides this James Philip's acquisitions already referred to, there are various records of others in Copgait (the lower part of the High Street); in Horner's Wynd (Commerce Street); in Lordburn; in Millgate; in Millgate Loan and in Grimsby.

James Philip and his wife, Margaret Grahame, enjoyed many years of wedded life, as we shall see further on. Meantime we will speak of their talented son,

JAMES PHILIP (3),

Author of "The Grameid."

BORN in Arbroath somewhere about 1654-5, James Philip received the rudiments of his education in the Grammar School of Arbroath, then, as we have said, in School Wynd. From the Grammar School of his native town he passed to the University of St Andrews, where he entered as a student in 1672. There he had as class-fellows young men bearing such well-known Scottish names as Grame, Campbell, Ramsay, Ogilvy, Menzies, Fotheringhame, Lindsay, Dougall, Kinloch, and Urquhart. He appears to have been a diligent student, and, judging from his subsequent work, his classical education had been well attended to. Taking his degree of M.A. in 1675, it is probable that, following the custom of the young men of his social position of that period, he had spent some time in foreign travel. However this may be, there is indirect evidence that in 1678 he was studying law in Edinburgh. In searching for information among the burgh records of Arbroath for the purposes of this sketch, a manuscript book of 345 pages of foolscap, closely written in a beautiful handwriting, has been found. It begins with " The Common Principalls off Law," and ends " Poynts Emergent." It is either a copy of a treatise on the " Early Principles of Law," or notes of some lectures on law.

Not only at the end of the book, but at the close of the different sections, it bears the signature of James Philip. There are various dates throughout the volume as the work of transscription proceeds—the rate of progress indicated by these dates, especially when the painstaking care with which the copyist has done his work is considered has been marvellously rapid, and shows much patient plodding industry on his part. The bulk of the work seems to have been done in the latter end of 1678, and closes thus :—" Finis duodecimo Novembris Anno Domini Incarnationis Millesimo Sexentesimo, Septuagesimo Octavo Edinburgh Scripsit Magister Jacobus Phillpphus, 12 November, 1678," and then follows his signature and the date repeated.

On the flyleaf are numerous scribblings of a later date, such as " James Philip of Almericlose " frequently repeated, and some sentences in Latin followed by " Jacobo Philipe De Almericlose." Also, in a different handwriting " Ex Libris Joannis Ouchterlony, 1693."—" J. Ouchterlony, 1700." Could this be the John Ouchterlony who wrote " The Account of the Shyre "? He was a contemporary of " Almerieclose," and it is not improbable that the book may have come into his possession for a time. On the other hand as the book appears to have lain in the Town House for about two centuries it may be that the John Ouchterlony whose name appears on it is that of the Town Clerk of that name.

THE PHILIPS OF ALMERIECLOSE.

The existence of this book and the nature of its contents suggest that some time after leaving college he had gone to Edinburgh, where he had entered as a law student and where it is certain he was in 1678. In further confirmation that he had some knowledge of law we find in the Arbroath Burgh Registers a deed under date 30th July, 1714, in which he grants a tack of certain subjects, which indicates that he had some knowledge of law, as the testing clause bears that the deed was prepared and written by himself. Some years before he succeeded to the estate of Almerieclose, and probably in 1684 or 1685, he married Jean Corbit, by whom he had two sons— James and John. From indirect evidence, he appears to have got his wife in the West country. In 1684 "Mr John Corbit of Tollcrosse" (near Glasgow) granted a factory to "Jean Corbit, my sister," for uplifting from James Philip, elder,. of Almerieclose, certain annual sums payable by the said "Mr James, elder," to "Mr James Philip, younger, of Almerieclose, his son," and sold and assigned by James Philip the younger to John Corbit by disposition, dated 3rd November, 1684. The factory is dated Glasgow, 24th July, 1686, and Peter Corbit, maltman in Glasgow, is a witness.

In 1686, James Philip (2) of Almerieclose, with consent of his sons, Walter and Peter, and in implement of his contract matrimonial with Margaret Grahame, settles the greater part of his properties on James Philip, his elder son, and he reserves the liferent of himself and Margaret Grahame, and power to burden Guthrieshill with 2000 merks to his son Peter; and he binds himself to pay, during his own lifetime, yearly to James Philip, his son, and Jean Corbit, his spouse, 300 merks Scots, also one chalder of bear, with £24 Scots according to the "decreit arbitrall past yeranent be Collonell John Grahame of Claverhouse and Robert Young of Auldbar of the dait 5 and 6 Oct., 1685." With the Philip and Grahame blood intermingled in his veins, and reared in such a loyal town as Arbroath, it is not to be wondered at that young Philip grew up a keen Episcopalian, and an enthusiastic Royalist. This enthusiasm led him to take arms under his kinsman, Grahame of Claverhouse, whose fortunes he followed in the capacity of standard-bearer till the death of "Clavers" at Killiecrankie.

We know the detestation in which Claverhouse was held by many of Scotland's worthiest sons—men who, for "Christ's Crown and Covenant," were willing to lose all their worldly possessions, and even to shed their last drop of blood.

The men whom Claverhouse led—the persecutors of the Covenanters—were mainly actuated by motives of self-aggrandisement. Grahame of Claverhouse, with all his faults—and these were not few—was a man cast in a different mould from the land-grabbing rabble whom he led. He appears not only to have been a brave and skilful soldier, but also a straight-forward and courtly gentleman ; just such a man as was likely to win the admiration and enlist the enthusiasm of young Philip. Joining his kinsman at Dudhope on his first raising the standard for King James, young Almericclose remained with Grahame till the close of his career.

"The Grameid," an heroic poem descriptive of the campaign of Viscount Dundee in 1689—the original MS. of which has been in the Advocates' Library since 1742, if not long before that date—was published in 1888 by the Scottish History Society under the editorship of Rev. Alexander D. Murdoch, F.S.A. Scot., of Edinburgh. The poem is in Latin, and is reproduced in the original in the Society's publications, but with it is given a translated paraphrase by Mr Murdoch, along with an interesting preface and valuable explanatory notes from the editor's pen.

From this volume has been gleaned much of the information which follows, relative to the poem, and for this privilege our warmest thanks are due to the learned editor.

"The Grameid," in which Philip sings the praises of his hero, affords a few details of his own personal history, and of the part he played in the civil war then raging in Scotland. But greater interest lies in the frequent allusions which the poet makes to the principal historical characters of the time and to the various topographical references to the most striking characteristic features of towns, rivers, roads, castles, cottages, and moors, and to the condition generally of the districts through which the army passed. In these particulars the poet shows his intimate knowledge of the history of the leading families in Scotland, and of the part they took in the politics of the period. He also shows a thorough acquaintance with the geography of his native country.

His description of the dress, weapons, and musical instruments, both of Saxon and Gael, are of great value to the student of social history, and his references to the manners, the customs, and the clan peculiarities are not without their interest and their use.

The superstitions of the times also find their place. The following passage as having a local reference is taken from Mr Murdoch's paraphrase of the poem :—"Already Mother Nature had given manifest presages of terrible war, and the heavens, and the elements of the world, are showing fatal signs of our ruin; and the lesser deities, sworn together for our destruction, terrify the breasts of men with marvellous prodigies. Not far from the ocean, where Scotland turns from the northern wain and verges towards the warming south, there is a place called the Land of Angus. Here, where Monromond [Montreathmont Muir] stretches itself towards the broad sea, the plain is clothed alone with thick heather. Through the deep silence of midnight in the sky are seen on every side menacing hosts, with bloody standards, rushing against each other with hostile arms. In the heavens there is heard varied clang of arms, sound of trumpets, shouts of men, neighing of horses, and rolling of drums. Through the dark distance, dread thunderings sound, with lightenings to be feared, and a voice following, of no mortal tone, rushes through the empty air with loud cry—'Why, O, Britain, dost thou evoke to thy bitter fate gods hostile to thee. Lo, thou shalt bear the dread calamities of war, and shall see havoc and the slaughter of men. But Ireland, first the more sorrowful, shall behold fierce battles, and the Grampian land shall see rivers flowing with blood, and will call out her sons to war.'"

The chief interest, of course, lies in the main purpose with which "The Grameid" was written, namely, as an epic in praise of his kinsman and leader,. the famous Viscount Dundee. But besides this, the poem bears evidence of the general culture and eminent classical scholarship of its author. The likelihood of its having been written in Arbroath gives it additional local interest.

Besides this poem, others from his pen have been preserved. On blank leaves of the MS. volume, presumably provided for a continuation of "The Grameid," is an epitaph in the author's handwriting on William Aikman of Cairnie, a contemporary and neighbour of Philip's, which Mr Murdoch conjectures was prepared before the day wanted, in a half playful, half serious spirit.

After the affair of Killiecrankie Philip may have been in hiding for a time; but soon thereafter he returned to Arbroath

THE PHILIPS OF ALMERIECLOSE.

where his father and mother were still living and where, no doubt, during his service under Claverhouse his wife and family continued to reside.

It is difficult to fix the date when he succeeded to the proprietorship of Almerieclose. His father and mother were living in 1693, as there is record of a bond granted by them on 4th July, and on 4th December of the same year "James Philip, *younger*, of Almerieclose, and Jean Corbit, his spouse," are parties to another bond.

The Philips seem to have had rather fiery tempers. So far back as 9th September, 1643, when James Philip, the father of the poet, was quite a young man he had to find caution for keeping the peace to John Henderson under the "paine" of £100; and three days later Thomas Piersone of Lochlands bound himself as cautioner for James Piersone keeping the peace to James Philip in a like penalty.

The poet was equally hot-tempered, and he too had to be hauled before the court. On 15th August, 1692, the Burgh Records bear that a declaration had been made that "Almerieclose, younger, and John Guthrie had, in a house in St Vigeans, abused the Magistrates, calling them base rascals, and that they were not worthy to sit in judgment, with many other opprobrious things." Philip had also abused the clerk, declaring that he was unworthy of his office. Both culprits were fined, and were ordered to be detained in prison till the fines were paid.

There is also evidence that serious family bickerings were not unusual. After the marriage of the poet, a dispute arose between him and his brothers and their father over the provision that was needful to be made to him and his spouse, Jean Corbit, and this dispute was only settled, as we have seen, by a decreet arbitral by Claverhouse and Young of Aldbar. But this did not end their quarrels, for on 29th May, 1686, James Philp, father and son, found it needful to enter into a "mutual obligment" whereby they bound themselves "that neither of them shall suite or persew ane vther before whatsomever Judge or Judges at law or vse any other diligence legally without the speical advyse and consent of Collonell John Grahame of Claverhous and Robert Young of oldbar, or any ane of them" "the pairtie failyen to pay 500 merks Scots."

With such a referee as "bluidy Clavers," one would naturally suppose that the two would still have pretty free scope for quarrelling, as what in the eyes of a milder man might be considered a serious offence, to one of Grahame's cruel and overbearing disposition would appear quite venial.

We have no record of the exact date of the death of either the father or the son. In a deed executed more than half a century later, and to which we will have occasion to refer further on, the father is said to have died in 1695 or 1696. As for the poet, we think we see evidence in the Burgh Records of his having been alive in 1714. He may have lived for a few years beyond this, but certainly he was dead in 1725. He was succeeded by his eldest son,

JAMES PHILIP (4).

THERE is little information to be obtained concerning him, and the little which can be gleaned is of no importance. He appears to have remained unmarried. In 1696, he was infeft in the estate in fee, and his father in liferent. The first record of his proprietorship is in a deed in 1725 in which he is described as "of Almericclose." In 1730, he acquires land in Gallowden,

THE PHILIPS OF ALMERIECLOSE. 101

in Muirlands, and in other parts of the town and neighbourhood. His death occurred somewhere about 1734, as in that year he was succeeded by his only brother,

JOHN PHILIP (5).

JOHN PHILIP is then described as Governor of the island of St Martins, in America. He had evidently been in business in Arbroath before going abroad; for in 1721, when he is described as "merchant in Aberbrothock," he is owner of the ship "Providence" of that port, and in 1727 he grants a factory to his brother James to recover debts due to him, "as he was going abroad." On the 15th May, 1734, while designed as Governor of St Martins, he signs a tack at Arbroath, so he must have been at home then—probably getting himself served heir to Almerieclose estate. There is no evidence of the place or date of his death; but in 1752 his only child, Susanna Philip, then wife of Alexander Wilson, merchant, Glasgow, completed her title to the Almerieclose estate, in consequence of the failure of all the heirs male of the marriage between James Philip (2), the entailer, and Margaret Grahame. The retour, which is dated 1st September, 1752, also speaks of her as heir of line and of provision to her great grandfather, James Philip of Almerieclose, in lands in Keptie, Dishland, and Lordburn, and that the lands had been in non-entry from the time of the decease of the said James Philip, great-grandfather of the said Susanna Philip, which was in the year 1695 or 1696.

In 1753 she sold Almerieclose to Robert Barclay, and so ended the connection with Arbroath of this branch of the Philip family.

EMINENT ARBROATHIANS.

With the exception of the founder of the family and his great-grandson, the poet, none of the Philips can be reckoned as men of mark ; still, holding for generations—as they did—a large stake in the town and neighbourhood, and performing important functions, both as citizens and civic rulers, they cannot be considered as out of place in a record such as this.

The building, which was so long their home, still bears the imposing name of Almerieclose Mansion House, but, alas, its glory has departed. While it bears some evidence of its former gentility, it presents but a shabby and dilapidated appearance.

In the Abbey Churchyard still stands the family tomb, a rather imposing structure, bearing the effigies of Henry Philip, the founder of the Arbroath branch of the family, and of Isabella Petersone his wife, together with the arms of the Philips and the Grahames.

JOHN OUCHTERLONY
Of the Guynd.

JOHN OUCHTERLONY, the author of "An Account of the Shire of Forfar," deserves to be gratefully remembered for his valuable contribution to local history.

The Ouchterlonys are a very ancient Angus family. The surname is said to have been assumed from the lands of Lownie, in the parish of Dunnichen. These lands were in possession of the Ouchterlonys down to 1226-39, when they were exchanged for those of Kenny in Kingoldrum, so that from then till now, a period of well-nigh seven centuries, the name, though variously spelt, has been more or less a familiar one in the county of Forfar.

William of Ouchterlony is mentioned in 1391 as having an interest in Melgund. In 1394, Alexander, son of William of Ouchterlony, married Janet, only daughter of Sir William Maule of Panmure, and received as part of her dowry the lands of Grenefurd [Greenford] on the 4th October of that year. The name of Ouchterlony is also occasionally found at charters as witness.

The Ouchterlonys for a time possessed the lands of Preyston in Ayrshire, and at the same time they had an interest in the lands of Kelly in Arbirlot. At what period they first acquired that interest it is difficult to determine, but in the first years of the fifteenth century we find them designed "of Kelly." On the 26th April, 1409, Alexander Ouchterlony of Kelly was served heir to his father, William Ouchterlony. On 20th November, 1442, they acquired an addition to their lands of Kelly, through an exchange of Preyston with Archibald de Crawford. The lands of Kelly remained in the possession of the Ouchterlonys till 1614, when they were disposed of to the Irvines of Drum, about or soon after which time the Ouchterlonys acquired the estate of the Guynd.

That they occupied an important position in the county, there can be no doubt. There is a tradition connected with the Ouchterlonys recorded by various old writers. James Thomson, at one time a teacher at Chapelton and afterwards at Dundee, wrote a "History of the Abbey of Aberbrothock," in which he gives the tradition at some length. It is that Ouchterlony of Kelly, at the head of a troop of his own name, family and retainers, three hundred in number, at the time of the Reformation, in order to clear off a heavy debt he was then owing to the steward of the Abbey, fired the monastery in different quarters, and so put an end to his debt and obligations of gratitude at one and the same time. This tradition further records that the leaden roof of the Abbey, fused by the immense heat, rolled in a continuous stream to the foot of Lordburn, and that scarcely an article in the least valuable or venerable was left.

There is no authentic historical proof that anything such as is here alleged, took place. We mention the tradition simply to show that the Ouchterlonys were considered a family of power and importance in the district, and without the aid of tradition there is ample proof of this.

Away back in the days when the struggle for our national independence was at its keenest, Ouchterlony of that ilk was one of those to whom Sir William Wallace, the champion of Scottish liberty, made a special appeal for help. In a letter which he addressed to his trusty and assured friend, the Laird of Ouchterlony, he asked him in all haste to repair to him with his friends and servants, adding, "for its lyke we will have use for you and other honest men in the countrey within a short tyme." This was shortly before that memorable adventure in the history of Wallace, the burning of the Barns of Ayr.

Not only in the field, but also in the Councils of the State were the services of the Ouchterlonys given to their country. In the third Parliament of Charles I., and first triennial Parliament which met at Edinburgh on 4th June, 1644, "John Auchterlony" sat as representative of Arbroath burgh, as did "John Ouchterlony, provost." in the Parliament of Charles II.

The estate of the Guynd is pleasantly situated on the banks of the Elliot in the parish of Carmyllie. Rising in Dilty Moss and receiving several small rivulets as tributaries, the Elliot flows through the Den of Guynd, and, passing into the Den of Cuthlie in the neighbouring parish of Arbirlot, it empties itself into the German Ocean within two miles west of Arbroath. On the high bank between the Den of the Guynd and the Black Den, and overlooking the stream, there are vestiges of what is supposed to have been an encampment or stronghold called Dunhead. It is supposed to have originally been a Caledonian fort, and that it may afterwards have been occupied by the Danes or Norwegians during some of their incursions.

The present Mansion House of the Guynd is a comparatively modern structure, having been built by the last Ouchterlony in the main line of the Guynd family, who died in 1843. The house and its surroundings show him to have been a man of considerable taste. Taking advantage of the configuration of the ground and the proximity of the stream, he has, by judicious planting and by the formation of an artificial lake, studded with wooded islets, made the Guynd one of the prettiest and most attractive spots in the neighbourhood of Arbroath.

The site of the high altar of the Abbey of Arbroath was long used by the Ouchterlony family as a private burying-ground, and a tablet, bearing date 1811, still to be seen there, records the fact. In or about the year, 1823, the Crown raised an action of interdict in the Court of Session to prevent it being longer used for such a purpose. The Court granted interdict, and the case was appealed by John Ouchterlony, the Laird of the Guynd, to the House of Lords, who, however, confirmed the decision. This John Ouchterlony died in 1843, when the lands of the Guynd passed into the hands of his nephew, James Alexander Pierson.

The present proprietor, Lieutenant-Colonel Thomas Heathcote Ouchterlony, belongs to another branch of the Ouchterlony family. One of the members of that branch married her second cousin, John Ouchterlony of the Guynd, their son, John Ouchterlony, being—as has already been mentioned—the last male representative of the main line of the Guynd family.

There are various branches of the Ouchterlony family. From the same stock sprang the Ouchterlonys of Kintrocket. Major-General Ouchterlony of the Russian army, who fell at the battle of Inkermann on 5th November, 1854, was a scion of the Kintrocket Ouchterlonys. He was a lineal descendant of Prince Rupert. Charles I. had a sister married to the Elector Palatine of Bohemia. Prince Rupert was the son of this marriage. Ruperta Skinner, a descendant of Prince Rupert, married John Ouchterlony of Montrose, whose son, General Ouchterlony's father, settled in Russia in 1794. General Ouchterlony's great-grandfather, Robert Ouchterlony of Kintrocket, married a daughter of Young of Auldbar, and so was allied to the family of Sir Peter Young of Seaton.

While we have a good deal of information about this and the other branches of the family and their possessions in the county of Forfar, much more than is needful for our present purpose, it is to be regretted that so little is known of the personal history of the subject of this sketch. He was laird of the Guynd in the latter part of the seventeenth century, having been served heir to his father, "John Auchterlonie," "in the lands of the Guynd with the teinds in the lordship of Arbroath," on the 12th April, 1676. In his "Account of the Shire of Foriar," he speaks thus of his domicile and of himself—"Guynd, a good house, with yards and planting, lying upon the water Ellot, belongs to John Ouchterlony, lineal successor and chief representative of the ancient familie of Ouchterlony of that ilk ;" and in another place he speaks of himself as "John Ouchterlony of the Guynd, only representative of Ouchterlony of that ilk." Of his family he says, "I will add no more of our familie of Ouchterlony of that ilk, but what I have said in the generall description of some places we have and had concern in, but that I have ane accompt of the marriages of the familie these fifteen generations, viz., 1. Stewart of Rosyth, in Fyffe; 2. Maull of Panmure; 3. Ogilvy of Lentrathene, predecessor to the Lords of Ogilvy; 4. Gray, of the Lord Gray; 5. Drummond of Stobhall, now Perth; 6. Keith, Lord Marishall; 7. Lyon, Lord Glames; 8. Cuninghame of Barnes; 9. Stewart of Innermeath; 10. Olyphant of the Lord Olyphant; 11. Scrimger of Dudope; 12. Beatoun of Westhall; 13. Peirsone of Lochlands; 14. Carnegy of Newgait; 15. Maull, cousine-germane to the deceist Patrick, Earl of Panmure. All these are daughters of the above written families. The familie is very ancient and very great, having above fourteen score chalders of victuall, which was a great estate in those days."

That the author of "The Account of the Shire" was a man of education, possessed of considerable powers of observation, and not lacking in literary skill, is evident by the fact of his having been engaged on the work which has been the chief means of preserving his memory alive. His authorship was brought about in this wise. In 1682 Sir Robert Sibbald of Kipps, an eminent physician and antiquary, was appointed physician-in-ordinary to Charles II. and geographer-royal for Scotland. Soon after his appointment, he received the royal command to write an account of the natural history and a geographical description of the various counties in Scotland. The projected work was one which it was impossible to execute unaided, and he naturally looked for assistance from qualified men in the different localities. It was to help him in this work that John Ouchterlony undertook to write "An Account of the Shire of Forfar." The entire work contemplated by Sibbald was never accomplished, but besides Ouchterlony's contribution, other portions of the work, including a history of Fife and Kinross, were printed.

John Ouchterlony's "Account of the Shire of Forfar," which was written in 1684-5, and which has been preserved in the Spottiswoode Miscellanies, is exceedingly interesting, and, written as it is by a gentleman born in the county of Forfar, and intimately connected with its various interests, it is considered as thoroughly trustworthy and reliable ; the plan of the work is admirable and methodical. Beginning with the divisions of the shire, geographical, ecclesiastical, municipal, and judicial, he goes on to enumerate the chief productions of the different localities, and to explain the natural history of the district. The five presbyteries into which the county is divided are carefully examined in rotation; the towns, villages, and parishes individually described; the various properties in the rural districts, together with the names and titles of their respective proprietors, are detailed, and any interesting historical facts connected therewith reviewed.

To those acquainted with the town, it affords the means of comparing the Arbroath of two centuries ago with that of to-day. Its municipal constitution, its situation and construction, as well as its commerce, are briefly, but graphically described. "Aberbrothock is a Burgh Royall, hath a Provost, two Bailzies, whereof the Earl of Panmure hath the electioun of the first. It is a pleasant and sweet place, and excellent good land about it, built upon the east syd of the water of Brothock; they have a shore, some shipping, and a little small trade, it hath one long, large street, and some bye-streets; it is tolerably well built, and hath some very good houses in it." Slezer's picture of the town, drawn about the time that this was written, helps us to realise the appearance of this little old-fashioned town, with its "one long large street, and some bye-streets." The Arbroathians of that day were as proud as their descendants are now of the grand old Abbey. There is really very little change on that edifice since Ouchterlony described it two hundred years ago. He says—"The beautie and decorement of the place [Arbroath] in tymes past, was that excellent fabrick and building of the Abbey thereof, built by King William, King of Scots, and endowed by him and others with great rents and revenues, and lyes buried there in a piece of very stately work built by himself for that purpose, and is a very stately piece of work of thrie storie high. The whole fabrick of the buriall-place is still entire as at first, and if it be not thrown downe, may continue so for many generations; the laigh storey is the buriall-place, and the second and third stories were employed for keeping the chartours of the Monastrie. There is one lodging remaining yet entire; it had a most stately church, with two great steeples on the west end thereof; most part of the church is ruined, but was the largest both for breadth and length, it is thought, in Scotland. There is much of the walls thereof as yet standing in many places; the tower, thrie storie high, is standing yet entire, and the roof on it; there was ane excellent roume, called the fish-hall, standing with ane excellent oak roof; but that with much more of the building by the avarice of the town's people about there, were all broken down, and taken away." This charge against our forefathers was quite true, for, for many years bye gone, and even to this day, when old buildings are demolished in various parts of the town, stones which at one time formed part of the Abbey are found. But the town's people were not alone to blame for these acts of despuliation. The monks, if they did not carry off her stones, robbed her of her furnishings. Speaking of St. Thomas Chapel, one of the four chapels attached to the Abbey, he says "it was richly furnished, and a gentleman told me he saw the verrie things in a chapple in Parish [Paris], and was told they were removed thither by the Monks of Arbroth the tyme of the Reformation, extraordinare rich, but of an antique fashion."

Besides this description of the town and Abbey, interesting glimpses are given of various places in the neighbourhood. Some of these, then in the outskirts, are now built on and form part of the town, as for example: "Hard by the towne upon the east syd, is Newgait, belonging to a gentlemen of the name of Carnegy, of the family of Southesk, a very good house and pleasant place."

His notice of St. Vigean's (except for the spelling) might have been written to-day. "St. Vigeans lyeth about a myll above Arbroth, on the water thereof; ane old great kirk built upon ane high artificial mount, as is famed, by one Vigeanus, a religious man, and was canonized and the church bears his name." Since then, in our own day, this ancient place of ecclesiastical architecture has been entirely renovated. In this work of restoration all the interest that attached to the ancient fabric has been carefully preserved, so that, thanks to the restorers, the edifice as it now stands has all the features of "ane old great kirk."

Other places in the neighbourhood are briefly, but graphically sketched. Thus, "Redcastle, ane old house, upon the sea-syde, under the walls whereof runs the river Lounane. King William, when he built the Abbey of Arbroath, dwelt there." "Hospitalfield and Kirktoune, a pleasant place, and good land, belonging to a gentleman of the name of Fraser . . . where they gather abundance of *alga marina*, wherewith they dung their land to their great advantage." Besides this special reference to the abundance of sea-ware, he has a general reference to its plentifulness along our coasts, and he remarks that it "occasions a great increase of corns where it is laid." Referring to the caves east of the town, he incidentally mentions that they formed a happy hunting ground for our forefathers. "There are," he says, "abundance of amphibious creatures bred in the rocks betwixt Arbroath and Ethie called sea calves [porpoises] who gender as other beasts doe, and bring forth their young ones in the dry caves, where there is abundance, and suck them there till they be of some bignesse and strength to swime in water; the old ones are of huge bignes, nigh to ane ordinare ox, but longer, have no leggs, but in place thereof four finnes, in shape much lyk to a man's hand, whereupon they go but slowly. In the end of September, which is the time they go a land for calving, several in the town of Aberbrothock goe to the caves with boates, and with lighted candles search the caves, where, apprehending, they kill diverse of them, both young and old, whereof they make very good oyll."

Some two hundred years have come and gone since John Ouchterlony trod the streets of our good old town, but in his "Account of the Shire of Forfar," he has raised a lasting memorial to his intelligence, industry, and literary skill.

HARRY MAULE.

HARRY MAULE
Of Kelly
("EARL HARIE" OF PANMURE.)

AMONG the many beautiful bits of scenery so fascinating to the eye of the painter, and dear to the heart of the poet, with which Arbroath and its neighbourhood abound, few claim a higher place than Kelly and its surroundings. While thus to the lover of nature Kelly is "a joy for ever," in no less degree to the student of history the associations connected with the name of Maule never lose their interest.

To Harry Maule of Kelly, who was an indefatigable antiquarian, and a diligent and painstaking student of Scottish history, and to his son, James, we are indebted for the collection and preservation of the family records. Besides this, their labours have resulted in the accumulation of a vast store of historical information of wider application, which has been of immense service to subsequent historians.

The Registrum de Panmure, as compiled by Harry Maule of Kelly, edited by Dr John Stuart, and printed at the expense of Fox Maule (Lord Dalhousie), is invaluable. For information obtained regarding the earlier history of the Maule family, we acknowledge our indebtedness to this work.

Great pains had been taken by Harry Maule, assisted by his brother, James, Earl of Panmure, to establish the identity of the family of Maule in France with their own branch. With this end in view, Earl James, while a fugitive in France, accompanied by his nephew and namesake, Harry's son, paid a visit to the castle and barony of Panmore, situate about eight leagues from Paris, the result of which visit was the acquisition of valuable evidence pointing clearly to the descent of the Scottish branch from the French stock of the Maule family.

From the researches then made, and from various other sources of information, the compiler of the Registrum has been able to present an exceedingly graphic and interesting account of the French Maules.

The earliest of the name of whom they found authentic record was that of Ansold, Lord of Maule, in 1015, but from the position which the family then held, it is self-evident that their origin was long anterior to that date.

Ansold was succeeded by Guarin, Lord of Maule, whose successor was another Ansold. This Ansold was designated "the rich Parisian," on account of his immense wealth. On his death his titles and fortune fell to his son, Peter. The character of Lord Peter Maule exhibited some of the features, which, in recent years, was characteristic of a bearer of the name of Maule in our own neighbourhood. Of a gay and liberal disposition, Lord Peter loved feasting much more than he loved fasting. He was easily induced to enter into any scheme, good or bad, for which he took a fancy.

During the eleventh century, many men of wealth became monks, making over their possessions to the church. One of these was Goisbert, physician to Ralph de Conches, son of Roger de Toni, the renowned standard bearer of Normandy. While on a visit to France in 1076, Goisbert became a guest of Peter, Lord of Maule. Easily fathoming Peter's facile dis-

position, Goisbert had little difficulty in inducing him to make
large grants to the monastry of St Evroulte at Ouche, of
which Goisbert had become a monk.

Not only was Lord Peter generous to the church, but his
tenants and neighbours were frequent recipients of his gifts.
On the whole, he appears to have led a jolly life.

> He, prudent, shrunk from war's alarms,
> And feasting pleased him more than arms;
> Good humoured, lavish, jovial, free,
> He spent his days in revelry.
> His liberal bounty never failed,
> He lived beloved, he died bewailed.

His son and successor, again an Ansold, was in many
respects unlike his father. In his youth a brave soldier, in
later years he became a diligent student of ancient history.
He was most frugal in his habits, practising fasting and bodily
abstinence; and while careful of his own property, he was most
punctilious in respecting the rights of others. Unlike many of
his contemporaries who were never pleased unless surrounded
by strolling players, buffoons, and dancing girls, he frowned on
all such amusements. In his later years he became more
devoted to his religious duties; indeed, so much so that he
entreated the monks to admit him to their brotherhood, and,
resigning all connection with the outer world, he was tonsured
and invested with the religious habit of the order, but he only
lived a few days after his admission. His eldest son and
successor, Peter, was a man of quite a different stamp, spending his youth in the company of gamblers and players, engaging
in rapine, ravaging his neighbours' property and squandering his

own. Entering the military service of his country, he held the rank of General at the battle of Breneville, fought by the French against Henry I. of England.

Such were some of the French forebears of the Maules. Not only Peter, but others of the old Lords of Maule fought against the Kings of England in France. But while this was so, some of the younger members of the family, following William the Conqueror, found their way to England, and were rewarded by large grants of land.

In course of time the tide of Norman settlers began to flow northwards, and among these Robert Maule is believed to have come to Scotland with King David First and to have obtained from that monarch various grants of land in the Lothians.

William, son of Robert, is said to have accompanied David to the battle of the Standard in 1138 and to have afterwards received from him grants of the lands of Easter Fowlis in Perthshire.

William Maule had no sons, and the succession fell to his younger brother, Roger. At Roger's death he was followed by Richard, his eldest son, who in turn was succeeded by his son, Sir Peter Maule.

Up to this point in the family history the order of succession has been considered a little hazy; but from the succession of Sir Peter onwards every link has been clearly established by the family records.

At this period begins the connection of the Maule family with Forfarshire.

Sir Peter Maule about the year 1224 married Christian de Valoniis, daughter and heiress of Sir William Valoniis, Lord of Panmure. The barony of Panmure had been gifted to Philip, father of Sir William Valoniis, by King William the Lion, the founder of Arbroath Abbey, who had also appointed him High Chamberlain of Scotland.

Sir Peter Maule thus became the lineal ancestor of the Maules of Panmure. The issue of this union was two sons, William and Thomas. The death of Sir Peter took place in 1254, but his wife survived him many years.

William, on the death of his father, became the chief of the Maules, and for a time held the office of Sheriff of Forfarshire. He was a great favourite of Edward I, who conferred on him various tokens of his friendship.

His brother, Thomas Maule, occupies a prominent niche in the annals of Scotland chiefly for his gallant defence of Brechin Castle against the English in 1303. In this year Edward I. made another effort to subdue Scotland. Marching as far north as Moray, he carried everything before him, till reaching Angus, on his way south, he met his first determined opposition at Brechin Castle, then held by the Scots under the command of Sir Thomas Maule. For twenty days did this brave soldier, against enormous odds, resist the seige. As a proof of his coolness and bravery it is told that he stood on the walls, in the face of the enemy, with a handkerchief or towel in his hand, and with irritating nonchalance he wiped off the dust raised by the English artillery. This fearless and daring action, while it inspirited the Scots, exasperated their foes. Profiting by the opportunities thus afforded them, the besiegers were able, by a well-directed stone projectile, thrown from an engine called the war-wolf—the propelling power being gunpowder, then coming into use for purposes of war—to wound him mortally while he was standing on a bastion directing operations.

When Maule's men saw that they were to lose their leader they asked him if they should not now surrender, to which he indignantly answered with his last breath—"What, cowards, yield up the Castle!" Being deprived, however, of the presence and guidance of their brave commander, the garrison capitulated on the morrow.

Sir William was succeeded by his son, Sir Henry Maule, who in turn was succeeded by Sir Walter Maule. Sir Walter is said to have been Governor of Kildrummy Castle in the reign of David II. He died in 1348, his son and successor being William.

In the person of this Sir William Maule, the family became allied to the then powerful house of Brechin.

In the genealogical table of the family of Panmure the line of Brechin is traced from David, Earl of Huntingdon and Gariock, brother of King William the Lion, and shows alliances among others with the house of Carrick, David de Briechen having married a sister of King Robert de Bruce. Their daughter, Margaret, was married to Sir David Barclay, of Lindores in Fife, and got a gift of the forfeited estate of Brechin from King Robert Bruce. Jean Barclay, their only daughter, married Sir David Fleming, whose daughter—Marion Fleming—became wife of William Maule.

The lordship of Brechin had become vested in Margaret Barclay, wife of Walter Stewart, Earl of Athole, the murderer of King James I. On her death, without issue, the succession reverted to the descendants of her aunt, Jean Barclay, whose grandson, Thomas Maule—the son of Sir William Maule of Panmure and Marion Fleming—became the undoubted heir to the lordship of Brechin. Besides this son, they had a daughter, Janet Maule, who became the wife of Alexander Ouchterlony, a progenitor of the Ouchterlonys of Kelly and the Guynd. Janet Maule, as a part of her dowry, received a grant of the lands of Greenford in Arbirlot.

On the death of Sir William, his son, Thomas, succeeded. He married Elizabeth, daughter of Sir Andrew Gray of Fowlis. Sir Thomas had not been long wed when he had to gird on his armour and take the field.

In 1411, Donald, Lord of the Isles, after having raised the standard of revolt, for a time threatened the dismemberment of the Kingdom of Scotland. Flushed with the success which at first attended his arms, he conceived the bold purpose of burning Aberdeen. With this end in view, he assembled his army at Inverness and marched through Moray without opposition. The governor, having been apprised of his intentions, at once set about raising forces to meet the enemy. Appealing to his nephew, the Earl of Mar, who bore a high military character, the Earl readily responded, and was soon at the head of a well-equipped army. He met the marauder and his fierce hordes at the village of Harlaw, where a most sanguinary battle was fought. In this most memorable of our internecine feuds, some of the bravest knights and gentlemen of Angus and Mearns fell, among these being Sir Thomas Maule. It has been said that at the battle of Harlaw there perished more noble and illustrious men than had fallen in foreign warfare during many previous years.

After the battle of Harlaw, his wife gave birth to a posthumous son, who was also named Thomas. This child, by virtue of an Act of Parliament dispensing with nonage of the heirs of those who fell in that battle, had a precept from the Duke of Albany infefting him in parts of Panlathy as heir of his father.

On coming to manhood, he advanced his claim to the estates of Brechin, and, while his title to the lordship thereof was indisputable, he failed to obtain possession of the whole estates; but he ultimately received certain small portions of the land. He married Margaret Abercrombie, daughter of Sir Thomas Abercrombie of that ilk, and died in 1450.

His son and successor, Sir Thomas Maule, was twice married; first to Elizabeth Lindsay, daughter of Alexander, first Earl of Crawford, and second to Catherine Cramond, daughter of the laird of Auldbar. By his first wife he had a son, Alexander. Alexander seems not to have been on good terms with his father, and is said to have been of dissolute habits. Besides the trouble and annoyance which he gave his father, he also quarrelled with his wife. She was a daughter of Sir David Guthrie of that ilk, who, for a time in the reign of James III., held the office of Justice-General and Lord High Treasurer of Scotland.

Alexander never came into possession of the estates, having predeceased his father, leaving two sons, Thomas and William. The father lived to a great age. He became blind in his later years, and was known all over the country as "the blind knight." Curiously, by his second wife he had a son who was also blind.

On the death of "the blind knight," his grandson, Thomas, son of Alexander, succeeded to the estates. Having been a great favourite with his grandfather, he had been put into actual possession of the bulk of the family estates and other property before his grandfather's death brought to him the titles.

Sir Thomas Maule, like his grandfather, was also twice married. By his first wife he had two sons, Robert, who afterwards succeeded to the title and estates, and William, who married Janet, daughter of John Carnegie, ancestor of the Earls of Southesk.

Sir Thomas Maule was among those who followed James IV. on his rash expedition against England, which ended so disastrously on the field of Flodden, where the flower of Scottish chivalry fell. As Drummond of Hawthornden has it : " Many brave Scots did here fall, esteemed to be about five thousand of the noblest and worthiest families of the Kingdom ; who choosed rather to die than to outlive their friends and compatriots." Among these brave Scots was Sir Thomas Maule.

Robert, his eldest son and successor, was only sixteen on the death of his father. He appears to have been a man of note. Tall and handsome in person, punctilious as to his dress ; brave and courageous in council and in action ; conversant with the laws of his country and expert in genealogical lore, yet he could neither read nor write, his education in these accomplishments having been neglected in his youth. Notwithstanding this drawback, so great were his natural abilities that he not only took an active and intelligent share in local government, but also in transactions of national importance. He was among those who attempted to rescue James V. from the custody of the Earl of Angus and Arran, and he also took part in opposing the proposed match between Queen Mary and Prince Edward of England. As a punishment for this, Panmure House was in 1548 attacked by the English, and after a gallant defence " he was schot with ane coulwerine in the chafts and evil hurt." He and his son, Thomas, were taken prisoners. The son was released, but Sir Robert was sent to, and kept confined in, the Tower of London, where he remained for a year. But this did not deter him from again engaging in local quarrels, for one of which he was summoned to appear at Edinburgh, and, having failed to comply with the order, he was denounced as a rebel and put to the horn.

At home he was a good landlord, and was well liked by his neighbours. His chief pastime was hawking and hunting, while he also took great pleasure in playing football and golf on the links of Barry.

In his later years he embraced the Reformed religion, and, although unable to read the Scriptures, he had the companionship of some of the leading ministers, and his son, Robert, was also very helpful to him in religious matters. Feeling the want of education himself, he took great care that his eldest son, Thomas, should not suffer in that respect. Sent to Edinburgh at the early age of seven, the boy was placed under the best masters, and received a liberal education.

Like his father, Thomas was handsome, and brave as he was handsome. When Panmure House was besieged he was along with his father. He was also engaged at the battle of Pinkie. When a young man, he was contracted in marriage to Margaret, a daughter of Cardinal Beaton, "bot on ane day, cwmand rydin in companie owt of Arbrothe with King James the Fyft, the King did cal him a syd, quha heawin afor hard of the contract, said to him, 'marie newir ane priest's geat,' quharwpon that mariage did ceas." While the Cardinal resented this, it did not come to an open breach, but it cost Maule 3000 merks. He still remained as one of Beaton's followers, but at the time of the Cardinal's death Maule was at home at Panlathy. Thomas Maule was twice married. There were no children by the first marriage, but by his second wife he had a large family. One of his sons, Robert, the fourth of this marriage, was Commissary of St. Andrews. Commissary Maule was a man of great learning, and was reputed to be one of the ablest antiquaries of his day. To him, as well as to Harry Maule of Kelly, are we indebted for various contributions towards the history of the Maules. He was author of a Latin treastise, "De Antiquitate Gentis Scotorum," and other works.

Patrick, the eldest son of Thomas, at the early age of fourteen, married Margaret Erskine, daughter of John Erskine of Dun, a well-known leader among the Reformers. At first, at Panmure, and afterwards at Bolshan, Patrick lived the life of a country gentleman, employing his time in hawking, hunting, and other rural sports. His father died in 1600, and as Patrick died five years thereafter, he did not long enjoy the family honours.

His son, also Patrick, was only nineteen at his father's death, and was then in England at the Court of James VI. He continued, after the death of his father, to serve the King, by whom and by other members of the Royal family he was held in high esteem. Both before and after his succession to the estates, he received many substantial marks of the Royal favour.

On the death of James and the accession of Charles I. to the throne, he continued his attendance at Court, and remained faithful to his Royal master in his darker days, "staying constantly with him all the time of his imprisonment till a little before the rebels did execute their lawful King, Charles." So writes Commissary Maule.

In 1634 Patrick Maule purchased from the Earl of Mar the Lordship of Brechin. He had already a hereditary right to the lordship through his descent from Marion Fleming, but, as we have seen, possession had not followed this. In 1635 he was appointed Sheriff of Forfarshire. In 1642 he purchased the Abbacy of Arbroath, and in 1646 he was created a peer by the title of Earl Panmure and Lord of Brechin and Navar. Earl Patrick, who was thrice married, left issue by his first wife only. She was a daughter of Sir Edward Stanhope of Grimston. His daughter, Lady Jean Maule, became the wife of David, Earl of Northesk. Earl Patrick was possessed of considerable literary tastes, as evidenced by his MS. history of Sir William Wallace. This history—the first forty-three folios of which are still preserved—is entirely in the handwriting of the Earl.

He died in 1661 and his son, George, Lord Brechin, became second Earl of Panmure. He too, like his father, was loyal to the house of Stuart, and took part in the attempt to restore that dynasty. He married Jane Campbell, eldest daughter of the Earl of Loudon, by whom he had a large family, only four of whom reached maturity. These were George, James, Harry, and Mary. Two of the sons succeeded to the title : George became third Earl, and at his death James succeeded as fourth Earl, while the third son was the brave and learned Harry Maule. The daughter, Mary, became wife of Charles, Earl of Mar, whose eldest son was John, Earl of Mar, who played such a prominent part in the rebellion of 1715.

James and Harry were drawn closely together, not only by the ties of consanguinity, but also by the similarity of their political views and literary tastes. Their brother George was a Privy Councillor to Charles II. and James VII., and died fifteen years after succeeding to the Earldom.

While yet young men, James and Harry travelled on the Continent, partly with the view of pursuing their studies and partly for love of adventure.

On the death of his brother, George, James Maule became fourth Earl of Panmure.

Both Earl James and his younger brother, Harry Maule of Kelly, adhered to the cause of the Stuarts, and when the Convention Parliament met at Edinburgh on 4th March, 1689, and declared that James Stuart had forfeited all title to the Crown and offering the royal dignity to William and Mary as next heirs, Earl James declined to take the oath of allegiance and never again appeared in Parliament.

But it was not merely a passive relation towards the reigning sovereigns which he assumed. He continued to take an active interest in the fortunes of the exiled monarch, not only keeping up a correspondence with the family but holding many communings with other nobles in the interest of the Stuarts.

In the plan of military operations for an expedition to Scotland, showing the advantages which would result to France in supporting a rebellion in Scotland, drawn up by Colonel Hooke in 1707 and presented by him to the French Court, and in the correspondence which passed between the Scottish and Irish Lords and Courts of Versailles and St. Germains, we find ample proof of the active part which the Earl of Panmure took in the movement.

Colonel Hooke made a tour through Scotland for the the purpose of submitting the memorial to the nobility and gentry favourable to the cause, and for obtaining their signatures thereto.

After visiting the Earl of Strathmore and securing his signature, as well as that of his brother Patrick Lyon, Laird of Auchterhouse, Hooke narrates—" From thence I went to the Earl of Panmure, brother-in-law to the Duke of Hamilton. He signed the memorial, and gave me a letter for His Majesty and another for the K—— of England. It was there that I first learned the news of the victory of Almanza, which gave great joy to all Scotland. I staid some days with the Laird of Powrie (Thomas Fotheringham), who signed for himself and for the whole shire of Angus, giving me a list of all the nobility of that shire of whom he said he was certain."

The letter referred to, which the Earl of Panmure addressed to "the King of England" (the chevalier de St George), is dated from Panmure the 12th of May, 1707, and is as follows:— "May it please your Majesty, Permit me to thank your Majesty for the honour of your letter last year and to return your Majesty my most humble thanks for your favourable opinion of me. I will endeavour to deserve it as much as I possibly can; and I shall esteem it my great happiness to find an opportunity to show my zeal and my fidelity towards your Majesty. I have seen your Majesty's letters of credence in favour of the Honourable Colonel Hoocke, who well deserves the confidence your Majesty has in him. I have represented, jointly with several others, the state of the nation in a memorial which we signed and delivered to the said Colonel. I, therefore, will not trouble your Majesty any further, but only take the liberty to assure your Majesty that I am truly, as is my duty to be, may it please your Majesty, your Majesty's most faithful, most humble, and most obedient subject and servant, PANMURE."

In another memorial we have it stated that "In Angus we are sure of all the nobility and gentry, the chief of which are the Earls of Strathmore and Panmure, with their brothers."

On the death of Queen Anne and the accession of George I. to the British throne, the imprudence of the new ministry intensified the hostility to the Hanoverian dynasty and increased the activity of the Jacobites. The King himself instead of trying to conciliate the adverse faction, which a wise man in his position would at least have attempted, identified himself so completely with the party through whose influence he had been raised to the throne that the feeling of discontent, already too prevalent, was alarmingly increased.

This spirit of general discontent and disaffection continued rapidly to grow and gather strength. The Earl of Mar, who, as he found it to suit his ambitious purposes, had made his politics subservient to his personal interests, endeavoured to ingratiate himself alternately with the opposing political parties. This deceitful and vacillating policy, ultimately, resulted in his abrupt dismissal from the court and service of George I. Smarting under the bitter feelings, insulted dignity, and pecuniary loss, and taking advantage of the prevailing discontent, he assumed the leadership of the Stuart faction. Before his return to Scotland his design had been known to the leading Jacobites, and secret preparations were being made to raise an insurrectionary force. Inviting a number of nobles and gentlemen, known to be favourable to the cause, to meet him at Aboyne, under the pretence of going on a hunting expedition, Mar harangued them on the injuries done to Scotland through the Treaty of Union, for his part in the carrying through of which he expressed his sorrow, and concluded by urging them to take up arms on behalf of James.

It is not very clear whether at this meeting Mar produced or only pretended he had a commission from James authorizing him to act as commander of the Jacobite forces; but that there had been some doubts on this score at the time is evident from a memorandum made some years thereafter by James Maule, Harry Maule's son, in which he says "John Ouchterlony of Guinde told me he was sent up to Braemar from Ja. E of Pan. to Lo. Mar in 1715. One of his principal instructions was to ask if he had a commission; to which Mar answered that he had not, but he had a plenipotentiary power, and shewed him as his credentials the chevalier's picture. When Guinde returned to the E of Panm. and told him this he said Mar had that picture 4 years ago to his knowledge, and that he knew him to be a very false body" ["From Guinde at Kelly, May, 1728."] The Master of Sinclair, in his memoirs of the rebellion, also refers to the same when he says, speaking of the meeting at Aboyne, that "he [Mar] shewed them the King's picture, which was all the credentials he had, kissed it frequently with the appearance of more than ordinary affection, and, to confirm all, told them it was an original which was sent him directly by his Master, for he judged there was some such thing needful to amuse them and get into credit with them, and make him pass for an honest man, which, if once allowed, he knew the people he had to do with too well to doubt that he would soon put himself at the head of them." It does not appear, however, that any difficulty on this score arose at this meeting. In any case, the proposal was taken up by those present, who pledged themselves to return to their estates and there take steps to have their followers in readiness to take the field.

While this was so, Harry Maule and his brother, Earl Panmure, had not much confidence in their nephew, for it is said that Mar had so little influence on Panmure that he returned several of Mar's letters to him with the greatest contempt without ever having opened them.

Meantime the Government, by the methods they adopted for putting down the rebellion, rather precipitated it. An Act was passed on the 30th of August, and immediately put into execution, by which about fifty of the most notable persons were summoned to appear at Edinburgh within a given period, under heavy penalties, to give bail for their allegiance to the Government. Among these was Harry Maule of Kelly. Buoyed up by Mar with the expectation that they might look daily for succour from France, very few had answered the summons. Some were in doubt how to act, and it is said that Harry Maule was one of these, and that he was twenty miles on his road southwards to deliver himself up when he was informed that the Government had intercepted letters to him from beyond the sea which, if he delivered himself up now, would as much as cost him his life. Sinclair, who tells this story, says that Mar found an absolute necessity of thus imposing on his uncle in this manner, being the man of the whole party whose example most of the people would follow, all having a good opinion of him. Thus influenced, Harry Maule returned and joined Mar, "who," Sinclair adds, "drew another advantage from it, which was informing the public that though Mr Maule, till then, had determined not to join, yet by letters of a fresh date he had received from beyond sea, he was at last convinced all was going well."

On the 6th of September Mar, having proclaimed the Chevalier at the Castleton of Braemar, raised his standard. Earl Panmure proclaimed "the King" at the Market Cross of Brechin, while the same was done at Montrose by Southesk and at Dundee by Strathmore.

To strengthen the cause of the Stuarts, Panmure had bought Edzell and the adjoining lands from David Lindsay, the last of the Lindsays of Edzell, thus greatly increasing his fighting strength. Many of the young men of Edzell, Lethnot, Navar, and Lochlee willingly followed their new chief to do battle for what they believed the rights of their lawful King, James VIII. While thus intent on promoting the cause of the Stuarts, the Earl was not blind to his own interests. Dr Thomas Guthrie, in his autobiography, tells that his great-grandfather,

David Guthrie, was a tenant of Panmure's. Guthrie, accounting his lease too dear, saw in the rebellion a favourable opportunity of getting rid of a bad bargain. So, when the Earl mustered his men he appeared among them on horseback, booted, spurred, and armed for battle. But he was foiled. "No, no!" said the Earl, dismissing him to more peaceful toils, "go home, David, and attend to your farm!"

The rendezvous was at Perth, where Forfarshire was soon well represented. The Earl of Southesk brought with him about thirty horse from Angus and a hundred and fifty foot. Panmure followed him with a hundred highlandmen and two hundred low-countrymen. It was suggested that Panmure should join his men to the Aboyne men, because they and the Glenesk men being neighbours would have confidence in each other. This arrangement was carried out, a regiment being formed under the name of Panmure's regiment, of which the Earl was placed in command; in the same way Strathmore taking command of his own and Southesk's low-country men.

From his camp at Perth, Mar was not slow to requisition men, money, and material from all quarters, Arbroath and the neighbouring towns being liberally drawn upon. From an order dated 24 Oct., 1715, addressed to Captain Thomas Lyell, we find him commanding this officer:—"You are hereby ordered to go to Arbroth and receive from the Magistrates a company of men which they have raised for his Majesty's service, but if they have appointed an officer of their own to bring them up to Perth, then you may proceed to Brechin and receive such men as the Magistrates have raised for the King's service and bring them along with you when ye return to Perth. You are also to go to Montrose and cause beat up volunteers. I have written to the Magistrates to assist you; and I desire you may tell the Magistrates that it is my express commands to them to give the freedom of their town, to all gentlemen and others who shall list themselves voluntarily with you, or any of his Majesty's officers hereafter, and half-a-crown to bring them up to the army, and what money they depurse on this account shall be repaid them out of the first subsidies raised in their town. For the doing whereof, this shall be your warrant. Dated at Perth the 24th Oct., 1715.   MAR."

These demands for men are frequent and imperative. Here is a sample of a requisition for money. It is addressed by Mar to the Magistrates and Town Council of Montrose. "John Earl of Mar, &c., commander in chief of His Majesty's Forces in Scotland. Our Sovereign, Lord James VIII., having been pleased to intrust me with the direction of his Affairs, and the command of his Forces in Scotland, and it being absolutely necessary to raise Money for their support and maintenance : These are therefore in His Majesty's Name, requiring and commanding you the Magistrates and Town Council of Montrose to Raise and Levy six Months' cess in full of all former cess, extending to the sum of fifty-six pounds, seventeen shillings and three pence sterling money, to be proportioned in the usual manner, and paid in to John Spence, Town-Clerk of the said Burgh of Montrose, Collector appointed for that end, upon the 10th of October instant, with certification if you fail therein that you will be quartered upon and poinded for the same, and ordains these presents to be published at the market-cross of Montrose that none May pretend ignorance.

" Given at the Camp at Perth the 6th day of October, 1715.—John Spence, you are ordered to transmit your collection to Alexander Watson of Wallace Craigie, General Collector appointed for the Shire of Forfar, for which he is empowered to give you receipt. MAR."

For material, the demands are frequent and varied. Here is one for arms. It is also issued by Mar, and addressed to the Magistrates of Montrose, similar commands being issued to other burghs.

"These are ordering and requiring you forthwith to cause make for the use of his Majesty's Forces, one hundred and fifty Lochaber Axes according to the directions herewith transmitted to you, and you are to take particular care that they be sufficient and fit for service, and how soon you have got fifty of them ready you are immediately to transmit them to Perth, or where the Army shall happen to be at the time : and so to continue to send them by fifty at a time, as they are got ready, until you have sent up the whole number above-mentioned, which shall be paid for as they are delivered.

"And for the more speedy execution of these our orders, we hereby require you to imploy all the workmen you can find in and about the toon of Montrose for making the said axes. Your punctual and speedy compliance with these our orders is expected, as you will answer at your Perils."

Nor had the soldiers encamped at Perth an idle time of it. A decree issued by the "Committee for Provision" sets forth "That forty men of Panmure's regiment, that have been accustomed to thresh, be sent out to Dalreoch and ordered to cast in what corns are standing there belonging to Glenagles, and thresh them out with all expedition ; that a captain and two subalterns be sent along with them to oversee the work, and that each man be allowed twopence a day over and above his ordinary pay for their encouragement to work." In the same order other forty men are told off to thresh.

At Perth some of the Highlanders threatened to mutiny for want of pay when Southesk and Panmure came to the rescue, each giving five hundred pounds.

Both the Earl Panmure and his brother, Harry Maule, were engaged with the Jacobite army at Sheriffmuir. Harry Maule was not with the Angus regiment on the day of battle. There is no authentic record of what part he took in the action, but it appears that his services were recognised in Mar's account of the battle. Sinclair, in his snarling way, endeavours to belittle Harry Maule's services, when he asks "Would not one believe that Mr Harry Maule had broke a wing of the Duke of Argyle's army in the action?" But it cannot be believed a Maule would remain inactive on such a day. It is beyond dispute, however, that his brother, the Earl, fought bravely, but eventually he was severely wounded and taken prisoner. Harry no sooner heard of this than, taking with him Dr Blair (a Coupar-Angus man) and accompanied by two or three of his men, he went in search of his brother. He found him at a cottar house guarded by six dragoons, who, on hearing the clatter of the hoofs of the horses of the rescue party and taking them for a large body of Jacobite cavalry, made off, leaving their prisoner in the hands of his friends. Harry had difficulty in persuading the Earl to accompany them, so severely did he feel his wounds, and though repeatedly urged, refused to do so on the score of inability to take the road. On the assurance of the doctor that his wounds would be no worse of the journey he consented. Mounted on a horse, on which he was supported by two of Harry's men who were walking up to the knees in snow—Harry himself riding before leading the way in the darkness—he made his way to Ardoch. This journey the Earl and his little rescue party accomplished not before time, as they were afterwards informed that a detachment of eighty horse came to carry the Earl to Stirling or Dunblane. Before starting, Harry had asked Mar for a party to go with him, but Mar went off without granting his request; he then, as ineffectually, asked assistance of all the troops he met. Nothing daunted, however, as we have seen, Harry Maule undertook the journey with the aid of only two or three domestics, thus running considerable risk of both himself and his brother falling into the enemy's hands, and so bringing ruin on themselves; and it is added by Harry Maule, " and Mar, beside the ingratitude to his 2 uncles, risked the K. and party's losing 2 of the most considerable men they had."

This battle of Sheriffmuir, as is well known, was a most indecisive one, each party claiming the victory. What took place between the battle of Sheriffmuir and the arrival of the Chevalier in Scotland is a matter of history. His presence and movements in this country had the effect of weakening instead of strengthening his cause, as was the intention. Sailing from Dunkirk, the Chevalier intended to land in the Firth of Tay, but, on sighting the coast of Angus, he conceived that it would be perilous to do so, so, steering northwards, he disembarked at Peterhead. From thence he came to Aberdeen, then to Fetteresso, where he held Court, exercising some of the functions of royalty. Continuing his journey, he arrived on Monday, 2nd January, at Brechin Castle, where he was royally entertained for two days as guest of the Earl of Panmure. After visiting Kinnaird on Wednesday and Glamis on Thursday, he reached Dundee on Friday forenoon, where he met with a very cordial reception. From thence he passed on to Scone, where he fixed his Court. From Scone, he made what was meant to be a triumphal entry into Perth, but in this he was disappointed, his reception being anything but cordial. Notwithstanding his assumption of royal prerogatives, from various causes, his councillors shewed great irresolution, his forces diminished, and it was at last resolved to abandon the undertaking as hopeless, and so, with a suite, the Chevalier embarked at Montrose for France. Shortly thereafter, he was followed by Earl Panmure, who was attainted for high treason and his estates forfeited.

It was while thus an exile on a foreign shore that his literary tastes led him, in company with his nephew and namesake, to pay the visit to the castle and barony of Maule in France, which resulted in the acquisition of so much valuable information as enabled them to establish the identity of the French with the Scottish family of Maule.

Earl James continued an exile till the day of his death, which took place on the 23rd of April, 1723. He had the opportunity of returning, but, had he availed himself of it, it would have been at the sacrifice of his loyalty to him to whom his fidelity was pledged; so, rather than take the oath of allegiance to the house of Hanover, which would be the means of restoring him to home and title, he preferred to remain true to the cause for which he had suffered.

Harry Maule had also to secure his safety by flight, taking refuge in Holland. Being, as already indicated, a man of considerable mental culture, instead of wasting his hours of exile in idleness, he not only diligently continued his previous studies, but he added largely to his knowledge of law, both civil and ecclesiastical, so much so that in later years he was acknowledged as a leading authority in canon law, in ancient church history, and especially in the history, laws, and constitution of Scotland. While abroad, and even after his return to Forfarshire, he carried on an extensive correspondence with the chief adherents of the Jacobite cause.

His love of literary pursuits brought him into contact with several men of similar tastes, and with these also he kept up a considerable correspondence. Much of this correspondence has been preserved, and the perusal thereof, in a measure, shows the high estimate of his legal and historical knowledge entertained by learned men of his day.

Harry Maule was twice married, his first wife being Lady Mary Fleming, daughter of the Earl of Wigton, by whom he had five children. The second son of this marriage—the first died in infancy—was James Maule. Like his father, he was endowed with rare mental accomplishments, and in all his genealogical, historical, and antiquarian pursuits, his father found in him an able and enthusiastic coadjutor. It was he who accompanied his uncle, Earl James, in his pilgrimage to the early home of the Maules in France in search of the evidence of the identity of the French with the Scottish Maules.

In the midst of all the political and financial troubles which his loyalty to the house of Stuart entailed, it must have been a great solace to Harry Maule to enjoy the companionship of such a worthy and accomplished son. When we think of the two in their charming home at Kelly—or in their library at Panmure, in the midst of their beloved books; or poring over and arranging their rich accumulation of historical documents, collected at so much labour and expense—we cannot help envying them.

During the collection of the material for, and the preparation of the chartulary or register of the families of, Maule, Valoniis, Brechin and Barclays of Brechin, and their cognate studies, Harry Maule and his son succeeded in amassing an amount of information, not only of interest and importance to themselves and to the descendants of these families, but they have brought together and preserved a store of historical lore which has been of immense value to subsequent students of Scottish history.

The pains taken by Harry Maule and his collaborator in verifying the historical incidents brought to their knowledge and in collating with the originals the copies of writs which had come into their possession, have materially enhanced the value of their work.

Besides the actual work performed by James Maule as a collector and literateur, his busy brain teemed with projects which he hoped to accomplish. One of these was a design for the formation of a reference library which would be free to literary men of his own and future times. His idea was to have a building erected at the foot of the garden at the Earl of Panmure's house in the Canongate of Edinburgh, and that he might secure the amenity of the site and assure quietness for study, he proposed to buy some ground at the east and west, to enlarge the garden, and also to feu a piece of the Calton Hill, the back of which he would plant with trees, so that the library thus standing free of all other buildings would be safe against fire.

In this building he would have one great room and a small one at each end; the principal room he would set apart for all the printed volumes, and in one of the small rooms all the MSS., and cabinets and presses with charters; while the other small room would be used as a sitting room or study, and there also would be stored the collection of medals, mathematical and astronomical instruments, Roman antiquities, and the like.

The building and contents which, while they would remain the property of, and be under the charge and at the disposal of the Panmure family, should by them be provided with such a sum as would cover the upkeep and pay the salary of a

EMINENT ARBROATHIANS.

librarian; and that this library should be open to the public during so many hours each day free of charge.

But besides his work in hand, James Maule had much literary work in contemplation. In a memorandum under his own hand he gives a list of work he had chalked out for himself.

In this memo., he proposes, if he has time and leisure, to write and compose several treatises under three general heads, viz.—(1st) relating to his family and himself; (2nd) to that state to which his family appertains, viz., the peerage; (3rd) to his country and king. "The books relating to the family of Panmure," he says, "are all scheemed out allready, as the History, Cartulary, &c., except the Chronicon and the Bibliotheca Panmoreana, or catalogue of books to which I would fall to when returned to Edinburgh; and to all these add a political testament of the family of Panmure, in which treat of how they are to manage with regard to publick affairs, their interest in the country, how to act towards other families, their neighbours, what alliances to make, &c.

"On the 2nd head, make a full and compleat Peerage, with an exact account of each dignity, and especially clear up the state of the Barons. The scheme of this may be blocked when I come to Edinburgh, having made good lists already. The other books to be made on this head are, collections of antient charters, patents, commissions, or relating to the nobility.

"As to the 3rd head, 1st country. Publish a compleat collection of Scotch historians, as Du Chesne's Historiæ Francorum Scriptores; then several volumes of other public and private acts and deeds, serving for proofs to a general history. Then write a history of Scotland, which may be blocked when at Edinburgh, with the dissertations which must go along with it ; and lastly, Political Memoires, like Jean de Witts Memoires, wherein treat of the ancient and modern state of Scotland, the reasons of its decay, and the proper way to recover it, &c. ; 2ndly, for the King and royal family, write a genealogical history of the royal family, like St Marth's of France's, beginning with the antient Fergusian race, and coming down, the Baliols, Bruces, and Stuarts, with their branches, and also giving the history of these families before they came to the Crown ; and, last of all, I would write a book addressed to the young C. of the S——t's, something like Matchiavel's Prince addressed to Laurence De Medicis, in which shew all the branches of his interest, and how he ought to govern, and the false steps and errors of his ancestors," and so on he goes laying out much more work for his pen.

But while thus deeply immersed in literary work he found time for improvements on the family lands—not theirs at this time by reason of the attaint, but held by them on a long lease in the hope of being regained one day, which hope, as we shall see, was happily realized. Here is a memorandum of his proposed improvements :—" Beside the great forest and other plantings at Panmure, I would make roes of trees on each side of the roads for a great way from Panmure, which will lead to the most remarkable places ; such as the road to Dundee and Bruchty, the road to Brechin, the road to Glames, the road to Kellie and Arbroath, the road to Panbride Church and Maulesbrough, &c. ; and also plant good bushes of planting at all the places formerly lairds' houses, and held of Panmure ; such as Carmylie, Skychen, Boath, Carncorthy, Auchrennie, Pitlivie, Balhousie, &c."

The woods and garden at Kelly were subjects of special interest to him ; and in a letter written to his father in September, 1724, he refers fully to them and says—" The planting at Kelly makes now a very good shew, ... and it will soon appear the best and greatest planting of this country after Panmure."

He seems not to have been very robust, and especially for some time before his death, which occurred on 16th April, 1729, in his twenty-ninth year, he was invalided. In consequence, many of his literary projects were never carried out. Judging, however, from what he was able to accomplish and from the testimony of those of his contemporaries well qualified to form a correct estimate of his work, he appears to have been a young man of great learning and promise.

The death of his son was a great blow to Harry Maule, but he had solace in his literary work, at which he continued with great assiduity. The compilation of the Registrum, at which he had now to labour alone, was finished in 1733, and in 1734 this brave soldier and accomplished scholar breathed his last.

His son, William, entered the army, and served with distinction in the wars that followed Frederick the Great's inroad into Silesia. He fought at Dettingen and Fountenay, and before he retired he had attained to the rank of General. In 1735, he was elected member of Parliament for the County of Forfar, a position which he retained till his death forty-seven years thereafter.

In 1743, he was created a peer of Ireland by the title of Earl Panmure of Forth and Viscount Maule of Whitechurch. Having amassed a considerable fortune, in 1764 he bought back the family estates in Forfarshire which had passed from the Maules through attainder in 1715. He died unmarried, the last of the race of the Maules in the male line, his titles thus becoming extinct.

In 1726, his sister, Jean Maule, Harry Maule's eldest daughter, married George, Lord Ramsay, eldest son of William, fifth Earl of Dalhousie, thus forming another of those illustrious unions into which the Maule family had entered.

Allan Ramsay, the poet, who, by the way, claimed kin to the Dalhousie Ramsays, in an ode, four verses of which are here quoted, thus signalizes the union of the houses of Maule and Ramsay :—

>Hail to the brave apparent chief,
>   Boast of the Ramsays' clannish name,
>Whose ancestors stood the relief
>   Of Scotland, ages known to fame.
>
>Hail to the lovely she, whose charms
>   Complete in graces, meets his love
>Adorn'd with all that greatness warms
>   And makes him graceful bow to Jove.
>
>Both from the line of patriots rise
>   Chief of Dalhousie and Panmure
>Whose loyal fame shall stains despise
>   While ocean flows and orbs endure.
>
>The Ramsays, Caledonia's prop.,
>   The Maules struck still her foes with dread
>Now join'd, we from the union hope
>   A race of heroes shall succeed.

Earl William, shortly before his death, settled his estates on his nephew, George, Earl of Dalhousie, in liferent, and on the Earl's second and other sons in fee.

This second son, who in time succeeded to the estate, was William Ramsay Maule, who at the time of his succession was only in his sixteenth year; at the same time his eldest brother inheriting the title and estates of Dalhousie. The younger, by his succession to the extensive estates of Panmure, became the richer of the two.

The Dalhousie family have been notable for talent, and William Ramsay Maule inherited that vigour of mind which for several generations distinguished the house of Ramsay.

In his youth, he gave evidence of the possession of a considerable mental grasp, and had his talents been put to some useful purpose, he was capable of doing great service to his country, as so many of his ancestors had done.

He entered Parliament as member for Forfarshire in 1796, and continued to represent the county till 1831, when he was created a British Peer by the title of Baron Panmure of Brechin and Navar.

As a member of the House of Commons, he took no part in its debates, but at home he took a share in the county business, in the management of which he showed some tact.

His large means he spent with an open hand, in some cases verging on prodigality. To his tenants, especially to those who entered into his whims and oddities, he acted on a liberal scale, so far as low rents were concerned. He spent little or nothing on drainage and buildings, consequently farm steadings and housing soon fell into a miserable state of disrepair. The beautiful beeches which adorned the avenue at Panmure, and large forests planted by his ancestors, were cut down, nothing being done to replace them. This neglect of his duties as a landed proprietor was openly attributed to his hostility to his family, especially to his eldest son, Fox Maule. While he is entitled to credit for many generous acts, much of his life was spent in amusements, many of which were anything but creditable, and few of which would have been tolerated in a poorer man. Naturally self-willed and impetuous, he was also very susceptible to flattery, and with ample means for the gratification of his desires, he found many sycophants ready to pander to his weaknesses. He held the estates for the long period of sixty-four years, and died at Brechin Castle on 13th April, 1852.

On the death of Lord Panmure his son, Fox Maule, succeeded to the title and estates. Born at Brechin Castle in 1801, he entered the army in his eighteenth year. He was a soldier for twelve years, latterly being attached to the staff of his uncle George, ninth Earl of Dalhousie, Governor General of Canada. Leaving the army in 1831, on the elevation of his father to the peerage, he turned his attention to politics, in which he was destined to play a distinguished part.

Having in 1835 successfully contested Perth in the Liberal interest, he was in the same year appointed Under Secretary of State for the Home Department. In 1837 he again contested Perth, but his opponent, Lord Stormont, managed to oust him. In 1838 he was elected to represent the Elgin Burghs, and continued to do so till 1841, when he again stood for Perth, and succeeded in winning the seat. He continued to represent Perth till called to the Upper House at the death of his father. In 1841 he was appointed Vice-President of the Board of Trade, which, however, in consequence of a change of Ministry, he held only for a few months. In 1846 he became Secretary of War, a post for which, from his previous military training he was well fitted. In 1852 he was transferred to the Presidency of the Board of Control; but which, from a change of Government, he held for a few weeks only. By the death of his father in that year, he became a British Peer, and took his seat in the House of Lords. In the following year he was appointed Lord Keeper of the Privy Seal of Scotland.

The most important function, however, which he was called upon to assume was that of Secretary of War in the Palmerston Administration at a critical period in the nation's history. The task of the reorganisation of the British army, which he was called upon to undertake, was a most difficult one. The gross mismanagement of affairs in the Crimea necessitated vigorous measures being taken. Lord Panmure, as War Secretary, with a seat in the Cabinet, proceeded with marked ability to rectify abuses, and reorganise the administration of that branch of the service. His success called forth varied feelings; feelings of resentment from those with whom he felt cause to find fault, and feelings of gratitude from the country generally, which was not slow to recognise the signal services which he had rendered, services which, besides being beneficial to the nation, brought considerable advantages to the rank and file of the army, thus gaining for him the title of "the soldier's friend." In 1860 he succeeded to the titles and estates of Dalhousie.

In all his services to the State, whether as Fox Maule, Lord Panmure, or Earl of Dalhousie, he displayed a ripe judgment and great administrative capacity — qualities which Her Majesty Queen Victoria was not slow to recognise and from time to time to reward. In 1849 he was appointed Lord Lieutenant of Forfarshire; in 1853 he was created a Knight of the Thistle; and in 1857 he became a Knight of the Grand Cross of the Bath.

Quite early in life he began to take a deep interest in ecclesiastical affairs. In the struggle between the Church and

State which eventuated in the Disruption of 1843, Fox Maule took an active part. When the separation of the evangelical party from the Church as established became imminent he was chosen to represent that party in petitioning Parliament with a view—even at the eleventh hour—to arrest the catastrophe. When the inevitable occurred, Fox Maule identified himself with the non-intrusionists, and from that day till the day of his death he continued a firm adherent to Free Church principles, taking an active part in the administrative work of the church. His services to the non-intrusion party of the Scottish Church, rendered at a time when the views he advocated were not popular with leading men on either side of politics, and the remarkable fidelity and steadfastness with which he adhered to that party, gained for him the gratitude and esteem of those whose principles he upheld; while his straightforward and manly avowal of these principles and the fairness which characterised his utterances on the questions then agitating Scotland secured the respect of many who differed from him on these matters.

He took a warm interest in Arbroath affairs, and was held in high esteem by her citizens. On 30th September, 1852, soon after his succession to the Barony of Panmure, he was presented with the freedom of the burgh, and four years thereafter he was entertained to a banquet in the Arbroath Public Hall by the citizens of Arbroath and the neighbouring burghs, and the gentlemen of the county, in recognition of the eminent services he had rendered to the country during the Crimean War. Again in 1871, the attainment of his seventieth birthday was seized as an opportunity for marking the esteem and respect in which he was held as a landlord and a neighbour, to entertain him at a banquet in the Arbroath Public Hall.

He was an enthusiastic Free Mason, and for a time held office as Provincial Grand Master of Forfarshire and Depute Grand Master of Scotland. In November, 1867, he was elevated to the Masonic throne of Scotland. During the three years in which he was Grand Master Mason for Scotland, he brought his usual energy to bear on the administration of its affairs, and it was mainly to his influence that the Scottish Order of Free Masons was indebted for the patronage of the Prince of Wales. On his demission of the office, he was presented with a testimonial in recognition of his services. The presentation took the form of a bust of his lordship by John Hutchison, R.S.A., and is now in the Masonic Hall, Edinburgh.

Till within a few weeks of his death he continued to discharge his parliamentary duties, and at the Free Church Assembly in the May previous he was in his usual place and took part in the business of the church.

His last public act was his official attendance, as Lord Lieutenant of the County, on the Queen at Bridge of Dun Station on Her Majesty's journey southward from Balmoral. In course of the following night he was seized with an illness which terminated fatally on the evening of Monday, the 6th of July, 1874, at Brechin Castle, where he was born seventy-three years before.

Throughout Forfarshire the loss of her foremost man caused a feeling of genuine sorrow. As a wise administrator and a fluent speaker, he left a blank in the House of Lords; and as one of her trusted friends and councillors, his death was deeply lamented by his royal mistress, Queen Victoria.

Fox Maule having died childless, and having been predeceased by his brother, he was succeeded by his cousin, George Ramsay, son of John Ramsay, fourth son of the eighth Earl of Dalhousie. Although he succeeded to the estates of Panmure, he did not succeed to the title of Baron Panmure, which became extinct on the death of Fox Maule.

Earl George was born at Kelly in 1805. He entered the Royal Navy at the age of fourteen, passing through the various grades of the service till he reached that of Admiral in 1875. He was present at the blockade of the Russian fleet at Helsingfors in 1854, then being Captain of the Euryalus. Besides obtaining the Baltic medal, he received in 1856 the order of Commander of the Bath. For some years he acted as Commander-in-Chief on the South American station. In 1845, he married Sarah Francis, daughter of William Robertson of Logan House, by whom he had four sons. In 1875, he was created a Peer of the United Kingdom, under the title of Baron Ramsay of Glenmark. The greater part of his life having been spent in the naval service of his country, he had but small opportunity of taking a share in the administration of his country's affairs. During the short period, however, between his accession to the estates and his death, he proved that he had the grit in him which goes to make a good landlord.

His predecessor, as we have seen, found that the dwelling houses and farm steadings on the estate had been allowed to fall into a miserable condition, and he had set himself in a measure to remedy this state of matters; but the improvements he was able to effect were quite inadequate to the requirements of the case. Earl George took up the work of improvement, and had succeeded in this, to a certain extent, when he was suddenly struck down. Up to the day of his death, he was in apparent good health, having been able to transact business in the early part of the day, and it was a great shock to his beloved wife when she found him sitting at an open window in his business room—dead! The sad event took place at Dalhousie Castle on the 20th of July, 1880.

His son, John William Ramsay, succeeded as thirteenth Earl of Dalhousie. Of the noble line whose history we have endeavoured to trace, and of which he was now the leading representative, a line famed for courage, daring, and administrative skill, John William Ramsay, on his succession to the estates, bade fair to maintain the prestige of his illustrious ancestry.

Born in 1847, it was resolved after he had received his early education, that he should follow the profession of his father. At the age of fourteen he was entered as a midshipman on board the training ship Britannia, where he at once showed a great aptitude in picking up the science of navigation. Joining a sea-going ship in further prosecution of his training as a naval officer, he soon earned a reputation for exceptional cleverness in acquiring a knowledge of his profession. In his examination for his Lieutenancy he had a most brilliant pass, his knowledge of the various duties being far above the average. His first appointment after obtaining the rank of Lieutenant was to H.M.S. Galatea, then commanded by H.R.H. the Duke of Edinburgh, and during the years from 1867 to 1871 he sailed twice round the world in that ship. From the Galatea he was promoted to be Flag Lieutenant to Admiral Hastings Yelverton, Commander in Chief in the Mediterranean; and in 1874 he was promoted to be Commander.

In that year Fox Maule's death brought the Earldom of Dalhousie to his father, and with it brought the title of Lord Ramsay and the prospect of succession to the Earldom to himself. Lord Ramsay acted as equery to the Duke of Edinburgh, and in that capacity he attended His Royal Highness on his visit to St Petersburg on the occasion of his marriage to the Grand Duchess Marie Alexandrovna.

His early training for a naval life was scarcely such as to fit Lord Ramsay for the position to which he had now the reasonable prospect of being called in the ordinary course of events. With that good sense which throughout his life was a distinguishing feature in his character, he set himself to make up for his want of such an education as was needful for one in the sphere which he might one day occupy. With this view he entered as a student at Oxford, where, under the guidance of Dr Jowett, he worked hard to overcome the difficulties which lay in his path, and in this he was eminently successful. In 1876, he was selected by the Prince of Wales to superintend the training of his two sons, Prince Albert Victor and Prince George, and during the two and a half years of their apprenticeship he was a great favourite, not only with these two cadets, but with all on board the Britannia. He married in 1877 Lady Ida Louisa Bennet, daughter of the sixth Earl of Tankerville, by whom he had five sons— Arthur George Maule, Patrick William Maule, Alexander Robert Maule, Ronald Edward Maule, and Charles Fox Maule.

The son of a staunch Tory, Lord Ramsay did not blindly adopt the political opinions of his father; but, after careful study and honest conviction, he gave his adherence to the Liberal party, and he very soon showed a considerable aptitude for political affairs.

His first public appearance as a politician was at the bye-election at Liverpool in the beginning of 1880, where he appeared as the Liberal candidate. It was considered very plucky for so young a politician to attempt to storm this Tory stronghold. The contest was a keen one, and Lord Ramsay entered the fight with characteristic vigour and thoroughness. As a canvasser, Lady Ramsay proved a valuable helper to her husband, and her presence along with him on the platform or wherever he appeared in public added a charm and grace to his meetings, which, along with his own frank and genial manner, enabled him to win his way to the hearts of many of the constituency. While success did not attend this effort, the result, under the circumstances, was considered eminently satisfactory, the successful candidate having obtained the seat only by a comparatively small majority. Such a favourable impression had Lord Ramsay made upon the constituency, that at the general election, which followed in April of the same year, he was returned unopposed as one of the members for Liverpool.

In July following his father died, so that his career as a Commoner was cut short, but even in the limited period which intervened between his entry to, and his exit from, the lower house he showed such a grasp of the leading questions of the day that his removal to the Upper Chamber was an acknowledged loss to the House of Commons. In the House of Lords as the Earl of Dalhousie, he continued to show his sympathy for the people, and in many ways he gave evidence that, if spared for a a few years, he was destined to play a conspicuous part in the conduct of national affairs.

The same thoroughness and enthusiasm which he brought to bear on his naval studies when a boy, and which then enabled him to outstrip his competitors, entered into the study of the various questions of public utility which now demanded his attention. Take, for example, the way in which he entered on his duties as chairman of the Trawling Commission. He visited the fishermen in their homes, took tea with them, and thus talking familiarly at their own firesides, set them at their ease, and so drew them out to state their grievances in their own simple way. He accompanied them to sea in their boats, as he did also the trawlers in their craft, so that he might have a practical knowledge of both sides of the question. In like manner, when he took up the measure for legalisation of marriage with a deceased wife's sister, he put himself into communication with the most eminent European scholars, Bible revisers and commentators, and with Greek and Hebrew professors, so as to obtain their opinion of the scriptural aspect of the question. So in every difficult subject on which he was required to form a judgment he approached its consideration with the same careful preparation.

The same conscientious thoroughness with which Lord Dalhousie entered on all his other duties was equally conspicuous in his endeavours to discharge his obligations as a landlord. The business of landowning was new to him, but he set about the administration of the affairs of his estates with the same earnest spirit which he invariably brought to bear on all his undertakings. He had many difficulties to contend with. We have already seen that the management of the estates during the many years they were in the hands of William Maule was of such a sort as to make the work of his successors anything but easy, and while the two immediate predecessors of Earl John did something to improve matters, their efforts fell far short of the accomplishment of the requirements of the case. Speaking at a banquet given to his tenantry at Edzell Castle in November 1882, Lord Dalhousie made pointed reference to the difficulties he had to encounter. One or two sentences may suffice. "I have not been," he said, "brought up to the business of landowning, and I have sometimes felt that I have taken command of a ship, so to say, in rather a gale of wind."

It would be a small pleasure to me to work my estate with the sole object of getting money out of it; any Edinburgh lawyer could do it a great deal better—more satisfactory to himself—than I should." Again, " It is uphill work trying to bring round an estate that has been allowed to run down, and that is also heavily burdened with debt—I might say up to the lips in debt. I daresay that many of you gentlemen, who no doubt take a look sometimes at the Forfar Valuation Roll, think I must be a precious rich fellow. Would you like to know exactly how much I have pocketed out of the estates during the last two years? Well, I will tell you. Not a single shilling. More than that, rather less than that. Not only have I been living on capital myself, but I have been borrowing money in order that the necessary improvements on the estate should go on." Thus cheerily did he meet his difficulties.

But these improvements were carried out in no perfunctory manner. He went as systematically to this work as was his custom in all his undertakings. He visited every farm, large and small, conversed with the farmer and the cottar, thus making himself thoroughly acquainted with the requirements of every individual case. So building and draining and dyking and planting went steadily on; the ploughman, no less than the tenant farmer, having his housing improved. Alongside of this came a handsome reduction of rents and a revaluation of his numerous farms, not by professional valuators from a distance, but by local practical men, in the choice of whom the tenants had a voice.

As an indication of his sincerity in this work, it was estimated at his death that in the short period during which he held the estates—over and above the money represented by abatements and reductions of rents—he had spent £150,000 on new buildings and other improvements.

Inheriting a good constitution, Lord Dalhousie had been able to perform a large amount of work, but latterly an attack of insomnia told on his health and gave fair warning that he must seek, in a cessation of his political and other labours and in a change of scene, a renewal of his former vigour. With this end in view, and accompanied by the Countess, he made a voyage to America. On their homeward journey they had reached Havre in November, 1887. Here Lady Dalhousie, who had been ill for only a very brief period, died suddenly. The shock thus caused to his Lordship's already weakened system was too much for him, and within twenty-four hours thereafter he too breathed his last. This tragic event sent a thrill of profound sorrow throughout Forfarshire, where it was looked upon as one of the most pathetic events which had occurred in the history of the county for many years.

The deep devotion of the beautiful Countess to her husband, the keen interest she manifested in all his undertakings, either for the good of his country or for the benefit of his tenantry, and the untiring help she gave him in his various undertakings, all tended to endear her to those who had the privilege of knowing her. By this sad event their eldest son— Arthur George Maule—then in his ninth year, became fourteenth Earl of Dalhousie.

In the death of John, Earl of Dalhousie, the loss to the country of one who during his comparatively short life had given such promise of great usefulness, and who as a landlord had shown above so many others of his class a full apprehension of the duties of a landed aristocracy, was keenly felt.

The earnest, conscientious devotion to every duty of life, either national or territorial, which he was called on by Providence to undertake, and the painstaking thoroughness which he brought to bear on the discharge of these duties, added to the unselfishness and generosity that permeated all his actions, won for him the esteem of his Sovereign and the gratitude and affection of his tenantry and friends, among whom he is deservedly remembered as "the Good Earl." His life was a short one, but he did not live in vain. He lived neither for himself nor for his own pleasure, but in his devotion to duty, he showed that he had the stuff in him of which heroes are made, and as an enduring legacy he has left a noble and a bright example to his descendants.

DAVID PIERSON
Of Lochlands
(AUTHOR OF "THE VARIETIES").

FOR nearly two hundred years from the beginning of the sixteenth century the name of Pierson was a familiar one in Arbroath. From time to time many members of the family filled one or other of the most important posts in the community. Even at that early date the Persons, Pearsons, Piersonnes, or Piersons—for the name is variously spelt — could claim to be of ancient Scottish lineage. Frequent mention is made of them in the public records. The earliest notice we have of the family is to be found in the Ragman Roll under date 28th August, 1296, when Wautier Pieresonne (del count de Berewyk) signs as land-owner in Berwickshire. It may, therefore, be inferred that the Piersons took rank as a Scottish family of distinction in, if not much earlier than, the thirteenth century.

In the reign of Edward II. of England, we find a notice of a safe conduct granted by that monarch and signed by the King at Westminster on 11th June, 1369, to David Perisone "meracator de Scotia," permitting him to pass through England, "cum quatuor sociis equitibus." Six others named in the same document have passes granted them for two mounted companions each. The safe conduct provides against the export of bows and arrows to the prejudice of England. About the same period, David Piersone and his brothers, Alexander and John, held office as comptrollers of customs in North Berwick, Dumfries, and Haddington, respectively.

On 27th June, 1396, "The King" (Richard II.) commands "his cousin, Henry Percy, Earl of Northumberland, to order the release of the Scots merchants and their goods, lately wrecked in a ship of Henry Pierson's on the coast of Werkworth last Lent, and said to be in his (the Earl's) custody, that the truce be not broken." In 1425, John de Perison, the then head of the family, was servitor to King James I. of Scotland, and twenty-five years later, Thomas, his eldest son, appears as a land-owner in Forfarshire, holding lands at Blackness, Eister Liff, now forming part of the west end of Dundee.

But it was not till the beginning of the sixteenth century that the Piersons took up their abode in Arbroath. In 1503-4, an illustrious Berwickshire man, George Hepburn, third son of the second Lord Hales, became Abbot of Arbroath—a post which he held till his death, which took place on the field of Flodden ten years thereafter. Abbot George, as was natural, did not forget his Berwickshire friends, and so we find at least one of them, in the person of Thomas Pierson, holding an important appointment under the new Abbot of Arbroath. A couple of years after his election to the Abbacy, Hepburn granted a charter in favour of "Thomas Piersone, servitor to George, Abbas de Arbroath, of ly rude, with pertinents in ly Almory de Arbroath." Besides this, the chartulary of the Abbey contains several other charters granting lands to the same Thomas Pierson and his successors.

This Thomas married, as his second wife, his cousin, Mariota, daughter and co-heiress (with her sister Sybilla) of

Thomas of Blackness, and in some of the grants of the Abbey lands during Hepburn's abbacy the name of Thomas Pierson's wife appears conjoined with his own. On the 13th October, 1508, " Thomas and Mariota Persoun " obtained a grant of the lands of Keptie, on a portion of which the Railway Station is now built. This, with other grants, formed the nucleus of the estate afterwards known as Lochlands, from which, as laird, David Pierson, the author of " The Varieties," took his designation. Thomas, who lost his second wife and married a third, Margareta Schort, died somewhere about 1524. He left four sons by his first wife and one by his third. The eldest of the four was John, who became a monk of Arbroath, his name appearing as a witness to charters granting Abbey lands during the abbacy of David Beaton. The second, Walter, was the ancestor of the Pearsons of Kippenross, Dunblane. Thomas, the third son, was the ancestor of the Pearsons of Clow ; and David, the fourth son, the ancestor of the Pearsons of Pierson's Baithe, Dunfermline. The Arbroath branch was continued in the person of Adam, son of Thomas, by his third wife.

Adam Pierson inherited the Abbey lands of Keptie and others. He married in 1529 Elizabeth Fethe, who deduced from Duncan de Fethyn, witness to a charter of Arbroath Abbey, 1254. Their second son, James—for the eldest, Bernard, died when quite young—inherited the Abbey lands of Keptie, Smithy Croft, and Lamblaw Croft, which included Lochlands as part of Cairnie. The third son was David Pierson of Barngreen, a man who took a leading part in the conduct of the affairs of the town. We find him as a magistrate sitting in judgment on 2nd September, 1564, along with Bailie William Scott, when " Willyam Crysty is amerciat for braking the comon statute, selling his aill derrer na iiid the pynt, and dowm gyffyn thairupon." Whether,

EMINENT ARBROATHIANS.

after the Court had skailled, the bailie and the brewer had adjourned to test the quality of the ale, or whether Bailie Scott had been attempting to carry out his own and his brother magistrate's sentence by confiscating the liquor, is not stated, but evidently a row had ensued, in which the brewer a second time that day had had the worst of it, for it is further recorded that, "The qlk day Willyeam Crysty maid the aith in judgment that he dreids bodelye harm of Willyeam Scott, bailyie and desyrit law bowrowis of hym; and David Pierson, bailyie, stud gude for his coleig, that the same Willyeam Crysty suld sustan na harm be the said Willyeam Scott."

By the way, this Crysty, the brewer, appears to have been rather thin-skinned, for shortly after this he again applies for the protection of the court, on a complaint that one George Bowar "hes doun wrang in myssaying of him," and the court ordaining "that the said George sall pass to the mercat cross and ask the said Wlm forgyfanis for amendis; and gif he duis siklyk in tym to cum to the said Wlm or ony uder honest man, he shall be banist the town."

In 1578, David Pierson had confirmation by King James V. at Stirling, of a charter granted by Sir John Hamilton, the last of the Abbots of Arbroath, of the Abbey lands of Barngreen. Besides fulfilling the duties of local magistrate, he was entrusted with more important functions. In 1574, he represented Arbroath at the Convention of Burghs held at Stirling, and again at Edinburgh in October, 1581. But a higher honour still was conferred upon him when in 1579 he was elected to represent Arbroath in Parliament. David Pierson was the first representative of Arbroath in the Scottish Parliament. This was brought about by the outlawry of Sir John Hamilton in that year, through which the abbacy and lordship of Arbroath became vacant, and consequently fell into the hands of the King, who accordingly became the immediate superior of the burgh. The King, being the feudal superior or lord of regality, it became the privilege of the burgh to send a representative to Parliament, and the choice fell on David Pierson, a leading citizen. He died before 1599, leaving behind him three sons, Thomas, Archibald, and George, each of whom, following the example of their father, took an active and important part in the management of the affairs of the town.

Thomas succeeded to the lands of Barngreen on the death of his father. He also acquired from his uncle, James, the lands of Lochlands including Keptie. He was infeft in these lands towards the end of the 16th century, which infeftment was ratified by Act of Scottish Parliament on 11th August, 1607. In this infeftment he is designated and infeft as follows, "Thomas Pierson of Lochlands, of his lands of Lochlands, with the tiend sheaves thereof included, and the loch belonging thereto: the lands of Barngreen, with the tiends and pertinents thereof lying within the regality of Aberbrothock and sheriffdom of Forfar, and of his house and tenement lying within the burgh of Aberbrothock." The loch here referred to does not now exist. The older inhabitants may remember it under the name of the Blind Loch, and recall the days when they enjoyed the exhilarating exercise of skating on its frozen surface.

Like his father, Thomas Pierson represented Arbroath at the Convention of Burghs, first at Aberdeen in 1590, then at Montrose in 1591, and again at Edinburgh in 1592. At the Convention held at Arbroath in 1612, he was chosen as its moderator or president. He was also the commissioner from Arbroath at the Kirkcaldy Convention in 1614.

But that which will connect his name with the history of the town in all time coming will be the important part he took in obtaining for Arbroath its charter as a Royal Burgh. Arbroath had long existed as a burgh of regality, and as such had enjoyed various privileges, but it was not till 1599 that it could boast of being ranked among the Royal Burghs of Scotland, and as such to possess the powers and privileges which this new charter conferred. In conducting the negotiations which led up to this Thomas Pierson of Lochlands took the leading part. His brother, Archibald, represented Arbroath at the Perth Convention in 1582. George, the third son of David of Barngreen, was the first Treasurer of the town after its creation as Royal Burgh.

This Thomas Pierson and his wife had a family of four sons and two daughters, of whom David Pierson, author of "The Varieties," was the oldest. The second son became minister of Forfar, and married Elizabeth Maule, and so became allied to the ancient family of the Maules of Panmure. Another son became, and long held the post of, Town Clerk of Arbroath. The eldest daughter, Janet, married John Ouchterlony of the Guynd, from whom descended the John Ouchterlony who wrote "The Account of the Shire of Forfar." The youngest daughter, Isobel, married her cousin, Archibald Pierson of Chapelton, Sheriff-Depute of Forfar.

On the death of Thomas Pierson he was succeeded as Laird of Lochlands by his son, David Pierson. As might be expected, the son of so distinguished a father had the advantage of the best education which the country could afford. On the completion of his elementary studies he was sent to the University. After taking his degree he added considerably to his knowledge of men and things by foreign travel. He also became acquainted with many distinguished men of his time. He was on terms of intimacy with William Drummond of Hawthornden; Arthur Johnstone, the king's physician, and other eminent men of the day. David Pierson was a man of sterling honesty and uprightness of character. While he appears to have taken considerably less interest in local affairs than his immediate ancestors, he gave great attention to questions of general interest. In 1635 he published a book under the title of "Varieties," which, so far as is known, is the oldest book in existence from the pen of an Arbroathian.

David Pierson's "Varieties" is, in many ways, a remarkable volume. The full title of the book is "Varieties : or a Surveigh of Rare and Excellent Matters, necessary and delectable for all sorts of persons ; Wherein the principall Heads of diverse sciences are illustrated ; Rare secrets of Naturall Things Unfoulded, &c." "By David Pierson of Loughlands in Scotland, gentleman." It was printed in London in 1635 by Richard Badger for Thomas Alchorn—"and are to be sold at his shop, in Paul's Church-yard, at the Signe of the green Dragon," saith the title page. The subject-matter of the volume is "digested into five bookes," and its character certainly justifies the title "Varieties." The first book deals with "the matter and nature of the Heaven, Sunne, Moone, Starres, Ayre, Sea, and Earth." The second book contains "A Discourse of Meteors, as of Comets, falling Starrs, and other fiery impressions ; of Winde, Clouds, Thunder, Haile, Snow, Raine, Deaw, Earth-quakes," &c. The third book treats of "Armies and Battels, Combats and Duels, Death and Burials, Laughing and Mourning, and Mentall Reservation." The fourth book is taken up with "Treatises on Curiosities, Divine Philosophy or Man's felicity, the Consonancie and agreement betwixt Ancient Philosophers and Christian

Professors, and on Sleepe and Dreams." The fifth book deals with the "Numbers Three and Seven, Miracles and Prodigies, Salamandra or the Philosopher's Stone, the World, and Metaphysicks." The sun, moon, and stars, the earth, and all that it contains, and, in fact, all that it does not contain, are Pierson's subjects. All phenomena natural, miraculous or prodigous, are discussed with an erudite sincerity which makes the numerous absurdities in the volume appear all the more absurd to the reader who peruses it under the new light which the centuries have thrown upon nature's secrets since Pierson wrote in 1635.

In reading Pierson's volume, it is necessary to keep in remembrance one or two red-letter dates in the history of scientific discovery in order to judge the book fairly. Copernicus published his great work, *De Revolutionibus Orbium*, in 1542, and Kepler's famous Three Laws were being discussed by scientific men a good many years before Pierson wrote. Bacon was dead nine years before Pierson's volume appeared, and in his travels on the continent our townsman might have had Descartes for a companion; for during the years he was gathering material for his "Varieties" in France, Italy, and other countries, Descartes, too, was wandering over Europe, bringing to maturity his great "Discourse on Method." Pierson does not seem to have known anything either of Kepler or his Laws, and though Galileo was a prisoner of the Inquisition from 1632 till his death in 1642, the author of "Varieties," writing in the very year of Galileo's trial and condemnation by the Roman Catholic Church for demonstrating the movement of our earth, never mentions him. Pierson does not seem to have regarded any writer as an authority who had not been dead and buried for more than a century. He does venture to mention Copernicus, but it is only to ridicule his "franticke and strange" notions, and to set him aside with contempt. "The globe of the earth," he says, "which (whatsoever fond conceit Copernicus had concerning the motion of it) yet remaineth firme and unmovable. And the heaven doth rolle still about this earth, and hath still as much below it as we see round about and above it."

All these facts seem to tell against Pierson; but let us not misjudge him. His notions concerning the earth and the stars were accepted by nineteen of every twenty educated men in his day. Newton was not born till 1642, and his full demonstration of the absolute truth of the law of gravitation was not published till 1684—half-a-century after Pierson's book had appeared. It is true that Bacon and Descartes had long before this sounded the battle-cry of rebellion against *authority*, and that it was responded to sympathetically by advanced men throughout Europe. Pierson was not an advanced man. He was an obedient son of the Roman Church, and his volume is duly certified to contain nothing "contra Catholicam fidem, aut bonos mores." His explanations of natural phenomena were those believed in by the vast majority of reading and thinking men up to the end of the seventeenth century. That the "Varieties" was regarded as the work of a more than ordinarily able man is fully proved by the congratulatory epistles from eminent men in Edinburgh and elsewhere, which are printed at the beginning of the volume. No less distinguished a person than William Drummond of Hawthornden—the good and worthy friend of rare Ben Jonson—in writing of Pierson's volume, tells us that—

> "The Lawyer here may learn Divinity,
> The Divine, Lawes, or faire Astrology;
> The Dammaret respectively to fight,
> The Duellist to court a mistress right;
> Such who their name take from the Rosie-Crosse,

May here by time learne to repaire their losse;
All learne may somewhat, if they be not fooles,
Arts quicklier here are lessoned than in schooles.
Distich of the same—
This booke a world is; here if errours be,
The like (nay worse) in the great world we see."

The lines do more credit to Drummond's goodness of heart than to his soundness of head, but they serve to show the respect in which Pierson and his volume were held by the distinguished men of his day.

The "Varieties" is chiefly interesting to us because it is the work of a townsman, and we will not be misunderstood if we say that Pierson's volume is really most interesting and amusing, where the author's facts and fancies are most absurd. Several quotations may best serve to give an idea of the volume at its worst, and, perhaps, at its best.

In his treatise on meteors, Pierson tells us that the appearance of a comet "portends some one evil or other," "as for death of princes, and change of estates foreshowne by them," he tells us, "experience of former ages can qualify, and by late miserable proofs it may be understood by that blazing star, which appeared in the year 1618, I being at that time in Florence, where an Italian astronomer, upon the third bridge, drawing in his table-bookes the height and aspect of it, was overheard by us who gazed on him, to cry although with a low voice, Vœ Germaniæ, 'Woe unto Germany,' and whoso is but never so little acquainted with the histories of diverse nations, shall soone perceive in them what lamentable accidents have ensued after extraordinary deluges, and overflowings of waters, and intollerable droughts; but more especially after the appearing of comets, what dreadful effects according to their affections; so we require that those Recusants would with the philosopher, who denied that the fire was hot, but put their finger into it to try the truth of his assertion." We laugh at such fancies now-a-days, but Zadkeil's Almanac has still an enormous circulation among us.

Pierson was conversant with the moon's influence on tides, and he also knew a good many of her other influences which have, since his day, got beyond our ken. "The ebbes and flowes of the sea," he says, "depend totally and constantly on the full and change of the moon, for accordingly her waters swell or decrease. Moreover, the braines and marrow in the bones of man and beaste doe augment or diminish as the moon increaseth or waneth, as doe likewise the flesh of all shell fishes. Dayly experience, too, hath taught your pruners of trees, gelders of cattle, gardners, and the like, to observe the moone's increase and decrease." Some readers may smile, and say that the moon must have been sadly on the wane when Pierson wrote that passage. We cannot say, for the passage is not dated; but we are old enough to remember the time when good people in our own county of Angus went out to look at the moon while they took their medicine. And you, my wise reader, who are smiling at the credulity of David Pierson, did you never, when the new moon caught your eye, thrust your hand into your pocket to see what money was there? Remember, before you laugh at Pierson, that you are nearly 300 years older than he; you ought to be wiser!

In our own day when theosophy has been so boomed, it is interesting to know that Pierson was a firm believer in, what Mr Gladstone calls, spiritism. There were no mahatmas in Pierson's day, but, to him the air was peopled with spirits who, if they could not write and post letters, could at least laugh and weep and make their voices heard by human ears. The whole earth was mysteriously living to Pierson's mind. In a curious passage in his first book he tells us that the earth may be compared to a living man's body—"the rocks and stones whereof are his bones, the brooks and rivers serpenting through it, the veins and sinews conveying moistness from their fountains unto all the members; the hollow of our bowels and of the trunk of our bodies, to the vast and spacious cavernes and caves within the body of this earth—within the which hollow of our bodies our vitious windes are enclosed, which if they have no vent, presently they beget in us iliak passions, collicks, &c., whereby our whole body is cast into a distemper and disturbed; even as the winds enclosed in these caverns, and hollow subterranean places, preassing to have vent, and not finding any, making way to themselves, do then beget these earthquakes, &c."

Pierson tells that the Adamant Stone is, of its own nature, so hard that neither fire nor iron can bruise or break it, but goes to pieces in a dishful of goats' blood, and he caps this absurdity by proceeding in dead earnest to give a recipe for making the Philosopher's Stone, the universal medicine and goldmaker. Those who care to try the recipe will find it very carefully stated in Pierson's fifth book.

One more item from Pierson's old curiosity shop must suffice. It is a curiosity this story. Pierson places it as a conclusion to his chapter on Curiosities, and we need hardly say that it is altogether a very striking conclusion. The story is quoted from an ancient author—all Pierson's authorities are very ancient—and Pierson's comment on the story is that Livia's singular curiosity was admirable. "Livia being with child of Tiberius fell into an inquisitive curiosity to know whether the child she went withal should prove male or female;

whereupon, repairing to Scribonius, the astrologer, she was advised by him to take an egg from under a sitting hen, and to hold it so long betwixt her hands till, through the heat of them, the egg should bird and break the shell; which accordingly she did, and thereout came a cock-chicken; whereupon the mathematician divined that she should be delivered of a man-child; who, as the bird was crested, should bear a crown and command over others: and so thereafter it happened."

But there is another side of the "Varieties" which deserves attention. Pierson had evidently superstition enough to serve a whole parish, but he had good sense too, plenty of it at times, and it is extremely interesting to watch his sense and superstition in conflict. As we have mentioned, Pierson was a faithful sheep in the fold of the Roman church. But his sense sometimes led him astray. When he was asked to worship the "Holy Tear," he had difficulties. The tear was said to be one received warm from Christ's cheek, and it was preserved in a vial in the church at Vendome in France. Pierson visited the church and saw the tear. Whether it has evaporated yet we cannot say. It may turn up again, perhaps, when the Holy Coat of Treves is worn out. Pierson is unable to be so "universally catholic" as to swallow the story of the holy tear. He protested mildly to begin with, and warms as his sense gains ground, and he concludes by declaring the tear "a gross invention." The Saints themselves become a little mysterious to him at times. "All the deeds of the Saints," he says, "are not to be obtruded as exemplary for all men to imitate," and, with a touch of admirable humour, he adds, "they are rather to be admired than followed." In this connection, too, we must mention a point which will lift Pierson in the estimation of every Arbroathian. He had a keen sense of personal honour. The Council of Constance decreed that no faith was to be kept with heretics or enemies of the Roman Church. Pierson scorns the authority of such a decree. He was evidently a valiant believer in Burns' principle—

> " Whaur you feel your honour grip,
> Lat that aye be your border,"

and he was prepared to defy even the authority of his church when it came between him and the dictates of his own conscience. There are autobiographical passages here and there in the "Varieties" which give us glimpses of a strong and kindly nature in the author, and these are interesting, and enable us to form some idea of the social character of David Pierson. "I think it one of the best fruits of my studies and travels," he tells us, "to be ever arming myself against death—and as in my morning and evening prayers I call for peace of conscience, in the assurance of my reconciliation with my God; and for peace on earth, for his blessing upon my children, his favour upon my king and country; so more specially for the favourable assistance of the Holy Ghost the Comforter to assist me then, that neither the terror of a present death may affright me, nor my trust and confidence breed in me presumption, nor my fear, despair; but there being a sweet harmony betwixt my soul and my God, 'I may lay down my life, in hope to re-assume it again for ever." There is a strong and generous personality behind a prayer like that.

One would imagine that Pierson must have been a man who could enjoy a hearty laugh—at himself. There are numerous indications in his volume of a power of honest introspection, not at all common in men of his position. He confesses to being wearied of his book, and betrays a fear that his subjects are "curiosities, more frivolous than necessary." He got over the difficulty of the language we are to speak in Heaven by foretelling an eternity of "Halleluiahs," but when he comes to perplex himself and his readers about the sex of angels, the size of Abraham's bosom, and at what time of the year the world began, he grows impatient, and begins to see that his problems are more curious than profitable, and he is frank enough to say that he thinks the best feature of his writings is their variety. Every reader will agree with him.

Whether David Pierson ever gave to the world any other of his prelections we have no evidence, but that he contemplated doing so will be seen from the following lines, which form the closing sentence of his "Varieties:"—"I feare to weary the Reader with these Generalls, For I intend hereafter (God willing) to put forth a small Treatise of Metaphysicks, wherein you shall finde that noble Science perspicuously delineated."

It would be interesting, but it is beyond our purpose here, to trace the history of this and the other branches of the Pierson family to the present day. Many of them have occupied distinguished positions in the army, in the navy, in the church, and on the bench, and not a few of them have, through marriage, become allied to some of the leading families in the kingdom. The last of the race in this district was James Alexander Pierson who, through his mother Margaret Ouchterlony, succeeded in 1849 to the estate of the Guynd and died in 1873. Worthy representatives of the family are still to be found both at home and abroad, among whom may be named Lord Pearson, one of the present Lords of Session, descended from the Pearsons of Clow, and David R. Pearson, M.D., of the Kippenross branch of the family, now of Kensington, London, to the latter of whom we are indebted for much of the genealogical information contained in this paper.

WILLIAM AIKMAN.

WILLIAM AIKMAN,

Of Lordburn and Cairnie.

WILLIAM AIKMAN, last of the long line of lairds of Lordburn and Cairnie of that name, more by his brilliant talents as an artist than by his lineage, has gained a niche in the temple of fame. His pedigree, however, was no mean one. Tradition tells that the progenitor of the family was the officer in Macduff's army under whose orders the soldiers cut down and armed themselves with branches of oak, and with these, like a moving forest, marched on Dunsinane Castle. It had been prophesied that Macbeth should never be slain by man born of any woman, or vanquished until the wood of Birnam came to the Castle of Dunsinane, and here in the advancing woods the usurper read his doom. The success of the stratagem is said to have earned for that officer the name of Oakman, or Aikman. Be this as it may, the family is an ancient one, and adopting the tradition as history, John Aikman of Cairnie, between 1672-78, registered the following arms :—Argent a sinister hand holding an oaken baton paleways proper, surmounted by a bend engrailed gules ; crest, an oaken tree proper ; motto, *sub robore virtus*—may be translated, valour under the oak, referring to the advance on Dunsinane.

The progenitors of the Aikman family appear to have been

free barons, and settled in Forfarshire several centuries ago. They are also to be met with in Lanarkshire and in the Stewartry of Kirkcudbright. Alysandre de Aikman, of Lanarkshire, was compelled to swear fealty to Edward I., 1296. We find reference to John Hekman, bailie of Montrose, in 1490. James Aikman, Dingwall Pursuivant 1460-88, sat in Parliament, 1473, and probably also in 1505.

The branch of the Aikman family with whom we have to do was long connected with Arbroath, and centuries ago its members occupied responsible positions in the town. John Aikman held land in Lordburn at least as early as, if not prior to, 1505. From that date, down to 1707, we find several local references to one or other of the family. At Michaelmas, 1564, "Jhon Akman" was elected to hold the office of lynar, and in the spring following he appears on the bench along with the "bailyies" acting as judge in a civil case. In 1566, he was one of the "quarter-maisters" appointed by the bailies during the "pest" to see "that na maner of parson within the broich resauve ane stranger or out man within thair hous day nor nycht without lecens asket and optenit of the bailyeis, onder the payn of tynsall of his fredom and comon landis." Within a month of the issue of this edict, Alexander Akman breaks the law by receiving "his gudebroder within his hous, quha cam fourth of Montross contrar the actes of this broich," and he is thereupon threatened with the loss of his freedom and banishment from the town "for yeir and day." But Alexander had cause to be thankful that he had a "friend in court," for, on the same day, "Jhon Akman in presens of the bailyeis and court oblish hym onder the payn of his life, lands, and guidis that thair sall cum na danger nor skaith to this town throw his rasaiving of George Brown or his wyf."

On 2nd June, 1570, "Jhon Akman, decane," is elected co-adjutor and helper to Thomas Lyndsay, reader, as " ane elimosiner for dew admynistration and distribution of the anuellis and yierlie apportionment of ald to the puyr," a most honourable and responsible office. For the next hundred years we meet from time to time the name of Aikman among the magistrates and council of the burgh. George Aikman of Lordburn (b. 1560 d. 1625), who was a bailie of the regality of Aberbrothock, was father of John Aikman, who acquired the lands of Cairnie. John Aikman married Margaret, sister of Sir Thomas Hamilton of Preston and Rossaven or Ross, by whom he had two daughters.

On the death of his first wife he married Euphemia Ouchterlony, daughter of Provost Ouchterlony of Arbroath, by whom he had several children. This lady seems to have had but a poor opinion of the municipal dignitaries. The Kirk Session Records of 17th October, 1693, bear that the Magistrates had complained that "Euphemia Ouchterlony, spouse to John Aikman of Cairnie, had scolded them publicly, they being sitting in judgment in a fenced court, calling them rascals, knaves, and carter fellows." The session, deeming this a heinous offence, summoned her to appear before them; but while she had had the temerity to flout the civic rulers, she shewed as little respect to her ecclesiastical superiors—so neither to the first nor to the two subsequent citations did she pay any heed. In consequence, the case was referred to the Presbytery, but, even then the difficulty was not so easily got over; and it was only after various modes of dealing with her had been tried that she consented to acknowledge that she was sorry for any offence she had given God in the matter, but no apology appears to have been drawn from her for the strong language she had used toward the magistrates.

On 15th July, 1661, John Aikman got a charter, under the Great Seal, of the lands of Cairnie. This John Aikman, who was locally known as "the gude laird o' Cairnie," was born in 1613, and died in 1693 at the ripe age of eighty. His eldest son, William Aikman, who married Margaret, the eldest daughter of John Clerk, the first laird of Penicuik, was an eminent advocate at the Scottish Bar, and for some time held the office of Sheriff-Depute of Forfarshire. He succeeded to the estate on the death of "the gude Laird," but was only in possession for six years when he died.

Thomas Aikman, the second son of John Aikman of Cairnie, was also a lawyer of good repute, and was Keeper of the Records of Scotland. He bought the lands of Bramelton, or Broomhilton, and afterwards the lands of Ross, in Lanarkshire.

Thomas Aikman, of Ross and Broomhilton, though he had eighteen children, was succeeded by two of his sons only, John and William, who both died unmarried, and the rest of his issue failing, the estates went to a grandson of William Aikman, the painter, and thus became the seat of the representatives of the family. Margaret Aikman, daughter of William, the painter, married Hugh Forbes, of Pittencrief; their son, John Forbes, succeeding to the estates in 1784, on the death of William, son of Thomas Aikman, took the name of Aikman. He married Marion Naysmith of Haughhead, but having no issue, the property passed to his sister Marion (Mrs David Robertson of Loretto), who was succeeded by her son, Captain George Robertson Aikman, H.E.I.C.S. (b., 1760 ; d., 1844) succeeded by his eldest son, also George Robertson Aikman (b. 1817, d. 1879). On his death, the second son, Hugh Henry Robertson Aikman (b. 1819) became heir. He did not live long to enjoy his possession, having died in 1882, when he was succeeded by his eldest son, Major Thomas Stokes George Hugh Robertson Aikman, the present proprietor of the estates and representative of the Aikman family.

In the Abbey burying-ground, about fifty-four yards from the sacristy door, and twenty yards from the tomb of the Philps, there was, until about a quarter-of-a-century ago, a chest tombstone which covered the last resting-place of the Aikmans of Lordburn and Cairnie. The tomb was then in a dilapidated condition, and the slabs were removed to, and are now lying against, the outside wall of the sacristy. Two of these measure over seven feet by three, the other portions being smaller and fragmentary. Each of the two larger stones bears an inscription—the one "HIC EST TVMVS AIKMNVM LORDBVRNE" (This is the tomb of the Aikmans of Lordburn), and the other "O FLVXVM DECOS HVMANVMET VARIABILE ET TEMPVS ET VMBRA SVMVS" (O fleeting and variable human beauty and opportunity, we are only a shadow). When these stones were removed to their present position, a brass tablet, bearing date 1st January, 1869, intended by the representative of the family to be "placed *on the stones* that covered the last resting-place in the Abbey grounds of ten John Aikmans," has since then, for its better preservation, been kept in the sacristy. The inscription, which is a long one, concludes with the statement that "this tablet is presented to the town by me, the great-great-great-great-grandson of the 'Gude Laird o' Cairnie,' in affectionate remembrance of the Aikmans of Lordburn and Cairnie, who resided in or near Arbroath for many centuries."

The Castle or Fort of Cairnie, the residence of the Aikmans, was situate on the rising ground a few hundred yards to the north-east of the present farmhouse of Cairnie, and was a very ancient building. It was beautifully situated, commanded a magnificent view of the German Ocean, the Firth of Tay, and the coast of Fife, and was approached by a fine avenue of trees. The old garden, enclosed by a stone wall, still remains. Some of the stones which formed part of the old castle had been built into the walls of the farm steading. One of these, which bore the initials "J. A." on each side of a shield, charged with the armorial bearings of the Aikmans, as already described, and with the date 1658, was, with the permission of Sir John Ogilvy, the then proprietor, removed in 1868 from the wall by the representative of the descendant of the family. It was then in an excellent state of preservation, and is now built into the mantel of the hall at Ross.

On the death of William Aikman in 1699, he was succeeded by his son, the subject of this sketch. William Aikman, the last laird of Cairnie of the name, was born at Cairnie, Arbroath,[*] on the 24th October, 1682. His father wished him to follow his own profession of a Scottish advocate, but he showed no great inclination to do so. The beautiful and romantic surroundings of the home of his childhood could not fail to foster within him a love of nature. He early developed a taste for poetical and artistic pursuits ; so, forsaking the study of law, he betook himself to the more congenial profession of painting, entering as a pupil under Sir John Medina, a celebrated painter of his day. After prosecuting his studies in Scotland for a time under Sir John, he proceeded to England, where he spent a brief period in study. In 1707, being then in his twenty-fifth year, he determined to go abroad in order still further to improve his education as an artist. In that year he disposed

---

[*] The Encyclopædia Britannica, ninth edition, erroneously states that he was born at Cairnie in Aberdeenshire, and the same mistake is made in Chambers's "Eminent Scotsmen."

of his ancestral estate of Cairnie, and so severed his connection with Arbroath. On leaving Arbroath, he proceeded to Rome, where for three years he had the opportunity of studying under the most celebrated masters, and of examining the best examples both of ancient and modern art. He also visited Constantinople and Smyrna, in each of which he remained for a short period, and afterwards returned for a time to Rome, where he renewed his studies.

After a five years' foreign residence, during which he acquired considerable skill, he returned to his native land. Taking up his residence in Edinburgh, he was soon recognised for his superior attainments by the few qualified to judge of the intrinsic merits of his work. But at that time money was not plentiful, nor was the taste for high-class art generally diffused, and consequently his commissions, although important, were few. His love of poetry was little short of his love of painting, and his refined tastes soon secured for him the warm friendship of the leading literary men of Edinburgh, and although we have seen no reference to it, we have little doubt he was a member of the "Easy Club," an association of young gentlemen of literary tastes. His intimate friendship with Allan Ramsay, who became one of the leading members of that Club, and who, at one period, was its poet laureate, would naturally bring him into contact with those of kindred tastes. The poet Thomson, then a young man, was also at this time a warm friend of Aikman's. While he enjoyed the literary kinships he had formed in Edinburgh, his professional talents were in a large measure unproductive.

The Duke of Argyle, with whom he was on intimate terms, and who not only thoroughly appreciated his abilities as an artist, but who also admired his personal character and literary attainments, urged him to try his fortune in the wider field which London afforded. In 1723, being then in his forty-first year, he removed to the metropolis along with his wife, Marion Lawson—daughter of Lawson of Cairnmuir—and his family.

His departure from Edinburgh formed the subject of one of those delightful pastoral poems from the pen of Allan Ramsay, for which that Scottish Horace was famed. Two of his old retainers, Betty and Kate, in alternate verse proclaim the virtues of their master. Betty, recalling his youthful days, as he amused himself on the bonnie braes of Cairnie, exclaims:—

> " Blyth I have stood frae morn to e'en,
>   To see how true and weel,
> He could delyt us on the green,
>   With a piece cawk and keel.
> On a slid stane, or smoother slate,
>   He can the picture draw,
> Of you or me, or sheep or gait,
>   The likest e'er you saw."

And Kate rehearses the domestic love and social virtues of Aikman, his wife and family:—

> " William and Mary never fail'd
>   To welcome with a smile,
> And hearten us, when aught we ail'd
>   Without designing guile;
> Lang may she happily possess
>   Wha's in his breast infeft;
> And may their bonny bairns increase,
>   And a' with rowth be left.
> Oh! William win your laurels fast,
>   And syne we'll a' be fain,
> Soon as your wand'ring days are past,
>   And you're returned again."

Two years before this was written Ramsay had addressed lines to Aikman, beginning thus :—

> " 'Tis granted, sir, pains may be spared
>   Your merit to set forth,
> When there's sae few to claim regard,
>   That disna ken your worth.
>
> . . .
>
> While frae originals of yours
>   Fair copies may be ta'en,
> And fixed on brass to busk our bowers,
>   Your memory shall remain."

Allan Ramsay was also on very friendly terms with William Aikman's cousin, Sir John Clerk of Penicuik, Baron of the Exchequer, whose memoirs were recently published by the Scottish History Society. In his journal, Sir John refers to a visit to him by Ramsay when he (Sir John) was sojourning with his wife and family at Drumcrief in August or September, 1754. He says—" Here I was very easy and happy. Mr Alan Ramsey, a very pleasant companion, staid with us." At Penicuik House there is a portrait of Allan Ramsay, painted by Aikman, on the back of which, in Sir John Clerk's handwriting, the following lines appear :—

A Roundlet in Mr Ramsay's own Way.

> Here, painted on this canvas clout
> By Aikman's hand, is Ramsay's snout ;
> The picture's value none may doubt ;
>   For ten to one I'll venture—
> The greatest critics could not tell
> Which of the two does not excel,
> Or in his way should bear the bell—
>   The poet or the painter.
>
> <div style="text-align:right">J.C., Penicuik, <i>5 May, 1723.</i></div>

The introductions which he carried with him to London from his friend the Duke of Argyle soon brought him into contact with the most celebrated British painters of the day, foremost among these being Sir Godfrey Kneller. Among his earliest acquaintances were also the Duke of Devonshire, Sir Robert Walpole, and other distinguished men of the time, with whom he continued on the most friendly terms. The Earl of Burlington, then one of the chief patrons of art to whom he was recommended by the Duke of Argyle, recognising his eminent skill, not only employed him himself, but obtained for him several valuable professional connections.

From the time of his settlement in London till his death, his professional services and his agreeable society were much sought after. His portraits of noblemen, ladies and, gentlemen, whose names retain no place in history, are still to be found, bearing ample evidence of the wonderful power of his pencil. But besides these, he has left portraits of many of the most distinguished men of the time—Fletcher of Saltoun, and William Carstairs, and also Somerville, Thomson, and Gay, the poets, the latter of which is believed to be one of the most successful of his works. He was commissioned by the Earl of Burlington to paint a large picture of the royal family of England, which, however, was never finished, owing to the death of the artist. This picture was in three compartments, all the younger branches being in the middle, while a full length portrait of Queen Caroline was on one end. The portrait of King George II. was intended for the third compartment, but it was never completed. This, which was one of his largest, was also allowed to be his best work. The picture is now in possession of the Duke of Devonshire.

As an artist, he attained a very high position, his style bearing close resemblance to Kneller's, so close, indeed, that it is said of his portraits that they may readily be mistaken for those of that great painter. His works found a place in the collections of the Dukes of Argyle, Hamilton, Devonshire, and Buckingham. In the Scottish National Portrait Gallery—of which John Ritchie Findlay, a native of Arbroath, was the originator, and to which he has been a most liberal contributor —there are some fine examples of Aikman's work. These are Patrick, first Earl of Marchmont ; John Gay, the poet and dramatist ; James Thomson, the author of "The Seasons;" and Allan Ramsay, the author of the "Gentle Shepherd." The latter is a small bust portrait in black chalk, touched with white. There is also a portrait there of Aikman by himself, said to be a most excellent likeness. It is that from which our portrait of Aikman is taken. There is another portrait of Aikman, also by himself, at Penicuik House, which is very similar to that in the Scottish National Portrait Gallery, the only difference being in the colouring of the costume. His portrait of Allan Ramsay at Penicuik House is in oil and shews the poet nearly to the waist, clad in a brown coat; the head is covered by a low-toned orange handkerchief wound round it.

As in Edinburgh, so in London, his society was sought by the leading men of the day. Pope, Swift, Gay, Thomson, Somerville, Arbuthnot, Mallet, and others of the brilliant literary circle of the period, being his intimate friends.

He died at his house in Leicesterfields, London, on the 4th June, 1731, before he had completed his forty-ninth year. His only son, John, had predeceased him by a few months. Throughout life he retained his love for his native country, and by his own expressed wish, his body and that of his son, were removed to Edinburgh, where they were buried together in one grave in Greyfriars Churchyard.

Thomson, the author of " The Seasons ;" Somerville, the author of " The Chase ;" and David Mallet, wrote elegiac verses on his death, and, as mentioned on page 98, James Philip of Almericlose, the author of " The Grameid," wrote an epitaph on Aikman.

A monument was erected over the tomb of the two Aikmans, which bore the following epitaph by Mallet:—

> Dear to the good and wise, dispraised by none,
> Here sleep in peace the father and the son ;
> By virtue as by nature close allied,
> The painter's genius, but without the pride ;
> Worth unambitious, wit afraid to shine,
> Honour's clear light, and friendship's warmth divine,
> The son, fair-rising, knew too short a date,
> But O, how more severe the parent's fate !
> He saw him torn untimely from his side,
> Felt all a father's anguish, wept, and died.

PROVOST JOHN WALLACE,

Pioneer of Local Enterprise.

UCHTERLONY, writing in 1684-5, says of the Arbroathians of his day, "they have a shore, some shipping, and a little small trade," and so it was then. The weavers and other tradesmen contented themselves with disposing of their respective commodities, the one to the other. Of commerce, in the general acceptance of the term, there was none.

In the early years of the eighteenth century, however, a spirit of enterprise sprang up, and business men began to look beyond the narrow limits of their own little burgh for a field for their commercial operations. To John Wallace may fairly be assigned the honour of being the pioneer of this new departure.

The Wallace family came to Arbroath from Kirkden in the beginning of the seventeenth century. No doubt they were there engaged in the weaving trade, but Arbroath offering a larger field for their business capabilities, and its sea-board greater facilities for communication with the big world beyond, a removal was made to the town. They very soon began to take a leading part, not only in the various business transactions of the burgh, but also in the management of its municipal affairs. In 1651 Patrick Wallace, then a leading citizen, took an active part in repelling Oliver Cromwell's attempt to land troops at Arbroath.

In the first years of the eighteenth century various members of the Wallace family are mentioned as having filled the highest municipal offices. The Provost's chair was filled in 1724 by William Wallace, and in the same year James Wallace was Town Treasurer, and John Wallace, who succeeded William Wallace in the Provostship had, prior to 1724, held the office of bailie. In that year—1724—Patrick Wallace, merchant in Aberbrothock, the father of John Wallace, appeared before the Commissioners at the Convention of Royal Burghs held at Edinburgh, as Commissioner for Arbroath, and presented a petition on behalf of the merchants in Arbroath, shewing that by Charter of Confirmation granted by King James VI., they were incorporated and created into a free royal burgh, with power to the free burgesses and inhabitants thereof to choose a provost, bailies, dean of guild and guild brethren, councillors, and other officers for governing the said burgh, and craving the Convention to ratify the Act, and ordain a dean of guild to be chosen. The prayer of the petition was granted, and they were accordingly empowered to elect a dean of guild at their next election of Magistrates. At a meeting held in September, 1725, at which Patrick Wallace presided, James Wallace was elected the first dean of guild under this edict. In 1727 John Wallace, provost, represented the Council at, and voted in, the election of a member of Parliament for this district of burghs. The office of commissioner at these elections was a most important one, the appointment of member of Parliament for the large district between Arbroath and Aberdeen, including both towns, being virtually in the hands of five commissioners, one each from Aberdeen, Bervie, Brechin, Montrose, and Arbroath. In this year, John Wallace, the subject of this sketch, occupied the then important office of Convener of the Trades. For many years after this, the Wallaces continued to fill the highest offices in the burgh. John Wallace, who was provost in 1727, retired in 1728, and William Wallace, who had previously held the office, was again called to the provost's chair. A year thereafter, he retired in favour of Patrick Wallace, John Wallace's father. His brother, Patrick Wallace, followed the fortunes, or rather the misfortunes, of Prince Charles Edward Stuart, and after '45 he was confined for a while in the Tower of London, where he was joined by his wife. A daughter was born to them while in the Tower, who was baptized by the name of Stuart Wallace. In "the List of Rebels from Montrose District" the following entry occurs:—"Patrick Wallace, Provost of Arbroath, Had a Commission as Governor of Arbroath for the Rebels, raised and commanded two companies of men in their service, and was active in landing French soldiers." This "rebel" was never provost of Arbroath; the compilers of the "List of Rebels" had confounded him with his father, Provost Patrick Wallace. He was, for a time, a bailie of the burgh.

The earliest record we have of John Wallace holding any public office is in April, 1733, when he is elected Dean of Guild. In 1735 he was a bailie. In 1738 he became provost, and in the same year Thomas Wallace and Patrick Wallace were chosen bailies, so that the entire Magistracy were Wallaces; and, as David Wallace was treasurer, and John Wallace, late provost, and John Wallace, shipmaster, were councillors, six of the seventeen councillors were Wallaces, three of them bearing the name of John Wallace. John Wallace continued in the provostship till 1741, and in 1764 he was again elected Chief Magistrate of the burgh. During the period he was in the council, both as bailie and as provost, the condition of the Harbour finances was causing considerable anxiety, and a rather novel plan was adopted to relieve the pressure. This was an application to Parliament for "An Act for laying a Duty of Two Penies Scots, or one sixth part of a peny Sterling, upon every Scots Pint of Ale and Beer, which shall be brewed for Sale, brought into, vended, tapped, or sold within the Town of Aberbrothock, and Liberties thereof." The case, as stated for the Town Council of the day, affords a glimpse of the state of matters, and the straits to which they were put for money, not only to carry on the business of the harbour, but also the other works in town. A quotation from the preamble to the bill will make this plain:—

"Whereas the Situation of the Town of Aberbrothock, in the Shire
"of Forfar, is such, that a commodious Harbour there will not
"only tend to the Advantage of the Trade within the said Town,
"but be of great Use to the Navigation in general upon the
"Northern Coasts of that Part of Great Britain called Scotland:
"And whereas some Years since the Harbour there became so
"decayed, that it was hazardous for small Vessels to sail into
"the same, whereupon the then Provost, Baillies, and Council
"of the said Town did cause the Foundation of a new Harbour
"to be laid, and the Work was carried on for some Years at
"the sole Expence of the said Town and Inhabitants thereof,
"whereby large Debts were contracted, and they being unable
"to proceed in the said Work, several charitable Contributions
"were made and duly applied towards carrying on the same:
"And whereas the said Town are uncapable to finish and com-
"pleat the Works of the said Harbour (so necessary for the
"Subsistence of the said Town, and useful to the Trade thereof)
"and to discharge the Debts already contracted on account
"thereof, and to rebuild the Town-house and Common Prison
"of the said Town, which are now very old and decayed, and
"to repair the Streets and Causeways, which are in a very
"ruinous Condition, unless some other Provision be made for

" raising Money for those Purposes:—To the end, therefore, that
" the Provost, Baillies, and Town-Council of the Burgh may be
" enabled to pay off the Debts already contracted for the publick
" Service of the said Town, and to perfect and compleat the said
" Harbour, and to rebuild the Town House and publick Prison,
" and to repair the Streets and Causeways, and to defray the
" Expence of other publick necessary Works of the said Town;
" your Majesty's most dutiful and loyal Subjects, the Provost,
" Baillies, and Town-Council of the Burgh of Aberbrothock, do
" most humbly beseech Your Majesty that it be enacted, and be
" it enacted by the King's most excellent Majesty, by and with
" the Advice and Consent of the Lords Spiritual and Temporal,
" and Commons, in this present Parliament assembled, and by
" the Authority of the same, That from and after the First
" Day of May, One thousand seven hundred and thirty eight,
" for the Term of Twenty-five years, and to the end of the
" then next Session of Parliament, there shall be laid an Imposi-
" tion or Duty of Two Penies Scots, or One Sixth Part of a
" Peny Sterling (over and above the Duty of Excise paid or
" payable to his Majesty, his Heirs, and Successors) upon every
" Scots Pint of Ale and Beer that shall be either brewed, brought
" in, tapped, or sold within the said Town, or Liberties thereof;
" and that the said Imposition or Duty shall be paid and made
" payable by the Brewers, for Sale, or Venders and Sellers of
" all such Ale and Beer, to the Magistrates and Town-Council
" of the said Town of Aberbrothock, and their Successors in
" Office for the time being, and their Assigns, or to such
" Collectors or Receivers as shall at any time during the Con-
" tinuance of this present Act be by them appointed, for the
" Uses and Purposes aforesaid."

The Magistrates and Council were appointed Trustees under the Act with power to levy the rates, and to execute the several purposes, for which the money was to be raised. In case of disputes between the parties so taxed and the Trustees, certain "overseers" were appointed, who should act as a sort of court of appeal. Among these were David, Earl of Northesk, John Carnegie, of Boysack, William Maule, of Panmure, John Maule, of Inverkeilor, Alexander Strachan, of Tarry, John Ouchterlony, of the Guynd, James Pierson, of Balmadies, and other local magnates. So impecunious were the Town Council that they experienced considerable difficulty in meeting the expense of procuring the passing of the Act, and the minutes bear such entries as these:—27th January, 1738, 500 merks are to be borrowed and applied "for a part of the charges . . . for obtaining ane Act of Parliament for two penies on the pint of ale," and another 500 merks for defraying the same charges. 10th Feb., 1738, another 500 merks are to be borrowed for same purpose. On 14th March, 1738, the minute bears that:—"It being represented to the Council that the expenses of obtaining the Act for laying a duty of two penies Scots on the pint of ale, would be much greater than at first imagined, so that it will be absolutely necessary to borrow money immediately for that purpose, since the bill for laying on the said duty is already depending before the Parliament," resolved to borrow 2000 merks. By the 25th of May following they had struggled through, for on that day a copy of the Act is produced to the Council, and David Mudie, the Town Clerk, is appointed collector of the duty.

The chief business in the town in these first years of the century was the weaving of linens. Under the energetic management of John Wallace, the staple trade grew rapidly in volume, and other departments of business shared in the general prosperity. To the trade of manufacturer, Wallace added that of shipowner, and he employed vessels belonging to himself, and others in importing flax for his own use as well as for that of others in the trade. He also, by means of his ships, exported the produce of his looms, not only to London and the other principal ports of the Kingdom, but to many foreign ports as well. The method of financing the flax purchases of his firm was different from the present method of carrying out such transactions. The flax was bought in Riga on the Arbroath firm's account by Provost Wallace's brother-in-law, John Mudie, one of the Mudies of Pitmuies. Mudie drew for the amount on a house in Amsterdam, Amsterdam paper being in favour with the Russian merchants. The Amsterdam firm protected themselves by drawing on a London House—each of course, charging a commission. The Arbroath firm met the payment of these bills by remitting to London from time to time, as they were in funds to do so. Besides flax, the firm also imported from Riga potash for their bleaching operations.

In a curious way, a new departure in the weaving business came about which, thanks to the energy and enterprise of John Wallace, was the means of giving a considerable impetus to the trade of the town. The story goes that in 1738, a weaver residing at the neighbouring hamlet of Marywell, or "The Law" as it is popularly called, having got a small quantity of yarn, which was unfit for the making of the usual article of Arbroath manufacture, made it into a web, and in order to get rid of it, offered it to Provost Wallace at a price which really meant a loss to the poor weaver. The Provost, who had had occasion in course of his business to visit foreign parts, noticed a strong resemblance between the article offered to him by the weaver, and fabrics manufactured in Osnaburg, so he not only purchased the web, but set about the systematic production of the article. Prior to this occurrence he had assumed as partner James Gardyne, the laird of Middleton, and at a subsequent period, John Gardiner. With the increased capital thus at command, under the energetic management of Provost Wallace, the business assumed large proportions, and the manufacture of the cloth thereafter known as Osnaburgs, soon became the staple industry of Arbroath, and gave employment to a great number of hands. In course of time other places in Scotland took to the manufacture of Osnaburgs.

The benefit the firm conferred on commerce by the introduction of this new article of manufacture was some years after this publicly acknowledged and rewarded. The Union in 1707 gave an impetus to trade in Scotland, and the Government wisely did much to encourage its manufacturing interests. Among other means used for this purpose was the institution in 1727 of a Board of Trustees for all Manufactures, with funds placed at its disposal for the encouragement of those employed in the various manufacturing industries. In a letter addressed to the secretary of this Board, dated 28th April, 1750, Wallace's firm write:—"We are very thankful to the Honourable Trustees that they have been pleased to order £100 for us towards indemnifying us in part of the expenses we have laid out on machinery. We have always been ready, and still are willing to communicate any small knowledge we have by our practice acquired in manufacturing, and shall at all times, when required, correspond with your Honourable Board, though we must tell you our little improvements, we have learned, are an expense upon ourselves not less than £1500 sterling, being the first undertakers in this country in making of Osnaburgs and white threads. . . None in the kingdom have done more towards the improving of the spinning as ourselves."

Shortly before this, Mr Wallace's energy found another outlet. Feuing a piece of ground from the town contiguous to

the harbour, at the west side, just about where the line of
railway now runs alongside the present quay, he erected thereon
a windmill for the sawing of timber, and for some years he
carried on a considerable timber trade. This feu, granted on
13th August, 1737, was at a very cheap rate. The minute of
Council bearing on this transaction is as follows :—" John Wallace,
baillie, having petitioned the Council for liberty to build a windmill for sawing of timber on the town's land lying contiguous
to the new shore, for payment of a feu-duty to the town,
equal in value to the yearly rent of the ground necessary for
building the said mill upon, the magistrates and councillors convened, unanimously agree to grant the desire of the said petition, and hereby appoint a piece of the said ground most
convenient for building, and contiguous to the harbour, to the
extent of twenty-four yards in length, and ten yards in breadth,
to be measured off and disponed by the members of Council
to the said John Wallace, his heirs and assignees, for payment
of a yearly feu of twelve shillings *Scots* money and doubling
thereof at the entry of every heir or singular successor *pro
omni alio onere*, excepting the minister's tiend, so far as the
same doth, or may extend to the ground to be disponed."
Within eighteen months thereafter the timber business had so
grown on his hands that he found it needful to take additional
ground to the extent of one rood and thirty falls, to form a
yard for the storage of the timber. Twenty-five years after this,
in a legal case which arose, and to which reference will be
made further on, the action of the magistrates and council in
granting this feu and other feus on such easy terms was strongly
animadverted on. In defence it was stated "that the Magistrates and Town Council have done no prejudice to the community, but have consulted the best means of advancing the

common good in granting the several feus . . . to Provost Wallace and Company for the special encouragement of the large manufactories carried on by them." From this it will be seen that, at this early date, through the Wallace's firm—of which John Wallace was the moving spirit—the prosperity of the town was largely increased, and by their example a spirit of emulation was kindled which was productive of great advancement in other branches of business, as well as in the staple trade of the town.

The introduction of the timber trade gave additional employment to the town's people. But Provost Wallace did not rest content with carrying on the businesses of linen manufacturer and wood merchant. His firm entered into large speculations in the grain trade, buying up not only the whole spare produce of various farms in Forfarshire and Kincardineshire, but carrying on their operations further north—Banff and Portsoy being ports at which frequent cargoes were shipped. These shipments of grain and meal were made to Norway, Sweden, and elsewhere on the Continent.

In a letter dated 15th October, 1749, Wallace refers to this branch of his firm's business. The following extract therefrom will show the nature and give some indication of the extent of this department. "My partner, James Gardyne, and I have, for a good many years past, bought up for our own account the victual of this neighbourhood, but now the quantity is much reduced since the farms of the forfeited Estates of Southesk and Panmure [which] lyes around us, are sold by contract, we missed that bargain by a post. It is believed the crop of bear may be plenty but some of it spoiled by the rains, the crop of oats thought to be but scanty. We have little wheat. If you have use for bear, we believe we might be able to pick up for you off farms, deliverable here, from 1200 to 1500 bolls, and for ready money, 800 to 1000 and the like quantity of meal." As an indication of the price then current, we find from a letter to Lord Arbuthnot that he accepts his Lordship's offer to sell the bear on his farm at "four pounds, twelve shillings Scots, pre boll, deliverable at your harbour of Gourdon." This bargain is made on 9th April, 1750, and the price is payable at "next Martinmas," but he expresses the hope that his Lordship will prevail on his tenants to deliver "as much as they can at Montrose, as the supply of it at Gourdon will be attended with a good deal of charge and other inconveniences, as no ship can take it in there that is fit to carry it any way abroad." From this it would appear that the landed proprietors not only sold their own grain, but acted in the capacity of agent for their tenants, in so far as the finding a market for their produce was concerned.

One would have imagined that these several and varied branches of business would have been sufficient to absorb all Provost Wallace's energies, and satisfy his ambition, but in 1744 he adds still another, and this time a very important branch to his already existing engagements, namely that of thread-making. In that year the Corporation, having a lease from the Crown of the Abbey House, sublet it to Provost Wallace's firm to be used by them as a thread factory. The application for this property was laid before a meeting of Town Council held on 28th January, 1744, on behalf of "Provost John Wallace who is wanting to take the same for seven years," and at a meeting held on 19th March following, the tack was granted. On the same day, an application was made by Wallace's partner, John Gardiner, for a tack of the Lordburn braes, and on 5th April, he got a tack thereof for three nineteen years, granting him liberty to build a mill for washing and knocking cloth and yarn, for which liberty, with the grass of Lordburn braes, he was to pay of rent 8 pound scots yearly, reserving to the inhabitants the privilege to wash, lay, and bleach made linen cloths, "from the top of the dam, to the corner of Thomas Watson's corn-yard dike, but not uncut webs or thread." On the 15th May, this tack was signed by the Council in favour of John Wallace, James Gardyne, and John Gardiner. In the same year they applied for, and obtained leave to enclose twenty square yards before the Abbey House for drying their thread, and this without additional rent.

This new branch of business expanded rapidly, and for upwards of half-a-century thereafter, it formed an important industry in the town, giving employment to a number of hands. The bulk of the produce of the thread factory was sold in London, and one would have thought that with the cheap accommodation, and the facilities possessed by the firm for the importation of flax the business would have been a profitable one. But if we were to judge from a rather acrimonious correspondence, which, in 1749, was carried on between the firm and the London house to whom they consigned their thread, we would come to the conclusion that it was far from being a money-making concern. In that year a difference of opinion as to the terms on which they had hitherto been dealing arose between the two houses, and the following extract of a letter written by John Wallace will show how he viewed the situation. After going thoroughly into the figures, shewing how unprofitable the business had been, he says, " but to brake its neck now, when we have done so much, its pity you and we both have stood the brunt of the battle. God knows if we shall ever have the applause of a victory. We have fought five years faithfully and stoutly, yet always beat, though we shall have one fair blow ere we give all up for lost, and not cowardlie retire till better cannot be." It had not after all been so bad as was represented, for we find them shortly after this proposing to enter into a fresh contract with the same firm for a term of *five* or *seven* years. As an additional proof that the business was not so bad as it was represented to be, it was continued as one of the industries of Arbroath till nearly the close of the last century.

To their trade of thread-making his firm in 1751 added that of stocking-making. Towards the close of the previous year they sent a young man to Glasgow to pick up what information he could in regard to the manufacture of thread stockings, with instructions to buy the necessary frames; they also ordered from Nottingham four additional frames. The stocking trade continued to be carried on in Arbroath for a much longer period than did the thread-making. In the end of last century, Robert Allan, father of the late Patrick Allan Fraser of Hospitalfield, came from Kirkden to Arbroath and engaged in the stocking-weaving trade. To the thread stocking-making Allan also added that of the manufacture of woollen stockings. In course of time he was joined by his sons, Alexander and James, and the business was continued by them—latterly by James alone—till 1847. It lingered in other hands for a few years longer, so that stocking-making continued an Arbroath industry for upwards of a century.

While engaged in these various branches of industry, the manufacture of linen goods, which still continued to be the staple trade of Arbroath, rapidly developed in the hands of Wallace's firm, and the growing demand for this class of goods led to its introduction to other districts of Scotland.

It may here be remarked in passing that a considerable impetus was given to the linen trade of the country by the establishment, in 1746, under Royal Charter, of the British Linen Company, not then as now a banking institution, but, as its name indicates, a company formed for the manufacture of linen cloth. The promoters however were chiefly actuated by patriotic motives, and as they believed that the settlement and prosperity of Scotland would best be promoted by the encouragement of such branches of industry, they not only entered into the trade themselves, but by advancing money to the poorer manufacturers in various districts they did much to provide steady and settled employment for the people, and this in no small measure helped to allay the spirit of unrest and insecurity which had been created by the rebellion.

While actively engaged in these different trades, Wallace's firm carried on a considerable business as general export and import merchants—salt, salmon, herrings, wines, tobacco, coals, linseed, fruit, and many other commodities passing through their hands. Their skippers acted in the double capacity of sailing masters and agents for the sale and purchase of their various articles of commerce. When they left a British port they were occasionally armed with powers to go from port to port till they found the best market for their cargo, and there they had similar powers to pick up the best bargains they could in certain specified articles. Referring to the export of salmon (or "salmond," as the Provost invariably spelt it) the following extract may be interesting :—" They,"—a firm with whom he had been corresponding,—" say the only ports in Spain for salmond are Cadiz, Alicant, or Barcelona. As this article is likely to be plenty and cheap with us this year [1749]—I believe may be sold for £20 Scots or under, per barrel—I propose, for an experiment, to send out a small vessel with 150 barrels salmond to last-mentioned places, where I apprehend such a small cargo may sell readyly." At this time herrings were a frequent article of import, but in 1750 a proposition is made to Wallace to share in a herring fishing adventure in Scotland. While profuse in his thanks to the brother provost who makes the overtures to him, he declines to enter into the undertaking, frankly confessing that he has already too many irons in the fire, adding "to keep them all hot my hands are full." He, however, expresses his best wishes for the success of the venture, as he considers it would confer a benefit on the whole kingdom. Although he does not see his way to join in the proposed undertaking, he has an eye to Arbroath sharing in any benefit that would result in connection with the movement, and he says —"If a few folks here were to take part in your chamber it would be upon condition to have a proportion of your trade carried on at this place."

It is no unusual thing for a successful man, especially in a small town, to find himself an object not only of envy, but of petty spite, and so it fared with Provost Wallace. In 1766 an action was raised in the Court of Session by the Convener of the Trades and others against Provost John Wallace and the other magistrates and members of the Town Council, charging them with committing great abuses in the management of the town, and with squandering and misapplying the revenues of the burgh. It was well-known that this action was chiefly directed against Wallace, and that it was largely actuated by trade jealousies. The action was defended with great spirit, and Provost Wallace brings out the motives which actuated its promoters in a rather amusing, but at the same time damaging statement, which he makes with reference to one of the pursuers.

After asserting that the attack which had been made on him arose from resentment of private and personal quarrels and disappointments, he says "one thing memorable, however, Provost John Wallace begs leave here to observe. On the day of election of magistrates at Michaelmas, 1764, when Mr Gellatly, one of the pursuers, understood that Provost Wallace was on the leet for Provost, he called the Provost aside, when going up to attend the meeting of Council, and told him that there was an action to be raised against the Magistrates and Council containing a very heavy charge for malversation, misapplication, and mismanagement of the public funds, that he and his partner, Mr Lyell, had been spoken to on this head, but that if Provost Wallace & Co., would make an easy bargain for so much yearly to be paid for scouring their yarn at the mill, Mr Gellatly would not only give up the claim he had against the town, but that his partner Mr Lyell and he would also give up having any concern with . . . the associations which was then forming." Besides this there is a good deal more of hard hitting. In defence he points out several instances where he and his firm have been benefactors to the town; in one instance where the town having become greatly embarrassed, and the interest of the debts being found in the year 1762 to exceed the annual income by between £200 and £300 sterling, that he was entreated to take part in the administration so as to help the community out of their difficulties; and that he did so contrary to a former resolution. At this time he and his partners in business, upon their own credit, reduced a considerable part of the Town's interest from 5 to 4½ per cent. and by otherwise making improvements, brought the revenue of the town to answer the interests. We have been unable to ascertain definitely how the case ended, but the business of the firm went on prosperously for many years after this. Meeting, however, with a heavy loss through the failure of a London house, with whom the firm had considerable dealings, the business was wound up.

Provost Wallace lived in a house on the High Street, the site of which is now occupied by the Public Hall. For a time he only occupied the upper storey as a dwelling-house, the lower storey being used as a warehouse. His son was in the army, and was an officer under Baron Maule. The regiment was stationed in Edinburgh, but having got the route for Aberdeen, young Wallace wrote to his father telling him that it was customary, when a regiment was passing through a town, for the Chief Magistrate to entertain the officers. The hint was taken, and in order to make an impression, the lower floor was quickly fitted up and furnished as a drawing-room—and it was said to be the first drawing-room ever seen in Arbroath, except in the town mansions of the landed aristocracy.

From the large orders for plants and flower roots, and for articles of clothing of a better class than could be got in Arbroath, occasionally to be met with in his business letter books, it is evident that Provost Wallace kept up a style befitting a city magnate. Here, for example, is an order sent to correspondents in London which will exemplify this. " Pray take ye trouble to buy and ship, per first opportunity to any our neighbouring towns, half a dozen hatts for boys from 7 to 14 years, let 5 be laced with a cheap silver lace, of small cost, except one of ye five of smallest size with broad open lace, for J. Gardyne's eldest son, ye young Laird, and ye largest hatt for my oldest son without lace, also 2 hatts for J. Gardyne and self."

Provost Wallace died at an advanced age, and his death

left a great blank in the community. To him more than to any man of his time, or generations after him, Arbroath owed the distinction of taking a fair position among the manufacturing towns of Scotland.

No representative of the family bearing the name of Wallace now remains in Arbroath, but there are still several of his descendants residing in the town.

W. F. LINDSAY-CARNEGIE.

WILLIAM FULLERTON LINDSAY CARNEGIE,

Of Spynie and Boysack.

WHILE the affairs of the burgh during centuries bygone have usually been administered by the burgesses themselves, now and then in the history of the town we find county magnates taking an active part in its government. Notable among these was Sir David Carnegie of Kinnaird, who in 1781 entered the Town Council of Arbroath, and continued to give to the town the benefit of his administrative skill for several years, notwithstanding more than one ineffectual protest against his election and continuance as councillor, on account of his being neither a trader or residenter in the burgh. Arbroath was not the only burgh where non-resident landed proprietors were chosen as councillors. The idea seemed to be that the office being mainly honorary, the affairs of the burgh could suffer no prejudice by the non-residence of councillors; and that by the assumption of gentlemen of property and high social standing in the neighbourhood they had in them men who were qualified to advise the burgh on important occasions. Such a man was Sir David Carnegie. Besides being an excellent man of business, Sir David was possessed of considerable literary attainments, and Arbroath was highly honoured by having one of his position and acknowledged ability among her leading burgesses.

To William Fullerton Lindsay Carnegie, however, Arbroath has been much more deeply indebted than to his kinsman, Sir David Carnegie. In several of her public institutions he took a lively interest as well as an active share in their management. But the pre-eminent service he rendered to the community in the promotion and successful introduction of the railway system insures for his name an honourable place among Arbroathians who have proved genuine benefactors to the town.

The very repetition of his name, William Fullerton Lindsay Carnegie, recalls to memory distinguished families who have played prominent parts in the leading events of Scottish history. A scion of the great historic family of the Lindsays, he also claims as his ancestors the noble house of Carnegie, and the ancient family of Foulerton of that ilk.

Tradition is fruitful in affording a fanciful history of the origin of many of our old families, and the Lindsays come in for their full share. Many are the apocryphal tales told of their pedigree. Rolt, in his life of John, 21st Earl of Crawford, says that the remote progenitors of the family were Anglo-Saxon kings. Whether this was so or not, it must be borne in mind that among the Anglo-Saxons the term king was not applied in the sense used now to convey the idea of a territorial chief, but merely as the head of a tribe or people. In a note to the author, the Earl of Southesk says :—" I have met with a pedigree of the Lindsays—I cannot remember where—in which the descent is traced with much plausibility through the centuries of the Northern occupation of Normandy back to an 'Earl' in Norway, in the 9th century. This, at all events, seems more likely than the Anglo-Saxon descent suggested by Rolt. The

Lindsays have always prided themselves on their Norman descent."

The earliest bearer of the name of whom anything is known in England was Randolph de Limesay, who came over at the Norman Conquest, and who was said to be a son of a sister of the Conqueror. Walter de Lindsey, whom Lord Lindsay in his "Lives" designates the "Anglo-Norman Colonist," was the first of the race to settle in Scotland, and his name frequently appears in the charters of David I.

To trace the history of the family would, in a great measure, be to narrate the leading events of Scottish history. More than once we find the Lindsays having particular connection with Arbroath affairs. One of these events marks an important epoch in the history of the town. Towards the close of Walter Panter's abbacy, the Benedictines of the monastery of Aberbrothock appointed Alexander Lindsay, the master of Crawford, their justiciar or supreme judge in civil affairs, but in course of time he rendered himself obnoxious to the Abbot and his monks, whereupon, as Lindsay of Pitscottie puts it, "Alexander Ogilvie, whether it came of his own ambition or if it was the Abbot's pleasure it is not certain, but he usurped the bailiary to himself and put this Alexander from the same." This act was looked upon as tantamount to a declaration of war between the two families, who had hitherto been fast friends. Lindsay and his men took forcible possession of the town and the Abbey, and preparations were hastily made for the conflict. To the aid of the Lindsays came the Douglases and the Hamiltons, while the Ogilvies had powerful allies among the Scottish nobility. On Sunday, the 13th January, 1445, the Ogilvies marched for Arbroath, also with the intention of taking the town, but they found the Lindsays not only in possession, but their forces drawn up in battle array. Here for a moment stood the opposing armies, in whose ranks were many of the best and bravest of Scotland's sons, each foeman eager for the fray. The signal for the onslaught had just been given, when the Earl of Crawford, who in Dundee had heard of the quarrel, galloped furiously to Arbroath, in the hope that he might be in time to stop the feud. The master of Crawford, who recognised his father, instantly drew rein, but ere the Earl could reach the chief of the Ogilvies, a soldier, not knowing the rank of the rider, nor the purpose with which he came, thrust at him with a spear, and he fell mortally wounded. This so enraged the Lindsays that they madly rushed to the charge. A desperate fight ensued, which ended in the total rout of the Ogilvies, who, it is said, left five hundred dead bodies on the field, while the loss of the Lindsays amounted to somewhere about a hundred men. The battle of Arbroath, which was fought on that eventful Sunday morning, was but the beginning of a feud which grew in bitterness and continued to devastate the country for many a day.

The Lindsay Carnegies of Spynie and Boysack are descended in direct line from David, tenth Earl of Crawford, whose younger son, Alexander Lindsay, was first Lord Spynie. This Alexander was a great favourite at the court of James VI., whose vice-chancellor he was. On the King's departure for Norway in quest of a wife, he was accompanied, amongst others, by Alexander Lindsay, who, besides his personal services, was otherwise useful to his royal master by lending him ten thousand gold crowns to help to pay the expense of the voyage. While on this matrimonial mission, Lindsay fell ill, and the King, with whom he was always on the most affectionate terms, was much grieved on account of his illness. To cheer him up he wrote to him very

kind letters, addressing him familiarly as "Sandie." In one
of these he pledges his royal word "that quhen God randeris me
in Skotlande, I sall irreuocablie, and with consent of Parliament,
erect you the temporalitie of Murraye in a temporall lordshipp,
with all honoures thairto apparteining"—and he jocularly adds,
"Lett this serue for cure to yure present disease." But not only
was the King anxious to confer honour on his friend "Sandie,"
but he also desired to help him in his wooing of Dame Jean
Lyon, daughter of Lord Glamis, to win whose hand Lindsay had
been using all his wiles with little apparent success. The King,
however, interceded on his behalf with her mother, the Countess
of Angus. But the maiden was coy, and it took more royal
communications than one to gain over the Countess to his aid.
Nor did he omit to urge Lindsay himself to persevere in his
suit, for we find him writing thus, "Sandie, we are going on
here in the auld way, and very merry. I'll not forget you
when I come hame—you shall be a Lord. But mind (remember)
Jean Lyon, for her auld tout will make you a new horn."
The King did not forget his promise, for on the day of
his arrival at Holyrood, he united the temporalities of Moray
into a free barony in Lindsay's favour, under the title of Lord
Spynie, and his royal master was also gratified by seeing him
united to Jean Lyon.

The connection of the Carnegies with this district has
existed for nearly seven centuries. Fraser, in his "History of
the Carnegies," traces their descent from John de Balinhard,
who was born about the year 1210, or towards the close of
the reign of King William the Lion. The name of Balinhard
was assumed from lands belonging to them in the parish of
Arbirlot. The great-grandson of John de Balinhard, also John,
acquired the lands of Carnegie—lying about midway between

Carmyllie and Panmure—from Walter Maule about the year 1340, and with the land, as was the custom, assumed the surname of Carnegie. From this main stem has sprung the various branches of the Carnegie family, of whom the Carnegies of Boysack form a not unimportant one.

The lands of Boysack, at a remote period, formed a portion of the possessions of the Abbey of Arbroath, and at a later date they were owned by the Earl of Argyle. Later still, they came into the possession of Alexander Lindsay, first Lord Spynie. They were subsequently acquired by Sir John Carnegie, afterwards Earl of Northesk. His eldest son, the second Carnegie of Boysack, acquired the lands of Kinblethmont in 1678. He had two children—John, who became the third laird of Boysack, and who was for some time Solicitor-General for Scotland, and M.P. for Forfarshire, in the first British Parliament; and Margaret, who married John Fullerton, and had issue a son, William Fullerton, and a daughter, Jean.

James Carnegie, the fourth laird of Boysack, was a keen Jacobite, and before succeeding to the estate, he threw in his lot with the Pretender. During Prince Charles Edward Stuart's expedition in 1745, he acted as one of the prince's private secretaries. The prince, after his escape from Culloden, wandered for five weary months among the rocks and glens of our Highland hills, and such was the steadfast loyalty of the Highlanders and their fidelity to the cause, that although thirty thousand pounds was set upon his head, not only did the offer of this large pecuniary reward fail to induce even the poorest of them to betray him, but they were willing to endure the greatest sufferings in order that they might protect him. Often was he at the point of being caught, and to avoid detection it was necessary to resort to frequent forms of disguise.

> Yestreen I met him in a glen,
> My heart near bursted fairly,
> For sadly changed indeed was he,
> Oh! waes me for Prince Charlie.

Yes! sadly changed indeed; for here the Prince, who had so recently ridden at the head of his victorious troops, in all the gay trappings of a royal commander-in-chief, was now fain to steal away from the banks of the Nairn in the humble attire of Ned Burke, an Irish serving man. Again we find him more than once during his highland wanderings rigged out in petticoats, acting Betty Burke, the Irish maid of Flora Macdonald; at another time having on a plaid without trews, or even a philibeg; and again in a short tartan coat, and vest of the same, a short kilt, tartan hose, and highland brogues—his shirt, hands, and face patched with soot. Shortly before making good his escape, he was the guest of the notorious "Seven men of Glenmoriston," who, distressed at the then miserable condition of his clothes, waylaid some servants carrying baggage to Fort Augustus, and shot them down, bearing off the spoils to the prince, in order to make him more decently presentable.

The young laird of Boysack, like many others of the Scottish nobility and gentry who were implicated in the rebellion, had to take refuge in France to save his neck. Among the Stuart papers is a letter addressed by the Marquis D'Argenson to Colonel O'Bryen, dated Fontainbleau, 16th Oct., 1746, in which he mentions that he had brought under the notice of the king the unfortunate condition in which many of the Scottish officers had found themselves in consequence of their adherence to the cause, and intimating that his majesty had agreed to make a grant of 34,000 livres for division among these Scottish exiles. The list of recipients contains the names of nineteen gentlemen, more than one of whom belonged to Forfarshire. These gratuities varied from 4000 to 1000 livres, and "Jacques Carnegy de Boissac, rang de Colonel," gets 3000 as his share. While in France, James Carnegie was presented by the prince with a wig and an old-fashioned tartan coat which formed part of his disguise during these Highland wanderings. These articles are still carefully preserved at Kinblethmont House, having escaped the ravages of fire which has thrice played havoc at the mansion house of the Carnegies of Boysack.

James Carnegie was the last male Carnegie of this branch of the family, having only one daughter, Stewart. This lady married her cousin, Colonel William Fullerton of Fullerton, who assumed the name of Lindsay, at the same time claiming the title of Lord Spynie. He proved his descent as heir of the line of the Lindsays of Spynie, but failed to make out his right to the title of Lord Spynie.

When, in 1781, Captain Fall made his memorable raid on the town of Arbroath, Colonel Lindsay came in to Arbroath from Kinblethmont, where he was then living, and, along with the Laird of Hospitalfield, assumed the command of the brave little company of inhabitants, who volunteered to defend the town against the attack of the famous privateer. As a relic of the bombardment of Arbroath, Colonel Lindsay secured one of the balls fired from the guns of the Dreadnought, and it is still preserved at Kinblethmont. Colonel Lindsay, or rather Fullerton, for, as just mentioned, he only changed his name to Lindsay when he tried for the Spynie peerage, served for many years in Lord Ogilvie's regiment in the French service, and after the regiment was disbanded he served for a few years as colonel in the Portuguese army.

William Fullerton Lindsay and his wife, Stewart Carnegie, had an only son, James, born in February, 1764. The grandfather of this child entailed him in the estates of Boysack and Kinblethmont, and, in conformity with the deed of entail, he assumed the name of Carnegie, thus becoming known as James Fullerton Lindsay Carnegie of Boysack and Spynie. In 1786, he married Mary Elizabeth, only daughter of James Strachan of Thornton, in Kincardineshire, by whom he had a large family. He died on 7th April, 1805, and was succeeded by his eldest son, James Lindsay Carnegie, commander R.N., who, however, only survived his father nine years. Commander Lindsay Carnegie had a distinguished career, having served with distinction at the battle of Trafalgar and other naval engagements. Having died unmarried, the titles and estates fell to his brother, William Fullerton Lindsay Carnegie, who was thus the direct and lineal descendant of Alexander Lindsay (Lord Spynie) of the Carnegies of Boysack and of the Fullertons of that ilk, and, as representing the latter family, was hereditary fowler to the Kings of Scotland.

Born on 13th May, 1788, William Fullerton Lindsay Carnegie was educated at St Andrews, and for a time attended the University there. On 20th July, 1804, having just completed his sixteenth year, he received a commission as lieutenant in the Royal Artillery, and was sent on service to Jamaica. He spent a considerable time as a soldier in the West Indies, and on 1st July, 1813, he was promoted to a captaincy. Under the Duke of Wellington, he served in the Peninsular War, where he commanded the Rocket Troop, and received the medal with clasp for the battle of Fuentes d'Honor.

At the close of the Peninsular War he retired from active service. Possessed of an immense amount of energy, and considerable intellectual attainments, and desiring before settling down as a country squire, to add to his already acquired knowledge, he spent a year or two in foreign travel.

On 27th December, 1820, he was married at St George's, Hanover Square, London, to Lady Jane-Christian Carnegie, daughter of William, seventh Earl of Northesk. He was not the first Lindsay to wed a Lady Jane Carnegie. A century before, Colin Lindsay—Earl Colin—coming home from the wars, fell in love with Lady Jane Carnegie, eldest daughter of the Earl of Northesk. Thinking to forward his suit, his royal master and intimate friend, King Charles II., entered into correspondence with her father, urging him to use his parental persuasion with his daughter, with the view of inducing her to accept of Lindsay as her husband. But the lady resented the royal interference, and declined the proposal. The king was anything but pleased at the failure of his self-imposed negotiations, and looked about for another bride for his friend. Colin, however, having occasion to be in Scotland, found opportunity to woo the fair lady, and she, discovering that the royal influence had been withdrawn, agreed to accept Lindsay as her husband on his own merits. This act so enraged the king that he forbade them the court. The marriage turned out a very happy one, and no less so did that union which took place in St George's at the Christmas of 1820.

William Fullerton Lindsay Carnegie now settled down at home, and his active temperament soon found plenty of outlets. He inaugurated his career as a country gentleman by applying the most approved scientific methods of agriculture to that portion of his lands which he farmed himself. But to further develop the resources of his estates, he opened the quarries of Leysmill and Border, which he kept in his own hands and worked on a large scale. James Hunter, the first manager of his quarries, proved a highly intelligent and enthusiastic coadjutor. To Hunter the country owes the conception of the idea of the stone-planing machines, an invention which has wrought such a revolution in the pavement trade. Had it not been, however, for the active co-operation and hearty financial support of the proprietor of the quarries, who patented the invention, these great improvements which gave such an impetus to the pavement industry of the country, would not probably have seen the light of day. The invention was of such vast importance that for a time Leysmill quarries became a place of pilgrimage to many of the leading scientific men of the day. This was in 1833-4. To the stone-planing machine was added — two years or so thereafter—the railway block boring machine, which Lindsay Carnegie also patented ; but however creditable this was to the inventive genius of Hunter, and the enterprise of his employer, the early introduction of wooden sleepers soon drove the stone blocks out of use in the railway system. It is difficult to estimate the large increase which the invention of these stone-cutting machines has added to the wealth of the nation. They are now in univeral use.

But his attention to his own immediate concerns did not prevent William Fullerton Carnegie from taking a lively interest in the town's affairs. In many of her public institutions he not only took a warm interest, but also an active share in their management. The Harbour, which has for so many years been "the old man of the sea" to the inhabitants of Arbroath, was about sixty years ago felt as an intolerable burden, and meetings were held and schemes devised for putting its finances on a better footing. One of these was the separation of the harbour interest from that of the burgh, and along with this the adoption of the General Police Act. At a meeting held in the Town Hall on 28th July, 1836, Lindsay Carnegie, who was one of the chief speakers, delivered an eloquent and effective speech in support of a resolution to the effect, that the entire revenue of the harbour ought to be applied to the proper purposes of the harbour instead of partially going, as it then did, towards the expense of lighting, paving, and watching the town. The resolution was unanimously carried, and in all the subsequent negotiations in connection with this movement, Lindsay Carnegie took a leading part. When the Harbour Act was passed he was one of the first trustees under whose management the harbour was placed, and he continued to act in that capacity up till the date of his death. A few years before this effort to put the harbour affairs on a better footing, the country had passed through a period of great commercial depression, but few towns in Scotland suffered as Arbroath did. Failures were the order of the day, and to such an extent that it might truly be said that the whole town was bankrupt. The immediate result of this was that the operatives were being discharged in hundreds. The idleness and want which followed produced a lawless activity. The unreasoning mob blamed the employers of labour for bringing about this condition of things, and, gathering in hundreds around the houses of the larger manufacturers, insulted and threatened them to such an extent as made it necessary for the magistrates to swear in the better class townsmen to act as special constables to protect those against whom the mob were vowing vengeance. One of the leading citizens, who was himself a severe pecuniary sufferer, in writing to a friend at the time, remarked that "never since Arbroath was a town has it known such wretchedness, such extensive desolation, and without one ray of hope to keep the spirits up." As might be looked for, it was some time before Arbroath recovered from the state of paralysis thus produced, but by that resoluteness and determination which characterised the leading men of the time, improvement set in—an improvement which received an immense impetus from the introduction to Arbroath of the railway system.

The need of increased facilities for communication between the county town and its natural seaport was no new idea. Away back in the last century the improvement of the means of conveyance was felt as a pressing want, and in 1788 Mr Whitworth, an eminent engineer of the time, surveyed the district, with the view of constructing a canal between Arbroath and Forfar. A similar survey was made by Mr Stevenson in 1817, and again in 1820, when that engineer recommended the construction of a railway. With this in view, a further survey was made in 1826, and an elaborate report was prepared by Stevenson, confirming his former recommendation, and showing the immense advantages which would accrue to the locality by the introduction of a railway system. This was all very good; no one disputed the advantages, and everybody admitted the need of such. But while this was so, the man possessed of sufficient courage to face all the difficulties that lay in the way of such an undertaking, and to lead the way towards the execution of the enterprise, had not yet been found.

Meantime William Fullerton Lindsay Carnegie, who had a quick perception, as has already been shown, of the value of certain inventions to the industries of the locality, was carefully watching the progress of the improvements on the locomotive engine, and so enthusiastic was he that he went to Liverpool, and was present at the opening of the Liverpool and Manchester Railway. What he saw and heard on that day impressed him not only with the importance to his native county of the benefits to be derived from the introduction of the railway system, but what was more, with its practicability. With that clear-headedness and strength of will, which were two of the leading features in his character, he at once set himself to overcome every difficulty —and these were not few—which stood in his way, to carry to a successful issue the floating of a local railway company. His first task was to prove to others the possibility of carrying out the scheme, and that if set agoing it would be remunerative to its promoters. For this purpose he employed first, on his own responsibility, the well-known firm of Grainger & Millar to survey a line of railway between Arbroath harbour and the town of Forfar. The Town Councils of these burghs, as well as the Guildry and other incorporations, appreciating the great importance of the undertaking, after a time subscribed towards the expense of the survey. The report which followed on a careful survey of the ground was ably drawn up, and gave very full details of the financial results which might be looked for. This was submitted to a meeting of the inhabitants, held in the Town Hall on Friday, the 7th August, 1835. The meeting was presided over by Lord Panmure, and was also attended by the magistrates and many of the leading citizens of Forfar. At this meeting resolutions were passed in favour of the undertaking, and with this view a subscription list was presented to procure funds for carrying out the project. Before the meeting closed it was found that £16,000 had been subscribed on the spot, and within a few weeks thereafter this had swelled up to £41,875, the largest individual subscriber being William Fullerton Lindsay Carnegie, the originator of the movement, against whose name stood the handsome sum of £3000. But this sum, handsome though it was, was small when compared with the gigantic labours—in season and out of season—which he gave to the furtherance of the scheme. Both by tongue and by pen, as well as by the influence of his enthusiasm, begot by his strong faith in the ultimate result, he was instrumental in arousing and stimulating others to take part in, and to push on, the enterprise. As a foretaste of the benefits which the formation of a railway would bring to the town of Arbroath, the promoters had the satisfaction of seeing, even at this early stage, that sales of property in the burgh realised prices fully one-third more than had been previously obtained.

It was first estimated that £60,000 would be sufficient to carry the scheme to a successful issue, but a sudden and unexpected rise on the price of iron having taken place, it was found needful to increase by £10,000 the sum required as capital by the company, which at a meeting held on 1st February, 1836, was fixed at £70,000. By the April following, not only was the full £70,000 subscribed, but several applications for shares had to be refused.

It was a proud day for its originator, when he found that sufficient financial support had been obtained to warrant the application which had been made to Parliament for power to proceed with the undertaking; but it was a prouder day still—and a fortunate one for Arbroath—when, on the 17th May, 1836, the Arbroath and Forfar Railway Act obtained the Royal assent. This result, however, was not gained without a keen fight. Opposition to the scheme arose from a quarter where it might have been least expected. Lindsay Carnegie's friends and neighbours, Gardyne of Middleton, Mudie of Pitmuies, Chaplin of Colliston, and Hay of Letham Grange, as landed proprietors and as Road Trustees, offered bitter—and in the case of some of them, relentless—opposition, and for a time it appeared as if the promoters were to be beaten. A deputation, headed by William Fullerton Lindsay Carnegie—who was in London at the time for the purpose of giving evidence before the Parliamentary Committee—by fighting skilfully and bravely, ultimately won the day. Great was the rejoicing in Forfarshire over the victory thus gained, the country residents vieing with those of the towns in doing honour to Lindsay Carnegie who was hailed as the hero of the day. On the 10th of May, 1836, the Arbroath Town Council, having met, passed the following resolution:—" That the Arbroath and Forfar Railway Bill had now passed into law, and William Fullerton Lindsay Carnegie, Esquire, of Spynie and Boysack, had bestowed great attention, and had been of vast service in bringing about this important object, so beneficial to the interest of this Burgh, unanimously resolved that the freedom of the Burgh should be bestowed on Mr Lindsay Carnegie as a mark of their estimation of his services and of the warm interest he takes in the welfare of the town." This resolution was carried into effect on the 27th of the same month. Enthusiastic demonstrations were held about the same time in Friockheim and in the surrounding parishes.

If the general inhabitants of the town were later than their country cousins in doing honour to William Fullerton Lindsay Carnegie, they chose a more appropriate time for their rejoicings. We have seen that immediately on the Railway Bill having received the Royal assent, the Town Council had promptly but quietly met and conferred on him the freedom of the Burgh, but Tuesday, the 20th of September following, was a red-letter day in the history of Arbroath. The public works were closed, business of every kind was suspended, and the

WILLIAM FULLERTON LINDSAY CARNEGIE.

entire population held high holiday, the occasion being the first breaking of ground for the new railway. Here again William Fullerton Lindsay Carnegie was the hero of the hour. During the early part of the day, the streets presented an animated appearance, the people turning out in crowds to witness and participate in the ceremonies of the day.

The public proceedings commenced with a meeting of the leading citizens in the Guild Hall, over which the Provost presided, Lord Douglas Hallyburton, member of Parliament for the County, and Patrick Chalmers of Aldbar, the member for the Burghs, taking a prominent part in the proceedings. Provost Goodall, on behalf of the railway proprietors, presented Lindsay Carnegie with a service of silver plate, which had been voted by them as a mark of their gratitude for his services. In making the presentation, the Provost referred to the fact that to the recipient of these gifts the railway company primarily and exclusively owed its existence, and that mainly to his indefatigable personal exertions in overcoming the various and formidable difficulties thrown in his way, the company owed its final establishment by Act of Parliament. To Arbroath and the district it was acknowledged to be of incalculable importance and value. On the same day a meeting was held in St Paul's Church, at which he was presented with a gold medal which had been subscribed for by the working people of Arbroath as a mark of their appreciation of his eminent services to the inhabitants—the gift, it was stated, being a spontaneous offering of the people to one whom they regarded as a genuine friend and disinterested benefactor. Not only was the presentation made to mark their sense of the enormous benefits which they expected the new railway would confer on the town, but for his exertions in many other directions, for whatever he considered would forward the interests of the burgh and the comfort and prosperity of the working classes. At the close of these meetings a procession was formed for the purpose of proceeding to Cairnie, where the ceremony of cutting the first sod of the Arbroath and Forfar Railway took place, that function being performed by Lindsay Carnegie. The ceremony over, he was entertained to a public dinner, other festive gatherings being held throughout the town. Seldom, indeed, in the history of the burgh has there been such a jubilation as was witnessed on that bright September day.

But the feasting and rejoicing over, the railway directors had to gird up their loins and set about the prosecution of their work in real earnest. The difficulties which, up to this time, had arisen and had been met and overcome, were nothing in comparison to those which followed. Those difficulties we have fully explained elsewhere.* With that courage, however, which acknowledged no defeat, Lindsay Carnegie and his coadjutors carried on the undertaking till they had the satisfaction of seeing the Arbroath and Forfar Railway one of the best paying lines in Scotland. It was a true remark of John Bright's that railways have rendered more service, and have received less gratitude than any of the other institutions in the land. No service of equal value to that of Lindsay Carnegie's in originating, and carrying out the introduction of the railway system had been previously or has since been rendered to the town of Arbroath by any single individual, and it is only right that such a service should continue to be held in grateful remembrance. He took an active share in the furtherance of the Dundee and Arbroath Railway construction, and it was in a large measure owing to his exertions that the turnpikes from

---
* Arbroath : Past and Present, pp. 205-207.

Friockheim to Brechin, and from Forfar to Kirriemuir were made. In all these and in other matters relating to the commercial progress of the county, he was, without doubt, one of the wisest and most far-seeing of the men of his time, and we of to-day are reaping the fruits of his skill, energy, and forethought.

It was not in business matters alone that his activity and philanthropy found outlet. The intellectual and moral advancement of the people found in him an ever-ready advocate. The early success of the Mechanics' Institute was largely indebted to his fostering care. The foundation stone of the building was laid by his wife, Lady Jane Carnegie, on the Reform Bill jubilee day, and before and after this he took part in its management. He was one of the originators and the first president of the Literary and Scientific Association, which was formed in 1835, and he took part in the starting of the Arbroath Museum Society, and was also its first president. The Arbroath Horticultural Society also had in him a keen supporter and an active president.

Indeed it would be difficult to find any good work of a public kind carried on in the town in which he did not share. All this could not fail to earn for him the esteem and admiration of every class in the community. It has already been shown that these sentiments found vent in the entertainments and presentations on the day on which the first sod of the railway was cut. But the citizens desired still further to mark their appreciation of his services and his worth, in such a way as would not only insure that his deeds would be remembered, but also that his lineaments should be made familiar to succeeding generations. Acting on behalf of numerous subscribers, Provost Mann wrote to Lindsay Carnegie intimating a desire on the part of the inhabitants that he should allow his portrait to be painted and placed in the Town Hall, as a mark, not only of their respect for his character, but as a public recognition of his services to the community and of the deep interest which he had so long taken in everything calculated to promote the public good. To this wish he gave ready assent, and what added additional local interest to the proceeding was that the work was entrusted to a then rising artist, a native of Arbroath, Patrick Allan, who in later years became so well-known as Patrick Allan-Fraser of Hospitalfield. Patrick Allan had just returned from Rome, where he had been studying, and this was his first commission of importance. The portrait was finished in the March following, and was placed on the walls of the Town Hall, which it still adorns.

On the 15th February, 1838, he was elected a member of the Society of Arts for Scotland. On the 30th April, 1846, in consequence of the death of Guthrie of Guthrie, he was on the nomination of the Earl of Airlie, the Lord-Lieutenant of the county, supported by the Vice-Lieutenant and by Lord Panmure, unanimously elected convener of the county of Forfar. This office he retained till the 30th of April, 1855, when, on account of failing health, he felt it his duty to resign. His resignation was very reluctantly received, and in accepting it, his brother Commissioners recorded their sense of the extremely able, energetic, and efficient manner in which he had discharged the duties, and the uniform courtesy which had characterised his conduct during the time he occupied the responsible office of convener. This resolution was conveyed to him by Viscount Duncan, accompanied by a very flattering letter, in which the writer expressed his personal regret at the great loss which the county sustained in being deprived of his services. On 10th

February, 1857, he was made Her Majesty's Vice-Lieutenant for Forfarshire, an office which he retained till his death.

In politics he was a thorough-going Liberal. A keen advocate of the principles of Free Trade, he was an active member of the Anti-Corn Law League, and attended the meetings in London of that body.

Whatever he believed was for the benefit of his countrymen found in him a ready promoter, and, although by many of his contemporaries—especially those of his own class—he was looked upon not only as a visionary, but as one holding opinions in some respects detrimental to public interest, still, the outcome of the opinions which he advocated, and the movements which he prosecuted, have proved how far-seeing and sound was his judgment.

Even to the end of his life he continued to take a warm interest in all the affairs of the burgh, and when (in 1859) the volunteer movement again sprung into prominence, although no longer able to take an active share in its organisation, he manifested great enthusiasm in the cause.

On the 13th day of March, 1860, he breathed his last, and amid universal mourning, he was laid to rest, without outward pomp or parade, in the family burying ground at Chapelton of Boysack, where twenty years before, on a pleasant autumn afternoon, he had left all that was mortal of his beloved and amiable wife. He was succeeded by his son, Henry Alexander Fullerton Lindsay Carnegie, who has worthily maintained the honour of the family, both as a soldier and a citizen. In early youth he entered the army, and took part in several of the engagements which followed on the Indian Mutiny. As Lieutenant in the Bengal Engineers, he was present at the siege of Delhi, and shared in the various actions fought with the rebels outside

Delhi, before the investing army began the siege. He also served under Lord Clyde in the operations which resulted in the capture of Lucknow. Afterwards in storming one of the feudal strongholds of Oudh, which followed on the fall of Lucknow, he displayed great valour. It being necessary to blow up the gate of one of these forts, in order to admit the storming party, the difficult duty of fixing a bag of powder to the gate was assigned to Lieutenant Lindsay Carnegie. The perilous undertaking was successfully carried out, but the premature explosion which followed nearly cost him his life. In consequence of his injuries he was forced to return home invalided. Since then he has taken an active part in the public work of the county, and has in this, as in other ways, followed in his father's footsteps.

THE ARROTT FAMILY,
Of Dumbarrow and Almericlose.

DURING the first three-quarters of the present century no name was more honoured in Arbroath, and no figures more familiar on its streets, than those of the Arrotts. The history of this old Forfarshire family carries us back at least six centuries. The surname of Arrott, Arrot, Arrat, Ariot, Arrade, Arroch, or Arrath—for the name is variously spelt—is derived from the lands so-called, situated in the Barony of Brechin, a territorial origin which is proof of the antiquity of the family. The earliest records to be found of the name is that of Richard of Arrath, who was owner of the lands of Balnamoon, and of William of Arrade or Arrath, whose name appears as a witness to the foundation charter of the hospital of Maisondieu in the town of Brechin. This charter, which was also witnessed by Albin, who was Bishop of Brechin from 1247 to 1269, is understood to have been granted about 1256.

In the Ragman Roll, among the chief men and tenants of the Crown in Scotland, who, at Berwick-on-Tweed, swore allegiance to Edward I. of England on the 28th of May, 1296, appears that of "John de Arrat, del Comte de Angoz," showing that the family was one of note at that early period. In 1378 David de Arroch sold to Thomas de Rate one-half of the family estate of Arrat, held by him of the lords of Brechin—a feudal dependence to which the arms of the Arrotts owe their origin.

The division of the Barony of Arrat into two parts, which thus appears so early as 1378, continued till 1695; in the latter year, the lords of Arbuthnot appear to have been in possession of both halves. At what particular period the second half passed out of the hands of the Arrotts we have been unable definitely to ascertain. The name, however, continued to occur among the land owners of Forfarshire. On 10th February, 1654, we find Andrew Arrott, of Dumbarrow, served heir in general to his father, William Arrott, of Dumbarrow. While the connection of the Arrotts was thus kept up with the county, as might be expected, branches of the family spread themselves elsewhere. On the 29th April, 1606, Christian Arrott, wife of William Murray, citizen of Brechin, was retoured heir to her sister, Elizabeth Arrott, in the half part of the Mill of Kincardine and mill lands thereof, and in the half of the town and lands of Reidheuch, in the Barony of Balmayne in the shire of Kincardine. The name of Arrott also occurs in the list of burgesses of Aberdeen in the sixteenth century. David Arrott was one of the assize in the Bailie Courts of that city on the 26th January, 1531, the 28th May, 1532, and the 25th February, 1538.

John Arrott of Baikie, Professor of Philosophy in the University of St Andrews, was one of the Forfarshire Arrotts. Warden, in his Angus or Forfarshire—referring to a note to Ouchterlony's account of the shire, in Spottiswood's Miscellany, which says that Baikie belonged to John Arrott—remarks that he has found no confirmation of one of his name being a proprietor of Baikie, but the following extract from the books of Council and Session, under date 27th February, 1729, confirms the statement in Spottiswood—" Compeared Mr Alexander Bruce, advocate, procurator for Mr John Arrott, afterdesigned, and gave in the disposition underwritten . . . . of the tenor following

—I, John Arrott of Baikie, late professor of philosophie in the University of St Andrews," and so on. A copy of this document is preserved among the papers of the Arrotts of Dumbarrow.

In 1682 William Arrott, son of Andrew Arrott, the laird of Dumbarrow, having finished his University studies, and being licensed to preach, became an "expectant" or probationer of the Church of Scotland. In that year he was one of the candidates for the position of parish minister of Channel Kirk, in the presbytery of Lauder. With this view he preached there on three Sabbaths namely, 4th June, 20th July, and 20th August. In this candidature he was successful, and was accordingly ordained. After fifteen years' service there, he was translated to Montrose. On the 6th January, 1697, he was inducted in the first charge of the parish of Montrose, where he continued till his death, which occurred on 15th August, 1730, having then attained the ripe age of seventy-five years. While parish minister of Montrose, he was also laird of Dumbarrow, having succeeded to the proprietorship of the estate on the death of his father. The Rev. William Arrott, by his wife, Magdalene Oliphant, had a son, Andrew, and two daughters, Margaret and Elizabeth. Margaret became the wife of John Willison, well-known as one of the ministers of Dundee, and Elizabeth was married to James Bell, the parish minister of Logie-Pert. His son, Andrew Arrott, also chose the church as his profession, and was ordained minister of Dunnichen, the parish in which the family estate was situated.

Before the old parish minister of Montrose had passed away, a spirit of unrest had appeared in the Established Church. The restoration of patronage in 1712, and the consequent settlement of ministers in opposition to the will of the people was, to a certain extent, the cause of this, and appeals to the Church

Courts were not infrequent. At the Assembly in May, 1731, an overture was presented which was a sort of supplement to the law of patronage. According to this overture, ministers were not to be chosen by the congregation, but were to be imposed upon them by the majority, in a conjunct meeting of heritors and elders. At the next Assembly, May, 1732, two representations of grievances were submitted to the Assembly—one by forty-two ministers, and the other by upwards of seventeen hundred of the people—both remonstrating against this overture. Notwithstanding these protests the Assembly turned the overture into a Standing Act. This was the beginning of a struggle which eventuated in the secession and deposition of a number of ministers who, on 5th December, 1733, constituted themselves into an Associated Presbytery. The work of Secession soon spread. Sentence of deposition was pronounced on a large number of ministers, among whom was Andrew Arrott of Dunnichen, upon whom the Established Church pronounced deposition in 1745. Being then the proprietor of Dumbarrow, he built a church on his own estate. In this church he officiated as minister of the Secession body to a considerable congregation, and here he continued to preach till his death, which occurred in 1760. The services were, however, continued in connection with the Secession denomination for a few years longer. When the building ceased to be used as a church, it was converted into and was afterwards known as the farm-house of Hill Kirk of Dumbarrow. The building was erected on an elevated and exposed situation, but was sheltered behind by a perpendicular rock.

On the death of the minister, his son, William, succeeded him as laird. This William Arrott was twice married. By his first wife, Catherine Chisholm, he had one son, Andrew, who

THE ARROTT FAMILY.

became Original Secession minister of Wick. By his second wife, Elizabeth, daughter of David Robertson, merchant in Perth, he had five sons—David, Robert, Colin, William, and James ; and five daughters—Catherine, Magdalene, Elizabeth, Grant, and Julia. Having disposed of the estate of Dumbarrow, he removed to Arbroath, where he resided for a few years, and died there on the 7th of October, 1811, at the patriarchal age of ninety-two years.

At the time when the old laird of Dumbarrow took up his abode in the town — the closing years of the last century— Arbroath was affording considerable evidence of commercial and literary activity. One of the leaders in all her enterprises was David Balfour, a member of an old Arbroath family. At this time Provost of the burgh, Balfour was also one of her most enterprising merchants. While energetically conducting a large and varied business, and thus contributing to the prosperity of the town, he was equally ready to defend the honour and interest of his country. When France threatened to invade Britain, and a thrill of patriotic enthusiasm pervaded the nation, Arbroath was no laggard in the cause. Chiefly through Balfour's exertions, a regular corps of volunteers was raised, and the command thereof was given to him with the rank of Major. Major Balfour was a most energetic officer, and was exceedingly popular with his men. He was also a great favourite with his brother officers, who showed their appreciation of his worth by presenting him with a piece of silver plate bearing the following inscription :— " Presented by the commissioned officers of the Royal Arbroath Volunteers to their commanding officer, Major Balfour. October, 1803." It is still in the possession of his descendants here, and is prized as an heirloom of one of Arbroath's honoured citizens.

But not only as an enterprising merchant and gallant officer did David Balfour foster and conserve the best interests of the town; he was also a leading spirit in the literary revival which took place in Arbroath in the end of the eighteenth century. One of the founders and most active promoters of the Arbroath Public Library, he was also its first president. He was not the only member of the Balfour family who showed the possession of literary tastes. His brother, Alexander, was the author of several poems of considerable merit, and his sister Mary, who formed the connecting link between the Balfour and the Arrott families, was a woman of rare accomplishments. Mary Balfour married Henry Sharpey, merchant in Arbroath, by whom she had three sons and two daughters. She was left a widow in 1801, and some time thereafter she became the wife of Dr William Arrott, the son of William Arrott, the last laird of Dumbarrow of that name.

WILLIAM ARROTT, M.A., M.D.

William Arrott was born at the paternal estate of Dumbarrow in 1774. He received a liberal education, having graduated in Arts at the University of St Andrews. He also studied medicine there and at Edinburgh University. While in the latter city, he resided with, and was considerably helped in his studies by, Dr James Arrott, a distant relative of the family. At the Edinburgh University, he had for a class-fellow Joseph Hume, who afterwards became a distinguished member of the House of Commons. The friendship thus formed in early life continued till Hume's death. After obtaining his diploma as surgeon, William Arrott commenced practice in Forfar in 1797,

WILLIAM ARROTT, M.A., M.D.

where he remained about two years. In 1798, he obtained his degree of M.D. from the University of St Andrews. He removed to Arbroath in 1799, where he remained till his death, which took place sixty-three years thereafter.

From the social position of his family—as well as owing to his skill as a physician—he soon acquired an extensive professional connection. In June, 1803, he was gazetted as surgeon to the Arbroath or First Forfarshire Corps of Volunteer Infantry, and in September, 1808, he was commissioned as surgeon of the eastern regiment of local militia of the county of Forfar. In the same year, he was admitted a free burgess of the burgh of Arbroath, and also a freeman of the Guildry, one of the qualifications for the latter being that he had married a freeman's daughter—his wife, Mary Balfour, being the daughter of a magistrate and merchant of Arbroath. In 1811 he acquired the mansion house and grounds of Almerieclose, which had been owned by several proprietors since it passed from the possession of the Philips.

On the establishment of the Arbroath Infirmary, which was opened on 12th January, 1845, Dr Arrott was appointed one of its consulting physicians, a post which he held till the close of his life. A member of Inverbrothock Established Church, he took a warm interest in, and a considerable share of, its management. So keen a supporter was he of everything that concerned its welfare that, among his friends, Inverbrothock Church was facetiously referred to as " St Arrott's."

In 1857, at a public meeting held in the Town Hall, under the presidency of Provost Lumgair, "Old Dr Arrott," as he was familiarly called, was presented with his portrait and a piece of silver plate, the latter bearing the inscription—" Presented to William Arrott, Esq., M.D. (with his portrait), by a number of friends, as a mark of the esteem and respect entertained for his character during a long, active, and useful life. 1857." The portrait now hangs in the Arbroath Picture Gallery, having been presented to the Directors of that institution some years ago by his only surviving daughter, Mrs Martin of Broughty Ferry. What adds to the value of the portrait is not only its faithful representation of the original, but that it was the production of A. Bell Middleton, a young Arbroath artist who gave great promise of a brilliant career as a portrait painter, and whose early death was much deplored.

After more than sixty years of active service as a medical practitioner and useful citizen, Dr William Arrott died on the 21st of September, 1862, in the old family mansion of the Arrotts at Almerieclose, at the advanced age of eighty-eight years.

His wife, Mary Balfour, who predeceased him, was possessed of fine literary tastes. Few had a better acquaintance with the old ballad literature of Scotland, and to her fine discrimination, and a powerfully retentive memory, we owe the preservation of many of our old Scottish ballads. When Robert Jamieson was collecting material for his "Popular Ballads and Songs," which was published in 1806, he found in Mrs Arrott an enthusiastic coadjutor. A mutual friend, Dr Jamieson, the author of "The Scottish Dictionary," introduced Robert Jamieson to Mrs Arrott, and a visit which he made to Arbroath resulted in his being able to take down, from her recitation, some of the finest specimens of our ancient Scottish minstrelsy. In an introductory note to "Sweet Willie and Fair Annie," one of the many ballads in his collection which he received from Mrs Arrott, Jamieson says :—" It is here given, rare and entire, as it was taken down from the recitation of a lady in Aberbrothock, to whose politeness and friendship this collection is under considerable obligations. She had no previous intimation of the compiler's visit, or of his undertaking, and the few hours that he spent at her friendly fireside were very busily employed in writing. As she had, when a child, learned the ballad from an elderly maid servant, and probably had not repeated it for a dozen years before I had the good fortune to be introduced to her, it may be depended upon that every line was recited to to me as nearly as possible in the exact form in which she learned it."

Although there is no direct evidence that Mrs Arrott performed a like service to Sir Walter Scott, it is highly probable that the author of the Antiquary, when he visited Fairport, had made the acquaintance of Mrs Arrott, possessing as she did tastes so similar to his own, so far as love of the old ballad literature of Scotland was concerned. There is a story, which was current in Arbroath at the period when Sir Walter visited this locality, and which, if narrated in his hearing—and in all probability it was—would readily suggest to him the scene in the Post Office at Fairport, where Mrs Mailsetter and her cronies "in order, from the outside of the epistles, and, if they are not belied, occasionally from the inside also, sought to amuse themselves with gleaning information." Mrs Arrott's brother, Provost Balfour, dealt largely in grain, cargoes of which he shipped to London and elsewhere. The then postmaster of the town, a member of the Ouchterlony family, also dealt in grain, but to a less extent than Balfour. On one occasion the Provost had written a letter to his London correspondents offering them a certain quantity and quality of grain at a price which he named. When the communication reached its destination, there was found to be written on the *outside* of the letter an offer by the postmaster of the same kind of grain, but at a shade less than the Provost's price. It must be borne in mind that in those days the postage of a letter to London cost over a shilling, so that the presumption is that the postmaster, by handling the letter in the same way as did Mrs Shortcake, till "it just cam open o' free will in his hand," he was able to anticipate his rival in the market by a few seconds, saving the heavy postage at the same time. No doubt he also eased his conscience with the reflection that "folk suld seal wi' better wax." Mrs Arrott died on 1st May, 1836, in the sixty-third year of her age. The issue of the marriage between William Arrott and Mary Balfour, the widow of Henry Sharpey, was four sons, William Henry, James, David, and Alexander, and two daughters, Mary and Jacobina, the latter of whom married David Martin, one of the leading merchants of Dundee.

DAVID ARROTT, M.D.

EXCEPT during the few years when attending the Universities of his own and other countries, David Arrott spent his life among his own people, and no one was better known, and few so universally beloved, as was "Doctor David." Handsome in person, highly cultured, and of a most genial disposition, he was ever a welcome visitor in the houses of rich and poor. He was born in Arbroath on the 9th of July, 1809. Having received such education as the schools of his native town afforded, he went, in 1825, to the University of Edinburgh, where he passed through the usual medical curriculum, and in due course received his diploma as surgeon. After practising for two years at home, he travelled abroad for a time, settling down for a year at

Berlin. At the University of that city, he continued his studies under several professors, some of whom at that period had gained European fame. While there, he was a diligent student, and gained well-merited commendation from more than one of his teachers. Before quitting the University of Berlin, he obtained the degree of doctor of medicine. His thesis for his M.D. degree was written in Latin, as was the rule in continental Universities in those days. On his return home, he joined his father, forming a partnership which subsisted till the death of the latter.

Both at Edinburgh and Berlin Universities, David Arrott was a most successful student, taking a high place in his classes, and few young men of his day started professional life under more favourable circumstances. Besides possessing a wide knowledge of general literature, his surgical and other scientific attainments were of such a high order that, had he settled in a place where he would have had a larger field for practice, his abilities would doubtless have enabled him to attain a position of more than ordinary eminence in his profession. As it was, he soon secured for himself an honourable place in the professional ranks of his native town. While he had a large practice among the more opulent citizens, his advice was much sought after by the working people. A pleasing feature in his character—indeed, it was characteristic of the family—was his kindness to the poor, for whom he freely prescribed without fee or reward. These acts of kindness were not fitful, but were of almost everyday occurrence during his lifetime, and endeared him to many, whose descendants still regard his memory with affection.

He was an excellent linguist, and was well versed in ancient and modern literature. His services were frequently taken advantage of in the translation of letters from foreign parts, and in acting as interpreter when occasion required. His literary tastes were well known, and it was often remarked, by competent judges, that had he chosen literature as a profession he would have made his mark. For many years no literary or scientific gathering in Arbroath was considered complete without his presence, and in the initiation of the various literary and scientific societies, which came into existence in his day, his advice and help were always sought. Of the Arbroath Literary and Scientific Association, instituted many years ago chiefly for the purpose of providing lectures during the winter months, he was one of the originators and office-bearers, and he frequently presided at the meetings. He was a fluent speaker, and an able public lecturer, brimful of pawky humour, and few men could hold an audience in thrall better than he could. The brilliancy of his humorous composition was very conspicuous during local elections, when he could throw off a "squib" which, while it afforded great amusement to his fellow-electors, was never known to hurt the feelings of the candidates. Himself a poet, he was one of the best reciters of poetry in Arbroath in his day.

Although Doctor David lived and died a bachelor, it was not in the nature of things that so kindly a heart as his could get through life without being touched by the tenderness of love. But the death of his loved one shattered his hopes, and he never again thought of entering into wedlock. Some time thereafter he met a young lady who in many respects reminded him of his early love. He took the poet's way of giving utterance to the secret of his inner heart, and there is no saying what depths of tender sorrow lay in the following lines, which, under the signature of "Alpha," he wrote away back in the forties:—

To———

Why do I love to linger near,
   To watch the soft light of thine eye?
How is it that no sound I hear
   But thy sweet voice, when thou art by?
Though there are many softer eyes,
   And many a voice as sweet as thine,
Yet thine and thine alone, I prize—
   I look and list alone to thine.

Thy look to me is like the sun
   That universal Nature cheers;
Thy voice the well-remember'd sound
   Of music heard in happier years.
Thy presence weaves a magic spell—
   A soft enchantment round my heart—
That chokes me when I'd say "farewell,"
   That chains me when I would depart.

And when I hold thy gentle hand,
   My faltering tongue would say "good-bye;"
But, gazing still, I ling'ring stand;
   Ah! gentle maiden, knowest thou why?
It is not that thy charms have power
   To win my yielding heart to love;
Believe me—no! 'tis past the hour
   When even *thou* this heart could'st move.

It is that thou resemblest one
   Whom (but it were in vain to tell)
I loved in days long past and gone;
   I loved her—ay, alas! too well.
But O! may happier days be thine,
   Sweet sunny days of faithful love;
And may a brighter star than mine
   Guide thee at length to peace above!

A young Arbroath lady, who was possessed of considerable literary ability, and who still lives, the widow of a long widely-known and popular baronet, shrewdly guessing who "Alpha" was, over the *nom de plume* of "Omega," wrote the following pungent reply to the doctor's verses :—

Answer to Alpha.

Is this the love you offer me?
  Is this the heart you give?
And, think you, true and lasting love
  On memory can live?
Is it but from reflected light
  Thy spirit turns to me?
Away! away! I cannot take
  Such paltry boon from thee.

Am I but as a moonbeam's light,
  To gild thy darkened way,
From whence the sun's rejoicing beams
  Hath long since passed away?
Must my voice but the echo be
  Of tones that now are still?
Must my smile but with vain regrets
  Thy aching spirit fill?

No, no! the love that I would prize
  Must be as morning bright;
It must not wear the chilling dews,
  Nor the dark shades of night.
Unsullied, pure must be the heart
  That worships at my shrine;
The incense that ariseth there
  Must bless no heart but mine.

> Go, weep beside thy loved one's grave —
>   Ay, weep in silence there,
> But bring not back her memory,
>   A living love to share.
> If still thy yearning spirit clings
>   Unto the faded past,
> Hope not another's smile will e'er
>   A radiance round thee cast.
>
> And know that woman's heart will spurn
>   Such cold and shadowy love;
> The heart she gives must cherished be—
>   All other hearts above.
> Then learn this wisdom from my rhyme,
>   And next your heart would woo,
> I pray thee tell the "ladye fair,"
>   That she is ALL to you.

In 1843 he was mainly instrumental in starting the Museum Society, and was chairman of the first public meeting held in connection therewith. At that meeting he was elected convener of the committee appointed to make arrangements for setting the society agoing, and for drawing up its rules and constitution. When the society was instituted, the doctor was chosen as one of its joint secretaries, an office which he filled for nearly twenty years. He continued his connection with the society down to the time of his death, filling more than once the office of vice-president.

He held several public appointments, among those being Medical Inspector of Factories, and Medical Officer of Health. He entered with great zest into the volunteer movement, and, from its institution in 1859 till the time of his death he held a commission as surgeon of the First Forfarshire Artillery Corps.

An enthusiastic mason, he was for a long period Master of the St Vigean Lodge of Free Masons, the mother lodge of the celebrated Dr Thomas Chalmers. Indeed, there was scarcely any society for the social or educational advancement of the community in which he did not take a part, and his talents and geniality gained for him in every sphere of influence a prominent and respected place.

Two years prior to his death, which occurred on the 27th December, 1876, he was laid aside from the active duties of his profession. When death came his loss was greatly felt, and the lines of David Carnegie, one of our local bards, well expressed the feeling of affection and veneration with which his memory was held among his fellow-townsmen. The first two lines of the sonnet refer to Thomas Watson, a well-known local poet, and a friend of the doctor's, who had predeceased him.

Sonnet.

Two years ago we mourned the loss of one,
  Whose genius to our hearts will aye be dear ;
And now another son of song is gone,
  Whose cheerful voice we never more may hear.
Although 'twas seldom he attuned his lyre,
  Yet well we knew he had a poet's soul ;
And in his breast there gleamed the heavenly fire,
  And from his pen the numbers sweet could roll.
But better, nobler far than poet's fame,
  He had a heart that for the poor could feel ;
And many a one will bless the doctor's name,
  And mourn for him who never grudged his skill ;
But often faced disease and death, without fee or reward,
  God pay thee now, physician kind ! Adieu, dear brother bard !

JAMES ARROTT, M.D.

JAMES ARROTT, M.D.

JAMES ARROTT was born in Arbroath on 13th February, 1808, and, like his brothers, was educated at the Academy, afterwards known as the High School. Choosing to follow his father's profession, he went to Edinburgh University to prosecute his medical studies. After completing the usual curriculum at the College of Surgeons, he obtained his diploma in 1827, and took his degree of Doctor of Medicine in 1829.

Instead, however, of commencing practice in his own country immediately on his graduation, as is frequently the case with young medicals, he continued his studies, and, with the view of adding to his already acquired knowledge of his profession, he travelled on the Continent, visiting Holland, Belgium, and France, spending some time in each. He settled in Paris, where, for a year or two, he studied under several of the celebrated professors in the great medical schools and hospitals of that city. Short as was the period of his residence there, from his mental acuteness, as well as from his steady and keen application, he profited largely by his studies, and few young men entered on the practice of their profession so well equipped in every respect as did James Arrott.

In 1831 he returned from France, and settled down in Dundee. Although then a complete stranger in that town, it was not long till he acquired a considerable practice. This was not to be wondered at, for, besides bringing with him introductions and testimonials of the highest merit from Sir Robert Christison and other distinguished men under whom he had studied, he early showed the possession of professional talents of an unusually high order. In private life he developed, in a marked degree, a social and exceedingly cheerful disposition, which did not fail to win for him a large circle of friends, so that very early in his career he became exceedingly popular. He did not, however, confine his activities to the enlargement of his medical practice and his social acquaintanceships, but he soon exhibited a deep interest in many of the public institutions of his adopted home. One of the first of these, to the furtherance of the interests of which he largely contributed, was the Watt Institution, where he delivered one or two lectures. So much were these appreciated that at the solicitation of the directors he, in 1834, delivered a course of nine lectures on "The Structure and Function of Animals." The reception which these got from all classes in the community was such as to increase very considerably the reputation of the lecturer. To mark their sense of the services thus rendered, the directors unanimously elected him a life member of the institution. Some time thereafter he was appointed one of the medical attendants of the Dundee Infirmary, and, in course of time, he became physician to that institution, Dr Crichton taking charge of the surgical cases. At this time the Infirmary was but a small concern—too small for such an important town as Dundee. Impressed with this, James Arrott, in season and out of season, eagerly and successfully advocated the erection of a larger building suitable to the wants of the town. In his efforts in this direction he was ably seconded by Sir John Ogilvy. So keen was the interest which the doctor took in the progress of the erection of the splendid building which superseded the former humble edifice in King Street that it was said he saw almost every stone in the structure as it was laid in its position.

Shortly after his connection with the Infirmary was formed, he was appointed physician to an institution which was started

THE ARROTT FAMILY.

for the treatment of consumption and diseases of the chest. It was located within the Watt Institute, and was under the presidency of Mr Erskine of Linlathen. For this he not only had special qualifications, but the occupation was very congenial to him, having, during his residence in France, had rare opportunities of acquiring a knowledge of chest diseases. Dr Arrott was the proud possessor of the stethoscope, which belonged to the French physician, Laennec, the inventor of that now universally used instrument. While prior to 1819 the process of auscultation was greatly aided by various methods and instruments introduced from time to time by different physicians, the invention of the stethoscope, possessing as it did such marked advantages over any of the previous aids to auscultation, soon became popular among medical men. Like many other inventions, its conception might be said to be due to accidental causes. It came about in this way. Laennec was consulted by a lady who had symptoms of disease of the heart, but, for certain reasons, he could not make an examination in the usual way by applying his ear to her breast. He recollected that it was a common amusement for a person to apply his ear to the end of a log of wood when the noise caused by the scratching of a pin at the other end could be distinctly heard. Immediately taking a quantity of paper which he held in his hand, rolling it up tightly and applying one end to the patient's chest and the other to his own ear, he was astonished and delighted to perceive how distinctly he could hear the beatings of the heart, and he became convinced that by the same means he would be able to hear, not only the heart's sounds, but also those of the other organs of the chest, and so to distinguish diseases of these parts of the human frame. Continuing his experiments, he tried various materials instead of the original roll of paper, and at length he constructed a wooden cylinder which he called a stethoscope, from the Greek words *stētheos*, the chest, and *skopeō*, to examine. This stethoscope was presented by Laennec to Dr. Sharpey, who had studied with him.

But Dr Arrott's active mind found other outlets. He was a frequent contributor to the medical journals, some of his articles attracting great attention. He also took a leading part in the establishment of the Dundee Free Library, and as a member of its first Board of Directors, he acted as chairman of committee for the selection of scientific books. On the passing of the Education (Scotland) Act in 1872, he was chosen as one of the members of the first School Board, and so satisfactory were his services to the community that, on the expiry of the first Board's term of office, he was elected a member of the second Board. In 1877, he had a similar honour paid to him by the citizens of Dundee as was conferred on his father by the inhabitants of Arbroath in 1862, to which reference was made in the sketch of Dr William Arrott's career. In September, 1877, at a public meeting held in the Albert Institute, he was presented with his portrait, along with a purse of three hundred sovereigns, on the completion of forty years professional life in that city. The presentation was made on behalf of the subscribers by his intimate friend, Sir John Ogilvy, who bore testimony to his high professional attainments, and the appreciation by his townsmen of the numerous and valuable services, which, in various capacities, he had rendered to Dundee. The portrait, after having been exhibited at the Fine Arts Exhibition, was presented by the doctor to the permanent collection of the Dundee Picture Gallery, where it now hangs.

James Arrott, distinguished for his eminent professional skill and scholarly attainments, possessed in a rare degree a frank and genial disposition, which made him equally at home with rich and poor. It is said that he never asked a fee from any of his patients, preferring to depend on their honour or sense of justice. For many of the poorer ones, not only did he advise and prescribe without fee, but it was no unusual thing for him to provide the necessary nourishment or luxuries which their circumstances required. Frequently in such cases, when the patient would ask for his bill, would he put him off with the remark that he would see about when he came back. His social qualities and lovable nature were such as to assure him a welcome wherever he went. While gentle and sympathetic in the house of mourning, he was brimful of fun in the house of mirth. His witty sallies and amusing stories made his company much sought after. At the time of the presentation of his portrait he was in delicate health, but he continued in practice for two or three years thereafter. About two years before his death, he retired into private life, and took up his residence in the neighbourhood of Perth.

He died on the 13th August, 1883, and when he was laid in the tomb in the family burying ground, beneath the shadow of the Round O, few men were more sincerely lamented. His kindness to the poor during his lifetime has been perpetuated in a way that is well fitted to keep his memory green in his native town. By his last will and testament he bequeathed the residue of his estate—amounting to between six and seven thousand pounds—in trust, the interest to be applied for the benefit of aged poor and deserving persons resident in Arbroath. Through the operation of this trust, the name of Arrott, so long an honoured one in Arbroath, will continue to be gratefully remembered in the days that are to come.

PROFESSOR WILLIAM SHARPEY,

M.D., LL.D., F.R.S.

OF Mary Balfour's talented family, William Sharpey was the most distinguished. He was born in Arbroath on the 1st of April, 1802, in a house which then occupied the site where the present Royal Hotel stands. His father, Henry Sharpey, an Englishman, who had migrated from Folkestone to Arbroath in the closing years of last century, died in 1801, leaving Mary Balfour a widow, with a family of four children, for William, her fifth child, was not born till five months after his father's death. The early death of her husband was a severe blow to one of such a sensitive nature, especially coming, as it did, at a time when she was in a delicate condition. The little posthumous stranger came into the world a very feeble creature, and for the first few hours after his birth his life was despaired of, the midwife declaring that the efforts to ensure his being kept alive were useless, as, in her opinion, although the child did live, he would be sure to prove an idiot! The crone's prognostications, however, were unfulfilled, for the infant continued to thrive, and in due course he became a sturdy fellow.

He was very early sent to school. At this period, besides the Grammar School, there were a number of adventure schools, some of which were taught by females. To one of these dame schools was William Sharpey sent as soon as he could toddle. This school was got at through an "entry" off the High Street, at that part where Hill Street now is, but which latter street was not then opened. It was quite a usual thing for better class children to attend these schools till they were old enough

WM. SHARPEY, M.D., LL.D., F.R.S.

to go to the Grammar School. While many of the dames were quite unqualified for the post, a few of them possessed a natural talent for teaching, one lady teacher, at least, being patronised and subsidized by the Magistrates and Town Council. To the influence and teaching of his talented mother, however, was William Sharpey mainly indebted for that love of learning and assiduity in its acquirement which were so characteristic of him throughout his life. From the dame school he went to the Hill School (the fore-runner of the Academy), then taught with a wonderful degree of efficiency by Mr Kirkland as rector, and other two masters.

Mrs Sharpey, when William was quite a child, became the wife of Dr. William Arrott. After gaining all the instruction he could at the Arbroath schools, William Sharpey chose to follow the profession of his stepfather; he accordingly proceeded to Edinburgh University at the early age of fifteen, attending the Greek and Natural Philosophy classes. In 1818 he commenced his medical studies, and in 1821 he obtained the diploma of the Royal College of Surgeons of Edinburgh. During the course of his college curriculum, he gave ample evidence of that natural ability and untiring zeal which continued to be his chief characteristics. In 1822 he went to London, where, for a time, he studied anatomy in the school of the celebrated Brookes. The following winter he spent in Paris, coming back to Edinburgh in 1823, when he obtained his degree of Doctor of Medicine. Returning to Arbroath, he spent two or three years as assistant to his step-father, Dr. William Arrott. But his ambition was to be something more than a country doctor, so in 1827 he set out for the Continent, partly with the view of improving his general culture and partly of training himself for his future scientific career. Knapsack on back, he travelled on foot through a large part of Germany, Switzerland, and Italy, entering into conversation with the people, thus laying up a store of varied information. But while adding to his stock of knowledge of men and places and things, he never forgot the main object of his life—a knowledge of his profession. At Berlin, where he remained for a considerable time, he devoted much of his attention to the study of anatomy and physiology. Under Rudolphi, he made himself master of topographical anatomy. It was there he laid the foundation of that success which so largely attended him in future years. He also studied at Paris, at Heidelberg, and at Vienna.

He returned to Edinburgh in 1829, and in 1830, he became a Fellow of the Royal College of Surgeons there. In the same year, he contributed his first paper to the medical journals. In 1831, he spent some time in Berlin, preparatory to commencing the teaching of anatomy, and in November of the same year, he became extra-mural teacher in the Medical School in Edinburgh, where he soon earned a high reputation for the depth and accuracy of his knowledge and the excellence of his methods of instruction. His colleague at this time was his friend, Allen Thomson, who was then lecturer on philosophy. Dr Sharpey's eminent services to medical science were early recognised, and his fame spread far beyond Edinburgh. His mother died in 1836, and he felt the loss very keenly. He was a most affectionate son, and while resident in Edinburgh, he was a frequent visitor to his parental home in Arbroath. In the same year (1836), on the death of Professor Jones Quain, he was appointed his successor in the chair of Anatomy and Physiology in University College, London—a post which he held for thirty-eight years, only relinquishing it when he felt that the physical infirmities of age prevented him from performing his duties with his accustomed vigour. During his tenure of office, he was held to be the most eminent teacher of anatomy and physiology in Great Britain. Among his pupils could be counted very many persons of the highest distinction in the medical profession and in biological science generally.

In 1839 he was made a Fellow of the Royal Society of London, and in 1859 he became one of its secretaries, a post which he held till he resigned when retiring from his professorial duties, when he was succeeded in the secretaryship by Professor Huxley. While Professor Sharpey held the office of secretary of the Royal Society, he was very popular, his kindness and courtesy added to his extensive knowledge and sound judgment, making him an invaluable guide in the affairs of the society. The Baly medal of the society was conferred upon him for physiological research. He acted as examiner to the University of London in anatomy and physiology between the years 1840 and 1863, and in 1864 he was appointed a member of the senate. He was also a trustee of the Hunterian Museum, and sat for fifteen years in the General Medical Council as one of the Crown nominees.

On the occasion of Lord Brougham's installation as Chancellor of the University of Edinburgh, Professor Sharpey was honoured with the degree of LL.D. In September, 1867, he was present at the meeting of the British Association held in Dundee, and as president of the Physiological Section, he delivered an able address. During its sittings a number of the members of the association, accompanied by Professor Sharpey, journeyed to Arbroath. The Abbey, the Cliffs and Caves, Auchmithie, Lunan Bay, Ethie, and other places of interest were visited. During the evening, the party was entertained to dinner by the Magistrates of the burgh. On the occasion Professor Sharpey was welcomed not only as one of the most distinguished scientific men of the age, but as a leal-hearted "Son of St Thomas." In replying to that welcome, the Professor spoke lovingly of the happy days of youth spent in his native town, which he remarked had multiplied three fold since he first remembered it, and referring to the many changes which had taken place in Arbroath during his absence, the retrospect he said produced in him a feeling of sadness. This was no mere sentiment, for he possessed a warm heart and a sensitive nature, and was well-known to have always been ready to do a kind turn and hold out a helping hand to any Arbroathian, who applied to him for assistance or advice. Indeed, his softness of heart and generous nature often led him to befriend those who were unworthy of his kindness. But this very feature of his character—a readiness to help and an unwillingness to think ill even of those of whose conduct he did not approve—endeared him all the more to his intimate friends. The circle of his friends was no narrow one, for the personal interest which he took in each of his pupils could not fail to add to that circle, his unvarying kindness and courtesy winning the hearts of his students. So deep and lasting was this feeling of gratitude and affection towards him on the part of his old pupils that they united in publicly testifying to their esteem for him as a man, and their appreciation of the benefits received by them from him as a teacher, by raising a fund known as the Sharpey Memorial Fund, which was applied to the foundation of a scholarship at University College, London, for students showing a proficiency in physiology. In 1874, feeling the infirmities of age creeping upon him, he resigned his chair, and the Government, recognising in him a teacher, than whom no one had done more for the advancement of physiological knowledge, bestowed on him a pension of £150 a-year.

As a writer on medical subjects, while his contributions were not so numerous as might have been looked for from one possessing so high literary and scientific tastes, everything that came from his pen bore the stamp of being the production of one who possessed large and accurate knowledge and sound judgment. Among these contributions to medical science, he published in 1830 a paper in the Edinburgh Medical and Surgical Journal "On a peculiar Motion excited in fluids by the Surfaces of certain Animals," which he followed up by other important papers on ciliary motion in continuation of the discoveries of Purkyne and Valentin in 1835. The results of his original investigations concerning the structure and growth of the bone, and numerous other histological problems were embodied in the later editions of Quain's "Anatomy," which has since become familiar to medical students as Quain and Sharpey's "Anatomy." But more as a teacher than as a writer was Professor Sharpey distinguished. The variety of his knowledge and the accuracy of his memory were invaluable, and were often called for in matters of doubt and controversy. While his scientific knowledge was profound, he was possessed of a fullness of information on general subjects, and possessing as he did a large share of shrewd Scottish penetration, together with that lively sense of humour which was a distinguishing feature in the family character, it is not to be wondered at that his social companionship was highly valued and much sought after. He was a frequent and welcome guest at those delightful little dinner parties given at the house of his old friend, Dr Neil Arnott, another of Arbroath's eminent sons.

Like his two step-brothers, whose careers have just been sketched, Professor Sharpey lived and died a bachelor. He survived his retirement from active life six years, his death taking place in London on the 11th of April, 1880. His body was removed to University College, where it was met by a large concourse of distinguished persons who came to pay the last mark of respect to the departed savant, the cortege accompanying it to Euston Station on its way to Scotland. The remains were brought to Arbroath, and were laid to rest beside his kindred in the Abbey Churchyard.

NEIL ARNOTT, M.D., LL.D., F.R.S., &c.

NEIL ARNOTT,

M.D., LL.D., F.R.S., &c.,

Physician Extraordinary to the Queen.

DURING the greater part of the eighteenth and the early years of the nineteenth centuries, the name of Arnott was a familiar one in Arbroath. The members of that family—besides engaging largely in different lines of business—took an active part in the management of the town's affairs. In 1726, Thomas Arnott was box-master of the Bakers' Corporation, and three years thereafter, he, being then a member of the Town Council, was elected burgh treasurer. The office of treasurer was then held for a year only. Evidently in those days, there was a want of promptitude in the making up and auditing of the public accounts, for, although Treasurer Arnott's term of office expired at Martinmas, 1730, his accounts were not submitted to the Council in audited form till the September following, ten months after the closing date. The ex-treasurer continued to give assiduous attendance at the Council meetings, and his name appears, not only in the Council records, but also in those of the Guildry and other incorporations till September, 1732. From the various transactions at which his name occurs—in lending money to the Corporation and otherwise—he must have been a man possessed of considerable means.

Another Thomas Arnott, presumably a son of the last-named, took a prominent part in municipal management, occupying at different periods various public offices in connection with the different incorporations. Elected a town councillor in 1750, he was stent master in the same year, and in the year following he was appointed burgh treasurer. In 1752 he was promoted to a bailieship, which office he appears to have discharged very faithfully. He, too, had many direct monetary transactions with the Corporation, besides being frequently accepted as cautioner for others. He retired from the Council in September, 1760, presumably in bad health, for, from the infeftment of his widow in May, 1762, it is known that he died between these dates. Thomas Arnott was twice married, first to Elizabeth Wallace, only child of James Wallace, merchant and Dean of Guild, Arbroath, and niece of Provost John Wallace. The Wallace family, as already shown, was a leading one in Arbroath in the eighteenth century. The names of Thomas Arnott and Elizabeth Wallace frequently occur in connection with properties held by them on the east and west sides of the High Street, in Newgate, and elsewhere throughout the town. Elizabeth Wallace, the first spouse of Thomas Arnott, died sometime prior to 1754, leaving one son, James Arnott, who on the death of his father, succeeded to heritable and other property of considerable value. This James Arnott, who is designated as merchant, is mentioned in connection with various transactions in the burgh, but he does not appear to have taken the same interest in municipal affairs as his father did. Thomas Arnott's second wife was a Janet Watson, who survived him. She also was possessed in her own right of some property in the burgh.

William Arnott, the grandfather of Neil Arnott, took to farming, but till his death, he continued his connection with

Arbroath as a proprietor of houses and lands, besides lending money on bond, as the burgh records testify. In early life, he became tenant of Over [now Upper] Dysart, then in the parish of Maryton, where he continued till his death, which occurred towards the close of the eighteenth century. It may here be mentioned in passing that while at the time of William Arnott's tenancy, Dysart was in the parish of Maryton, it had not always been so. Prior to 1649, Dysart (Over and Nether) was ecclesiastically a separate parish, and for nearly a century after the Reformation, it was attached to the parish of Brechin. At the General Assembly of 1649, an Act was passed recommending to "the Commissioners for planting of kirks," the desirability of disjoining the lands of Over and Nether Dysart from Brechin. This was given effect to, and on the petition of the residenters— who found "The Kirk of Brechin, quilk was their paroche kirk," to be most inconvenient for their attendance — Dysart was attached to Maryton. In 1891, the Boundary Commissioners separated Dysart from Maryton, and joined it to Lunan civilly, the former ecclesiastical division, however, remaining. The earliest mention of William Arnott's name, so far as can be traced from the public records of the town, is an entry in the burgh register of sasines, in which a sasine in favour of "William Arnott, tenant of Over Dysart, in a tenement on east side of High Street," is recorded on 2nd December, 1748. Another deed is recorded in his favour on 13th June, 1754. On 17th May, 1760, the register bears record of a bond by "John Gairdner, merchant, and one of the present bailies of Aberbrothock, and Thomas Arnott, merchant, in the said burgh, in favour of William Arnott, tenant in Over Dysart," and, on 15th August, 1785, there is a record of a sasine in favour of William Arnott tenant in Over Dysart, in a tenement on the east side of Copegate [High Street.]

Alexander Arnott, eldest son of this William Arnott, became a merchant in Arbroath, and continued so for some years, indeed, till he succeeded to the lease of Over Dysart on the death of his father. He married Ann MacLean, a daughter of MacLean, chieftain of Borreray, who was connected by the ties of blood to the Clan Macdonald, the celebrated Flora Macdonald, of "Bonnie Prince Charlie" fame, being a kinswoman. It is said that the couple became acquainted while the young lady was at a boarding school, and that they made a runaway marriage. The precise date of Alexander Arnott's succession to the tenancy of Over Dysart farm cannot be fixed, but on the 3rd February, 1792, "Alexander Arnott, late merchant in Arbroath, now tenant in Over Dysart, eldest lawful son of the deceased William Arnott, sometime tenant in Over Dysart, was infeft in the tenement on the east side of Copegate," so that Alexander must have left Arbroath and become tenant of the farm of Upper Dysart some time between the date of the birth of his second son, Neil, in 1788, and the beginning of the year 1792. In this house "on the east side of Copegate" [High Street] situated a short way below the White Hart Hotel, and then owned by the family, Neil Arnott was born, and only a few doors from the house in which Professor Sharpey first saw the light. In an article which appeared in the *Times* newspaper two days after Dr Arnott's death, it is stated that Dr Arnott was "a native of Upper Dysart, near Montrose." This article seems to have caused other writers who have made reference to Neil Arnott to have doubts as to the place of his birth, but, in addition to the family history given above, showing as it does the long connection of his progenitors with the burgh, the following extract from the register of births of the parish of Arbroath thoroughly dispels all doubts as to the place of his nativity :

Dates— Births, Baptism.	Parents.	Children.	Witnesses.	1788.
May, Born 15th. Bap. 18th.	ALEX. ARNOT, Merchant. ANN M'LEAN.	NEIL.	JAMES ARNOT. DAVID ARNOT.	ARNOT

Whatever good fortune may have attended Alexander Arnott as an Arbroath merchant, it seems to have deserted him after he took to farming, for, notwithstanding the fact that he held the farm at an exceedingly moderate rent, he did not remain long in its occupancy. It is conjectured that while carrying on the farm he did not entirely relinquish his mercantile pursuits, and that, with a divided attention, in the latter he ultimately became unsuccessful. Getting into difficulties, he had to dispose of his interest in the lease of Upper Dysart, and he and his family removed therefrom to Blairs, about four miles from Aberdeen, where he became tenant of a small farm ; but fortune still frowned, and this farm had in turn to be given up also, after a tenancy of less than three years.

Although descended from an old Arbroath family, and born within our ancient burgh, Neil Arnott's youthful days were spent in the parish of Maryton. His first lessons were got from his mother, who was an accomplished woman ; but, as her family rapidly increased, her domestic duties prevented her from giving that attention to the education of the boys, which, in point of ability and acquirements, she was well fitted to give. Neil was sent to the parish school of Lunan, some two miles from his home at Upper Dysart. Lunan parish school was, for many years, taught by a man who gained more than local fame—Robert Huddleston, who, besides being a teacher of more than ordinary ability, was known for his literary attainments. In addition to other good work, he edited and published "Toland's History of the Druids." He died in 1820.

But fully as much to the teaching of nature, as to the instruction gained at the parish school of Lunan, was Neil Arnott indebted for that scientific bent which was so early displayed in his character. To his mother, however, who as already indicated was possessed of considerable mental endowments, might be traced many of those qualities which characterized him in after life. She died in Edinburgh in 1860 at the advanced age of 93 years.

After the removal of the family to Blairs, Neil for a time attended the parish school of Maryculter. On the relinquishment of the lease of the Blairs farm, the household took up their abode in Aberdeen, when the father attempted to make a livelihood by opening a small grocer's shop, but instead of attending to his customers, he preferred to sit behind the counter and read, so that he was as unsuccessful at shopkeeping as he was at farming. In consequence of this want of energy on the part of her husband, the maintenance of the family chiefly devolved on Mrs Arnott, who started business as a corset and stay maker. But Alexander Arnott did not long survive his unsuccessful attempt at shopkeeping, and his widow was left with a large family to provide for. In November, 1708, Neil, then in his eleventh year, entered the Aberdeen Grammar School, at which he remained three years. While there, he made considerable progress, taking a high place in his classes. Gaining a bursary, he left the Grammar School, and entered Marischal College as a student. Four years thereafter he took his degree of M.A.

While attending the University classes, he managed to serve a sort of apprenticeship to a chemist and druggist. This was done, not so much from choice as from the necessity to help, in however small a measure, the replenishment of the family purse. Truly, the help was small, but, as far as it went, it was acceptable. But this did not exhaust the benefits derived from his shopkeeping. While he was gaining a little money, he was also gaining a little—possibly a very little—still a certain amount of skill in the pharmaceutical art. Denied the benefit of better opportunities of gaining a knowledge of medical science—which lads of his own age in more fortunate circumstances were able to procure—he had to pick up his initiatory information as best he could. But this he did amidst such difficulties as would have disheartened many a less determined lad. Bringing to bear on these difficulties that singular energy and indomitable perseverance, which so eminently characterised his after life, he made rapid progress in his various studies.

In the Natural Philosophy Class, under Professor Copeland (himself a highly-cultured and talented enthusiast), he soon proved to be one of the most distinguished students. Copeland had the knack of enlisting the interest of his class, but in young Arnott he found an unusually bright, intelligent, and enthusiastic pupil. The insight which he here acquired, and the taste for physical research, which Professor Copeland's lectures begot in Arnott, laid the foundation for his future achievements in this department of science. The writer of the article in the *Times*, to which reference has already been made, says that while at the Aberdeen Grammer School, Arnott had Lord Byron for a fellow pupil; and in Chambers' Biographical Dictionary of Eminent Scotsmen, he is represented as a contemporary of Byron at the Aberdeen University. But neither of these statements is correct, for Neil Arnott, as already mentioned, entered the Grammar School in November, 1798, while Byron left it and Aberdeen, on the death of his grand-uncle and his accession to the peerage in May or June of the same year. Lord Byron was Arnott's senior by four months, and having left Aberdeen at the age of ten after attending the Grammar School for four years, was too young to be, and never was, at the university of that city.

To the knowledge acquired at Aberdeen, Arnott was desirous of adding the practical experience to be gained in a London hospital, his intention being to qualify himself for obtaining the diploma of the Royal College of Surgeons. With this view, he set out for London, where he arrived on the 29th September, 1806. There he commenced his studies as a pupil of Sir Everard Home at St George's Hospital. Throwing himself, with his usual vigour and enthusiasm, into the work of his class, and exhibiting, as he soon did, a ready appreciation and mastery of that special mode of treatment of stricture, which owed its inception to Sir Everard's skill, he attracted the notice of that distinguished surgeon, who at once manifested a warm interest in his brilliant pupil, and, under him, Arnott made rapid progress in his studies.

It was his original intention, after obtaining his diploma, to return to Scotland, and there commence practice, but after he had been a year in London, quite an unexpected change was made on his plans for the future. The captain of an East Indiaman who was suffering from stricture, and who was under the treatment of Sir Everard Home, but who before the cure was perfected, had, in the exercise of his profession, to go to sea, was desirous of having, on board his ship, the services of a surgeon possessed of sufficient knowledge of Sir Everard's method of treatment and able to continue it aboard ship. It at once occurred to Sir Everard that no one was better qualified to do so than young Arnott, but unfortunately, one of the rules of the company was that their medical officer should serve at least one year as assistant before being appointed full surgeon. This difficulty was got over however, through the influence of the captain and of Sir Everard Home, the latter being one of the Board of Examiners of the College of Surgeons. Arnott being able to pass all the necessary examinations, found himself before he had attained the age of nineteen years in possession of his diploma as a fully qualified surgeon, and as such was appointed to the "Surat Castle." While this was satisfactory to the master of the vessel, and to young Arnott, it did not at first give satisfaction all round. Besides carrying merchandise, the vessel carried troops, and the officer in charge of the soldiers was not at all pleased when he saw the youthful appearance of the doctor, and he reported to his superiors that the men were to be under the medical care of a boy, but the "boy" soon proved himself to be a man. While attending assiduously to his official duties, he not only continued his own studies, but incited others to join him in such of these as were not purely professional. Delivering lectures on natural philosophy and political economy, and playing the fiddle to the dancing of the Jack Tars, no wonder that he became most popular with all aboard from the captain to the cabin boy. One day the captain, during a terrific storm, inadvertently let the ship's chronometers run down, and in attempting to re-wind them found that they would not go. His dismay at the prospect of what might be the fate of the ship and those on board in such a dilemma may be imagined. Arnott, however, who, when studying under Professor Copeland, had learned the mechanism of clockwork, was able to set the chronometers agoing to the no small delight of the captain and the other officers. At another time we find him improving the ventilators of the ship, by making a couple of funnels out of pieces of old sails, one to admit the fresh, and the other to emit the foul air, and so, in many little ways, was he constantly contriving some plan for the comfort, the convenience, and the entertainment of his fellow-voyagers.

The "Surat Castle" touched at various ports, and Arnott made ample use of the opportunities thus afforded him, not only to pick up a knowledge of different languages, but to add to his stock of general information. During these voyages he also accumulated a vast amount of material to enable him to prosecute his favourite studies in natural philosophy, and of these he made good use in after years. In the medical superintendence of the troops under his care, both in the outward and inward voyages, he was most successful in having a less percentage of sickness than was to be met with in any other transport ship, and so marked was this, that he was specially complimented and thanked by the military authorities.

He relinquished the sea in 1811, and commenced the exercise of his profession in London, where he soon gathered a good practice. His knowledge of the French, Italian, and Spanish languages gave him ready access to the houses of better-class foreigners, and among these he found many patients. While he was gathering his practice he could not be idle, and he found fit field for his powers in the delivery of a course of lectures on chemistry and natural philosophy. The course was eminently successful and added considerably to his reputation. At its close he was presented with a valuable set of philosophical instruments. In 1814 the degree of M.D. was conferred on him by the Senatus of Marischal College, Aberdeen. In 1816 he was appointed physician to the French Embassy, and at a later period he received the appointment of physician to the Spanish Embassy. In the years which followed, his practice increased in extent and value. But it is to his scientific researches and the writings and inventions resulting therefrom, that he owes that fame which will long preserve his memory as a public benefactor.

In 1823 he delivered a course of lectures on medical physics which formed the basis of his famous work, "The Elements of Physics." The book was published in 1827, and was at once hailed as one of the most important contributions to scientific teaching which had issued from the press for many a day. Its style, while erudite, being at the same time lucid and fascinating, it at once became immensely popular. In a highly appreciative review which appeared in the *Lancet*, the following paragraph occurs:—" Dr Arnott has contrived to invest physics with the charms of poetry and romance, and to melt down the rugged and uncouth technicalities into language the most smooth, energetic, and harmonious." The *Times* also spoke of it in these most laudatory terms:—" This great desideratum (the simplifying of the greatly increased knowledge of the day) as far as the elements of physics are concerned, Dr Arnott has at length supplied, and with a degree of success and completeness, not merely which has never before been arrived at, but which, we may venture to predict, will not be surpassed." The first edition was sold off within a week after its publication, and a second appeared the same year, a third next year, a fourth in the year following, and a fifth soon thereafter. Within a few years' time the book was translated into every language of civilized Europe, besides being several times reprinted in America.

It not only added to his fame, but was a means of still further increasing his practice. Notwithstanding of this great success, its author did not consider it complete, but pressure of purely professional work prevented him from giving it those finishing touches which would make it satisfactory to himself. This, however, he accomplished in 1865, when he issued a sixth edition, revised and considerably extended.

In 1838 appeared his treatise on "Warming and Ventilation," which passed through a second and improved edition in 1855. He also published other two works, the one entitled "A Survey of Human Progress," and the other under the title of "National Education," the latter of these appearing when he was over eighty years of age. In 1836, when the University of London was founded, he was nominated a member of the Senatus, and it was largely due to his efforts that the new scientific degrees were introduced to that institution. He was elected a Fellow of the Royal Society in 1838, and in the same year he was appointed Physician Extraordinary to the Queen. But not only as an author was he distinguished, but also as an inventor. His ventilating chimney valve—an easy and ready method of ventilating rooms—the smokeless grate; in connection with which he was the recipient of the Rumford Medal; the water bed, for the prevention of bed sores, and other highly scientific and useful inventions. For these, and for other novel applications of science to the treatment of disease and the preservation of public health, the jurors of one of the departments of the Universal Exposition of Paris 1855 awarded to him a gold medal, to which the Emperor added the Cross of the Legion of Honour.

He married, in 1856, Mrs Knight, the widow of an old

friend. This step, although taken late in life, was an exceedingly happy one. Not forgetting his own early difficulties, he spared no effort to make the path of his young fellow-countrymen towards the acquirement of scientific knowledge a smoother one than he himself had trod, and among other means to this end he founded a scholarship in experimental physics in connection with the London University, giving an endowment of £2000 for the purpose. Following her husband's example, Mrs Arnott presented two Ladies' Colleges in London with £1000 each, to institute scholarships for encouraging the study of natural philosophy. Besides the endowment of £2000 to the London University, Dr Arnott gave each of the four Scottish universities an endowment of £1000 for the founding of a similar scholarship. In 1871 he expressed, through Dr Lyon Playfair, his intention of repeating his gift of £1000 to each of the four Scottish universities, but in consequence of an unfortunate accident with which he met, he was never able to carry his intention into effect, but after his death his widow made good his promise.

Dr Arnott died in London on the 2nd March, 1874, in his eighty-sixth year, and was buried in the Dean Cemetery, Edinburgh, his widow following him to the grave two years later. Few men led a busier or more useful life than did Neil Arnott. In a remarkably strong, vigorous, and active frame—a vigour and activity which he retained till within a few years of his death—he carried a warm and generous heart. In the social circle he was the "king of good fellows"; and at the weekly parties held at his own house, to which his most intimate friends, Professor Sharpey among the number, had a standing invitation, he entertained some of the most distinguished men of the day.

He was held in the highest regard among those who came under his care professionally. Many were the simple yet efficacious mechanical appliances for the relief of his patients which owed their origin to his inventive skill, and many sufferers beyond the circle of his own patients had reason to be grateful to him for the alleviation of their pain through the use of the means thus suggested by him. Among the many distinguished sons of St. Thomas few deserve a more honoured place than Dr Neil Arnott.

ALEXANDER BALFOUR,
Poet and Novelist.

TOWARDS the close of the last century, and the opening years of this, Arbroath was the centre of considerable literary activity. As an outcome of this, we have still a relic in the Arbroath Public Library, an institution dating back to 1797. Besides the Library, the town possessed a good literary society, and a prolific printing press. The leaders in the literary movements of the period were chiefly young men engaged in mercantile pursuits, one of the most energetic of whom was Alexander Balfour.

Alexander Balfour was not a native of Arbroath, but twenty-one of the best years of his life were spent in it, and while a citizen of the burgh, he earned for himself a more than local literary fame. He was born on the first of March, 1767, in a humble dwelling in the parish of Monikie. His parents were in poor circumstances, and, as on his arrival, he was accompanied by another addition to the household, the parents, from their scanty store, felt it hard to fill two additional mouths. So a relative of the family, not much richer than themselves, but possessing that kindliness of heart, so frequently found among the poor toward the poor, relieved them of one of the twins, by adopting Alexander. In this relative, the child found one who well supplied the place of a faithful and affectionate father. Not only did his foster father show him a good example, but he otherwise bestowed on him such training as materially helped to develop his talents. Besides giving him such an education as the parish school afforded, by wise counsel, he instilled into his mind sound Christian principles. Writing many years after to his friend, David Carey, another literary Arbroathian, with whom Balfour kept up a life-long correspondence, he refers in warm and grateful terms to his foster father, through whose pious care he had had those principles of religion and virtue instilled into his young mind, which throughout life served to guide and keep him in the paths of rectitude and probity.

Balfour seemed early to have developed a love of nature, and a desire to commit his thoughts to writing, as is shown by the fact of his having at the age of twelve attempted English composition in the shape of verses descriptive of the natural scenery of his native parish. These he read to a group of school-fellows, feeling not a little proud when his recital gained for him the applause of his juvenile audience. On leaving school, he was apprenticed to the weaving trade. But whilst working hard at the hand-loom, his mental training was not forgotten. He continued by diligent private study to increase his knowledge. While thus engaged, his earnest efforts at self-education attracted the notice of the Rev. Dr Maule, the parish minister, through whose influence he obtained the appointment of teacher of a side school in the parish, and in this position he continued for a few years. In 1793, being then in his twenty-sixth year, Balfour resigned his scholastic appointment, having obtained a situation as clerk in a manufacturer's office in Arbroath, and in the year following, he married. He remained four years in his first Arbroath situation, and then changed into the employment of another manufacturer in the town. After two years, this employer died, and Balfour joined the widow in partnership. The lady did not live long, and the business on her death fell into Balfour's hands. He then assumed another partner. In the hands of the new firm, who had secured some large Government contracts for canvas, the business increased to such an extent that Balfour in time became possessed of property of considerable value.

Before leaving Monikie, he had been cultivating his literary tastes, occasionally sending articles to the *British Chronicle*, but it was not till his settlement in Arbroath in 1793 that he gained any literary distinction. About this time he became a contributor to various provincial publications, amongst others to the *Dundee Repository* and the *Aberdeen Magazine*. Soon after he took up his abode in Arbroath, he set about diffusing a taste for literature among his fellow-townsmen. A Literary Society was formed, of which he at once became the life and soul. From a paper read by Balfour at one of the meetings of this club, we can form a fair estimate of the subjects which engaged the attention of the members. This particular paper is a poem in the Scottish dialect consisting of about five hundred lines, and in its introductory stanzas the subjects of some of the former papers and discussions are set down. The whole piece is rich in humour and the author shows in it, as he does in other of his writings, a rare command of "the mither tongue." Besides the interest he took in the Arbroath Literary Club, he also took an active share in the founding and subsequent management of the Arbroath Subscription Library. The Library, which still exists but which will soon be merged in the new Free Public Library, was instituted on the 24th August, 1797, four years after Balfour settled in Arbroath. The initial expenses were considerable, and to meet these a subscription of five pounds was required from each member. The members, who represented the *elite* of society in Arbroath and neighbourhood, were neither slow to discern nor unwilling to acknowledge the distinguished position which Balfour was earning for himself in the ranks of the literary men of the day. The institution was not many months old when he was admitted an honorary member—the first to hold that position. Although an honorary, he was one of the most active of its members during the first seventeen years of its existence, filling the offices of secretary and treasurer. Possessed, as he was, not only of energetic business habits, but of rare enthusiasm and fine literary tastes, his services were exceedingly valuable to the institution, placing it, from its foundation, on such a firm basis as has ensured its continuous existence for a hundred years.

Another Arbroath literary undertaking to which he lent valuable aid was the first production of the periodical press of the burgh, *The Arbroath Magazine*, 1799-1800. Balfour was one of the chief contributors, and there is reason to believe that he acted in the capacity of editor. His contributions to that magazine were both in poetry and in prose. Only two of them bear his initials, but some of the best articles in that publication are reproduced in his collected works, which removes any doubt as to their identity. During Balfour's residence here, many standard works were issued from the Arbroath press, and while this is mainly attributable to the commercial enterprise of John Findlay, the printer and publisher of these works, Findlay was largely helped and encouraged by Alexander Balfour. We have already, in referring to one of his poetical pieces, said that he possessed a rich vein of humour. We find the same quality exhibited in some of his prose writings. In a satirical article in *The Arbroath Magazine*, entitled " A new and most excellent method of preserving a wife," we have a good example of this.

While attending assiduously to his manufacturing business, which, as we have already seen, continued to thrive and extend, his literary undertakings became more numerous and important. In addition to this, he carried on an extensive correspondence with literary men in London, Edinburgh, and elsewhere. An ardent admirer—nay, a worshipper—of Burns, he shewed by his frequent allusions to him how much he loved, and how thoroughly he appreciated his genius. When the death of Scotia's greatest poet became known, the soul of Balfour was stirred to its depths, and his feelings found vent in a noble elegy which appeared in *The Edinburgh Magazine*. It was warmly received at the time, and some years afterwards Alexander Campbell, in his "History of Scottish Poetry," characterised it as by far the best that had been produced.

He was a frequent contributor to the magazine in which the elegy appeared, and his contributions to other magazines were also numerous. *The Dundee Magazine* published by Francis Colville; *The Temple of the Muses*, a poetical miscellany by Vernon & Hood, London; *The Poetical Register* by Davenport; *The Edinburgh Literary Gazette*; *The Edinburgh Literary Journal*; the Scots magazine *Forget-me-not*; *The Literary Souvenir*; *The Literary Mirror*, published in Montrose, and other magazines were frequently enriched by articles from his pen. "When wild war's deadly blast was blawn" and our soldiers had gone forth to try their mettle against the armies of France, Balfour wrote a large number of patriotic songs which appeared chiefly in *The Dundee Advertiser*. So appropriate were they to the temper of the times that a number of them were re-published in London, set to music, and sung in theatres and concert rooms of the metropolis, besides being very popular throughout the country. This gained for him considerable fame as a song writer, and he was solicited by the editors of various publications to write songs for them. To the *Northern Minstrel*, published in Newcastle, he contributed some twenty songs, and for the Montrose *Literary Mirror* he also wrote a few. The article "Arbroath," in Sir David Brewster's Encyclopædia, was written by Balfour, and he also wrote several papers for *Tilloch's Philosophical Journal*. As might be expected, his writings brought him into public notice far beyond Arbroath. While resident there he was elected an honorary member of the Newcastle Philosophical Society.

In 1814, he left Arbroath, as already stated after a residence of twenty-one years, years both of commercial and literary activity, and took up his abode at Trottock, near Dundee, having relinquished his business in Arbroath, and joined a London House, with whom his firm had long had extensive dealings. Placing all his means in the concern, he took the management of their Dundee branch. The result of the war terminating in the peace of 1815 brought disaster to many a commercial concern, and, among others, the house with which Balfour had a year before connected himself, became bankrupt. Thus he, who, before leaving Arbroath, was in comparative affluence, and who naturally looked forward to that leisure which an arduous and thrifty life deserved—a leisure in course of which he might be able to devote himself to his loved literary labours—was now reduced to poverty. Misfortunes seldom come singly, and so it befel Balfour. About this time, typhus fever broke out in his family, and continued for some months to harass them—himself not entirely escaping. Broken in health and bankrupt in fortune, to such a sensitive nature these ills were hard to bear, but, with that Christian fortitude for which he was distinguished, he set himself to face the world in the position of a servant once more. He was offered and accepted an appointment as manager to a manufacturer at Balgonie in Fife, which he retained till 1818. Anxious however about the education of his family, he was desirous of removing to a locality where better educational advantages could be had, so he applied for and obtained a situation in the publishing firm of Blackwood of Edinburgh, and so became a resident in that city. He had not been long in Edinburgh, however, before worse than financial bankruptcy overtook him. Accustomed to a life of activity, he was now tied down to his desk from morning till night. Missing the free air of the country and his walks among the sylvan scenes of Fife and Angus which he loved so well, his health began to give way, and in 1819 the symptoms of paralysis appeared. Before the close of that year, he became a confirmed invalid, and had to be moved about in a wheeled chair. Not only were his limbs affected, but his speech also, and it was with the greatest difficulty that he was able to articulate.

While thus a wreck physically, his mental qualities were as active as ever, and now that literature, which had formerly but lent a charm to his hours of relaxation, was henceforth to be pursued as a means of earning his daily bread, he set himself resolutely to the task. Although the loss of his worldly fortune and of his physical health had naturally a depressing influence, and would have had a tendency to produce inaction in a mind differently constituted, in the case of Balfour it but served to stimulate his mental faculties to greater exertion, and so he bravely girded himself for the task. From this time till his death, which occurred ten years later, it may be judged from the following list how hard he wrought. His "Campbell or the Scottish Probationer," a novel in three volumes appeared in 1819, as did "Richard Gall's Poems," which he edited, and for which he wrote a memoir; in 1820 "Contemplation and other poems"; in 1822 his second novel, "The Farmer's Daughter," in three volumes; and in 1823, "The Foundling of Glenthorne, or the Smuggler's Cave," a romance in three volumes. In 1825, he republished from *Constable's Magazine*, where they had previously appeared in serial form his "Character's omitted in Crabbe's Parish Register," and his "Highland Mary," a novel in four volumes. All the while he made considerable contributions to the periodical press. It is said that his contributions to *Constable's Edinburgh Magazine* alone would have filled three goodly octavo volumes. His first novel, "Campbell," was published anonymously, and it at once became exceedingly popular. It contains an account of the literary labours and the privations and sorrows of a licentiate of the Church of Scotland, scrambling for the bare means of subsistence in his search for a living. This book was very favourably received by the press. The biographical sketch affixed to the poems of his friend Richard Gall, the author of the popular song, "My only Joe and dearie O," was written in a genial and highly appreciative style. The "Characters omitted in Crabbe's Parish Register" are admirably drawn, and the versification is excellent. The "Foundling of Glenthorne," and "Highland Mary" became exceedingly popular, and the fact that the circulating library copies were dog-eared and thumbed almost to tatters may be taken as a proof of their success. His tales and sketches were admirably written and warmly welcomed. As might be expected, several of his poems make special reference to Arbroath, and most of his legendary poems are founded on local traditions. The Brothock, Cairnie Hill, the Abbey, the Bell Rock, the Cliffs, and St. Vigeans are made to pass with panoramic vividness before the mental vision of the Arbroathian. "Mary Scott of Edenknow," "The Piper of Dickmontlaw," and "The Legend of the Bell Rock" are founded entirely on local traditional tales. Besides telling their own story, in highly poetical language, they abound in passages descriptive of local scenery.

In the summer of 1824 he was removed temporarily to the village of Liberton. The house was beautifully situated in the midst of an extensive garden, through the walks of which he was wheeled, and under the canopy of a tree, while enjoying the sunshine and fresh air, he was protected from the heat. The change from the city to this lovely spot acted like magic on one born and brought up in the country, and who loved nature so well. His "Elegy by an Invalid" exhibits the intensity of the pleasurable feelings experienced during his brief stay in this sweet village. The last three years of his life were spent in Lauriston Place, Edinburgh. Here, shut up by the walls on the opposite side from a single glimpse of nature, he felt the deprivation intensely. To make up as far as possible for the loss to him of the green fields, the running brooks, and the other beauties of nature in which his soul delighted, there was collected for him in his sitting-room an extensive assortment of greenhouse plants and exotics in which he took a lively interest.

In 1827, through the influence of Joseph Hume, M.P. for the Aberdeen district of burghs, which then included Arbroath, a donation of £100 from the Treasury, "in consideration of his talents and misfortunes," was sent him by the Prime Minister, Mr Canning. This was only one of the many services unostentatiously rendered by Joseph Hume to Balfour and his family. Until within twelve days of his death Balfour continued to work, and his last piece of composition was transcribed and sent to *The Edinburgh*

Gazette two or three days before he died. To the end he retained his calm composure, and bore with meek resignation and uncomplaining patience the severe physical sufferings with which he was afflicted. As his death drew near his bodily sufferings appeared to abate, and on the 12th September, 1829, he departed as in a sleep.

As a writer, Alexander Balfour was far above the average. His imagination was always made subservient to correct taste, and his works accordingly, while never common-place, were rather sensible than sparkling. He was a close observer of life and manners, which made his sketches both pleasing and natural. Possessed of fine genius, a gentle and amiable nature, and imbued with pure Christian sentiment, he was loved by all who were brought into contact with him. To vice in every form he was an inexorable foe, a feature of his character frequently reflected in his writings. Arbroath has reason to feel honoured that she numbers among her former citizens one possessed of such fine literary tastes, and who, by his numerous productions, both in prose and verse, has earned a worthy place on the roll of literary Scotsmen.

JAMES CHALMERS.

JAMES CHALMERS,

Inventor of the Adhesive Postage Stamp.

IT is now more than half-a-century since the introduction of the penny postal system. The enormous benefits, not only to the commerce of the world, but to social intercourse, which the uniform small charge for the transmission of correspondence has conferred, are simply incalculable. But wanting the adhesive postage stamp the penny postal system could never have been successfully wrought, and the benefits flowing from that system, which are now universally acknowledged, are due in large measure to the invention of the adhesive stamp. It is only fair therefore that all honour should be given to its inventor.

In paying such honour, we throw a lustre on Arbroath, the birth-place of James Chalmers, the inventor of the adhesive postage stamp. Not only was Chalmers the inventor; he was, further, the man who urged the adoption of this stamp, when at a critical moment, all was dismay as to how the new penny postal system could be carried out in practice.

For a considerable number of years this invention was very unfairly claimed for Sir Rowland Hill, but now, by all but universal consent, the honour is given to him to whom it is undoubtedly due. It is not needful to detract from the credit due to Rowland Hill for the ability and energy he displayed in connection with the organisation and introduction of the penny postal system of the country, in order that others, who contributed so largely to its success, should receive the credit due to them. It is not creditable to that portion of the British press, nor to some of the descendants of Sir Rowland Hill, who continue either to ignore or deny the fact, which has been proved beyond dispute, that to James Chalmers, and to James Chalmers alone, we owe this important invention and proposal. James Chalmers was an exceedingly modest man, and it was quite foreign to his nature to blow his own trumpet. Had he been a little less retiring in his disposition, and had he been half as anxious about his own interests as he was about the interests of his country, he would have made sure that his contribution to the great cause of postal reform should have been as publicly admitted at the time, and as adequately recompensed, as was the contribution thereto of Rowland Hill. Now, however, his claim to the honour of being the inventor of the adhesive postage stamp has been established beyond dispute. It is not therefore needful that we should here waste a single line in offering proof of what has otherwise been incontestibly proved.

It may, however, be interesting to our readers, if we give a brief sketch of his life. James Chalmers was born in Arbroath on the second day of February, 1782. He was the second son of William Chalmers. We have been unable to ascertain in what part of the town James Chalmers first saw the light. His father was a member of the Glassite church. The building in which that body worshipped, although long since disused for that purpose, is still standing in Church Street. Here he was baptised, but as the local records of the denomination have gone amissing, we have failed to obtain the information which these records would undoubtedly have afforded. In early life he was bred to the occupation of handloom weaving, then the leading industry of Arbroath ; but his elder brother, William, having settled in Dundee as a bookseller, James forsook the loom, joined his brother, and, at a later date, he carried on the business on his own account. As bookseller, printer, and publisher, he met with considerable success. In early life he married Barbara, daughter of Bailie Dickson of Montrose, by whom he had a numerous family. One of Bailie Dickson's grandsons was Baron Oscar Dickson, who some years ago fitted out the "Vega," renowned for its successful arctic voyages.

In June, 1820, *The Caledonian*, a quarterly journal, bearing Chalmers's name on the title page, appeared in Dundee. On No. VIII. of *The Dundee Magazine and Caledonian Review* (the first number of which came out in July, 1822), he appears as the publisher. He was also printer and publisher of *The Dundee Chronicle*. His enterprise as a publisher was not confined to periodical literature, but works of a more permanent nature were issued from his press. But while he was thus diligent in the prosecution of his business, he did not overlook the claims which the community had upon him as a prominent citizen, so we find him taking an active interest in the various local charities and philanthropic movements in the burgh, as well as in the various public projects, having for their object the furtherance of the interests of his adopted town. When in 1819 the Bill for the improvement of the Tay Ferries was before Parliament a difficulty presented itself. The estimated expense of the improvement was £25,000, and it was found that by the standing orders of the House of Lords, four-fifths of the estimated cost had to be subscribed before the Bill could be passed into law. It was calculated that the Government would give a grant of £10,000, as they had done in the case of Kinghorn and Queensferry, thus necessitating the raising locally of £10,000. An appeal for contributions to this scheme was made, and was heartily responded to, and among the subscribers to the fund we find the name of James Chalmers.

In the agitation for Burgh Reform, he took a distinguished part, and as deacon, and afterwards as convener of the Nine Incorporated Trades, he manifested an active interest in public affairs. Subsequent to that he served the community faithfully and well in the capacity of Town Councillor, and for several years he filled the honourable office of Treasurer. His connection with the press brought prominently before him the iniquity of the Excise duty on paper, as well as the tax on newspaper advertisements, and the stamp duty on newspapers themselves, and he threw himself heartily into the agitation for the repeal of these obnoxious taxes on knowledge.

To a reform of the postal system, he devoted much attention, and in the furtherance of this, he entered into correspondence with the various postal reformers of the day, both in and out of Parliament. Locally, he won the gratitude of the business men of his time by his strenuous and successful efforts for the acceleration of the Scottish mail to and from London. In this case, after a protracted correspondence, he succeeded in convincing the Government that, without additional expense to the nation, two days could be saved in the transmission of letters between Dundee and the great commercial towns of England—a day each way. The boon thus gained by his persistent efforts was much appreciated by the commercial community. But the crowning service—for which his name should be gratefully remembered in all time coming — was that of his invention of the adhesive postage stamp, and his persistent and successful endeavours in having it adopted.

We remember the time when the charge for the conveyance of letters was so exorbitant as to make it almost prohibitive to poor people to correspond with their friends, and business concerns felt greatly hampered by the excessive rates exigible for the transmission of letters. For example, a letter from Arbroath to Dundee, a distance of seventeen miles, cost fivepence; to Edinburgh or Glasgow ninepence. Even for the shortest distance fourpence was the minimum charge. These heavy rates had a very prejudicial effect not only on the commerce of the country but on the public revenue itself. The idea of a uniform rate of postage for the transmission of letters over the whole kingdom, originated with the Rev. Samuel Roberts, M.A., Conway, and he not only promulgated his views through the press for a number of years, but urged them on the post office authorities. By his enthusiastic and persistent advocacy of the subject, others were enlisted in the cause, and strenuous efforts to induce the Government to make a trial of the uniform rate of postage were put forth. Confirmation of this assertion, with reference to the important services rendered by Mr Roberts in initiating this movement so early as 1829, may be found in the Treasury Minute of 11th March, 1864, where it is admitted that *others* urged the adoption of uniform penny postage *before* the development of the plans of Sir Rowland Hill, as well as in interesting articles which appeared in *The Times* newspaper of 30th September, 1885, in *Walford's Antiquarian*, and in *The Glasgow Post Office Magazine* for 1887, and other papers.

While this agitation was going on, James Chalmers was industriously working in the interests of postal reform. In 1834 he conceived the idea of an adhesive stamp for postal purposes, and the result of his efforts in this direction was well known at the time to many in Dundee, Arbroath, and elsewhere. Some years ago ample testimony was borne to the fact, not only by workmen who were then in his employment, but by many other most reliable witnesses. William Whitelaw, a bookbinder in Glasgow, stated in a letter to *The People's Journal* that he entered the service of James Chalmers on 22nd November, 1825, as an apprentice, and continued with him till 17th July, 1839; he affirms that Chalmers was the sole inventor of the adhesive stamp, and he details the various steps, including his own (the narrator's) part in the work, namely, the dissolving of and brushing on the gum. These stamps, he says, were exhibited to many of the leading men in Dundee, whose names he gives. Another old servant, who left Chalmers's employment shortly before 1st November, 1834, tells that previous to his apprenticeship as an engineer, at the date stated, he was P.D. in the printing establishment of James Chalmers, and he has a distinct recollection of clipping the sample stamps apart after they had been printed on slips containing about a dozen stamps, and the backs gummed over. To the testimony of these men who performed their part of the work of preparation of these stamps can be added that of a gentleman who, in 1834 and onwards, saw them in Mr Chalmers's possession. Mr Prain, who for many years was one of the best known and most highly-respected citizens of Brechin, testified to having been shown the invention in Chalmers's premises prior to his leaving Dundee for Brechin towards the end of 1834. They were also submitted to many business men in Dundee, and to some in Arbroath, for we are credibly informed that about the same period they were exhibited by Chalmers to Patrick Wilson, a well-known bookseller in Arbroath.

In course of time the agitation for a uniform penny postal rate having taken definite shape, the consideration of the subject was remitted to a Select Committee of the House of Commons.

JAMES CHALMERS.

When that Committee met in November, 1837, Chalmers submitted his plan of an adhesive stamp to the Committee, and in February, 1838, he sent it to the Secretary of the Mercantile Committee of the City of London, and at the same time to Rowland Hill. It was clearly seen that the adoption of the penny postal system would involve considerable difficulties in the collection of the revenue in that department. Rowland Hill's first plan was to pay the penny or money with the letters, and his next plan for the prepayment of postage was by sheets of impressed stamped writing paper or by stamped covers.

When the question was being discussed in Parliament on the introduction of the Penny Post Bill on 5th July, 1839, it was admitted on all hands that either of Hill's plans would not only be very complicated, but would involve considerable expense and responsibility on the part of the Government, being liable to fraud or forgery; besides, the latter would give a monopoly of the production of the covers to one manufacturer under strict excise supervision. In this dilemma as to how to carry out the scheme, Mr Wallace, M.P. for Greenock, chairman of the Select Committee of the House of Commons already referred to, an ardent postal reformer, with whom Chalmers had been corresponding, favourably suggested the adoption of the adhesive stamp. By a Treasury minute of 23rd August, 1839, plans were invited from the public to show how the scheme could be practically carried out, when Chalmers again sent in his plan—accompanied by a certificate from the merchants, bankers, and other leading citizens of Dundee—to the Lords of the Treasury. A copy of this certificate appeared in the *Arbroath Herald* of 11th October, 1839. After detailing Chalmers's many services to postal reform, the certificate says, "Since the proposal to establish a uniform rate of postage was announced, Mr Chalmers has devoted much attention to the subject and has been at great pains to discover the best method of carrying the scheme into effect. We have seen a specimen, along with his description of his plan of using stamped slips, which appear to us to possess several peculiar and important advantages. We beg, therefore, respectfully to recommend his plan to the favourable consideration of the Right Honourable the Lords of Her Majesty's Treasury." A Treasury minute of 26th December, 1839, provided for the issue of both stamps—the impressed and the adhesive. After a fair trial, the Mulready envelope issued on the impressed stamp system proved a failure, but the adhesive stamp, invented by Chalmers, turned out a complete success and so saved the penny postal scheme.

The enormous expansion of the postal system, not only of this country, but of the civilised world, which has resulted from the adoption of the penny post would never have been realised but for the invention of the adhesive postage stamp by James Chalmers. Chalmers received no official recognition or reward from the Government, although Joseph Hume and other eminent men of the day held that he was entitled to both. Chalmers's easy disposition, careless of personal advantage, prevented him from pushing his claims to recognition or reward. So to Rowland Hill, whose official position necessarily brought him into prominence in connection with the introduction of the scheme, was the merit of the conception of the adhesive postage stamp unjustly attributed. Besides the certificate, an extract of which is given above, Chalmers's fellow-citizens bore public testimony to their appreciation of his valuable services to commerce, and on New Year's day, 1846, he was publicly presented in the Town Hall of Dundee with a handsome testimonial.

Although not yet officially recognised by the Government, a large proportion of the Philatelic Societies of the world have investigated and admitted the claim of James Chalmers as the sole inventor of the adhesive stamp. The "Encyclopædia Britannica," and the "Dictionary of National Biography," both acknowledge the claim which has been made on his behalf, "Blackie's Modern Encyclopædia" also admits this. It is a significant fact that neither the London press in their jubilee articles, nor the Postmaster-General in his jubilee speech, made any claim whatever as to Sir Rowland Hill having been the originator of the adhesive postage stamp; while the London and other Philatelic Societies, after searching inquiry, have felt constrained to admit that Sir Rowland Hill was not its inventor.

Hence our assertion that James Chalmers's title to be considered the inventor is now incontestably proved, and all but universally admitted; and Arbroath may well be proud of having given birth to a man who has thus been a benefactor to the human race — proud that to the genius of one of her sons the civilized world is so deeply indebted. It cannot be denied that this achievement of James Chalmers has contributed, in an immeasurable degree, to bring about the realisation of the dream of our national poet when he looked forward to the time—

> "When man to man the warld ower
> Shall brithers be, an' a' that."

And what has the nation done to show her appreciation of the service rendered by James Chalmers? Had he been a military officer who had had the fortune to lead the army under him to victory, even though the benefit arising from that victory had been somewhat doubtful, he might, years ago, have had a national column erected in his honour; and, in addition to a vote of thanks in Parliament, he, and his decendants after him, might have been in the enjoyment of a pension from the public purse;

but his contribution to the wealth and well-being of the world has only been rewarded by cold neglect, which is anything but creditable to the British nation. Justice to his memory, justice to Scotland, the land of his birth, demands that even yet the British Parliament should acknowledge the fact, and should put on record the admission that to the genius and perseverance of James Chalmers, Britain owes the distinction of having been the pioneer of that improvement on the postal system which has made it easy for all nations to conduct their correspondence, and which has thus conferred such an enormous benefit on internal and international commerce, as well as on social intercourse, throughout the civilized world.

After a long and highly honourable career, James Chalmers died in Dundee on 26th August, 1853. The local press contained appreciative obituary notices, in which were fully recognised his various services to the community, but specially his services to our own and other nations in connection with his invention of the adhesive postage stamp.

His remains lie in the "Howff," the old cemetery of Dundee, and over his grave has recently been erected (with the consent of the Magistrates and Town Council of that city) a granite monument bearing the following inscription:—" To the memory of James Chalmers, bookseller, Dundee. Born, 1782; died, 1853. Originator of the adhesive postage stamp, which saved the penny postage scheme of 1840 from collapse, rendering it an unqualified success, and which has since been adopted throughout the postal systems of the world."

Rev. THOMAS GUTHRIE, D.D.

THOMAS GUTHRIE,
Of Arbirlot.

THE eighteenth century witnessed a remarkable decline of the evangelical spirit which had formerly been a distinguishing feature in the character of Scotsmen. Many causes contributed to this, but there is no reason to doubt that this low tone in the religion and morals of the country, in a great measure, lay at the door of the clergy, who formed the majority in the councils of the church during a period, which has been fitly designated as the "dark age" of the Kirk of Scotland, culminating in the days of Robertson and Hill. The evangelical party towards the close of last century, although small in number, was strong in zeal for the cause of religion, and under the leadership and advocacy of such men as John Erskine and his successors, Henry Moncrieff, Andrew Thomson, and Thomas Chalmers, the beginning of the present century saw the revival and growth of the evangelical spirit in the Church of Scotland.

Under the teaching and example of such men as these, many became candidates for the ministry, not for the sake of ".the loaves and fishes," but from a higher and holier motive. The Presbytery of Arbroath was fortunate in having a number of such young men as candidates for the pulpits of parish churches in the town and neighbourhood. Besides these, there were churches in Arbroath in which the ministers were chosen by the people and not by patrons, and as vacancies occurred, not a few talented young men became candidates for, and were elected to, office. The consequence was that during "the thirties" there was quite a constellation of bright young ministers in the burgh and throughout the bounds of the Presbytery—Thomas Guthrie, J. M. M'Culloch, Robert Lee, James M'Cosh, William Stevenson, John Laird, James Lumsden, John Kirk, William Wilson, and others, who in after years became more or less famous.

With such a body of spirited young men in Arbroath and its immediate neighbourhood, at a time when Scotland was being stirred to its depths by questions of ecclesiastical polity of the greatest moment, there could not but be the keenest discussion. Already the Dissenters were beginning to demand the separation of Church and State. Lee, Guthrie, and Stevenson, at somewhat boisterous public meetings held in Arbroath, defended the existence of the Established Church against Davidson of the U. P. Church, backed by the arch-voluntary, Ritchie of Potterow. M'Cosh, although upholding the Church of Scotland, as by law established, did not publicly take an active part in the Voluntary contest. He held that with such a growing division of sects, the country would not long continue the endowments to any one denomination. But following in the wake of the Voluntary controversy, the discussions which most moved the whole of Scotland were those on the subjects of non-intrusion and spiritual independence. The Civil Courts were insisting on settling ministers in parishes against the expressed will of the people, and each minister had now to take his side in the battle which has since been known as "The Ten Years' Conflict."

All the young men already referred to were bent on abandoning the cold Moderatism of the previous century. But when the day for decision came, it was found that these young men, who, throughout the war against the Voluntaries had fought shoulder to shoulder, now on the non-intrusion question took opposite sides; Lee, Stevenson, and others taking part with the "Moderates;" while Guthrie, M'Cosh, Lumsden, and others of their set declared emphatically that they would part with their livings rather than allow what they conceived to be the rights of the people and the freedom of the Church to be interfered with. The battle was a keen and bitter one, culminating as it did in what is known as "the Disruption day," on the 18th of May, 1843. It is not, however, with these ecclesiastical disputes we have to do, except in so far as these were the means of developing qualities in the various combatants whose characters we here endeavour to sketch.

It might be interesting to speak of many of the young men who, about the period referred to, filled the Arbroath pulpits, and who afterwards, in one way or another, became outstanding men; but we shall only deal with a very few who attained to more than ordinary eminence.

Among these young men, Thomas Guthrie, parish minister of Arbirlot, was the acknowledged leader, his great vigour, his ready wit, and his moving eloquence marking him out as one who could do valiant battle for any cause he espoused. Arbirlot was not only his first charge, but it was here he laid the foundation of that fame which in after years made his name a familiar one throughout Christendom. Although a Brechiner by birth, we may be pardoned if we claim him as an Arbroathian, seeing that this was the scene of his early triumphs and the ground on which he won his spurs. The prominent part which Thomas Guthrie played in the ecclesiastical battles then raging in Scotland drew the attention of leading men, both in church and state, to the splendid capabilities of the young minister of the parish of Arbirlot, ultimately leading to his removal from the quiet of his country parish to the larger arena of the metropolis.

Thomas Guthrie sprang from a highly reputable and pious family in the neighbouring city of Brechin. His ancestors for many generations were farmers on the Braes of Angus, and the frequent references which he makes in his autobiography to incidents in their history are intensely interesting. The twelfth child and the sixth son of David Guthrie and Clementina Cay, his wife, Thomas Guthrie was born on the 12th of July, 1803. His father, a merchant and banker in Brechin, was the first of a long line of Provost Guthries who ruled over that city. David Guthrie took up his abode in "the ancient city" in the closing years of the eighteenth century, and there for generations the name of Guthrie was synonymous with all that was upright and loveable. A clear-headed, shrewd man of business, and at the same time a man of sterling piety, David Guthrie was well mated—his wife, Clementina, being not only a godly woman, but a person of strongly-marked individuality. In a home presided over by such a couple was Thomas Guthrie reared. Sent early to school, if school it could be called, he was in some respects fortunate in being placed under a remarkably pious teacher. Jamie Stewart was a weaver by trade, and while little Guthrie and some half-dozen others sat learning their letters, Jamie industriously plied the shuttle. This scene in the weaver's shop—which also served as bedroom, kitchen, and parlour—was never effaced from the memory of Thomas Guthrie. After mastering the alphabet and words of small syllables printed on the cover of the Shorter Catechism, Jamie led them on to the Book of Proverbs, then a text book in all the common schools in Scotland. From the school in Jamie Stewart's weaving shop, Guthrie was transferred to another, belonging to the Seceder body. At one time this school was taught by the afterwards celebrated Dr M'Crie, then a very young man. During M'Crie's residence in Brechin, young although he then was, he gave evidence of many of those qualities for which he was afterwards so distinguished. His successors in the dominieship of this little school, if they were not men of such heavy calibre as to scholarship, were men who bore a high character for personal worth. Here Guthrie made considerable progress. From this school he passed to one where the higher branches were taught. This was a private school kept up by a few of the more influential citizens, the teacher, a University man and a licentiate of the church, being thoroughly capable of preparing his pupils for college. While a diligent scholar, Tom Guthrie was no milksop. The same combative spirit which led him in after life to face his foes in the stormy debates on public platforms and in church courts manifested itself in a readiness to fight any fellow bigger or older than himself who attempted to act the bully either to himself or to any of his weaker class fellows.

At the early age of twelve, accompanied by Robert Simpson, afterwards Professor of Hebrew in Aberdeen University, and in later years well known as Dr Simpson of Kintore, he set out for Edinburgh there to enter as a divinity student. For a boy of his age he made excellent progress, but it was no easy matter to compete with fellow-students so much his senior. His college curriculum of eight years was finished two years before he was of age to receive license. While this, in a certain measure, was a disadvantage he was still able to turn the interval to good account. He returned to the University, taking classes not required for the clerical profession but which nevertheless turned out greatly to his advantage in after years.

In 1825 he was licensed to preach by the Presbytery of

Brechin, delivering his popular discourse in the Cathedral Church there, in the presence of a crowded congregation of his fellow townsmen, a very severe ordeal. He was now a full-fledged preacher, but the next thing was to get a charge. In consequence of his father's position as Provost of Brechin, he was able to command a considerable amount of political influence. In ordinary circumstances this would have made his prospects of preferment very good, and so it was that within four months after his license he had almost within his grasp one of the best livings in Scotland. But there was a fly in the ointment. The struggle between the opposing parties in the church was now exceedingly bitter, and the Moderate party being backed up by those in power in the State, it became almost impossible for any one with evangelical leanings to obtain an appointment to a church where the Crown was patron. And so Guthrie found that unless he pledged himself to support the Moderate party with his vote in the church courts, this appointment could not be conferred upon him. This pledge he could not allow himself to give either tacitly or directly, and so he had still to remain a probationer. At this period, his leanings to either side were not very pronounced, but his manly nature recoiled from thus selling his freedom of action for a piece of bread. This was not the last disappointment of the same kind, arising from the same cause, he had to bear, but as he afterwards acknowledged, though bitter pills to swallow at the time, they had a salutary effect.

His two years' extra studies at the University and at the celebrated Sorbonne, and his Continental travels were to be followed by a training of quite a different sort, but one which, taken with his other experiences, would add largely to his knowledge of men and things, and so give him such a splendid training for his life-work as few young men have an opportunity of enjoying before entering on the work of the ministry. The bank agency in Brechin, started by his father, and afterwards managed by his elder brother John, became vacant by the death of his brother. A valuable business had been gathered, and it was very desirable to keep it in the family, but his nephew—the deceased's only son, David, afterwards well known in Forfarshire as Colonel Guthrie, commissioner to the Earl of Dalhousie—was at the time rather young to be entrusted with the responsibility of such an appointment. It was needful, therefore, that some arrangement should be made to keep it open till he was qualified to fill it. To accomplish this, it was proposed that Thomas Guthrie should take his dead brother's place. This he did, and the result was that not only was a commendable action done in the keeping of the seat warm for his nephew, but that Guthrie himself gained an experience that was most valuable to him in his after career. While carefully discharging his duties as a banker, he did not neglect the chief object of his life. Three or four times a year he occupied the pulpit of one or other of the neighbouring parishes, thus not only keeping himself well up in the work, but also letting it be known that he had not abandoned his original profession. So, while plodding on in the routine of the banking business, he was patiently awaiting the time when his hopes of "getting a kirk" would be realised.

It was now five years since he was licensed, and he was yet without a call; but the time was approaching when his patience was to be rewarded and his hopes realised. On the seventh of September, 1829, Richard Watson, the venerable incumbent of Arbirlot, died at the manse of that parish, at the advanced age of eighty-seven, having filled the ministerial office worthily and well for the long period of fifty-three years. It has often been remarked that the ministers of the Church of Scotland are noted for their longevity. Richard Watson was the eighth parish minister in succession who died within the presbytery of Arbroath, the average of whose ages was upwards of eighty-four years. In the same year in which Watson was removed, the parish minister of Banchory died in his eighty-third year, and the minister of Monimail in his ninetieth year.

Richard Watson, previous to his translation to Arbirlot (1790), had been for seventeen years assistant minister in Arbroath. On the death of Alexander Mackie, the parish minister, in 1787, the Arbroath Council and the Kirk-Session petitioned the Crown to have Richard Watson appointed as his successor, but other influences prevailed, and the appointment was conferred on George Gleig. Both in Arbroath and Arbirlot Watson was highly esteemed as an able and earnest preacher, and he was long remembered as one of the most faithful ministers of the Church of Scotland. Notwithstanding his advanced age, Richard Watson continued to preach till within a fortnight of his death. His pulpit Bible is in the possession of the present writer, and the innumerable annotations it bears, afford evidence of the themes on which he loved to speak to his parishioners. With the exception of the Psalms and Isaiah, which have been much used, the Old Testament was seldom drawn upon; but the marginal columns of the New Testament are thickly annotated. The text Col. iii., v. 3, "For ye are dead, and your life is hid with Christ in God," bearing the year 1829, the last of his life, shows that to the end he continued to preach "Christ and Him crucified." It would have been good for the cause of religion in the district if all his co-presbyters had been animated by the same evangelical spirit as Richard Watson exhibited, but a few of them, at least, were true representatives of the cold Moderatism of the previous century. Many ludicrous instances were told of formality in worship on the part of some of these. An aged minister in Arbroath had used the same prayer during all his incumbency. A deaf woman who used to stand on the pulpit stair had committed it to memory, and she had got into the habit of uttering it, always a few words in advance of the minister, without being conscious that she was heard by the congregation. A minister of the Presbytery on a visit to a neighbour's house was asked to pray in the family, and while doing so he fell into the prayer which he used at the dispensation of the sacrament of the Lord's Supper, and was not arrested till he had consecrated the elements of bread and wine.

The death of Richard Watson caused a vacancy in Arbirlot, and through the influence of Lord Panmure, Thomas Guthrie obtained a presentation to that parish. Up to this time there was nothing remarkable about his style of preaching. But when he was fairly settled in Arbirlot, he threw his whole heart into the work. Instead of two ordinary diets of worship each Sabbath, he introduced certain changes. In the forenoon a discourse was given to the general congregation, and in the afternoon he had a special service for the young people, whom he catechised on the service of the morning. Notwithstanding these changes and the earnestness which he brought to bear on his work he felt disappointed. So far as outward evidences indicated he appeared to be making no marked impression on the young men and women. Instead of blaming them, as some might be apt to do, he took the blame to himself. Consequently he made an entire change in his style of preaching and mode of address, becoming what might be called a pictorial preacher. Drawing illustrations from the events of common life and scenes familiar to the people, and talking to them in a most practical manner, he soon aroused the whole parish. The old as well as the young now attended his afternoon class, and his forenoon service was also more largely attended. He was yet unknown in the great cities, but his fame spread throughout the district, and wherever he preached he had a crowded audience. But it was not in the pulpit only that he could move the people, he was equally effective on the platform. In "Arbroath: Past and Present" the part taken by Guthrie in the Voluntary controversy is told at some length, and need not therefore be repeated here, but the following description of a missionary meeting held at Barry, which was communicated to the author by an old parishioner, is interesting. We give it in his own words: " I revere the memory of Dr. Guthrie. He was kind to me, and gave me books to read. I lived in Arbirlot when Richard Watson died, and for nearly four years after Mr Guthrie came to it. The last time I saw him was at a missionary meeting in Barry Church. I remember it as if it had been yesterday, though nigh sixty years have passed since. The Committee of the Barry Missionary Society were at loggerheads. The famous Voluntary agitation was beginning to estrange the sympathies of the Barry Auld Kirkers from the Seceders, who had before acted in concord with them, and Dr. Guthrie was sent for to heal the breach—or to widen it. Speaking at the meeting, he said, 'There is only one Dissenter in my parish, and she is a Voluntary; nay more, a strong-minded woman. Well, I employed her and a few more auld wives to reap a field of barley on the manse glebe;' and, continued the Doctor, 'on going out after breakfast to see the reapers, judge my surprise to find only a few sheaves cut. They had thrown down the sickles—it is well they did so—and were argey-bargeyin' wi' a' their micht about Voluntaryism, the Dissenter holding her ground stoutly against all the rest. I tell you what I did. I put the Dissenter with the long tongue at a corner of the field by herself, and the barley was all in the stook by mid afternoon. Now, I say, let the Red Kirkers or Carnoustie Seceders take one corner of the Mission field, the Evangelicals of Barry Links another, and things will go on beautifully, for truly the harvest is great, and the labourers are few. You can imagine the effect of Dr. Guthrie's story.'" The narration of this incident so tickled the audience that they began to laugh, and as he proceeded they were fairly convulsed. So oppressive did it become that one old man stood up and, holding his sides all the while, stuttered, "Oh! stop, Maister Guthrie, we can stand this nae langer." At once changing his subject, Guthrie drew a harrowing picture of a shipwreck which he had recently witnessed on the neighbouring coast, when every head was bent and the tears were brought to many eyes. In his wanderings throughout the parish, he had a kind and cheery word for every one he met, and in his visits to the homes of his parishioners he was an ever-welcome guest. He was particularly fond of talking to country people, to farmers, their wives, and servants, and he had a happy way of drawing them into conversation. On one occasion he and Dr M'Cosh went together in a cart to the funeral of a minister at Carmyllie, six miles off, and Guthrie employed most of the time in conversing familiarly with the boy who drove the cart about what he knew of the nature of the soil, and of the character of the families all along the route. It was in such ways, more than by reading, that he acquired his extensive knowledge of men and their manners. With his clerical brethren in town and country he was a general favourite, his frank and winning manner and perennial good humour bringing sunshine wherever he went. But it was not his brother ministers and others of like social standing alone who experienced the warmth of his large heart, the poorest parishioner in Arbirlot felt that in their young pastor they had secured a friend who took a keen and intelligent interest, not only in their spiritual, but also in their temporal well-being.

He established a library and a savings bank which were much appreciated and largely taken advantage of by the Arbirlot folks, the savings bank having been continued for many years after he left Arbirlot. In the parish were many highly intelligent men, chiefly among the hand-loom weavers, and by them the library was heartily welcomed and regularly resorted to. The memoir by his sons, as well as his autobiography, contain many interesting reminiscences of his intercourse with his parishioners in humble life, with some of whom he kept up a correspondence long after his removal to Edinburgh.

In 1834 he gave great satisfaction to his parishioners in giving them the right of choosing their own elders. The system of popular election of Kirk-Sessions, if it had ever been the practice in the church, had fallen into desuetude in this district at anyrate. So gratifying was this concession to the members of Arbirlot Church that they declared they saw in it the dawn of a better day for the Church of Scotland, and they gave hearty expression to their feeling of gratitude to Thomas Guthrie for so generously transferring to the communicants the power of nominating and electing to the eldership a body of men well qualified for the office. When he entered on his duties as minister of Arbirlot he found the church in a very dilapidated condition, and through his instrumentality the present parish church was built.

But while discharging with remarkable fidelity his parochial duties, he felt that his energies should embrace a wider range of usefulness. Elsewhere we have referred to the active part he took, along with Lee, Stevenson, and others, in the campaign against the champions of Voluntaryism. He also took a prominent part in the discussions in the presbytery on the various public topics then agitating the church. In Arbirlot, Arbroath, Montrose, Dundee, and elsewhere he advocated the abolition of the Act of Queen Anne, imposing patronage on the Church of Scotland, and he successfully moved in the same direction in the Arbroath presbytery. He also took up with great keenness the movement on behalf of Church Extension, and in various places throughout the district, he pleaded the claims of the fund being raised for this scheme. His rich humour and his powerful eloquence made him one of the most successful public speakers in the district. Wherever he appeared either in the pulpit or on the platform, he was sure to draw a crowded audience, and it was felt that a man possessed of such qualities could not long remain the pastor of a country parish. His removal from Arbirlot came about as follows :—

In June, 1837, Dr M'Cosh, then the minister of Abbey Church, and afterwards the distinguished president of Princeton College, New Jersey, was asked by the Kirk-Session of Old Greyfriars, Edinburgh, to preach before that congregation with a view to filling the then vacancy. This he declined, but in doing so, he strongly recommended his friend and neighbour, Thomas Guthrie, for the vacant office, stating that he was sure to interest the people, and would soon fill the church. In his letter he stated that they would not find in Mr Guthrie the polished style of preacher they were accustomed to call to Edinburgh, but that they would find a powerful gospel preacher, and an orator who would move the people as O'Connell did. As O'Connell was at that time a bugbear in Scotland, this unfortunate statement alarmed a number of the Edinburgh councillors, and M'Cosh had to write an explanation to the effect that he compared Guthrie to O'Connell simply as a moving popular orator. Guthrie was asked to preach, but at once declined. Meanwhile, Alexander Dunlop, the eminent church lawyer, who was, with others, bent on filling the Edinburgh pulpits with evangelical ministers, had great difficulty in dealing with Thomas Guthrie. Guthrie was most unwilling to leave his country people and parish, so beloved was he by all, and he declined to be regarded as a candidate for any office which would remove him from Arbirlot. He wrote peremptorily asking his name to be withdrawn. To this, however, the Edinburgh folks would not listen, but resolved to send down a deputation to hear him preach. Dr M'Cosh gave him a hint of this, on which Guthrie wrote him: "I have a plan in my head of fleeing, not just my country, but my parish next Sabbath, to avoid the deputation." To this M'Cosh replied that his doing so would be as bad as the deed of Jonah in fleeing when called on to preach in Nineveh, "that great city." The deputation duly came and heard him in the forenoon in Arbirlot Church, and in the evening in Arbroath where he happened to preach, and strongly recommended that he should be appointed. He wrote to M'Cosh: "If I am elected, I must go, as it would be a call in providence and a duty," but he added that he would be greatly relieved if the election fell on another. In spite of these remonstrances, he was elected. He felt the responsibility of leaving his quiet country sphere to engage in a great work in the capital of Scotland, and he remarked to his friend M'Cosh, "I will give it a fair trial, and if I do not succeed, I will go down at once to some country parish."

Before leaving Arbroath some of his co-presbyters urged him to change his style of preaching when he appeared before a refined Edinburgh audience, but M'Cosh implored him to do nothing of the kind, assuring him that human nature was much the same everywhere, and that what moved the people of Arbirlot and Arbroath would move the people of Edinburgh. So it turned out, as his friend predicted, he at once gained the people, and he kept them during all his future ministry. But his love for his Arbirlot flock threw another difficulty in his way—he could not think of leaving them, unless he was assured that he would be followed by a thoroughly evangelical minister. He therefore felt it to be his duty before accepting the presentation to Old Greyfriars, to use his influence with Lord Panmure, to have a man of the type indicated appointed in his place. In this he was successful, and in due course a very suitable successor was found, in the person of John Kirk, the parish minister of Barry, the father of Sir John Kirk, and of the late Alexander Kirk, LL.D., the eminent engineer. Mr Kirk, who was highly esteemed for his many able and amiable qualities, proved most acceptable to the parishioners of Arbirlot.

Although Thomas Guthrie went to Old Greyfriars as colleague of Mr Sym it was really the intention of those who were the means of bringing him to Edinburgh, that he should assist in working out the idea of the old parochial system, with a view to arousing and elevating the lapsed masses, and so bringing them within the hearing of the gospel. In accepting the presentation it was understood, that as soon as arrangements could be effected he should sever his connection with Old

Greyfriars, and devote himself entirely to the work of evangelisation. During the three years he was joint-pastor of Old Greyfriars, his time was chiefly spent among the poor people, who were afterwards to form his new congregation. The scenes of poverty, squalor, misery, and vice which met him in the old town of Edinburgh contrasted with the beautiful scenery of his dear Arbirlot, and the contented, happy, and comparatively comfortable lot of even the poorest of his country parishioners, almost overwhelmed him. But his large, loving heart yearned to alleviate their temporal, and to elevate their moral and spiritual condition, and he threw himself with vigour into the work of reclamation. It was early brought home to him, when coming into contact with the degraded and criminal classes, that if he was to do any permanent work it must be among the young. He felt convinced that the "city," with "its sins and sorrows," contained no more sorrowful sight than the multitude of boys and girls growing up—in the very heart of civilisation and Christianity—in practical heathenism; and although for two or three years after his settlement in Edinburgh his hands were quite full of other work, the sad condition of the poor, neglected children was ever and again occupying his thoughts.

The Church Extension scheme, which in him had had such an able advocate in Arbroath, he still more vigorously prosecuted in Edinburgh, and his powerful appeals and moving eloquence—the outcome of the practical acquaintance he had gained in the Cowgate—aroused not only Christian Edinburgh, but re-echoed far and near throughout the land. No one appreciated the value of his advocacy of this scheme more than did Dr. Chalmers, its originator. One of the fruits of this scheme, Thomas Guthrie's own church—St. John's—was opened in November, 1840. While labouring with unabated zeal in his own parish, the keen interest he took in every Christian effort and the powerful and persuasive eloquence which he brought to bear on any cause which he advocated made his services to be in great demand. During the whole period of the "Ten Years' Conflict," the leaders of the non-intrusion cause found in Thomas Guthrie a doughty champion, and when the Disruption came, he left St. John's, and for a time worshipped with those who adhered to him in a building in Nicholson Square till a new church, Free St. John's was built for him.

The Disruption did not bring idleness to those who had taken a foremost part in the events which led up to it. Congregations had to be consolidated, financial arrangements for the maintenance of the minister had to be made, churches for the newly-formed congregations and manses for their pastors had to be built. This latter part of the work was in a large measure committed to Thomas Guthrie. In carrying out the task thus imposed on him he travelled all over Scotland addressing innumerable public meetings, and by his eloquence arousing an immense amount of enthusiasm, his labours resulting in the production, within one year, of one hundred and sixteen thousand three hundred and seventy pounds. While his labours had brought comfort to the households of the Free Church ministers, they told heavily on his own health, and it was soon found needful to give him a colleague, an arrangement which was made, and continued till his retirement from active duty some years thereafter. His work was not confined to his own congregation or church; in almost every movement for the moral or social well-being of his fellow-citizens, he took an active hand. He had long had a hankering after doing something to alleviate the misery of the poor children, and in 1847 his famous "Plea for Ragged Schools" appeared. So great was the effect produced by this powerful and pathetic plea that forthwith committees were formed and meetings held which resulted in the establishment of the well-known Edinburgh Ragged School —an institution which has conferred incalculable benefits on thousands of poor children, and largely helped to reduce juvenile crime in the city. His efforts on behalf of the Total Abstinence cause was also productive of lasting good.

In 1862 he was the recipient of the highest honour his church had to bestow in being elected as Moderator of the General Assembly of the Free Church of Scotland. In 1864 he felt constrained by increasing infirmity to withdraw from the active duties of the pastorate. This was not only a great disappointment to one who had led such a busy life but also to his attached congregation. Their affection for him was testified by the presentation to him of the house he had occupied for some years. In further recognition of his services, not only to the church but to the general public, he was presented with a service of silver plate and £5000. During the many years of his busy life he found time to make a considerable contribution to the religious literature of the country, and for some years he edited the *Sunday Magazine*. The news of his death, which took place at St Leonards-on-the-Sea, on Sabbath, the 23rd February, 1873, was received with sorrow by all creeds and classes throughout the Kingdom from the Queen to the cottar.

Rev ROBERT LEE, D.D.

ROBERT LEE,
Of Inverbrothock.

AT the village of Tweedmouth, now a thriving suburb of the famous border town of Berwick-on-Tweed, where in the olden days many a tough fight took place between the Saxons and the Scots, was born on the 11th November, 1804, Robert Lee, the eldest son of George Lee and Jane Lambert, his wife. George Lee was a man of considerable intelligence and an excellent tradesman. Entering, in early manhood, business on his own account, he became a fairly prosperous man, and in course of time was able to employ from eight to ten men besides apprentices. While diligent in business, he found time to make himself otherwise useful. At the age of nineteen, he became precentor to the Scotch church at Tweedmouth, and at a later period he was elected successively to the offices of collector of seat rents, elder, and session-clerk. In these various offices he continued for the long period of forty years.

George's father, Robert Lee, also a boatbuilder at Tweedmouth, had married Lilly, daughter of Isaac Davidson. Lilly Lee was a very clever woman, a sweet singer, and an excellent performer on the violin. Her son, George, inherited her love of music, and while precentor of the Scotch Church, he did much to improve the psalmody. In those days it was the custom for the precentor to read the psalm line by line in a drawling monotone. George, however, was a bit of an "innovator" in his way, and among his other improvements, he started to read two lines at a time, and that, too, instead of in the customary monotonous style, in a way which brought out more clearly the meaning of the verses being sung. This was not the only improvement he introduced into kirk affairs. On taking office as seat rent collector and elder, he found the financial affairs of the congregation very unsatisfactory, the books and accounts having been very irregularly kept, and everything connected with them in a confused condition. He at once set himself to inaugurate a systematic method of book-keeping, and thus gradually got the congregational affairs into an orderly state, much to the satisfaction of the minister and other office-bearers.

Jane Lee, the mother of Robert Lee, was the youngest daughter of Robert Lambert and Joanna, his wife. The father was a staunch member of the Church of England, and the mother, Joanna, was a pious Dissenter. Though born and bred a Presbyterian, Robert Lee was brought up under the shadow of the Church of England as the State Establishment. He lived within a few yards of Tweedmouth Parish Church, and he is known from his youth to have admired the book of Common Prayer; and from his environment in his young days, would gradually grow up tolerant, nay, attached to the more ornate service of the Anglican Church as contrasted with what he considered the bald and unattractive service of the Church of Scotland. This account of his parentage and early surroundings, brief as it is, gives us considerable insight into what contributed so materially to mould the character, and give the leanings towards those ritualistic reforms which in after years brought Robert Lee into such sharp conflict with his brethren on this side of the Tweed.

He was educated under a famous grammar schoolmaster, Guy Gardiner, an excellent classical scholar who turned out more than one man who was afterwards known to fame. At the close of his school career at Berwick-on-Tweed, Lee was apprenticed to his father's business of boatbuilding, and with him he served six years. As might be expected from one so sharp and intelligent he became most proficient at the trade. Not only could he build a boat, but he could handle one in the bay with a steadiness and nimbleness that made it quite a pleasure to go out with him as sailing master, as in later life did many of his student and clerical friends who accompanied him on his periodical visits to the home of his youth. While working as a boatbuilder his aspirations were higher, and in the intervals of his business he diligently pursued his studies, and even then so great was his early promise of a distinguished career that Mr Grieve, of Ord, a neighbouring squire, used to say, that if Robert Lee was taken care of he would one day be a .bishop of the Church of England. But trained in a Presbyterian home, when he did think of turning to the church as a profession it was to the Scottish, not to the English, Church that he looked. One of his brothers, however—Anthony Pye Lee—became a clergyman of the Church of England. He died at Torquay on the 21st January, 1842, at the early age of twenty-five. Another brother, William, an engineer went to Russia, and was employed in the mint at St Petersburg. During the time of the Crimean War he fell under the suspicion of the government of the Czar Nicholas, was transported to Siberia, and, like many more, was never again heard of.

Having made up his mind to study for the church, Robert Lee chose St Andrews as his Alma Mater. His biographer, Dr Story, makes it appear as if want of funds interfered with his designs in this respect, but such was not the case. As we have seen, his father was a prosperous tradesman, and when Robert was a boy of nine, besides having sufficient means for carrying on a considerable business, George Lee was able to purchase for himself a substantial dwelling house looking out on the Tweed, a house which is still occupied by a near relative. The story of Robert Lee building a boat and selling it, in order to provide funds wherewith to pay his entrance fees, is a very pretty but at the same time an apocryphal one. It is quite true that he built a boat and that with his own hands and for his own use, but this was done in his student days when at home from college on holiday. In this boat he and his friends and fellow students had many a pleasant sail in the bay. He matriculated at St Andrew's University in the session of 1824-25, and, thanks to his early training under Guy Gardiner, he at once took a high place in the Greek and Latin classes there. As a student, his career was a brilliant one, carrying, as he is said to have done, all before him—gaining the highest encomiums from so distinguished a man as Dr Chalmers, as well as from the other professors under whom he studied.

He spent the summer of 1826 at Exeter with a Mr Vicar, at whose house he acted as tutor. In his correspondence with his Tweedmouth friends at this period, he gave evidence of an earnest desire to further the cause of religion to which he had devoted his life. Writing to his brother George, he first counsels him, while attending to his daily toil, not to neglect his intellectual improvement. "I know," he says, "at night you are tired and unfit for anything like arduous study, at the same time I should wish to convince you that reading what is instructive fatigues almost as little as talking of that which is unimportant; the knowledge which I have been recommending makes a man an interesting, and it may be a useful, member of society, but"—and here he leads on to higher and more important things—" but there is another knowledge which has a far higher claim upon you, and that is derived from the Bible. I hope you do not fail to read it privately, for it contains whatever is requisite to direct your conduct, whether in respect to time or eternity. You are young, and I know your imagination pictures to itself scenes of future happiness, which I can confidently assure you will never arrive. The only possible means of securing real enjoyment is by fixing your affections upon that which cannot deceive you. This, I hope, you are endeavouring by God's grace to do," and with many more exhortations to persevere in prayer, and to trust himself to God's guidance in all his worldly affairs, he does his best to encourage his brother to lead a truly Christian life. Mr Vicar, with whom he appears to have lived for more than one summer session, had not failed to observe that young Lee was a lad of bright promise, for, in one of his letters home, he says: "Mr Vicar wants me to enter at Oxford," and he jocularly adds, "which, if you would lend me some two or three hundred pounds, I should have no objection to do!"

During the later period of his St. Andrew's curriculum he resided at Mount Melville, where he acted as tutor to George John Whyte Melville, the eldest son of Mr Whyte Melville. His pupil, afterwards well known as a sportsman and literateur, is regarded as the founder of a school of novels — the fashionable sporting novel. It is said of him that "he exerted a considerable and a wholesome influence on the manners and morals of the gilded youth of his time," and we may reasonably suppose that his early contact with such a fine personality as that of Robert Lee helped so to form his own character as to make his influence felt on those with whom he was brought into contact in after years. When Lee left the college the Principal said of him—" This University has not for many years sent forth a more distinguished student. He has gained during a succession of years the highest honours which the University can award."

It may readily be imagined that a young man with such a distinguished college record and possessing considerable mental and physical activity, added to an effective style of preaching, would not long remain a probationer. And so it was that a few months after being licensed to preach, he was unanimously elected—out of a leet of four candidates—minister of St Vigeans Chapel of Ease at Arbroath, or, as it is now known, Inverbrothock Parish Church. This was on 13th November, 1833, and on the 10th April following, the Presbytery of Arbroath, under the presidency of Thomas Guthrie, of Arbirlot, ordained him as minister of St. Vigeans Chapel. His predecessor, and the first minister of this Chapel of Ease, was also a man who became widely known, among other things for the educational works which he edited—James Melville M'Culloch, afterwards Dr. M'Culloch, of Greenock, where he enjoyed one of the richest livings in the church.

Robert Lee soon won his way to the hearts of the Arbroath people. Frank in manner, with a large fund of good humour, he was received as a favourite, not only into the houses of the members of his own congregation, but into the best circles in the town. Both as a preacher and as a citizen, he was exceedingly well liked. In his preaching, he was sharp and pointed, his sermons were chiefly homely and practical; indeed, so pointed and practical, that they were oftener than once the cause of offence, some of his hearers having been known to wait on him and suggest "that he should preach the gospel and not these practical things." One sermon especially which he preached from the text "Owe no man anything" gave great offence in some quarters. From this text he drew the lesson that it is much easier to make high professions than to act as honest men ; to make long prayers and pious speeches than to make restitution of unjust gains. Instead of attempting to allay the murmurs against him for the strong and pointed statements in this sermon, with that contempt of opposition which was so characteristic of him in later years, he had the sermon printed and published under the title of "The virtue of common honesty."

He early showed a tendency to relax the forms of public worship which then prevailed in the Church of Scotland. A distinguished Arbroath contemporary referring to this tendency remarked that it was as difficult to determine whether Lee was a Presbyterian or an Episcopalian as to settle whether he was a Scotsman or an Englishman. When in after years, public attention was being directed to what by some was called his "devisive courses," Dr Story tells that he (the biographer) was informed by a member of Old Greyfriars, and a close friend of Dr Lee's, that he was taken when a boy to Inverbrothock Church. What there impressed him most was the minister's copious reading of the Scriptures and his repeating of the Lord's Prayer, a rare formula which the youthful worshipper had never heard used in any church.

Along with Guthrie, Stevenson, Kirk, and Whitson, Lee took an active share in defending the Established Church from the attacks of the Voluntaries, and at various public meetings held in Arbroath from 1834 onward, his great powers as a debater, and his singular readiness of repartee, made him a formidable opponent to Dr Ritchie and Mr Davidson, the champions of Voluntaryism. At one of the meetings—which we have fully described in "Arbroath: Past and Present,"—Lee was speaking amid much interruption, and in course of his remarks, he made an incidental reference to Jeroboam, when a voice from the gallery shouted that Jeroboam was an Establishment man. Lee, with his usual readiness, replied, "No, no; Jeroboam was a Voluntary for he upset the Established Church and set up his own." With this and similar smart sayings, he gained the sympathy of a large portion of his audience and was able to influence the meeting. It was to their able advocacy of the principles of Establishment at this period that Dr Guthrie attributed his own and Dr Lee's rapid promotion which they both speedily attained in the service of the church. During his pastorate in Arbroath, he was most assiduous in his attention to the young people of his congregation, by whom he was affectionately regarded, and his classes, male and female, were largely attended.

In 1834 his congregation and his classes showed their appreciation of his services, the one by increasing his stipend, and the other by the presentation to him of a piece of silver plate. While attending assiduously to his ministerial duties he took a full share in public work. Among other offices which he held were those of president of committee of the Infant School, and a director of the Arbroath Library. He was also one of the lecturers in connection with the Arbroath Scientific Association. While in Arbroath he began a practice, which he kept up throughout his life, of delivering courses of lectures on special subjects, a practice which gave great satisfaction to his Inverbrothock congregation, as it did to those to whom he ministered in after years. When in Arbroath he contributed some excellent articles to the *Scottish Christian Herald*, a paper chiefly conducted by the evangelical party in the Church. When it is noted that this publication had a weekly issue of forty thousand copies, the influence it had throughout Scotland will readily be understood. In the few years he remained in Arbroath he succeeded, by his great mental activity, his frank geniality, and his independence of action, in gaining a fame more than local, and his call to Campsie, and afterwards to Edinburgh, was the natural outcome. He made more than one visit to Arbroath after this, to one of which he refers in his diary under date 13th July, 1852, "To-day returned from Arbroath, whither I went to re-open the Abbey Church, which has been closed since the Disruption in 1843. I never preached to such a crowd, and almost never saw such a crowd in a church. I was told that five or six hundred people went away for want of room."

Doubtless the esteem in which he was held during his residence in Arbroath had helped to draw the people out on this occasion. If he was a favourite with the people so was he also with his co-presbyters. On his leaving Arbroath for Campsie, Thomas Guthrie, of Arbirlot, wrote him as follows:—

"Many, many thanks for all your kindness to me. I have enjoyed much pleasure in your friendship, and am sensible of no little profit from it; and you carry my respect, my affection, and my very best wishes along with you. I almost play the woman while I write this farewell note. Fare thee well, my good friend, again I say fare thee well. May the Lord bless you and make you a blessing, and I have now only to say that at the very sight of you my door will swing wide open on its hinges, and that I am, and ever will be your most affectionate friend,

THOMAS GUTHRIE.

MANSE OF ARBIRLOT, *April 18, 1836.*

The bitter controversies of the times, which increased during the few following years, and which separated friend from friend and brother from brother, prevented the realisation of the vision of the hospitable door of Guthrie swinging open on its hinges at the approach of the genial Lee.

During the years spent in Campsie, the battle between the opposing parties in the church grew fierce, but Lee took little or no part in the warfare. Any part he did take was more in the way of attempted conciliation between the opposing parties. As the time of disruption drew nearer, with his characteristic straight-forwardness he felt that he must take a side, and he therefore ranked himself on the side of "the Moderates," but his speeches did not savour of that bitterness which characterised many on each of the sides of the discussion.

On settling in Campsie, he married in June, 1836, Isabella Buchanan, whose father carried on business in St. Ninian's, near Stirling. His brother-in-law, Dr. Robert Buchanan of Glasgow, was a well-known leader of the "non-intrusion" party in the church, and the author of the "Ten Years' Conflict: a History of the Disruption of the Church of Scotland," and other works. Robert Lee's domestic life was a happy one, and his intercourse among his parishioners, whose affection his kindly interest in their temporal and spiritual welfare drew forth, was exceedingly pleasant.

In 1840 he became a candidate for the chair of Theology in the Glasgow University, the other candidates being Dr. Thomas Chalmers and Dr. Hill, the latter being successful. That Hill should have been preferred to Chalmers, a man so much his superior, can only be accounted for by the fact that not to attainments, but to party spirit Hill owed his success.

The Disruption day of 1843 made many blanks in the

kirk, and among others the pulpit of Old Greyfriars, of Edinburgh, became vacant through the secession of the Rev. John Sym, and to this church, where his former friend and co-presbyter, Thomas Guthrie, had ministered, was Robert Lee called. Here he set himself with great zeal to his work. In 1844, the degree of Doctor of Divinity was conferred on him by the University of St Andrews. In the following year Old Greyfriars was burned, and until the erection of a new church in its stead, his congregation worshipped in the Assembly Hall.

When the Chair of Biblical Criticism in the University of Edinburgh was founded in 1846, Dr Lee was the first to fill it. He was also appointed Dean of the Chapel Royal of Holyrood, and Chaplain in ordinary to the Queen. These high honours did not bring immunity from cares and troubles. On the contrary, from this time onward it may be said that the current of Robert Lee's life flowed less smoothly than heretofore. While discharging the duties of his professorial office, he continued in the pastorate of Greyfriars, and as there was a strong party opposed to pluralities in the Church, he had from time to time, both in the Presbytery and in the General Assembly, to defend his position. This was only one of the battles he had to fight, the position he took up on ecclesiastical questions bringing him into sharp conflict, not only with his professional brethren, but with many leading laymen. But the chief conflict which he had to engage in, and which only ended with his death, was in connection with his endeavour to extend what he held to be the freedom of worship and thought within the Church of Scotland.

This was no new idea to him. We have seen that heredity and early environment had done something to implant within him a love for what he considered the more ornate forms of public worship, as practised in the Church of England, and we have also seen that the tendency of his teaching in the early years of his Arbroath ministry was in this direction. From the time he stood apart from his brethren, and, single-handed took upon himself the role of ritualistic reformer, he became one of the best-abused men not only in his own but in other Presbyterian communities throughout Scotland. Not a few of the changes he advocated, and the "innovations" he introduced which were the cause of bringing him into such disrepute, are now practised by many congregations in Scotland, among these being kneeling at prayer, standing when singing, the use of instrumental music as an aid to worship, reading prayers from a book which contained a series of church services which he had prepared, and the performance of the marriage ceremony in church; making these changes at his own hand without consulting the Church Courts being considered an aggravation of his offence. He did not stop short at making these alterations in the method of conducting the worship in Greyfriars, but by voice and pen he urged their adoption throughout the Church. His contention, however, was that the reforms he advocated were really not "innovations," but, as he explained, they "only tend for the most part to restore those customs and practices which the fathers of Presbytery thought expedient, and which they established and themselves practised."

It is needless here to trace the struggle with the Church Courts on which he had now embarked, and which was carried on with more or less acrimony, and almost without intermission till the day of his death. The whole has been fully and well told by Dr Story in his "Life and Remains of Dr Lee," and need not be repeated here. The contumely brought on him through his "innovating" propensities was not the only cause of his being eyed with suspicion by a number of the "fathers and brethren." It was more than hinted that his teaching and preaching were tinged with Socinianism. This pained him very keenly. It was asserted that from the earliest years of his ministry, his preaching gave evidence of Unitarian leanings. A landed proprietor in the neighbourhood of Arbroath, well known for his godly character and Christian benevolence, who was a member of Inverbrothock Church during Dr Lee's incumbency, and who was then and afterwards an attached personal friend of the doctor's, on being asked by the author whether there was any sign or suspicion of Lee's preaching such doctrines when in Arbroath, indignantly declared that the insinuation was a base one, and that it had no foundation in fact. All the same, these charges and suspicions were for years a source of pain and worry to Dr. Lee. Added to all this, death had time after time entered his dwelling, and had taken one and another of his beloved ones from him. The death of his only son George, a promising young man, which took place at Stirling on 13th September, 1862, was a heavy blow, but the bereavement was softened by the Christian resignation which the sufferer displayed. Writing to his brother in Tweedmouth, two days before his son's death, Dr. Lee says, "I can give you no good news of our dear George as to his outward man, which is hastening rapidly to the dust, and is not far from it to all appearance, but in a more important respect we have every possible reason to be comforted aud thankful, for his behaviour all through his long sickness has been exemplary, and now that he is looking death in the face it is most beautiful, full of humility, patience, resignation, and hope in God. When it arrives, I feel confident that his will be a blessed change. . . . These are bitter dispensations, my dear brother, but we will not let go our confidence in Him who abideth faithful."

In addition to the discharge of his ministerial and professorial duties he took an ample share of other work, taking part in the discussion of many topics of public interest. All this was a pleasure to him, but the turmoil of the Church Courts and the harassing work of defending his position, and the consequent labour of preparing therefor, in the end began to tell on his health. He gives indication of this feeling of worry in an entry in his diary on 28th March, 1867, in which he says: "Finished my twentieth session, having not lost one hour with sickness, though with Presbytery meetings I have lost several. I hope eventually they will be found not to have been lost."

But there was little rest for him on earth; the bickering and fighting went on which eventually wearied him out. The Assembly of 1868 was looked forward to, by the opposing parties in what was known as the Greyfriars' case, as the scene of a decisive battlefield, but to Robert Lee it never came. On the 12th of March, he was a second time struck down by paralysis, and three days thereafter his fearless spirit had taken its flight. Great were the lamentations over him, amongst all classes and conditions of people. To us who view his work at a distance of time, and who in a measure participate in what some of us consider the benefits of the changes in the mode of conducting our Presbyterian worship, of which he was such a persistent advocate, he appears as a man who has done something to leave his mark on the religious thought and life of the Church.

REV. JAMES M'COSH, D.D., LL.D., &c

JAMES M'COSH,

Of the Abbey Church.

JAMES M'COSH, one of the ablest philosophers and profoundest thinkers of the latter half of the nineteenth century, became a minister of the Church of Scotland in Arbroath in 1835. In a letter to the author, written many years ago, when Dr M'Cosh was a professor in Queen's College, Belfast, he says: "Arbroath is a place which must ever be dear to me; there I began my ministry in the church when yet a very young man." Frequently since then he has expressed his love for the old place, and when revisiting Scotland he never failed to spend a day in Arbroath. On his return to America from his last visit to his native land, after referring to the work carried on by him as a minister of the Abbey Church, he writes: "I remember many of my old people, but was deeply affected when I visited Arbroath two years ago to find so very few of them living. Nothing seemed permanent but these rocky promontories, among which I took such pleasure in walking."

The son of a wealthy Ayrshire farmer, James M'Cosh was born on the banks of the Doon on the first of April, 1811. Burns was dead, leaving behind him a rich legacy to future generations; but the romantic scenery of "the banks and braes o' bonnie Doon" which had lent inspiration to the soul of the poet could not fail to make a deep impression on the mind of the future philosopher, as it had done on that of the poet. In after years, when far removed from the land of his birth, the scenery among which he had spent his youth would often rise in vision before him, supplying him with a wealth of illustration, of which he was not slow to avail himself. Carskeoch (hill of the hawthorn), the farm where President M'Cosh spent his boyhood, is in Straiton parish, looking down on the "bonnie Doon." There is a village called Patna, now built near it, with two churches; but in those days there was no village, and the M'Coshs travelled across the moor four miles to the Straiton church on Sundays.

In early youth he gave proof of the possession of that pluck which in later years he more than once found it necessary to exhibit in the intellectual combats in which he took part when defending the tenets of his faith. When about nine years old he on one occasion accompanied his mother to the neighbouring market town. While she was shopping, he, growing wearied of leaning on the counter, was allowed to go to the shop door, but with strict instructions to meddle with nothing. Standing there in all the glory of a new suit of clothes, of which he was the proud possessor, a young sweep, begrimed with soot, espying the little dandy thought fit to mock and tease him for his own amusement and that of other little ragamuffins. It was not easy to endure such insults, so, notwithstanding that the sweep was older and bigger than himself, he fell to, and succeeded in giving him a sound thrashing, much to the amusement of the bystanders, who gave audible expression to their appreciation of his pluck. Not so his mother, however, who, attracted by the crowd outside, found her young hopeful with hands and face nearly as black as the sweep's, while his new suit was rather the worse of the encounter.

After passing through the usual curriculum of the parish school, the teacher of which was Quintin Smith, a man of more than ordinary ability, he was sent at the age of thirteen to the University of Glasgow, where he studied for five years. From thence he passed to Edinburgh University, where he remained for other five years, in each of which he proved to be a diligent and apt student. At Edinburgh, he studied theology under Chalmers and Welsh. Sir William Hamilton was then delivering lectures on civil history and literature, and M'Cosh benefited much by his attendance at these lectures. An essay which he wrote on Stoic Philosophy led to his receiving from the University of Edinburgh the honorary degree of Master of Arts. After the death of his father, his mother removed to a neighbouring farm called Auchenroy, where she lived with an unmarried brother, and on his death she went to reside in Maybole. There she died, and was buried at Straiton. In his probationer days he was very popular in that quarter, and would have been appointed to the Church of Kirkmichael, four miles distant, had the wishes of the people been consulted.

In October, 1835, he was elected minister of the Abbey Church, Arbroath, by a large majority over the other candidates. The previous minister had been deposed for drunkenness, and in consequence there was a considerable distraction in the congregation, but notwithstanding, the settlement was a most harmonious one. The young minister took his position, at once setting himself devotedly to his pastoral work, and by his kindness and independence soon brought the people into harmony. There were about seven hundred communicants on the roll, and, being chiefly a working class congregation, all the stipend they could afford was the modest sum of one hundred pounds, which they afterwards raised to one hundred and twenty.

The Abbey Church, originally a Chapel of Ease, in the progressive movements of the period, had been turned into a *Quoad Sacra* Parish Church, about two thousand people being allotted to the new minister. He visited from house to house, according to the parochial system of Scotland, waiting even on the Dissenters, but disclaiming all jurisdiction over them. He usually spent a day each week in this general visitation, and another day a week in visiting the sick. In this way, he became intimately acquainted with, and was affectionately trusted by his parishioners, and as he had considerable tact in speaking to the families he visited, he soon became a universal favourite, and was lovingly remembered for many a year after he left Arbroath. He organised Sabbath Schools, carefully looking out for competent and pious teachers. His adult class—the special class for young men and women—was largely attended, and was a great success. He prepared for the teaching of this class with the greatest care, and gave instruction of a kind not usually communicated to classes of this sort. His examinations were systematic, calling forth the intelligence of the members of the class, and leading them to read extensively. In instructing and catechising these advanced classes, he was really preparing himself for his higher work in after years in the colleges of Belfast and Princeton. At these classes he got acquainted with the character of the young men and women, and was thus able to deal with them personally, and not a few of these in after years bore testimony to the immense benefits which he was instrumental in conferring upon them. Besides attending assiduously to the various departments of his congregational work, he took an active part in all the movements in the town having for their object the intellectual and moral advancement of his fellow-townsmen.

In June, 1837, M'Cosh very unexpectedly received from the

session-clerk of Old Greyfriars, Edinburgh, a letter asking him to preach there on the following Sabbath, with a view of filling up the vacancy in that church. This was a high compliment to one so young. Than Old Greyfriars few churches in the land had a more interesting history. Here in 1638 *The Covenant*, after prayer and exhortation, was solemnly signed by a multitude of Scotland's worthiest sons of all ranks and conditions. Here in 1679 many of those who had been taken at the Battle of Bothwell Brig were kept as prisoners, and here also more than one distinguished man had held office. It was therefore no little honour to be called to occupy the position of minister of such a church. But besides all this, the young preacher saw that a wide field of usefulness might thus be opened up to him in such an important charge as the successor of Dr Inglis, the leader of the Moderate party in the Church of Scotland, but after seriously weighing the matter, he failed to convince himself that it was his duty to undertake such a responsible charge. In looking back in his later years on this event in his early history, he felt constrained to express his conviction that he had acted rightly in declining the offer, feeling that the work to which he was afterwards called in Queen's University, Ireland, and in Princeton was better suited to him. In the letter which he wrote, declining the invitation, he strongly recommended for the vacant office his friend and neighbour Thomas Guthrie, of Arbirlot, who in due time, as we have seen, was translated to Old Greyfriars.

Although M'Cosh refused to encourage the advances of the Old Greyfriars, other and more influential congregations than the Arbroath Abbey Church had their eyes upon him. In 1838 he was presented to Brechin Parish. Here, as in the case of the Abbey Church, when he was elected to it, the congregation had just passed through a sea of troubles, the previous presentee having been accused of plagiarism, the case dragging a long and weary course through all the church courts, from the Presbytery to the General Assembly. After much bickering and fighting between the opposing factions in "the Ancient City," James M'Cosh was relieved from his Arbroath charge, much to the disappointment of his attached people there, and inducted to the Parish Church of Brechin. The objections on the part of his opponents in the Brechin Presbytery were feeble, and in more than one instance very amusing. As an example of the opposition, it may be mentioned that Mr Harris, the parish minister of Fearn, in contending that they had young men nearer home equally well qualified, proceeded to say that he had statements to make in regard to Mr M'Cosh. With great sorrow did he make these charges—he hoped they were not true—most happy should he be to hear them contradicted. Here the speaker assumed an air of great solemnity, and the audience waited in breathless suspense to hear the awful charges; but the effect may be imagined when he proceeded to say—"It is notoriously well-known that Mr M'Cosh is an anti-patronage man; and moreover, he has not called upon ME, has not given me even five minutes' conversation since he got his presentation!" The announcement of these dreadful accusations caused much amusement to both sides of the house.

As in Arbroath, so in Brechin, James M'Cosh threw himself heartily into his work, and very soon gained the esteem and affection of the congregation. But the times were troublous, and as the charge levelled against him by Mr Harris, that he was an anti-patronage man, was true, he was soon in the heart of the conflict, doing yeoman service to his party. Far and near, but chiefly throughout Angus and Mearns, he addressed crowded meetings, explaining and expounding the position taken up by the non-intrusionists, and when the Disruption was an accomplished fact, he did much to build up and consolidate the newly-formed congregations. Everywhere he was heartily welcomed; and in later years his reminiscences of these exciting times, which he was fond of recounting, were exceedingly interesting. His stories lost nothing of their freshness in the graphic way in which he told them. The district specially assigned to him was a wide one, and lay in the heart of the Grampians at their eastern end. For the various localities in the district it was part of his work to provide preachers, and frequently he had to do duty himself. His journeys were generally made on horseback, and it was no uncommon thing for him to ride thirty miles and preach two or even three times in one day. It was not by the farmers and trades people alone that he was well received; many of the landed proprietors, whether they agreed with his views or not, shewed him marked attention.

Some of his stories of Sir John Gladstone, father of Mr W. E. Gladstone, are worth repeating. At the laying of the foundation stone of one of the new Free churches, Sir John, who had just come down from Liverpool, was riding through among the people assembled to witness the ceremony, observing the apparent pleasure they were taking in the event. Returning to the Castle he wrote to Sir James Graham, the Home Secretary, telling that what he had witnessed that day, had convinced him that a great mistake had been committed. "I have," he said, "passed through the people at the laying of the foundation of their Free church, and I saw among them the great body of my best servants and tenants." And so it was that shortly thereafter Sir James Graham was reported in the *Times* as having in his place in Parliament said, "I have committed the blunder of my life in allowing these people to be driven out of the Church of Scotland."

In one of these journeys he passed a scholarly-looking gentleman walking thoughtfully along the road, and on asking at the first farm-house he came to who this was, he was told that it was "Sir John Gladstone's clever son." Although W. E. Gladstone usually passed his summer holidays at Fasque, this was the first time M'Cosh had seen him. Another day, as M'Cosh was passing an Episcopal Chapel, in course of erection, he stepped in to see it, and as he was there, Sir John and a friend also came in. Continuing a conversation the Baronet, not noticing who was present beside themselves, remarked to his friend, "We would have got on very well in this district had it not been for a young fellow of the name of M'Cosh, who is troubling us very much." But when the excitement attendant on this work of building up and consolidating the new congregations was over, and the Church had in a measure settled down to her ordinary work, James M'Cosh, then the minister of the East Free Church, became a power in Brechin, especially among young men. As has already been shown, he had exercised a powerful influence among the same class in Arbroath.

But while preaching and teaching in the little city of Brechin, he was, in the solitude of his study, preparing himself for the great work of his life. Many articles from his pen appeared in the different theological and philosophical magazines, but that which brought him most prominently to the front was the publication in 1850 of his famous work, "The Method of Divine Government," a production which at once stamped him as one of the foremost philosophical thinkers of the day. It was eagerly sought after by learned men both at home and abroad, the first edition having been sold out in six months. On a Sabbath morning it fell into the hands of the Earl of Clarendon, the then Lord-Lieutenant of Ireland, who was so taken with its contents that he spent the whole forenoon in reading it, and did not manage to get to church that day. His study of the book set him to find out more about its author, the result being that he offered him the Professorship of Logic and Metaphysics in Queen's College, Belfast. The appointment of a Scotchman was looked upon as another "Irish grievance," and a good deal of indignation was expressed. This is commemorated in one of Thackeray's ballads in which Master Molloy Molony in a "pome" of nine verses gives vent to his indignation after this manner :—

> As I think of the insult that's done to this nation,
> Red tears of revinge from me faytures I wash;
> And uphold in this pome to the world's daytistation,
> The sleeves that appointed Professor M'Cosh.
>
> . . .
>
> O! false Sir John Kayne; is it thus that you praych me,
> I think all your Queen's Universitees bosh;
> And if you've no neetive Professor to taych me,
> I scawurn to be learned by the Saxon M'Cosh.

For sixteen years, during which he filled that chair—his lectures embracing metaphysics, ethics, psychology, and logic—his success as a teacher greatly added to his reputation, but what contributed most to spread his fame was the publication while there of his "Intuitions of the Mind Inductively Investigated," a book of which it was said that no philosophic student could afford to be ignorant of its contents. While his best energies were devoted to his professional work, and to his literary and philosophical studies which were most prolific, he did not neglect his duties as a citizen. He took an active part in defending the national system of education. He also rendered considerable assistance in the organisation of the English Civil Service, and took a prominent part in the agitation for the disestablishment of the Irish Church.

One evening in the month of May, 1868, on returning home from his work in Queen's College, he found a despatch awaiting him conveying the announcement that he had been elected President of Princeton College in America, a call that was quite unexpected on his part. The announcement was not at all agreeable to the authorities of Queen's College, who did what they could to induce him to remain where he was. But after carefully weighing the whole circumstances he decided to accept the appointment as he saw in it the acquisition of a wider field of usefulness. When his decision became known there was a feeling of keen disappointment that the services of one, who was acknowledged as a leading representative of the philosophy which had made Scotland famous, should not have been retained in this country. Before settling down in his new sphere he visited the chief seats of learning in Germany and America. On the 27th October, 1868, he delivered his inaugural speech before the trustees, and the faculty and students of Princeton College, and from that day till the 20th June, 1888, when he gave his farewell address on his voluntarily relinquishing the presidency, he not only upheld the reputation of an institution, which for many years before his advent had held a high rank among the educational seminaries of America, but by his profound learning, backed up by the energy and enthusiasm which he brought to bear on his work, he secured for Princeton College a world-wide fame.

Although trained in the Scottish school, Dr M'Cosh from his early manhood followed an independent course, accepting truths from ancient philosophers, from the French and German schools, and from other sources, but bringing all the ideas— their's and his own to the test of reality. His own testimony on this point is interesting. He says, "I am represented as being of the Scottish school of philosophy, I am not ashamed of my country, certainly not of my country's philosophy. I was trained in it. I adhere to it in one important principle. I believe that the truths of mental philosophy are to be discovered by a careful observation and induction of what passes in the mind. Not that our observation and induction gives them their authority, they have their authority in themselves, but it is thus we discover them. But in other respects I differ from the Scottish school. I profess to get my philosophy from the study of the human mind directly, and not from the teaching of others. The Scottish school maintains that we know all the qualities of things. I say we know the things themselves. Hamilton makes our knowledge relative. I make it positive. So I call my philosophy realism, and by help of a few distinctions I hope to establish it." It will thus be seen that there was a thoroughness, and at the same time a freshness, in his teaching which could not fail to gain for him a place in the first rank of great teachers.

Princeton with its theological seminary, and its university or college, under such men as Dr Charles Hodge and Dr James M'Cosh has had a distinguished history. As a seat of learning it has been said of it that if it were transplanted bodily to Britain it would stand a fair comparison with the best of the colleges of the old country. It is told of the late Principal Cunningham who had visited the spot, that on being asked by a student of divinity whether, supposing he went to Princeton for a session, would that be allowed to count as a part of his curriculum. "Count," exclaimed the Principal, "of course it will. My only difficulty is as to whether a session at Princeton ought not to be taken as equivalent to two at home." A native of Arbroath, the Rev. C. A. Salmond, in his "Princetonia," gives a delineation of the character, and an interesting account of the life-work of Dr. Charles Hodge and his son, who have done so much for the theological part of the work carried on at Princeton.

Under Dr. M'Cosh's presidency, the college rapidly increased, not only intellectually, but also materially. Students flocked to it from all quarters, and every year saw a steady addition to the numbers on the roll, the annual attendances growing gradually from two hundred and sixty-four in the first year of his office to six hundred and four in the last. During the same period the teaching staff increased proportionately. In 1868 there were ten professors, four tutors, two teachers, and three extra-ordinary lecturers. To these there was a steady accession, the number in his last year being thirty-five professors and several tutors and assistants, in all a staff of upwards of forty. Along with this increase in the teaching staff, a large addition was made to the scientific apparatus. During President M'Cosh's twenty years of office, through the munificence of various American citizens, immense additions were made to the College buildings—a gymnasium, a library, a school of science, a museum, a chapel, a university hall, and other college buildings, besides a residence for the president, and houses for some of the professors having been provided. But the material was nothing compared to the moral, intellectual, and spiritual growth in the work carried on during his presidency. His resolution on taking office was on the one hand to keep all that was good in the old studies, but on the other hand to place new branches alongside of these, to introduce into the college every department of scholarship and knowledge, and to leave out all that was fictitious and pretentious. How well he succeeded in this is now a matter of history. When he retired from active work in Princeton, he had attained his seventy-seventh year, but in doing so he was able to say, "I leave the college, thanks be to God and man, in a healthy state, intellectually, morally, and religiously." But he did not retire to a life of complete idleness. Such was not his nature. He continued both by voice and pen to serve the cause of philosophy and religion, of which he was a life-long champion.

Outside his professional duties, he took a large share in the work of the church. In the movement for the federation of the churches he took an active part, attending conferences not only in America, but in this country as well. His great aim in labouring for the federation of all the evangelical churches was, that while leaving them as they are in their own ecclesiastical doctrines on forms of polity, they should so blend visibly before men as one great body of believers in the unity of one faith, one God, one Christ, and one common brotherhood of Christian workers together. From this he looked for a larger and far more effective preaching of the gospel in a united church than could ever be attained in a divided one. This he held as the highest development of the church on earth in that large, broad, and benevolent spirit which should characterise its life. He also took a considerable share in the discussions with reference to a revision of the Confession. While declaring emphatically that in any revision he would not take one jot or tittle from the great cardinals of religious truth, as they are formulated in our Confession, he held that the formulas of our faith should not be burdened with what the Romans would call "impedimenta." Our standards should be made as perfect as possible; if the scholars of the seventeenth century have made any imperfect statements it is for the scholars of the nineteenth century to correct them. In carrying out this, he, however, held that there must be the exercise of great carefulness, delicacy, and tenderness. Excessive care, he says, must be taken that every article in thought and language be founded on the Word of God, and be in strict accordance with it. There must be no inferential theology, no speculative process of interpretation. Further, those who subscribe to a creed must do so in good faith. Ministers must be able to believe absolutely what they preach and teach.

Frequently his students, his co-workers, and his many admirers showed their appreciation of the great work he has accomplished in the land of his adoption. On Exhibition Day in June, 1889, after the usual college exercises had been gone through, and the other formalities of the day completed, a mural statue of President M'Cosh, the decennial gift of the class of 1879, was unveiled. The statue, which cost 12,500 dollars, forms the most handsome decennial gift ever made by any class to Princeton College. The doctor is represented as standing beside a reading-desk, on which rests one hand. He is in the act of addressing an audience. The figure is a most impressive one. Placed on the wall of the chapel to the left of the apse it will be, for all time, a lasting tribute to the vigorous administration of Dr M'Cosh. On the attainment of his eightieth birthday he was the recipient not only of the warmest congratulations of all classes, but of numerous presents, the chief of which, a massive silver pitcher, was the gift of former pupils in Princeton, and who were then teachers in various American colleges, who had been under his personal instruction and had graduated during his twenty years' administration.

Along with the wife of his youth, Isabella Guthrie (second daughter of Dr Alexander Guthrie of Brechin, a medical practitioner of considerable repute, and a niece of the Rev. Dr Guthrie), to whom he was married in September, 1845—who had been his companion and solace during his long and laborious life—he spent his declining years in his beloved Princeton, not in idleness, however, for, till nearly the end, he devoted a few hours daily to the studies which had been so dear to him all his life. Till the close of his life his heart continued warm to "Auld Scotland," and this he showed in many ways. In November, 1892, he founded a bursary in connection with the East Free Church in Brechin, in which city he passed some of the pleasantest days of his life. This bursary, which is known as the "M'Cosh Bursary," is founded for the purpose of assisting young men connected with that congregation to prosecute their studies at any Scottish University or theological hall. He also founded a similar bursary, to be awarded annually to the scholar attaining the highest eminence at the Public School of Patna, the village nearest his birth-place. Some years ago, when on a visit to this country, he spent a few days in the home of his youth. Preaching in Straiton Church, at the close of his discourse, he recalled a few incidents of his early connection with the church, and pointed to the pew in which he sat as a worshipper when a boy. Though then his home was far away from Scotland he had still, he said, a warm side to his native parish and to the Old Church round which his fathers were resting, and he expressed the pleasure it had afforded him of saying these things within its walls. In the churchyard, among other monuments, is one in memory of Jaspar M'Cosh, who died in 1729, the oldest member of the M'Cosh family buried there, and on retiring from the church he visited the hallowed spot, and stooping down the aged president affectionately patted the time-worn memorial as he took a final leave of the Auld Kirkyard.

Till the last he also retained a pleasing recollection of Arbroath, where the first years of his professional life were spent. Writing, within three months of his death, to the author of these sketches, with whom he had kept up a correspondence, extending over nearly half-a-century, he remarked, with reference to those of the clerical sketches in this volume, which had previously appeared in serial form, under the title of "Arbroath Ecclesiastics of the Thirties," all of which he had read, "I am glad you have written the lives of these ministers and are keeping up the remembrance of us in Arbroath, in which I still feel an interest. I should have liked," he continued, "to visit Scotland one more summer, but I was afraid of getting a stormy passage going and coming home, and so I have remained in America. I am afraid there are few who remember me in the Abbey Church, but if there be any remember me to them." The letter from which these sentences are extracted was a long and interesting one, and was among the last he wrote. He was then among the White Mountains, in the hope of gathering a little strength for the coming winter, but this hope was not realized; life with him was drawing to a close, and on the 16th November, 1894, he fell peacefully asleep, and was laid to rest, with fitting ceremony, in the cemetery of his beloved Princeton.

REV JAMES LUMSDEN D.D.

JAMES LUMSDEN,

Of Inverbrothock and of Barry.

JAMES LUMSDEN, who like Dr J. M. M'Culloch and Dr Robert Lee, commenced his ministerial career in Inverbrothock Parish Church, was born at Dysart in Fife in January, 1810, the eldest of a family of three sons and two daughters. His father, James Lumsden, was a native of Falkland, but in early life he removed to Dysart, where he joined his uncle, James Dryburgh, in business. His mother, Margaret Oswald, was the daughter of Robert Oswald, shipmaster and shipowner in Dysart. By the death of their father in 1827 the care of the family devolved upon their mother, a woman of quiet energy, great prudence, and deep unobtrusive piety.

On leaving the Burgh School, which was taught by James Maclaren, a good scholar and a very able teacher, young Lumsden, at the early age of fourteen, entered the University of St Andrews, and was thus a contemporary of Robert Lee, whom he followed in the Inverbrothock Church. He took a high place in his classes, especially in that of Moral Philosophy, then crowded by students, eager to listen to the lectures of Dr Thomas Chalmers. He entered the Divinity Hall in 1828, and carried off the first prize in the Hebrew class. During his first session at St Andrews, he formed friendships, some of which continued through life, especially that of Alexander Duff afterwards the famous missionary. He completed his theological curriculum in the University of Edinburgh, to which Dr Chalmers had removed. As a student, he was distinguished for application, ability, and success. In October, 1831, he was licensed by the Presbytery of Kirkcaldy. In 1833, he was chosen as assistant to the Rev. John Bonar, of Larbert and Dunnipace. The population, which consisted chiefly of colliers and workmen at the Carron Iron Works, made the place a good training field for mission work, to which for a time he was afterwards called. His selection for the assistantship at Larbert was an indication that he was even then considered well qualified for the ministry, as Mr Bonar was well-known for the careful selection of his assistants, Lumsden's successor being the saintly Robert Murray M'Cheyne, and Dr Hanna, of Edinburgh, also acted in that capacity. In 1835, a city missionary was wanted in Dunfermline, and for this office James Lumsden was recommended by Dr Chalmers as one " having such enduring worth that he will surely and rapidly grow in the estimation of any people among whom he may be settled, by sound judgment, by scriptural theology, and withal by persevering assiduity in the labour of Christian usefulness." The experience in mission work which he gained in these early years of his life was put to good use towards the close of his days, when he took a deep interest, and an active part, in Home Mission work in Aberdeen.

Through the translation in 1836 of Robert Lee to Campsie, a vacancy occurred in Inverbrothock Church. For the appointment there were three applicants, M'Beth, Lumsden, and Gillis. Considerable diversity of opinion prevailed in the congregation as to who should succeed Lee, a large number of the members favouring M'Beth, while the bulk of the heritors or pew proprietors preferred Lumsden. Great were the bickerings which ensued, resulting in a miniature "disruption." On the matter coming formally before the Presbytery, James Lumsden was found to be duly elected. The supporters of M'Beth, however, were so dissatisfied that they resolved to break their connection with Inverbrothock, and form themselves into a new congregation. In this they were encouraged by a section of the Presbytery, led on by Thomas Guthrie of Arbirlot, and the result was the building of Ladyloan Church and the election of James M'Beth to the pastorate thereof. The action of this section of the Presbytery was not so much antagonism to James Lumsden as the desire to forward the movement for church extension which had been before the country for some years, and which had been strongly advocated by Thomas Guthrie and other members of the Arbroath Presbytery. On the 22nd December, 1836, James Lumsden was ordained minister of Inverbrothock. He entered on his duties with a zeal which soon won for him the affection and hearty co-operation of his office-bearers and members. His pulpit services were most acceptable, and were much appreciated by his people. It was remarked by one well able to express an opinion, that when minister of Inverbrothock he preached in an able and elaborate manner the Calvinistic creed and defended the Confession of Faith in seventeenth century language. Throughout life, he remained an uncompromising Calvinist, but all the same he was ever ready to acknowledge the sincerity of other Christians who differed from him on these points. Under his fostering care the various departments of congregational work in Inverbrothock Church were largely developed. The library, which had been closed for nearly two years was freed from debt, rearranged, about a hundred volumes added to it, and opened for gratuitous circulation in the district, thus in a small way foreshadowing the Free Libraries of the present day.

Thomas Guthrie's call to Old Greyfriars, and John Kirk's transference to Arbirlot, caused a vacancy in Barry. Various names were suggested as successors to Kirk, among these being James M'Cosh of the Abbey, and James Lumsden of Inverbrothock. A majority of the parishioners having indicated a preference for Lumsden, he was recommended to the Crown, and in due course received the presentation. He was inducted to Barry in 1838, but this did not remove him from the Arbroath district. On being settled in Barry he set himself zealously to eradicate, what he considered, existing evils and unseemly customs which prevailed in the district. At that period an annual horse race meeting was held on Barry Links, in connection with which many discreditable scenes were enacted. To rid the district of this annual carnival, Lumsden set vigorously to work, preaching powerfully against its attendant evils and its demoralising tendency, and warning his parishioners to give the races a wide berth, an advice which large numbers acted on. As might be expected, the promoters of these meetings were highly indignant at these attacks on their favourite sport, and retaliated after their own fashion. Notwithstanding all this vapouring, James Lumsden's denunciations had the desired effect; in the year following the race course was almost entirely deserted, and the whole affair thereupon collapsed. Previous to his connection with Barry, Sunday funerals, with their attendant drinking customs, were very common in the locality. Against this custom he rigidly set his face. But old customs die hard, and here he met with strenuous opposition. The Kirk Session, acting on his advice, issued a recommendation to the parishioners that no funerals should be fixed for Sunday except in cases of necessity. At this period party feeling in the church was running high, and anything that could be construed into a *casus belli* was eagerly seized on. Here an opportunity for a fight arose. Lumsden having been asked by a ploughman to officiate at the funeral of his child on a Sunday refused. Out of this refusal arose what became a rather famous case. After playing for a time at cross purposes with the Kirk Session the man was declared contumacious, and the case was referred to the Presbytery. While the ploughman was put forward as the principal, it was well-known that he was only a lay figure, the strings being pulled by the real instigator of the opposition, the factor on the estate on which the man was employed. The case became one of more than local interest and was fought out in the arena of the various Church Courts with great keenness and bitterness. In the interests of the man, an Arbroath solicitor and an Edinburgh advocate were employed, James Lumsden defending his own position with marked ability and legal acumen, and in the end winning his case. Coming out of the court, a solicitor who was present was heard to remark, "Well, I am ashamed of my profession; an Arbroath lawyer and an Edinburgh advocate floored by a country minister!" The result of this case proved the death knell of Sunday funerals at Barry.

While ready to attack prevalent malpractices in the parish he was not slow to discern faults within the Church. Prior to his taking the oversight of Barry congregation it had been the custom to cause parties undergoing church discipline, if not actually to "sit the cutty stool," to do what was equally disagreeable, namely, to be publicly rebuked in the face of the congregation. Against the continuance of this practice the minister of Barry set his face, maintaining that such an ordeal was not only painfully oppressive, but demoralising, and especially so in the case of a sensitive female. His protest was effectual, and this mode of punishment was abandoned. The fruit of his ministerial work at Barry was perceptible for many years after his removal, the Barry folks being noted as hard-headed theologians. Some of his old parishioners still bear testimony to the highly doctrinal, argumentative, and logical style of his sermons. These were prepared with great care, and delivered from memory. It was no uncommon occurrence on a Saturday afternoon to have overheard him, in some sequestered corner, rehearsing his Sabbath sermon with considerable vehemence to the trees and bushes. He took care never to "practise" in the manse, however, at least to the annoyance or inconvenience of the other inmates, nor would he tolerate such conduct in others. On one occasion, on a Saturday evening, when a young minister, who was to officiate on the morrow, vigorously rehearsed his sermon in his bedroom, stumping the floor during the greater part of the night, to the no small annoyance of the household, Lumsden took him severely to task on the Sunday morning. As a preacher and public speaker, he was powerful and logical. His delivery had a pleasant swing and rhythm, combined with a slight nasal twang, but his manner was better calculated to convince than to draw forth the enthusiasm of an audience; he wanted that depth of pathos, quick susceptibility, and burning fervour of preachers of a more nervous temperament to arouse his hearers. Still there are those living who remember some of his more powerful orations, especially about Disruption times, when his oratory rose almost to the sublime.

Fearless in debate, and quick at intellectual fence, he was equally ready to defend his person as he was to defend his principles. He gave an amusing example of this on one occasion. The appointment of a parochial teacher was under consideration; there were two candidates, each aspirant having his own set of supporters, James Lumsden being the leader of one clique, and a landed proprietor of the other. As the minister, so far as argument was concerned, was making the greatest impression, his opponent losing his temper flourished a huge walking-stick, and held it menacingly over the minister's head. Lumsden, not a bit put about, quietly informed his audience that he had also come provided with a similar argument, and drawing forth a ponderous walking-stick he placed himself in a fighting attitude. The humour of the proceeding so tickled the laird that he abandoned his opposition and shook hands heartily with the minister, thus ending what at first threatened to become a disagreeable incident. Although there was a good deal of the stern in his character he was by no means devoid of a keen sense of the ludicrous. No one was fonder of a joke or readier to crack one. On one occasion, at a Presbytery dinner, it was suggested that they should finish up with a round of toddy, but in response to the order, the waiter announced that they were out of hot water, to which Lumsden gravely responded "Well, it's the first time I have known the Presbytery of Arbroath to be out of hot water." Even in church he could see the humorous side of things. One Sunday an old woman, a member of another denomination, thought she would give the parish minister "a hearing." As was her custom in her own church she took her seat on the pulpit stair. It appears that she had a habit of repeating certain passages of Scripture or of the sermon after the minister in a mumbling tone, or even going before him when the context suggested to her any line of thought. Though in a "strange kirk" she could not control herself on this occasion, but did a fair share of the speaking. When descending the pulpit stair at the close of the service, the preacher addressing his visitor said, "Well,——we've got on very well together ; on the whole I think you would make not a bad assistant."

Guthrie, Lee, and M'Cosh having one by one left the locality, Lumsden began to take a prominent part in the business of the church courts. His knowledge of ecclesiastical law, his practical sagacity, his force of character and his strong will, added to a readiness in debate, secured for him the acknowledged leadership of the non-intrusion party in the Arbroath Presbytery. As the battle of parties waged warmer James Lumsden threw himself into the thick of the fight, and few men in the church did more efficient service to their party. He did not confine his energies to his own locality, but here and there and everywhere he lectured, and spoke, and debated, and wrote with a skill and power which won for him the admiration of his friends, aud the execration of his foes. The "conflict" between the contending parties in the church was much the same here as elsewhere throughout Scotland, and is now a matter of history; it is needless therefore to detail the action of the local contingents in the opposing forces. When the Disruption day came it did not bring rest—to the non-intrusionists at least. The battle of the sites had to be fought —and, as will be shewn further on, no more keenly anywhere than in this locality—the new church organisations had to be set agoing, funds had to be raised, and a multitude of other functions had to be performed, and in all these Lumsden proved himself to be a man of energy, skill, and ample resource.

So far as his own parish was concerned, he carried a large majority of the congregation along with him, the attendance at his services—held in an old plash mill which was hastily fitted up for his use—being nearly as numerous as formerly. At the meeting held in Barry Parish Church for the settlement of a successor, Robert Barclay, of Lunan, who presided, called repeatedly on the elders to come forward to sign, raising the pitch of his voice at each call, but with no response. At last one of his co-presbyters whispered to him that there were no elders to sign the call, as they had all gone out with Mr Lumsden, whereupon Mr Barclay brought the meeting to such a sudden close that, in his confusion, he forgot to pronounce the benediction. Probably Barclay was not altogether disappointed when he found so few signatures to the call, as prior to the Disruption, he had always acted with the evangelical party, and professed to hold the principles of non-intrusion and spiritual independence. He was, however, frank enough to confess that he did not care to suffer for these principles. When urged at the Disruption by some of his seceding co-presbyters, to come out, his answer—expressed in his native Doric which he was fond of using—was, " Hoo could I leave my bonnie Lunan," and when told that he would get another charge, he naively remarked, " Wha wid ha'e me ? "

In the Free Presbytery and Synod, as in the Established, James Lumsden naturally took a leading part in the business of the Church. In this he found an able coadjutor in William Wilson, then minister of Carmyllie, afterwards the well-known Dr William Wilson, clerk to the General Assembly. In January, 1843, the " Presbyterian," the organ of the non-intrusion party in Forfarshire, was started. The editorship was for various reasons kept secret, but it was believed on fairly good evidence that these two members of the Arbroath Presbytery were joint editors, and that the heaviest part of the work of conducting the journal devolved on James Lumsden. The paper, which ran for three years, was ably managed and did considerable service to the cause at this important epoch in the history of the Free Church.

Of his acknowledged literary works, his earliest was a treatise on " Infant Baptism, its nature and objects." In this treatise, Alexander Hislop, of the East Church, Arbroath, the learned author of the "Two Babylons," and other works, thought he discovered a tendency to heretical teaching. In the local press and through the Courts of the Church, till the case ultimately reached the General Assembly, he impugned the book. Lumsden defended himself from the charge preferred against him, repudiating the meaning put on some of the expressions by his co-presbyter, but to avoid further trouble he agreed to withdraw the book from circulation.

During his residence at Barry, James Lumsden became acquainted with several young gentlemen who came from Sweden to study Scottish agriculture. The interest he took in them developed into his visiting their country, where he formed friendships with many leading clergymen and professors, with whom he kept up intercourse personally and by correspondence, notwithstanding their fear of him as a Calvinist. One of the results of the knowledge which he thus gained of, and the deep interest he took in, the religious life of Sweden, was the issue of a book entitled, "Sweden: Its Religious State and Prospects," in which he noticed the persecutions then in progress owing to the close connection of the Church with the State. During one of his many visits to Sweden, where he was familiarly known as the "Scotch Professor," the King, in 1871, conferred on him the Order of Knight of the North Star. In later years, although he held no official appointment, he was recognised as a sort of consul-general and Secretary for Sweden in Scotland, it being quite customary for natives of Sweden visiting this country to bring letters of introduction to Dr Lumsden.

While his excellence as a pastor and his great capacity as a leader in Church Courts were locally recognised, his fame travelled far beyond the limits of the Synod of Angus and

Mearns. The Church was not slow to discern the many eminent qualifications he possessed for higher office in her service, so, in 1856, he was elected Professor of Systematic and Pastoral Theology and Early Church History in the College at Aberdeen. To a ripe scholarship he added a clear and concise method of imparting instruction to his classes, and the deep interest he took in the students, not in the mass only, but individually, enabled him to exercise a powerful influence on the intellect and Christian life of the young men committed to his care. Few men were better qualified to deal with those subtle intellectual doubts which often assail the earnest enquirer after truth than was Professor Lumsden, and frequent testimony has been borne to the ready access which his students had to him on such occasions. One of his old students, referring to this, says: — "How approachable Dr Lumsden was to students struggling with difficulties. . . . how willing he was to hear their story; with what patience he could enter into it; with what gentleness he could speak of it and feel, and weigh, and consider it; with what light he was able to surround the matter of difficulty, and to exhibit the various points of it, and to find for his young friends a way out of it—sometimes on a totally different side from that expected, yet by a wholly satisfactory gate some of us who studied with him had abundant opportunity of experiencing." But it was not in the College alone that Dr Lumsden showed his interest in the students. Knowing that many of these young men were far from home and home influences, his interest in them reached beyond the mere duty towards them which he felt he had to discharge as their teacher. In the Young Men's Christian Association and in the Free Church Students' Association he was their "guide, philosopher, and friend." The influence he brought to bear on them in these institutions and as his guests at his own fireside left deep impressions on many of them in after years.

When, in 1864, the office of Principal in the Free Church College was endowed, Professor Lumsden was selected by the General Assembly as the first Principal, an office which he retained till his death. While attending faithfully to his official duties, he did not shirk the responsibilities of citizenship. In the various local missionary enterprises he took an active share, and as a member of the Aberdeen School Board, at a time when more than ordinary skill was required in the adjustment and starting of the educational machinery of the city, his services were eminently valuable. A long, busy, and useful life was suddenly brought to a close. He had attended and taken part in the proceedings of the Synod on 12th October, 1875, but feeling unwell, he was obliged to leave the hall, and during the ensuing night he was seized with illness, which terminated fatally on the Sabbath following. In the death of Principal Lumsden, not only did the Free Church lose one of her ablest and most faithful servants, but Scotland also lost one of her most leal-hearted and patriotic sons.

REV. WILLIAM WILSON, D.D.

WILLIAM WILSON,
Of Carmyllie.

WE have already described the conflict carried on between the different parties in the Church of Scotland in our own locality during "the thirties." We have seen that from 1830 and onwards during that conflict the Arbroath Presbytery possessed some of the ablest young men then in the Church of Scotland. But the very brilliancy of their talents drew the attention of other parts of the country to them, with the result that to one after the other came calls to more important charges. In this way Thomas Guthrie, Robert Lee, and James M'Cosh were removed from Arbroath. But the blanks so made were filled up by such men as John Kirk, James Lumsden, and William Wilson, so that during the whole of the "Ten Years Conflict" Arbroath was never without men of light and leading, men whose scholarship, energy, and perseverance fitted them admirably for assuming the leadership and for carrying on the work and warfare of the Church, with a zeal and ability equal to that which had characterised the men who had preceded them.

Born in 1808 at the homestead of Blawearie in the ancient parish of Bassendean in Berwickshire, William Wilson inherited, in a marked degree, the fighting propensities of the famous borderers whose blood ran in his veins. Blawearie still stands, a shepherd's house, on the north side of the Gordon and

Whitburn road, within a mile to the west of the old ruined kirk of Bassendean. A single thatched house is all that remains, but there had been other buildings in connection with it at the beginning of the century. The name Blawearie is most appropriate, situated, as the house is, in an exposed position, frequently liable to be swept at either end by the north-west and southeast gales which rush with full force through the gully or hope. There were other Blawearies in the same quarter, besides places with equally dismal names, such as Windy Winshiel and Mount Misery. Uninviting although these names appear, in such places have been reared many of Scotland's hardiest sons. Among these uplands William Wilson spent his childhood. He received his elementary education at the school of his native parish, where, from his mental and physical superiority, he not only stood at the head of his classes, but became a recognised leader of his schoolmates in all their outdoor sports. In 1825, he entered the University of Edinburgh, and that intellectual energy and enthusiasm of which he had given such evidence when a pupil at the parish school of Westruther, soon enabled him to take a foremost place in his University classes. It was his good fortune on entering on his college career to fall on a time when Edinburgh could boast of such distinguished teachers as Professor Wilson (Christopher North), Professor Pillans, and Drs Chalmers and Welsh. The mental stimulus which Wilson received from these intellectual giants, so quickened and developed his inner life that he was able not only to pass through his literary and philosophical, but also through his theological course with marked distinction. Among his fellow-students, whom he reckoned as his personal friends, were such men as John Laird, Robert Murray M'Cheyne, Alexander Somerville, Henry Moncrieff, and Horatius and Andrew Bonar

The closest of these friends was John Laird, between whom and William Wilson there sprang up an affectionate intercourse, which was only interrupted by death. Laird and Wilson afterwards became co-presbyters at Arbroath, and both in after years obtained the highest distinction which their Church could bestow; indeed, it is noteworthy that of the coterie of young students just named all attained to the same distinction, with the exception of M'Cheyne, who died young.

Having completed his University career, Wilson was licensed by the Presbytery of Lauder in 1838, and in the following year he was appointed a parochial missionary in Glasgow. While discharging his duties with remarkable assiduity and success, he was urged to undertake the editorship of the *Scottish Guardian*, a bi-weekly paper, the organ of the Evangelical party in the Church of Scotland. Nothing could have been more congenial to one of his recognised literary tastes. He accordingly accepted the post, and entered on his editorial duties with that zeal and sagacity which were so characteristic of the man in his later undertakings. In this work of editorship and consequent contact with the ablest men of his party in the west country, he had an excellent training for the position which afterwards fell to him as a leader in the church courts.

After four years' missionary and literary labour, in both of which positions he displayed an amount of energy and devotion, which were highly appreciated and heartily acknowledged in the west country, he was ordained as parish minister of Carmyllie in the Presbytery of Arbroath. But the settlement was not effected without a keen and bitter struggle between the parishioners of Carmyllie and the Crown, who held the patronage. We noted in the case of Thomas Guthrie the difficulties which beset the path of a probationer with evangelical leanings who became a candidate for an appointment to any charge of which the Crown was patron. In the case of Carmyllie, William Robertson, who had been parish minister for nineteen years, died in the end of November, 1836. Shortly after his death the Home Secretary, in reply to a resident heritor, stated that in any appointment that would be made attention would be given to the wishes of the resident heritors and the people. The parishioners who were deeply imbued with evangelical views were desirous of obtaining as their minister one holding these views. With this end in view it was agreed to support the appointment of James M'Cosh, of the Abbey Church, if he would consent to become a candidate, but M'Cosh did not see his way to accept the invitation. The parishioners then turned their eyes to William Wilson, who, as editor of the *Scottish Guardian*, was well known in the church. He was accordingly invited to preach before them, which he did, and so satisfied were they that out of about one hundred and seventy male heads of families, one hundred and thirty, trusting to the pledges of the Home Secretary, petitioned the Crown to issue a presentation to the parish in favour of William Wilson. The remaining forty who did not sign the petition were not antagonistic to his appointment, but preferred not to interfere. While these negotiations were going on, a letter was received from the Home Secretary intimating that the Government having heard that there were dissensions in the parish had resolved to take the nomination of candidates into their own hands, and that a presentation would not be issued in favour of William Wilson, "however well qualified he may be." They accordingly nominated four candidates of their own, who in due course preached before the congregation.

Thereafter a meeting of the male heads of families was held, Mr Gardyne of Middleton presiding. The roll having been called, there voted for two of the Government nominees, none; for another, four, and for the fourth twenty-nine; while for William Wilson, "the man of the people," as he was locally called, there voted one hundred and nineteen. This was the second time that an overwhelming majority of the representatives of the parishioners had spontaneously and urgently appealed to the Crown as patron for the appointment of William Wilson, and a petition to that effect signed by three-fourths of the male heads of families was forwarded to the Home Secretary.

In reply to this petition a letter was received from Lord John Russell positively refusing to recognise Wilson as a candidate, and at the same time an intimation was sent to the Presbytery that a presentation had been issued in favour of Mr Watson, minister at Embleton, near Alnwick, to be minister of Carmyllie, Watson being one of the two Government nominees who did not secure a single vote at the meeting of parishioners. The indignation of the Carmyllie folks may well be imagined; their denunciations were loud and deep, and the question was asked: "Does the Home Secretary take the parishioners of Carmyllie for a set of clodpolls, and the Arbroath Presbytery for a set of fools?"

The Presbytery soon made it clear that they were no fools. At their next meeting held early in June the presentation was laid before the Presbytery in favour of Mr Watson; but the Presbytery rejected it in respect that more than six months had elapsed between the occurrence of the vacancy and the issue of the presentation, and they resolved to appoint William Wilson, who had been twice petitioned for by a very great majority of the people. After some further fighting, Mr Watson, the Crown presentee, intimated that he would not persevere in his attempt to be inducted, and the Presbytery in virtue of the *jus devolutum* presented William Wilson to the parish, to the pastorate of which he was in due time ordained.

Wilson soon became exceedingly popular in the parish and beyond its bounds. He was not long a member of the Presbytery of Arbroath till he gave evidence of the possession of those qualities which fitted him to take a prominent place among the leaders of the Evangelical party in the Church of Scotland. For the next few years he was one of the busiest members of the Presbytery of Arbroath, delivering lectures, addressing meetings, and writing pamphlets on the all-absorbing topics of the time; and this not in his own Presbytery only, for his services were sought in many parishes throughout the length and breadth of the counties of Forfar and Kincardine.

The party to which Wilson belonged included in its ranks many of the most brilliant intellects of the day, but their most strenuous efforts to roll back the tide of civil invasion of the spiritual liberty of the Church proved unavailing, and the 18th of May, 1843, saw the Disruption of the Church. On that memorable day, the Moderator, after laying the Protest on the table, and, bowing respectfully to the Lord High Commissioner as the representative of Royalty, left the chair, followed by the leaders of the movement. This was expected; what else could they do? But the question naturally arose in the minds of the spectators—What of the crowds of country ministers, who throng the back benches, will they seek to follow? Yes; slowly but deliberately they followed their leaders, leaving behind them, not only the yawning benches of the Assembly Hall, but leaving also their State emoluments, their manses and glebes, with the many pleasant associations which clustered around their happy homes. Whatever may now be thought of the movement which led to the Disruption, no one can deny that the men of that time made a noble sacrifice for their principles. The city of Edinburgh was that day stirred to its depths. As the procession wended its way to Canonmills Hall many a tear was shed by the spectators of the solemn scene. It is told that Lord Jeffrey, who was sitting quietly in his room, when informed that "more than four hundred of them were out," flung the book he was reading aside, and, springing to his feet, exclaimed, "I am proud of my country! There is not another country upon earth where such a deed could have been done!" But among all the four hundred and odd men who had relinquished their livings there was no feeling of regret on that score. They had counted the cost, and were willing to endure hardship for what they considered the honour of their Lord and Master.

In many parts of Scotland the persecutions and sufferings which followed required the greatest Christian faith and fortitude to bear. The proceedings in the parish of Carmyllie are a fair representation of what took place in many parishes throughout Scotland. The persecution of those who were known to favour non-intrusion principles began in Carmyllie before the Disruption took place. As a sample of these persecutions it may be mentioned that at Martinmas, 1842, the factor, acting no doubt on the instructions of the proprietor, refused to pay the stipend of the minister and the salary of the parochial teacher (who had also given in his adherence to the Evangelical party), and it was only after strong remonstrances, and the discovery that he was acting illegally, that the payments were made. But it was not the minister and the dominie only who were made to "thole the factor's snash." Three of the Carmyllie elders, and other farmers and crofters, whose leases expired at Whitsunday, 1843, were informed that these would not be renewed because of their non-intrusion views. Acting on the example set by their superiors, some of the "Moderate" farmers threatened to expel from their houses those cottars who were known to favour non-intrusion principles. But the full force of the storm of persecution set in when the Disruption became an accomplished fact. Six of the farms and pendicles already referred to, the leases of which expired at Whitsunday, were advertised to let, and when the outgoing tenants offered to re-take them, they were told that they could only get a renewal of their leases on condition that they turned their backs on the Free Kirk. Some of them did get renewals ultimately, but these were got at an advanced rent. For some days the Sheriff-officers were kept busy serving summonses of removal on sundry tenants of houses and other holdings, and it was said that in one week upwards of thirty summonses were served in the parish of Carmyllie. As a miserable attempt at a disguise of the motives for serving these summonses, a few were served on persons who had remained in the Established Church, but the parishioners understood very well the meaning of this action. This was manifest from the reception given to a Sheriff-officer by one old woman who had not espoused the non-intrusion cause, and who, when the document was served upon her, exclaimed, "Gae awa', min; I've naething to do wi't; I'm a Moderate!"

As may be readily imagined, the battle of the sites was keenly fought here. In anticipation of the severance of the church from the state, the non-intrusion party applied unsuccessfully to the proprietor for a piece of ground on which to build a place of worship. In their straits, they contemplated petitioning a neighbouring proprietor to grant them a site; but, as such a site, even if granted, would be most inconveniently situated for the bulk of the people, the idea was abandoned. At this juncture, a worthy widow came generously forward and offered her garden as a site, so long as she might have a right thereto, she being only in the position of what might be termed a life-tenant. Her tenancy was based on a promise made by the proprietor that "as long as she lives she will have a house from me." In making the offer of this site, Mrs Gardyne well knew the risk she was running; but she was quite willing, for the sake of the cause, to risk the loss of her all. Her house being in a central part of the parish and not far from the parish kirk, her garden was thus most conveniently situated for the purpose, so her offer was readily accepted. A wooden building was speedily erected on the site thus obtained, and there the congregation met for the first time in September, 1843. This proceeding put the proprietor in a fix. So long as by his dogged silence he prevented the congregation from having a shelter he was pleased, but now that, through the generosity of the poor widow, they had procured a place of meeting, which, though humble, was at least moderately comfortable, he felt that he must either tolerate the church or set himself to destroy it.

To do the latter openly would be detrimental to his reputation; so he fell upon the expedient of offering a site, but in such a locality as, if accepted, would only have the effect of preventing many members of the congregation from availing themselves of the regular opportunity of worshipping there, and thus in a large measure damaging the congregation, the proposed site being on the extreme verge of the parish. As in further proof that the offer was made in no good will to the congregation, there came to Widow Gardyne a summons to remove from her humble home. At first it was thought that this was simply a threat and nothing more. The old lady had lived for nearly seventy years on the estate, and when she got the house she had been promised to have it for her lifetime. That one so aged and helpless, and for no other fault than this, should be forcibly ejected could scarcely be believed. But so it was. At the Whitsunday following the Sheriff Officers, at the instance of Lord Panmure, proceeded to eject her. They found her prepared to submit with becoming firmness and resignation. The neighbours drew near to see the strange sight—the officers of the law, at the bidding of him who boasted that his motto was "Live and let live," casting out to the highway the furniture of the widow of one of his old and respected tenants. The old lady bore her part in the scene with great calmness and dignity, counting it an honour to suffer for what she believed to be the cause of Christ. Willing hands stored the furniture in a neighbouring barn, and she herself found refuge in the house of a friend till her removal to Arbroath could be effected. Thus getting rid of the widow he at once interdicted the congregation from worshipping in the wooden erection in her garden, and so they were once more driven to the roadside. Here again they worshipped, in the open air in fine weather and in a canvas tent as the winter came on. This was all very well when the days were moderately quiet, but in wet and boisterous weather they could not erect their tent. On such days they were thankful to find refuge in a barn at the Mains of Carmyllie. Not only was the congregation thus deprived of a settled place of worship, but William Wilson was refused a house to live in, and was glad to accept a residence at the old farm-house at Westhaven, seven miles from the scene of his labours.

During all this time he was not only preaching with

enthusiasm, but was actively engaged in building up the church in the district, and thus not only by his voice, but also by his pen, doing yeoman service to the cause. His people were proud of their minister, as one of them tersely put it, "Oor minister can haud the gully o'er the dyke to ony ane o' them." A story is told of this period when the congregation was worshipping in the barn. It was a very stormy Sabbath day, and the folks were on their way to the service when, as usual, they met a number of their fellow parishioners making for the Parish Kirk. One of the latter, accosting a Free Kirk elder, remarked "Weel John, ye're awa' to the barn to get a thrashin'," alluding to the reputed severity of Wilson's preaching. "Na, na," said John, "the thrashin's ower, and we're noo at the dichtin' (winnowing); do ye no see the chaff blawin' doon yonder," pointing to the Parish Kirk. It was not considered enough to eject Mrs Gardyne. Lord Panmure's agent, in writing to William Wilson, under date 20th May, 1844, says, "I think it right to inform you that Lord Panmure will consider every erection found on the ground let to Mrs Gardyne at Milton of Carmyllie as his own property after Monday 27th instant, and will treat it accordingly." To this paragraph Wilson, in his reply of 27th, remarks, "you tell me that Lord Panmure will consider our church as his property after this day. We cannot help it. It is hard that a building, for the erection of which, out of our deep poverty, we willingly contributed, should be forcibly seized and the rightful owners expelled from it. But we cannot meet force with force. Lord Panmure is too powerful for us, and we must patiently bear what we cannot shun. His Lordship will not be greatly enriched, either in property or in character, by his dealings with us in this matter. I believe most of us are prepared to take 'joyfully the spoiling of our goods.' To yourself, in the way of remonstrance and warning, I would say that you will not find it good to be an instrument, however humble, in forcing from their possession the widow and the fatherless, and in denying to a people the highest right which God and nature alike claim—the right of worshipping according to the light of our own consciences." This wooden erection was not immediately pulled down, but the congregation were interdicted from using it, and, as already mentioned, they were once more driven to the roadside.

The bitter struggle of the earlier stages of which we have here attempted to give a feeble outline, continued without abatement till 1845, when at last a suitable site was obtained, and William Wilson, and his congregation, were allowed to worship God in peace. But while this was so, the neighbouring parishes of Arbirlot and Panbride—which had also to bear similar hardships at the hands of the same site-refusing proprietor—did not find rest for a considerable time after the Carmyllie affair was settled. While this struggle was going on, the "Arbroath Central Congregation," as it was then called, but now known as the East Free Church, gave a call to William Wilson to become their pastor, but neither he nor the Presbytery would accede to this request, as they could not think of his deserting the Carmyllie congregation in their time of trouble. So he continued in Carmyllie till 1848, when he was called to the Mariner's Church (now Free St. Paul's), Dundee.

It is chiefly with William Wilson's connection with Arbroath that we have here to deal, but it is needful to add that his after career was such as might have been looked for in one, the early years of whose ministry were marked by so much strength of will and enthusiasm, tempered as these qualities were in so remarkable a degree by great wisdom and sagacity. While exceedingly cautious, his was not a standstill policy. He advanced with the age, and was quite open to the influences of the times, and was thus all the better fitted for the post of a prudent leader in the current controversies.

In Dundee, he was early recognised as an able, attractive, and polished preacher, and he soon gathered around him a large and influential congregation. As a citizen, he took a leading part in the various organisations, having for their object the moral and social well-being of the community. He took a deep interest in Mission work, and his services in this respect so drew the attention of the church to his capacity in the management of this branch of Christian endeavour, that it led to his election to the important office of Convener of the Home Mission Committee of the Free Church, an office which he held for ten years. When we consider that in his younger days he was a most prolific writer, and even in later life made important contributions to periodical literature, it is to be regretted that he left behind him so little of permanent value. Besides two volumes of sermons, his chief work was a memoir of Dr Candlish.

In 1866, the Church conferred on him her highest gift, that of Moderator of the General Assembly, an office which he filled with great dignity and with marked ability. In 1870, the University of Edinburgh conferred on him the degree of Doctor of Divinity. In 1875, he was elected to act, along with Dr Rainy, as joint convener of the Sustentation Fund Committee, and in 1877, he was unanimously chosen to fill the important post of Secretary to that Fund. This appointment necessitated his withdrawal from the active ministry of Free St. Paul's and his removal to Edinburgh, but he continued his connection with the congregation as *emeritus* minister till his death. In 1868, he had been elected Junior Clerk to the Assembly, and in 1884, he was appointed Principal Clerk in succession to Sir Henry Moncrieff. To a thorough knowledge of Church history and ecclesiastical law, Dr Wilson added business qualifications of a high order, all of which rendered him eminently qualified for these important offices. He died in Edinburgh on the 14th January, 1888, at the ripe age of eighty, and in his death, the Church lost one of her noblest and most devoted servants.

JAMES BOWMAN LINDSAY,
Of Carmyllie

(ELECTRICIAN AND LINGUIST.)

IN the early years of the present century there might be seen almost weekly, a slender lad trudging along the road from Carmyllie to Arbroath with a web of linen slung over his shoulder, and a book in his hand. This youthful weaver-student was destined in later years to make for himself an honoured name in the literary and scientific world.

James Bowman Lindsay was born in Carmyllie on the 8th September, 1799. The rudiments of his education were acquired at the Public School of his native parish. At the close of the eighteenth century the income of the Parochial Schoolmaster of Carmyllie was a very meagre one, not exceeding twenty pounds sterling a year. But even in these days the parishioners, who have long been acknowledged as a hard-headed race, had begun to show a desire to improve matters in this respect. With this view, they subscribed among themselves a sum sufficient for the building of a schoolhouse, and otherwise made decent provision for the maintenance of a fairly-well qualified teacher. It was not, however, so much to the ability of the schoolmaster as to the studious habits of the scholar that young Lindsay made so rapid progress with his learning. When he left school it was necessary that he should find suitable employment with the view to earn a living, but in these days in a country place the choice was very limited. Being of a delicate constitution, he was unfit for the physical exertion required from the ploughman, the blacksmith, or the joiner, so he was apprenticed to the weaving trade; but though he had left school he did not leave off his studies. These he pursued with redoubled diligence, his books being seldom off his loom as he drove the shuttle, or out of his hand when the clatter of the loom had ceased; and, even as we have seen, the book was his constant companion in his periodical visits to the town.

Discerning the bent of his mind, his parents very wisely encouraged him in the prosecution of his studies, and with this view he was sent, in his twenty-second year, to the University of St Andrews. As a self-taught student, his favourite subjects had been mathematics and physical science, and so much had he profited from these home studies that he was able on entering on his college career to take a foremost place in these departments. During his earlier university vacations he returned to Carmyllie and resumed his work at the loom, but latterly he employed the recess in the more congenial work of teaching. At first he had some thoughts of entering the Church, so when he had completed his first four years' course, he entered as a student of theology in the Divinity Hall of St Andrews. If, however, he had ever seriously entertained the intention of adopting the church as a profession he never carried it out, his inclination leaning more to scientific pursuits than to theological studies. On the completion of his university course he took up his residence permanently in Dundee, where he entered on the profession of teaching, in which vocation he was eminently successful. He did not, however, allow his duties as a teacher to interfere with his scientific investigations, but continued to pursue them with untiring energy. In the course of these investigations he set himself among other things—to rectify, adjust, and verify the dates of outstanding events in ancient history, the outcome of which was the publication, in 1858, of his "Chrono Astrolabe," a book which attracted the attention of the most eminent scientific men of the day, and in the preparation of which the author spent nine or ten years.

It is claimed for him that he was one of the first, if not the very first, to make the important discovery of the electric light. So early as 1831, he had turned his attention to the subject, and in 1835, he succeeded in obtaining a constant and steady electric light, a full description of which appeared in the local newspapers of the time. In 1845—a dozen years before the project was seriously entertained—he propounded a scheme for connecting this country with America by means of electricity. Although the honour of being the originator of the idea of an electric telegraph between the two countries was claimed by an American, James Bowman Lindsay was really the first to propose it, and to show its practicability. In later years, he advocated the establishment of electrical communication through the water without wires, and in demonstration of the feasibility of the scheme, he succeeded in sending messages across the Tay at Glencarse, where the river is about half-a-mile broad.

His great work, on which he laboured for many years—having begun it in 1828, and continued it till his death in 1862—was his Pentecontaglossal Dictionary, a dictionary in fifty languages. It is understood that he originally intended this work to contain the equivalents of at least one hundred different languages, but ultimately he confined it to fifty. This wonderful polyglottal dictionary was in October, 1894, handed over for preservation to the Trustees of the Albert Institute in Dundee. The MS. is contained in one volume of upwards of one thousand pages, having special ruled lines for the various languages, and columns with head lines for the English words interpreted. It is a perfect marvel of philological research.

This remarkable man was as modest and retiring as he was laboriously studious. Though frugal in his habits, and simple in his mode of living, he never managed to acquire much means. What he did acquire usually went in the purchase of rare books, and in the furtherance of his favourite studies. In 1858, Her Majesty, on the recommendation of Lord Derby, granted him an annual pension of £100 in recognition of his learning and extraordinary attainments, but he did not live long to enjoy it, having died on the 24th June, 1862.

Rev. PATRICK BELL, LL.D.

PATRICK BELL, LL.D.,

Of Carmyllie

(INVENTOR OF THE REAPING MACHINE.)

THE rapid progress which mechanical invention has made in the present century, has quite revolutionized the methods of carrying on the world's work. The number of labour-saving machines which have been produced, is something marvellous. Almost every department of industry has been benefited thereby, but none more so than that of agriculture.

Those who are old enough to remember the droves of Highland and Irish peasantry who, forty or fifty years ago, flocked to this and other quarters of the country every year to assist in harvest operations, will see a mighty contrast between then and now. "The Hair'st Rig," a humorous poem written by a Lothian farmer, in 1786, gives a graphic picture of the hard work and merry sayings and doings of the harvesters of the olden days. In those days, and for long after, there was no difficulty in finding harvest hands, for not only was there this large influx of Highland and Irish labour, but many of the villagers and town's folk—the shoemakers, the tailors, and the handloom weavers with their wives and daughters were always ready to "tak' a hairst."

Patrick Bell, the inventor of the reaping machine, was born in 1801, at the farm of Mid Leoch, in the parish of Auchterhouse, of which farm his father was tenant. He obtained his elementary education at the parish school of Auchterhouse, and, after being for a time under the tuition of a Mr Horne at Murroes, he entered the University of St Andrews, where he went through the usual course of Arts and Divinity. After being licensed as a preacher in connection with the Church of Scotland, he became tutor to Charles Baillie—afterwards Lord Jerviswoode—one of the Senators of the College of Justice. Here he formed a friendship with some of the members of that distinguished family which lasted during the remainder of his life. In 1833 he went to Canada as tutor to the family of a Scotch resident of the name of Ferguson, where he remained till 1837. Fergus, the residence of Mr Ferguson, was very much in the "backwoods" in those days. While resident there, Bell did not forget the main object of his life—the preaching of the Gospel—but took every opportunity to expound the Word of God in the neighbourhood.

After returning home he spent the interval in teaching, and in 1843, when the Parish Church of Carmyllie was left vacant by the relinquishment of the charge by the previous incumbent, William Wilson, who had thrown in his lot with the non-intrusion party, Patrick Bell was presented to the parish, and in that parish he spent the remainder of his life.

From boyhood he had a taste for mechanics, and was fond of tools. But in these days, to him at least, tools were not so easily got. Necessity, however, is said to be the mother of invention. So it was that to get a cutting tool he had to set his wits to work, with the result that he made a handy instrument out of an old hoop. In many other directions he showed his ingenuity. When quite a young man he made a ton of sugar from beetroot which he had grown, and he sold it at the rate of £40 a ton. To produce it, he had to make, and in some respects to invent, his apparatus. He also about this time illuminated his father's house with gas.

His love for mechanics followed him to the manse. There he had his workshop fitted up, in which he made nearly all the manse furniture, including a handsome sideboard and dining table. He also brewed his own beer, and manufactured his cheese from an improved churn of his own making. Receiving an afternoon visit from three of his co-presbyters, he set one to grind the coffee in a coffee mill of his own handiwork, the chicory having been grown in the manse garden; the other two he despatched to the attic to work a mill he had erected there to reduce his wheat to flour for scone-making, his guests having thus had to bear a share in the preparation of their afternoon refreshments. When the evening fell, the dining-room was lit up with a candle of his manufacture, the candle being about four inches in circumference, had a considerable illuminating power, and from its unusual bulk had to be accommodated in a ponderous candlestick which he had turned for the purpose. The neighbouring farmers' wives were ever welcome to bowls, "caps," and other wooden kitchen utensils, the produce of his turning-lathe. With these and such like occupations he employed his leisure time as a country minister.

But to go back to the story of the reaping machine. In early youth, both from observation and experience, he became painfully aware of the severe nature of the toil of the harvest workers, and having, as we have seen, a predilection for mechanics, it occurred to him that there was a possibility of performing at least a portion of the work by horse power, through the medium of machinery. But the more he pondered, the greater appeared the difficulties to be overcome. One evening, however, while walking in the garden, his eye fell on a pair of gardeners' shears. Seizing this, he commenced to snap at the twigs of the thorn hedge. Not content with this, he brushed through the hedge into a field of young oats, and there, with the shears, he commenced to cut right and left. For weeks and months after this, by night and by day, a-field or in his study, or when lying awake during the night, his mind was full of the subject on which he kept continually ruminating. Method after method presented itself, till, at length, in 1827, while he was still a divinity student, he evolved a plan which eventually resulted in the construction of a rude model—the precursor of the reaping machine which still bears his name.

Having had no regular mechanical training, and being without the requisite tools to work out his idea, a very difficult task lay before him; but with an energy and perseverance, begotten of a strong conviction that he had made a discovery, which, if carried to a successful issue, would so revolutionize the work of the harvest field as to mitigate the excessive labour of the cultivator of the soil and promote the speedier ingathering of the crops. His first step was to construct a model in wood, and it was while making his little wooden frame and tiny cutters that the idea of a sloping canvas for conveying the cut corn to the side occurred to him. His model finished, the next step was to have a machine constructed on a sufficiently large scale for practical purposes. Having made his calculations as to dimensions, and cut out pieces of board to the various sizes and shapes, he fitted them together, thus making his frame. In the same way he formed his cutters of wood, sending them bit by bit to the neighbouring smithy, with instructions to the blacksmith to make things of iron exactly like the wooden models. When he got these from the smith they were in a rude state; but by dint of hammering and grinding and filing, he managed to make them fit into their respective positions. This, however, was no easy task, but at length he had the satisfaction of seeing the machine in what he considered a workable condition. All this was done with as much secrecy as possible. But the student's visits to the smithy and his mysterious doings in his little workshop excited the curiosity of the ploughmen on his father's and on the neighbouring farms, and there was consequently frequent peering into his sanctum, and much speculation as to what it was all about.

The next thing was to test the efficiency of his rude machine; but to do this, and yet to preserve secrecy was no easy matter. The scene of operations of this testing process was the outhouse, which he had appropriated as his workshop, and the day chosen for the trial was a quiet one when most of the farm-folks were afield. By the help of a wheelbarrow, he conveyed a quantity of earth into his workshop, spreading it on the floor to the depth of six inches, compressing the loose mould with his feet. This done, from an old stack in the farm-yard he drew a sheaf of oats. Carrying it to his newly-formed field on the floor of his workshop, he planted the oats therein, stalk by stalk, at about the same distances as they had been when growing. Barring the door to keep out intruders, and all being in readiness, he went behind his machine, pushing it forward through his improvised field of oats. This required a considerable force, which nearly took away his breath. On pausing to see the result, he was gratified to find that the cutting part of the process had been well done; but the grain was lying in such a "higgeldy-piggeldy" state as would have disgraced a regular harvest field. The cutting, however, was perfect; and thus, so far,

x

his invention was a success; but yet it was only a cutting machine, and nothing more. His ambition was not satisfied: he must achieve more than this. So he again set to work. His machine must be so constructed that, besides cutting the grain, it should deliver it in an orderly condition; in fact, it must be a reaping machine—not a cutting machine only. So, putting the rollers in position, adjusting the wheels for driving and stretching the canvas on the rollers, he thought all was right; but, on pushing the machine forward only the length of the house, he found the canvas twisted, and on the point of being torn to shreds. He next proceeded to make grooves at the end of the rollers, in which he placed a small rope, and to this he sewed the canvas, expecting that the ropes and the canvas would move simultaneously. Not so: the ropes, from inequality in the grooves, moved irregularly, and the canvas was twisted as before. At first, he was nonplussed and dispirited; but, setting his mechanical wits to work, he bethought him of trying pitched chains instead of ropes; and having made a pattern chain from a piece of old hoop iron, the services of the blacksmith were again called in, with the result that a chain was prepared, and affixed to the machine, and all was in readiness for a third attempt. The wheelbarrow was once more in evidence, the old stack was requisitioned, the dibbling process gone through, and all made ready for the reaper. Pushing with might and main through his indoor field, to his inexpressible joy, the oats were not only nicely cut, but were laid in perfect order alongside of the machine, ready for the binder. This was in 1828. But the harvest was not yet, and it was needful that he should possess his soul in patience till he could experiment in earnest when the grain was ripe for the operation. Meantime he had discovered a flaw, for, though elated with his success so far, he was quite conscious that his machine was not yet perfect. He had noticed that even in the calm of his artificial field some stalks had capriciously straggled in different directions, so, to remedy this, he constructed what he called his reel or collector. All being in readiness, he longed for the day when he should be able to bring to a practical test the offspring of his brain.

The day has come! no, not the day; day shall not behold it yet, the trial must be by night when none except himself and his brother George shall witness the success or failure of his invention. The long-wished-for night has arrived.

"The hour approaches . . . .
That hour o' night's black arch the Key-stane."

The "farm town" has gone to bed, and all is still; the brothers steal out of the house not even daring to speak to each other except in whispers. Taking the machine from its hiding place, and yoking the good naig "Jock," they quietly wend their way to a field of standing wheat where the machine is set in motion; the inventor goes before to direct operations, while brother George guides "Jock." They have not gone far—not many yards, when a halt has to be made. Something is wrong. Again, as at the first trial on the miniature field on the workshop floor, the grain is well cut, but it lies in a heap before the machine. For a moment both men are cast down—is this the outcome of all our toil? Ah! stupid, we have forgot to bring the reel. Running across the field as fast as the darkness will allow, the inventor soon finds his missing gear, and hoisting it on his shoulder hurries back to the field. Having made his attachments, "gee up, Jock," away goes the reaper, the wheat is now cut and laid beautifully along-side; and the sight sends a thrill of joy to the heart of the youthful inventor. Such is briefly the simple story of his difficulties and how he overcame them, as told by Dr Bell at a meeting of the British Association held at Dundee in 1867.

The reaping machine so constructed was at once put to practical use on his father's farm, where, afterwards, and at his brother's farm of Inchmichael it continued to produce excellent results for many years, and as might be expected it attracted considerable attention. Very soon after its invention it was introduced into the Arbroath district, a public exhibition and trial of its capabilities having been held on the farm of Panlathy in September, 1830, the machine used on this occasion having been manufactured by John Petrie, Salmond's Muir. The wheat in the field where the trial was made was in many places considerably lodged, but this circumstance did not materially mar the efficiency of the reaper, the cutting, collecting, and laying down having been accomplished to the entire satisfaction of a large assemblage of Forfarshire agriculturists.

That it did not come immediately into general use may be accounted for on various grounds. Among others, it has been alleged that the reaping machine, even at that period, had come somewhat before its time. In the early years of the century, furrow-draining, levelling, high ridges, and filling up old deep intervening furrows were only beginning to assume their due prominence in the practice of agriculture, and so long as these improvements remained in abeyance, the surface of the land was ill-suited for the operations of the reaping machine. Besides this, manual labour was neither so scarce nor so costly as in the years that followed, and so the demand for mechanical aid was not then so pressing as it afterwards became.

The attention of British agriculturists was drawn to the importance of the reapers as a powerful aid to harvesting operations when, at the Great Exhibition of 1851, the rival American reapers of M'Cormick and Hussey were exhibited. For a time their respective merits were keenly discussed, and trials of their capabilities made at various parts of the country.

At this juncture, James Slight, the curator of the Highland Society's models, in an able paper—to be found in the transactions of the Society, 1851-53—after tracing the history of the various reaping machines, and narrating and describing those brought out during the first half of the present century, drew special attention to the one invented by Patrick Bell of Carmyllie in 1828, and for which he had gained the Society's premium of fifty guineas. In this article, Mr Slight, who was a most competent authority on the subject, speaks of "the perfection of Bell's reaper." He mentions that, shortly after its invention, four reapers had been sent to America, and he said that he considered it highly probable that these became the models from which the so-called American reapers have since sprung. Whether this was so or not, it is certain that a description of the machine had found its way to America very shortly after the date of its invention. In the quarterly *Journal of Agriculture*, published in August, 1828, there appeared a plan of Bell's reaper and a minute description of every part of it; so full and minute, indeed, that any ordinary mechanic, without difficulty, could have constructed a machine from the details therein given. Again, in 1830, an article, descriptive of the machine, from Bell's own pen, appeared in the *Gardeners' Magazine and Encyclopædia of Agriculture*. These papers found their way, in the ordinary course, to America, and it is a remarkable fact that it was a considerable time after these papers had been circulated there that the Americans took up the idea and commenced the construction of reaping machines. In an American publication in 1834, it is stated "that, however, after the trial and notice of Bell's machine, several individuals in different parts of this country (America) gave attention nearly simultaneously to getting up reaping machines."

At the Great Fair held in New York in 1851, no fewer than six reapers were exhibited by different firms, each claiming to be a special invention, yet in all of them, as Mr Slight shows, the principal feature—the cutting apparatus—bears the strongest evidence of having been copied from Bell's machine.

At the Highland Society's show held at Perth in August, 1852, Bell's machine was successfully put into competition with its American rivals. Immediately following on this, Hugh Watson of Keillor, one of the foremost agriculturists of the day, in conjunction with George Bell, gave a challenge to the makers of the other reapers then attracting attention, for a sweepstake of fifty sovereigns each, to test the merits of the different machines. Judges were selected from among the most competent authorities in Scotland, England, and Ireland. The trial took place at Mr Watson's farm of Keillor on 4th September, 1852. Only three reapers appeared on the field—Hussey's, as improved and exhibited by Croskill; a similar machine, with some important improvements, exhibited by Lord Kinnaird; and the old original reaping machine invented by Patrick Bell of Carmyllie, which had been worked by his brother, George Bell, on his farm of Inchmichael for upwards of twenty years. Another machine, constructed by an ingenious mechanic at Invergowrie, near Dundee, was also expected, but it had met with an accident on the previous evening. Mr M'Cormick was present, but the machine which bore his name was not brought forward.

Mr Croskill's agent, who superintended the Hussey machine, stated before the commencement of the competition that after the decision of such a high and competent tribunal as the Highland Society at Perth, and after witnessing a previous trial of the machine, Mr Croskill considered that it would be useless to contend against Bell's machine any longer, as he considered it a far superior and more effective implement than any he had yet seen, but that he would give every assistance to work the "Hussey" for the satisfaction of the large and influential body who had assembled.

The contest was entered on. The report of the judges is very interesting. After giving a minute description of the ground, the nature and condition of the crop to be operated upon, and the various difficulties with which the machines had to contend, the report goes on to give a detailed account of the manner in which each performed its function. With regard to the relative merits of the different reapers, the judges declared that two of them were imitations of, but not improvements on, Bell's, and this they showed by reference to various parts of the mechanism of the respective machines. The report concludes in these words—"We have no hesitation in pronouncing Mr Bell's to be the best and most effective reaping machine that has yet been submitted to our notice: That it is superior in every respect, both in principle and practice, to any of its rivals, which, in our minds, are only humble and defective imitations of the original, and it is not only deserving the confidence of the farming classes of these countries, but likely, even in its present form, and under proper and judicious management, to be a powerful auxiliary in saving the vast and priceless crops of this country, which, from obvious reasons, are becoming more precarious and difficult every successive season. We cannot, however, close this most interesting and important investigation without expressing the deep obligation which we owe, in common with the country at large, to Mr Hugh Watson of Keillor for the energy and zeal he has displayed on this occasion, not only in procuring tardy justice to the merits of Mr Bell, the now undisputed inventor of this most important implement, but also for the vast and inestimable benefit he has conferred upon the whole community by asserting its utility at this most critical and eventful period, and by securing the confidence of the public in its use, to prepare them to meet those fluctuations in the labour market, which are becoming daily more inevitable." Thus, after nearly a quarter of a century of comparative neglect, was this important implement brought into prominence, and placed in the forefront of all its imitators, the value of the invention being publicly acknowledged.

That Bell occupied the same position in relation to the reaping machine as Watt did to the steam engine cannot be denied. All the reaping machines that were invented before the days of Bell turned out to be failures, and it was his invention that rendered them serviceable, just as in the case of Watt with the steam engine. Even to this day, the improvements made on reapers are merely modifications of the original machine invented by Patrick Bell, as the improvements on the steam engine have been but modifications of Watt's engine.

By the invention of the reaper, Dr Bell did more than revolutionise the work of the harvest field. He inaugurated an entire change in the system of the agriculturist. His invention led the way to others of equal importance. If the grain could be cut down and gathered in by machinery, why could not other parts of the farm work be performed by mechanical means; and so, by degrees, at first slowly and then in rapid succession, came the many machines which now perform nearly every department of agricultural work.

The benefits conferred by Dr Bell's invention were not confined to his native land; but England, Ireland, America, and the Continent of Europe participated in the boon. While this was so, and while Dr Bell was gratified by the acknowledged success of his invention, pecuniarily he had reaped no advantage. Had he patented the machine, which his modesty prevented him from doing, the inventor might have made a fortune. It was an open secret that Lord Panmure offered him the requisite sum to enable him to procure a patent, and an offer was also made by a machinist who wished to purchase the patent after it had been recorded. Both these offers he respectfully declined. But he was not allowed to go unrewarded. In 1867, a movement, inaugurated by the Highland and Agricultural Society, to present him with a tangible token of the gratitude of the nation was set on foot, and at the half-yearly meeting of the Society held at Edinburgh in January, 1868, Dr Bell was presented with a piece of silver plate and £1000, the salver bearing that the presentation was made "by a large number of his countrymen in token of their appreciation of his pre-eminent services as the inventor of an efficient reaping machine, constructed in 1827."

The presentation was made in a highly eulogistic speech by the Marquis of Tweeddale, K.T. The congratulations of his Arbroath neighbours on this occasion were fully as much appreciated by him as the encomiums of the members of the Highland Society. The University of St Andrews conferred on him the degree of LL.D., but so modest was he that he was very averse to accept the honour. It was only on being strongly urged by a friend in Arbroath to do so that he intimated his acquiescence in the resolution of his Alma Mater. He died on the 22nd April, 1869.

DAVID MILLER.

DAVID MILLER

(AUTHOR OF "ARBROATH AND ITS ABBEY.")

"OF making many books," saith the Preacher, "there is no end." While of the nineteenth century this is pre-eminently true, it appears astonishing that it was not till the latter half of the century that a beginning was made in the making of a book, which should give an account of the ancient Abbey of Arbroath —one of the most important institutions of the kind in the kingdom—and of the busy little town which existed before the Abbey was founded, and which during these seven centuries has grown around its walls. In "Arbroath and its Abbey," which was published in 1860, we have the first popular history of the burgh and its belongings. Scattered here and there over many publications could be found incidental references to the outstanding events in national history, in which Arbroath has played so prominent a part ; but no connected narrative of these events, or of others of a more local nature, had previously been written. Consequently, Miller's book, on its appearance, was welcomed as a most valuable contribution to the history of the town and the ancient monastery with which it specially deals, as well as to the ecclesiastical history of the kingdom at a most important period. The Chartulary of the Abbey, published some years before by the Bannatyne Club, while of immense value to the historian and the antiquary, was of little use to the general reader. What was desiderated was a popular history of the Abbey and the town. To the laborious research, the antiquarian enthusiasm, and the literary skill of David Miller, we are indebted for a work which has thrown a flood of light on the early history of the Abbey and the burgh, a book which has taken its place among the standard literature in its own department.

While Miller acknowledges the recently-published Chartulary as the basis of his work, it is quite evident that he brought to bear on its production and elucidation a mind well-furnished by long years of study in legal and antiquarian lore. A careful examination of the old burgh records, taken along with what he found recorded in these monastic writings, has enabled him to present his readers with a vivid picture of the manners and customs, not only of the monks of old, but also of the honest burghers of a byegone day. In speaking of the Chartulary, Miller pronounces it as perhaps the completest specimen of records of one of the most complete monastic establishments in the kingdom, exhibiting, as it does, a full register of charters from kings and nobles down to private burgesses; of papal bulls, grants, and concessions of every description in favour of the convent, during a period of three centuries and a half. This being so, it will be seen what a valuable repository of information he has had from which to draw his supplies. That he has made a splendid use of his material will be admitted by all who peruse his volume. He has also, as already indicated, been largely helped in the elucidation of his subject by his intimate acquaintance with the contents of the old Burgh records. His book does not profess to deal with the history of modern Arbroath; Miller has left this to later writers, but to him these later historians are deeply indebted, as his work, so full and so accurate in its own department, has saved them a great amount of original research.

It is impossible in this short sketch to follow Miller in his numerous interesting details. In the opening chapters, he deals with the introduction of surnames, the material changes in the pronunciation of the names of towns, farms, streams, and muirs during the last seven centuries. He treats of the Anglo-Norman and other settlers in Angus, of the Royal residences, of the introduction of shires and sheriffs, and of the formation of parishes. Before proceeding to give the history of the Abbey and town, he refers to the Culdees, who had their location in the neighbourhood of Arbroath; and of the extinction of their order, caused in a measure by the enforced celibacy of their priesthood, destroying as it did, the Levitical custom of the descent of the heritage to their children. Besides a very full history of the erection and endowment of the Abbey and of the other conventual buildings, ecclesiastical and civil, connected therewith — of its many chapels and altars in the neighbourhood of the town, and of the rich possessions of the monastery—he gives an account of the origin and condition of the town, prior to the foundation of the Abbey. This is followed by a vivid picture of the condition of the rural and urban populations at the same period, and of the subsequent history and growth of the burgh. A biographical sketch of the Abbots of Arbroath from 1178 to 1606 forms a most interesting part of the work, and his notes on the decay of feudal power and the emancipation of the rural inhabitants of Scotland are exceedingly helpful to the student of history.

David Miller belonged to a family long settled in the little town of Strathmiglo in Fife, where he was born in 1809. He very early developed a taste for acquiring a knowledge of local history, and while quite a young man he had stored up an unusual amount of information relative to the ancient town of his birth. Removing to Edinburgh in the prosecution of his legal studies, he continued his topographical and antiquarian researches. These he afterwards put to practical use in the construction of an "Archæological Map of Fife," which was pronounced to be strictly accurate, but, so far as we know, it was never published. After passing his examinations, he obtained an appointment in Cupar Fife, and in 1840 he came to Arbroath, where he acted for a time as principal assistant to Scott & Ritchie, one of the leading legal firms. Early in "the fifties" he commenced practice on his own account. In Arbroath he found a rich field for his antiquarian researches, of which he was not slow to avail himself, and in time these culminated in the publication of the book which will link his name with that of the burgh in all coming years. "Arbroath and its Abbey" was heartily welcomed by the press, and the entire issue was speedily absorbed. When a stray copy turns up in the catalogues of the dealers in second-hand books, it is quickly picked up at a considerable advance on its original cost. Shortly after its publication he was elected a corresponding member of the Society of Antiquaries of Scotland, and he was frequently consulted on antiquarian and topographical matters by many of the leading Scottish antiquaries. He was a diligent student of Church history, and few had a more thorough knowledge of the history of the Church of Scotland than David Miller. During the non-intrusion controversy he took a prominent part in the discussions then going on, and at the Disruption he became a member of the Free Church, of which, for many years before his death, he was an active and efficient office-bearer. While a staunch Free Churchman, he belonged to what is known as the constitutional party, and by his pen he strongly supported the contendings of that party in the Church. As a director of the Educational Institute, before and at the time of its amalgamation with the Academy, under the title of the High School, his interest in educational matters and his legal knowledge made his services of great value to his co-directors. As secretary to the Town Mission Board, from the institution of the society in 1849 till within a year or two of his death, he did much to consolidate the work of the Mission. He also acted for many years as local secretary to the Bible Society of Scotland. In his capacity of legal adviser to David Duncan of Greenbank, a gentleman who bequeathed considerable sums for educational, charitable, and other public purposes, David Miller rendered valuable service in counselling, directing, and assisting the testator in the preparation of the comprehensive schemes. The perspicuity with which the deeds in relation to the Duncan mortifications were drawn up have frequently been remarked upon, and in this respect are in marked contrast to the documents relating to many similar bequests. As the result of ambiguous expressions, expensive litigation has not infrequently taken place, and the funds intended for special beneficent purposes have too often been frittered away in settling endless legal quibbles over doubtful intrepretions of the donor's wishes. So clear and explicit were the testamentary writings drawn up by David Miller, however, that the Duncan Trustees experienced no difficulty in setting agoing and carrying into practical effect the various objects contemplated by Mr Duncan. These benefactions embraced a scheme for providing bursaries to assist young men in attending a university with the view of preparing them to enter the ministry of the Free Church; a scheme for providing supplements to the stipends of the ministers of the Free Church within the bounds of the Arbroath Presbytery; and the institution of a fund, now known as the Duncan Charity, from which aged persons, being natives of, or old residenters in the burgh, should, on certain conditions, be granted annuities of ten pounds. At the present time there are nearly forty annuitants receiving the benefit of this fund. For a few years he filled the office of Town Councillor, and took a very active share in the management of the town's affairs. His ample knowledge of the manners and customs of Scottish life in byegone days made him a most interesting and agreeable companion. In consequence of failing health he retired from business, and removed with his family to Dundee; but he only survived for a few months thereafter. He died there on the 9th February, 1879, and lies buried in the grounds of the Arbroath Abbey, over the history of which he has cast such a charm.

FRANCIS ORMOND, M.L.C

FRANCIS ORMOND,

M.L.C. of Victoria.

IT is undeniable that a considerable share of the success of our British Colonies is due to the industrious and frugal habits, to the indomitable courage, and to the intellectual superiority of the hardy Scot. The rapid growth of Australia especially during the present century has been most remarkable. In an incredibly short space of time enormous tracts of land have been brought under cultivation ; farms of vast extent, some of them as large as an average-sized Scottish county, have been formed and fenced. What had been swamps and forests have been drained and cleared ; and, where solitude so long had reigned, villages, towns, and cities, with all the modern equipments of advanced civilization have sprung up. The accomplishment of all these mighty changes, wrought out mainly during the reign of Queen Victoria, has been materially helped forward by the skill and intrepidity of our adventurous countrymen.

Towards the end of the last, and the beginning of the present century, James Ormond and Ann Ritchie, his wife, were toiling on a small croft, on the anything but fertile soil of Boysack Muir. The struggle to make both ends meet was a severe and, as it turned out, an unsuccessful one. In the end, they were forced to relinquish their little holding, and for a time to take up their abode at the Cairnconan or " Blind " Toll on the Boysack Muir road.

To the hardy upbringing, and to the Christian example of the parents were the young Ormonds indebted for the success in life which attended them. To the couple, on their little croft at Boysack Muir, were born a family of eight children, six sons and two daughters. Of the sons, five took to seafaring, more than one of them attaining to the rank of skipper. On their periodical visits to their home at the Blind Toll, or in Arbroath, to which the old folks had removed in the closing years of their life, the sailor lads were able, by their kindly help, to increase the comfort, and by their tales of travel and adventure, to cheer the hearts, and to brighten the declining days of the aged couple. But the closing years of the life of James Ormond and his wife were not all sunshine. Robert, their eldest son, who had become master and owner of a vessel hailing from Arbroath, was unfortunately drowned; their son George was accidentally killed, while with his vessel, at Archangel; and a third son, Thomas, who left on what proved to be a last voyage, was never more heard of. After a life of honest toil, James Ormond and Ann Ritchie, his wife, sleep peacefully in the ancient churchyard of St. Vigeans.

Francis Ormond, the third son of the Boysack Muir family, after finishing his apprenticeship as a sailor, went several voyages in various capacities. Somewhere about 1840, then being captain of an emigrant ship, he sailed for Port Philip, and after a successful voyage he arrived in safety. Anchoring off the red bluff to the south of St Kilda — which in commemoration of the event was named, and has since been known as Port Ormond—the captain was quite struck with the beauty, salubrity, and fertility of the country, and he secretly formed the resolution that this should one day be his home. About this time sheep farming had become a profitable industry in Australia, and Captain Ormond

—thanks to his early training on Boysack Muir—was much impressed with the prospects which were open to any one with some knowledge of agricultural pursuits and with sufficient courage to brave the dangers of squatter life, so he determined that one day he should give such a life a trial. Returning home, and keeping this object steadily in view, he made several voyages, and in two or three years thereafter he found himself in a position to become the owner of a schooner of a hundred and eighty tons, and with his wife and family on board, and freighted with such articles as were suitable for the new career on which he had determined to enter, he set sail for his adopted country, arriving at Port Adelaide in 1842.

The life of the pioneer emigrant was no easy one. Many of the squatters were convicts who had served their time, and were by no means very desirable neighbours. Encounters with black men and bushrangers were not rare occurrences. Cattle reiving and sheep stealing were among the difficulties which the early settlers had to face. Of all these dangers and hardships which the intrepid settler had to encounter, Francis Ormond had his full share. But with that doggedness and determination to overcome difficulties so characteristic of his race, he accepted the disappointments and discouragements as incentives to increased efforts to overcome them, and when many around him failed, he in time became the possessor of a large fortune. His son Francis, with whom here we have most to do, was only twelve years of age when he left Scotland. He soon became his father's right hand, and, at a time when he should still have been at school, he was actively engaged in the management of one of his father's largest stations. When still quite a lad, Francis Ormond, the younger, took up land on his own account. His first station was situated between Buninyong and Scarsdale, to the south-west of Ballarat, and subsequently he acquired the fine estate of Borrivolock, about thirty-five miles from Ballarat, comprising about 30,000 acres of first-class grazing land. His father retired many years ago, taking up his abode in Geelong, where he died. On his father's retirement, young Francis assumed the full charge of the business. By prudent management, Francis Ormond, the younger, became one of the wealthiest men in the Colony. But it is not because of his wealth that we seek to give him a place in these pages, but rather to the noble use he made of that wealth that we seek to call attention. Instead of hoarding up his acquisitions, he formed the resolution of choosing to spend what he had so industriously acquired, and that freely, in making provision for the intellectual welfare and mental advancement of his adopted country. This was, however, no mere fad of a wealthy man. His interest in the education and social advancement of those around him was early manifested. When quite young, before he was out of his teens, being then, as we have seen, at the head of a large station far from educational facilities, he saw around him a great number of children entirely left to themselves and growing up in ignorance. Recognising his own responsibility in the matter, he formed a class, and nightly, at much inconvenience to himself, he instructed, trained, and disciplined the young people, and so fitted them for a more intelligent discharge of the duties of life. The work thus begun increased his interest in educational matters. Finding it too great a strain on him to continue the personal supervision of the work, he made arrangements for carrying it on under a properly qualified teacher. In 1860 he paid a visit to Europe, and during a brief stay, he took a keen and observant interest in the work of Sabbath, Industrial, and Technical Schools, as well as in the methods of Secondary Education.

It now became one of the main ideas of his life to devote a large proportion of his wealth towards the furtherance of the educational facilities of the colony. From the moment that his mind was set on this most laudable object, he entered enthusiastically upon the carrying of it out. Scheme after scheme was suggested, each requiring greater pecuniary outlay on his part to bring them to a successful issue. The first of his educational projects on a large scale, was the College which now bears his name. When the University of Melbourne was incorporated, now upwards of forty years ago, ground was reserved for four denominations. For more than twenty years after this, no attempt had been made by the Presbyterian Church at Victoria to carry out the intention of the founders of the University. In 1877 the Minister of Public Instruction brought the subject before the church authorities in a letter in which he asked if they intended to take steps towards the erection of a college for their denomination on the ground reserved for the purpose, and in the event of such action not being contemplated, whether the Church would be disposed to make an arrangement with the State, by which the land might be sold, half the proceeds going to the State for University purposes, and the other half to the Presbyterian Church. The Church chose the former alternative, and resolved to proceed with the erection of a College, the funds for which, estimated at first at £10,000, they set about raising. In the first subscription list Francis Ormond's name appears for £300, but it was soon seen that £10,000 would be quite inadequate for the purpose. Ormond offered to subscribe an additional £1000, provided £9000 was provided by others. When £6000 had been reached, he intimated that he would raise his contribution to £10,000, if a like amount was otherwise subscribed. This generosity on his part was contagious, the other £10,000 being readily forthcoming, and Francis Ormond thereupon gave his cheque for £10,000. The College was opened in 1880, but Francis Ormond's benefactions had not ceased. A College Tower was erected at a cost of £2570, the expense of which he entirely met, in addition to which he contributed handsomely to the Endowment Fund. In 1883, and again in the Jubilee year, additions were made to the structure, the additional wing receiving the name of Victoria, in honour of Her Majesty. The total sum contributed to the building fund alone was upwards of £40,000, and the Ormond College is now acknowledged to be the most imposing, and one of the most flourishing of the educational establishments in Victoria.

Francis Ormond next turned his attention to technical education, and to him was due the idea of establishing in Melbourne a college for the general technical education of the working classes. At a meeting held in 1881 he propounded his scheme, giving the result of his observations in this connection, during his visit to this country. His proposal was coldly received at first, even by the very class for whose benefit it was intended. But once more his enthusiasm became contagious. At a public meeting, held subsequently, and addressed by some of the leading public men, it was resolved to accept his offer. In due time, the Working Men's College was founded, with Francis Ormond as its first President. The College was inaugurated in 1887, and before the founder's death it was attended by over two thousand students. In the same year which saw the opening of the Working Men's College, Francis Ormond announced his intention of giving £20,000 as the endowment of a fund for the promotion of musical culture in Victoria, and he invited the co-operation of musical experts and representatives of the general public to decide on the best means of realising the object in view. After careful consideration, it was resolved to endow a Chair of Music in the University, and he offered to hand over the £20,000 to the University Council on a further sum of £3500 being raised by public subscription for the endowment of a scholarship. The stipulated amount was readily raised, and Francis Ormond paid his £20,000 into the bank to the credit of the University Council.

But Francis Ormond's munificence was not confined to educational purposes. He was a liberal contributor to other public objects. To the various schemes of the Presbyterian Church, of which he was a leading member, he gave unstintedly. In his Church connection he otherwise rendered valuable service, on different occasions representing the Victorian Church at the General Assemblies of the Presbyterian Church in Britain, and at the Pan-Presbyterian Council at Philadelphia. Although a staunch Presbyterian, he was by no means a bigoted one. He was mainly instrumental in starting the Anglican Cathedral Fund. When Bishop Moorhouse was almost in despair, and it seemed as if an Anglican Cathedral, worthy of the Church and the city of Melbourne, must be indefinitely postponed, he received an anonymous offer of £5000 on condition that a certain amount was subscribed by others. The Bishop took the hint, and the result was the erection of the present handsome edifice. It came out afterwards that Francis Ormond was the contributor of the £5000. Taken together his benefactions to his adopted country for public purposes have been estimated at a quarter of a million sterling.

Francis Ormond did not take a very prominent part in politics, although for some years he was a member of the Legislative Council, representing the South Western Province, but his thorough knowledge of business, especially in the department of agriculture, and his keen appreciation of the various points connected with the educational requirements of the Colony, led to his being acknowledged as a wise and useful legislator. Such are some of the leading incidents in the life of one of the greatest benefactors of Victoria, who, instead of spending his means, as many modern millionaires do, on questionable objects, had the pleasure during his life time of distributing his money in such a way as should promote the happiness and prosperity of his fellow-men for generations to come. His death took place at Pau, in France, on the 5th of May, 1889.

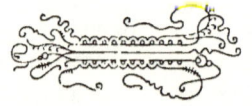

PATRICK ALLAN-FRASER, *ll*. R.S.A.

PATRICK ALLAN FRASER,
Of Hospitalfield.

NEXT to the Abbey and the Abbot's house, there is no building connected with Arbroath, more historically interesting than the Mansion House of Hospitalfield. Founded by King William the Lion, and dedicated by him to Thomas á Becket in 1178, the Abbey of Arbroath, one of the wealthiest religious houses in Scotland, soon gained a European fame. Devotees from many lands, attracted by its magnificence, made pilgrimages to the altar of St. Thomas, its patron saint. As the number of these pilgrims increased, it was found necessary to make more ample provision for their reception and entertainment, than the original hospice of the Abbey afforded.

For obvious reasons, the monks deemed it prudent that the new hospital should be placed at a reasonable distance from the Abbey buildings, around which clustered the dwellings of the inhabitants of the town. The land now known as Hospitalfield, situate nearly two miles from the Abbey, from its fertile situation and salubrious surroundings, suggested itself as a suitable site. Here the hospital or infirmary of the Abbey was built, and, as the number of occupants increased, a chapel dedicated to St. John the Baptist was erected for their use.

So recently as 1861, and again in 1892, while digging operations were going on on a knoll in a field not far from the present mansion house, human remains were discovered. It was computed that at least from a hundred to a hundred and twenty skeletons were found at the spot, one of these being of massive build, evidently that of a powerful man. Excavations were made under the supervision of Patrick Allan Fraser, the proprietor, and Andrew Jervise, F.S.A. Scot., discovering old whin stone walls on the south-east and west of the knoll. It was conjectured that the spot where these remains were found was the site of this old Chapel of St. John the Baptist.

In 1325—by which time the revenues of the Abbey had been greatly augmented—Abbot Bernard, finding it necessary to have storage for the produce of the land, took two of the tenants of the hospital lands bound to build during the first year of the five of their lease a barn and byre, each of forty feet in length. On the site of this barn the hall of the present mansion house of Hospitalfield is built. It is conjectured, with a considerable show of reason, that this suggested to Sir Walter Scott the name of "Monkbarns" as the residence of Jonathan Oldbuck. During a brief stay in this locality, Sir Walter visited Hospitalfield, in the walls of which was distinctly traceable a portion of the old barn erected by order of the monks, and, as in many other respects, the building, its situation, and surroundings fit in with the description of "Monkbarns" as given in the pages of Scott, the claim of Arbroath to be the "Fairport" of "The Antiquary" receives the strongest support.

While during its earlier years it was used as a resort for sick pilgrims, in course of time, its beautiful situation and its salubrious surroundings pointed it out as a desirable retreat for the leading ecclesiastics and their friends, and so it ceased to be a place of refuge for the poor, the sick, and the stranger.

Before the dissolution of the Abbacy, the estate of

Hospitalfield, with its beautiful mansion house as well as other properties belonging to the Abbey, passed into secular hands. As already stated, David Beaton, the Abbot of Arbroath, bestowed on his mistress, Marion Ogilvy, the lands of Hospitalfield, and the property remained in her possession and occupation after Beaton's death. Since passing out of her hands it has been owned by several of the leading Forfarshire families till 1656, when it came into the hands of the Frasers.

James Fraser, who, as we have seen, succeeded Simon Durie as minister of Arbroath in 1653, and who married Isobel, younger daughter of Dr Henry Philip, shortly after his marriage became proprietor of Hospitalfield. He continued minister of Arbroath for sixteen years, but during that time he does not appear to have got on smoothly with the civic authorities. He had a quarrel with the Provost of the burgh, the cause of which is not very clear, but the offence in his eyes is so great that he complains to the Presbytery of the Provost's "carriage towards him on some particulars," and he asked them "to notice it and think upon redress." This appeal the Presbytery thought of so much importance that they appointed their moderator and other two of their number to proceed to St Andrews and submit the case to Archbishop Sharp. The result of this interview appears to have been unfavourable to the parish minister, and the Presbytery, proceeding no doubt on the advice they got at St. Andrews, temporarily suspended James Fraser from the exercise of his ministerial functions. In the meantime, however, and evidently to save further trouble, he demitted his office, and retired into private life, preferring rather to spend the remainder of his days in his quiet home at Hospitalfield, as a county gentleman, than in bickering and fighting with the city fathers.

On his death, he was succeeded in the proprietorship of Hospitalfield and Kirkton by his son James, who in turn was succeeded by his eldest son John, but neither of these made up titles to the property. Captain David Fraser, son of · John Fraser, having succeeded his father, made up a title to the estate in 1766 and 1767. We have been unable to glean any particulars of his history. The only incident we know is that when Captain Fall made his memorable attack on Arbroath in 1781, Captain Fraser of Hospitalfield, along with Colonel Lindsay of Kinblethmont, assumed the command of the burghers in their successful defence of the town against the attack of this famous buccaneer. Captain Fraser married Mary Barclay, and in 1759 had a son John, who in due course succeeded to the estate. When in 1793 war was declared by France against Britain, and an appeal was made to the country to arm in her defence, John Fraser, the laird of Hospitalfield, offered his services. These were accepted, and in 1794, having locally raised a regiment of four or five companies, under the designation of the Angus Fencibles, he was appointed Major and assumed the command. During the four following years the regiment was stationed in different parts of the country. When Burns died, the Angus Fencibles were at Dumfries, and a detachment of the regiment took part in the funeral obsequies of the poet, the Major putting the first shovelful of earth on the coffin of the bard.

Major Fraser married Elizabeth, daughter of Francis Perrot of Hawkesbury Hall. The Perrots trace their descent from the blood-royal of England, and in many ways were a most distinguished family. By the marriage one daughter, Elizabeth, was born, and in September, 1843, she became the wife of Patrick Allan. Robert Allan, father of Patrick, was a stocking-weaver at a time when that industry was a flourishing one in

Arbroath. He carried on business in the premises now occupied as the High Street Foundry, his dwelling being in the house connected with the works and facing the street. His wife was Isabella Macdonald, a daughter of Alexander Macdonald, the senior partner of the firm of Alexander Macdonald & Sons, house painters. Patrick, their third son, was born in 1813, and was educated at the Arbroath Academy. After completing his course at school, he was apprenticed to his grandfather's firm, and to the trade of house painting he served a full apprenticeship. When quite young he developed considerable artistic tastes, and at the termination of his apprenticeship he was sent to Edinburgh to study art. As an art student, under Robert Scott Lauder and others, he made rapid progress. Leaving Edinburgh, he proceeded to the Continent, and in different schools where he continued his studies, he added to his experience. After studying for a time in Rome, he returned to Arbroath somewhere about 1839, where he commenced the practice of his profession, obtaining some good commissions. Not satisfied with his attainments, however, he determined to take another spell of study, and with this view he took up his residence in Paris and London, in the former place studying the *chef d'œuvres* of the great masters that line the walls of the Louvre. He returned to Arbroath in 1841, resuming his professional duties. As one of his first commissions, he was employed on a series of sketches for Cadell's edition of the Waverley novels. In particular, the illustrations for " The Antiquary" were entrusted to him, his intimate knowledge of the scenery of " Fairport" and its neighbourhood enabling him to give a truthful delineation of the exquisite views to be obtained in this picturesque locality. The original sketches now hang in one of the Hospitalfield galleries, and are adjudged among the best work that Allan-Fraser produced during his career as an artist. About this time some of his pictures were shown at the Glasgow Exhibition, and were very favourably criticised. His first important commission was the presentation portrait of Mr Lindsay-Carnegie, to which reference is made at page 220. He also painted the portrait of Provost Mann, which hangs on the walls of the Arbroath Town Hall, alongside of that of Mr Lindsay-Carnegie. But his professional career was cut short by his marriage with Elizabeth Fraser, although he did some excellent work in later years.

Eight years after his marriage, he assumed, by royal license, the name of Fraser. To the estate of Hospitalfield, and later on of Hawkesbury Hall, to which he succeeded through his marriage, Patrick Allan-Fraser, from time to time, added various estates both in Scotland and England, ultimately becoming a large landed proprietor. Having now plenty of leisure, and ample means to indulge in his predilection for art, he set about the reconstruction and adornment of the mansion-house of Hospitalfield and its surroundings. In the reconstruction of the house he showed great architectural and artistic taste. An exceedingly interesting description of the mansion-house as it now appears, may be found in A. H. Millar's "Historical Castles and Mansions of Scotland." His art collection is exceedingly valuable, consisting as it does of some of the finest examples of modern pictures to be found in Scotland. These include many fine specimens of the work of Sir William Fettes Douglas, P.R.S.A.; R. Scott Lauder; John Pettie; David Farquharson; Keeley Halswell; Alexander Fraser; James Lauder; James Cassie; Arthur Perigal; George Hay; and D. O. Hill.

A number of Allan-Fraser's pictures also find a place on

the walls of the Hospitalfield Art Gallery, among these being portraits of his wife; of John Philip, R.A.; Andrew Jervise, F.S.A. Scot.; Patrick Bell, LL.D., the inventor of the reaping machine; and of Tom Watson, a well-known local poet.

In one respect the Hospitalfield Art Gallery is quite unique, that is in the collection of portraits of celebrated artists painted by themselves. In connection with this W. P. Frith, R.A., in his Autobiography and Reminiscences, makes a humorous reference to Patrick Allan-Fraser, under the name of "MacIlray, a Scotchman," whom he met in Paris, when studying in the Louvre in 1840. He tells that he was attracted to the young Scotsman by his pleasant manner, and by some excellent copying on which he was engaged. On his return to London, Frith again met "MacIlray" whom he introduced to a set of young men with whom he was intimate, and he says that the Scotsman soon became a great favourite with them all. After referring to his marriage which occurred shortly after this, and on which he warmly congratulated him, he adds, "There is no blessing, I suppose, that is quite unalloyed, and the drawback to my friend's perfect bliss, was the impossibility of a Scottish Laird, with all the duties connected with the position, being able to devote himself to a profession which requires all a man's energies to ensure success. But if MacIlray could no longer paint, he could be the cause of painting in others; and this took the kind and graceful form of commissions for pictures to all his friends. The price to be paid for each work was a hundred guineas. We might take what subject we pleased, but each picture must contain a portrait of the artist, painted by himself. I think everyone, in course of time, executed MacIlray's order, and I hear that the pictures are intended to become the nucleus of a national collection in a Scottish town. . . . If my old friend—who will easily recognise himself under the pseudonym I have used —should read these lines, I hope he will forgive the introduction of them for the sake of 'Auld Lang Syne.'" In Frith's portrait—one of the collection of artists painted by themselves— he is represented as standing in a London street in walking costume, while a flower-girl offers him a bouquet. Another is by John Philip, R.A.—"Spanish Philip"—the protegé of Lord Panmure, who represents himself as standing in a group of Spanish figures; John Ballantyne, R.S.A., whose brother, R. M. Ballantyne, the well-known novelist, is portrayed on the same canvas. Among the others of this collection are those of E. M. Ward, R.A.; Robert Scott Lauder, R.S.A.; W. B. Johnstone, R.S.A.; Henry O'Neill, A.R.A.; Augustus L. Egg, R.A.; and A. Bell Middleton, a rising Arbroath artist, who died young.

Among the other art treasures at Hospitalfield are several valuable pieces of sculpture and some exquisite examples of wood-carving. The Library contains some rare works, including a copy of the first folio edition of Shakespeare, as well as a number of old charters and historical documents, one of the deeds, as already mentioned, bearing the autograph signature of David Beaton, Abbot of Arbroath, a *fac simile* of which is attached to his portrait at page 33 of this volume.

The Mortuary Chapel in the Western Cemetery of Arbroath was erected by Patrick Allan-Fraser as a memorial of his wife, and her father and mother. The work of erection occupied nine years. The building is quite unique, both as to its style of architecture, and its wealth of carving in stone. A full description of it is given in the author's "Arbroath: Past and Present," and need not therefore be repeated here. Patrick

Allan-Fraser was the architect of this fine building, and he also superintended its erection. It is believed to have cost him somewhere about £20,000. On its completion, it was made over to the Town Council of Arbroath in trust for the community, together with funds for its maintenance. It is now used for funeral services of any and every denomination. This interesting building is an adornment to one of the most beautiful cemeteries in Scotland.

Patrick Allan-Fraser also entered the lists of authorship. Of his "An Unpopular View of our Times" and "Christianity and Churchism," it is not necessary to say much. Though books in format, these works would be classed by the bibliographer and literary critic as mere essays by an amateur pamphleteer, dealing with subjects in great measure beyond the sphere of his knowledge. Churchism has hurt and hindered Christianity at every turn, according to Allan-Fraser's reading of history. He preaches a materialistic gospel which he believes to be the true interpretation of the doctrines of Christ. The Kingdom of Heaven is to be obtained, according to the "view" taken in these pamphlets, by knowledge of God's laws and commandments acquired through the study of physical science. The saving of Shadrach, Meshach, and Abednego, from the fury and fire of Nebuchadnezzar, was more than likely effected by use of "fibrous mineral asbestos," and Elijah's historic triumph over the prophets of Baal was due to a superior knowledge of the nature of oxygen and hydrogen. Salvation for men is to be found only in "a sound, well-balanced brain and its righteousness." The best that can now be said of these pamphlets is that here and there in them Allan-Fraser has varied his attacks upon clergymen by effective paraphrases of passages which had evidently impressed him in perusing the works of John Ruskin. "An Unpopular View" and "Christianity and Churchism" have passed into the great library of the unknown. As writings, they are now only of value as giving glimpses of the religious and social views of the subject of our sketch.

To Patrick Allan-Fraser the town owes the inception of the idea of procuring a supply of good pure water for domestic use. Having reason to believe that there were constantly flowing underground streams of water, finding their way from the higher land to the sea, he proceeded to sink a well on his own estate, and by continuous pumping over a considerable period, he came to the conclusion that the supply was practically inexhaustible. This result led him to suggest to the civic authorities of Arbroath that it would be worth their while to make a similar experiment. This hint was acted on, a well was sunk, works were erected, and on the 25th September, 1871, the water was turned on, and from then till now the town's supply has been solely obtained from this source.

Patrick Allan-Fraser took an interest in various local institutions—the Public Library, the Infirmary, and others, receiving the benefit of his personal services, as well as his pecuniary support.

He was an Honorary Member of the Royal Scottish Academy, was President of the British Academy of Arts in Rome—an institution of which he was the main instrument in founding—and a Fellow of the Society of Antiquaries of Scotland. As a Commissioner of Supply and a Justice of the Peace, he took an active share in the business of his native county. On the 13th October, 1886, he was presented with the freedom of the Burgh of Arbroath, an honour which he appeared to value more highly than any of the others which had been conferred upon him. His death took place on the 18th October, 1890. By his settlement, his property in England was devoted to the payment of legacies and annuities to relatives and personal friends; while the free income from the whole of his Scottish estates and Scottish movable property was left permanently and in all time coming as follows :—

(1) For the assistance and encouragement of young men not having sufficient means of their own who shall be desirous of following out one or more of the professions of painting, sculpture, carving in wood, architecture, and engraving.

(2) To provide for the comfortable maintenance and support of aged or infirm professional men, and those who from physical defects are incapable of supporting themselves in comfortable circumstances, being painters, sculptors, and literary men (that is, men who have devoted the greater part of their lives to literature as a profession), and to all who, when engaged in their respective professions, were men held in esteem for their moral conduct as well as for their artistic or literary talents, and who, from unavoidable causes, have been unable to provide or lay up for themselves sufficient means wherewith to secure comforts and requirements in their declining years or infirmities.

For the carrying out of the first purpose of the trust, the deed provides that thirty young men shall be comfortably lodged, boarded, and clothed in the house of Hospitalfield, under the conditions of the trust, which are specified with great detail in regard to almost every matter of house management. The age of the applicants for admission is to be not less than sixteen and not more than eighteen, and there is a test specified in order to satisfy the trustees of every applicant's fitness for the profession he desires to follow. The students admitted are to be indentured for a period of four years, and bound to conform to the rules of the house. A thoroughly qualified certificated teacher in the South Kensington Art Department, or otherwise qualified in painting or sculpture, is to be appointed governor of the house, and is to reside in a separate wing, to be built to Hospitalfield House. A matron is also to be appointed, and an assistant governor, to reside in the house and exercise supervision over the students. A sum of £150 is directed to be paid annually to the directors or managers of the Infirmary in Arbroath towards the salary of a resident medical attendant, if the directors have appointed such an officer, and this gentleman is to medically examine each applicant for admission, and to give weekly attendance and medical advice to all the students and others resident at Hospitalfield. Provision is made for an annual expenditure to permit of students visiting objects of nature at a distance, and exhibitions of science and art at Edinburgh or elsewhere. The students are also to be provided with summer quarters at Blackcraig or Glenkilrie, in Perthshire. The students may also be sent by the trustees to classes in Arbroath for the improvement of their general education, and the trustees are to engage carvers and engravers to teach the students the use of tools; also to engage lecturers on subjects of science and art, or natural history. Power is also given to send students who have completed their indentures at Hospitalfield to the Continent for the completion of their education as artists, and an allowance is provided to each student for this purpose. Lastly, young people resident in Arbroath, between the ages of sixteen and twenty, may also be received and taught along with the students in Hospitalfield House, and allowed to lunch with the students free of charge.

For the carrying out of the second object of the trust—

viz., the assisting of aged or infirm professional men—the following are the provisions :—

(1) That the number of recipients shall be ten, to consist of four painters, three sculptors, and three literary men, to be selected by the trustees.
(2) The annuitants selected shall each receive £50 per annum during their lifetime, or so long as the trustees shall think proper.

The following additional bequests are made by the deed :—

(1) Should revenue permit after the fulfilment of the two first objects of the trust, a donation of £50 per annum is directed to be given to the Artists' Benevolent Institution, London, for the education of orphan children in connection with that Institution.
(2) Should revenue permit after providing for the first and second objects of the trust and the above donation to the Artists' Benevolent Fund, a sum of £200 per annum at least is directed to be paid to the Magistrates and Town Council of Arbroath, as a contribution towards maintaining and extending the present system of water supply for the burgh, but this only so long as the present water supply scheme is continued in operation.
(3) Should surplus revenue still remain after providing for the purposes before enumerated, the trustees are directed to extend the benefits under the first and second main objects of the trust in the proportion of receiving three additional students into Hospitalfield House for one additional annuity granted. The testator further empowers his trustees to make subscriptions from the trust funds in periods of extraordinary distress, local or national, to an amount not exceeding £100 per annum.

In various quarters disappointment was expressed that Allan-Fraser had not devoted a part of his means to the erection of some public institution which would have spread and nourished among the common people a knowledge and love of things beautiful. The fact that the country is already fairly well supplied with agencies for the training of all youths of artistic genius, and that under existing circumstances the supply of professional artists has really outrun the public demand for fine art, naturally gave rise to a feeling that some institution, devoted to the excitement and cultivation of an intelligent love of the fine arts among the great body of the people, would have been a fit memorial of one whose talents and whole life-work were devoted to purposes associated with art. The Hospitalfield Trustees have recognised this, and have earned public gratitude by the opening of Hospitalfield Picture Galleries and Grounds to a certain number of visitors one afternoon a week during the summer months. A quiet hour or two spent in these galleries amid their art treasures may give to many a dweller in a humble home artistic pleasure and impulse which cannot fail to manifest themselves in efforts towards beautifying the surroundings and conduct of everyday life.

ALEXANDER CARNEGIE KIRK, LL.D.

ALEXANDER CARNEGIE KIRK,

LL.D., F.R.S.E.,

Naval Engineer.

ALEXANDER CARNEGIE KIRK was born on the 6th July, 1830, in the manse of Barry, and when a child of seven summers he was brought to the manse of Arbirlot, where, as we have already seen, his father, John Kirk, succeeded Thomas Guthrie as parish minister. The manses of Scotland have reared and sent out to the world many able men, and to these Arbirlot, in Dr Alexander Carnegie Kirk and his talented brother, Sir John Kirk, has made no mean contribution. Few sweeter spots can be found than the charming village of Arbirlot on the banks of the Elliot, near the grey tower of Kelly Castle; the lovely dell, the wimpling stream, the one-arched bridge, the pretty cottages embowered among the trees, above which peep the spires of the two churches, the village smithy and the old mill, presenting many picturesque points for the pencil of the artist. Above this quiet and cosy village stands the beautifully-situated manse, commanding a fine view of the German Ocean, while raising its tall form in the distance may be seen the Bell Rock, keeping watch and ward over the lives of the many mariners who traverse the blue waters. In this quiet and lovely spot was reared the subject of this sketch, until the "Disruption," when his father "came out," and, with his family, temporarily took up his abode in the town.

Not only was Alexander Carnegie Kirk a son of the manse, but, on his mother's side, he descended from a levitical family. His great-grandfather, John Carnegie, was for half-a-century parish minister of Inverkeilor. John Carnegie's wife, Catherine, was the youngest daughter of William Walker, minister of Collessie, in Fife, third son of Alexander Walker, third baron of St Fort. According to Douglas, there were free barons of the surname of Walker settled in the county of Fife upwards of three hundred and fifty years ago. From one of these, Catherine or Katherine Walker, the wife of John Carnegie, traced her descent. Two of her uncles were related by marriage, the one to the Earl of Lauderdale and the other to the Earl of Leven. It may also be locally interesting to mention in passing that Helen Walker, grand-aunt of Catherine Walker, married Alexander Pearson of Clow, whose family connection with Arbroath has already been referred to.

John Carnegie, who died in 1805, was succeeded as incumbent of Inverkeilor by his son Alexander, the grandfather of Alexander Carnegie Kirk. Alexander Carnegie married a daughter of Adam Skirving, the author of the well-known song "Johnnie Cope," and other lyric poems. Skirving was a wealthy farmer, having long held a lease of Garleton, near Haddington. Handsome in person, of robust constitution, he was foremost in every manly sport. He was also recognised as a man of vigorous intellect, of ready wit, and of a genial and happy temperament. He died in April, 1803, in his eighty-fourth year, and was buried in the Parish Church of Athelstaneford, where a metrical epitaph, in the fashion of the period, records his merits.

His two songs "Tranent Muir" and "Johnnie Cope" have

earned for him undying fame. Burns, in his notes to "Johnston's Musical Museum," tells a good story, which he says he often heard in connection with the first of these songs, in which Skirving speaks in scathing terms of the pusillanimity of several of the officers engaged in the battle of Preston, and, among others, of an Irishman—Lieutenant Smith. The Lieutenant, as might be expected, was greatly enraged at the author, and sent him a challenge to meet him in mortal combat. "Gang back," said Skirving to the officer who was the bearer of the challenge, "Gang back and tell Lieutenant Smith that I ha'e nae leisure to come to Haddington, but tell him to come here and I'll tak' a look o' him, and if I think I'm fit to fecht, I'll fecht him, and, if no—I'll do as he did—I'll rin awa'!"

Archibald Skirving, a son of the author of "Johnnie Cope," and grand-uncle of Dr Kirk, was a painter of some note. The most popular portrait of Burns is the crayon sketch by Archibald Skirving, who, although there is no record of his having sketched the poet from life, is believed by many to have met him in Edinburgh.

Alexander Carnegie held the office of parish minister till his death in 1836, so that father and son had ministered to the spiritual wants of the parishioners of Inverkeilor for the long period of eighty-one years. Besides being parish minister of Inverkeilor, Alexander Carnegie was proprietor of the estate of Redhall, having purchased it from George Fullarton Carnegie of Pitarrow and Charlton in 1825. At his death in 1836, he was succeeded as laird of Redhall by his son, John Carnegie, on whose death in 1879 he was succeeded by his elder son, Captain Alexander Carnegie, the present proprietor. But the connection of the Carnegies with the parish of Inverkeilor has continued unbroken. The smithy, the smith's house, and another cottage adjoining, with about a Scots acre of land bought from the estate of Anniston by Alexander Carnegie, the parish minister, is still in the family, being now owned by Captain Carnegie, his grandson.

John Kirk, the parish minister first, and afterwards the Free Church minister of Arbirlot, as already mentioned, was one of the able young members of the Presbytery of Arbroath, in the stirring years of the "thirties." He was a man of refined and well cultivated mind, and dignified demeanour. For some years after the Disruption he suffered no little privation, but throughout those troublous times he was cheered and helped and encouraged by his worthy helpmate Christian Carnegie. In a home presided over by such a couple, was Alexander Carnegie Kirk reared.

At an early age he was sent to the Arbroath Academy, where he received an excellent education. From the Academy he went to Edinburgh University, where he attended the mathematical and natural philosophy classes. He also for a time attended the engineering classes in Heriot-Watt College. Deciding to follow engineering as a profession, he returned to Arbroath. Here, in the joiner's shop of Nicol & Wallace, he first learned to handle tools. Some of the workmen who stood at the same bench with him have a pleasant recollection of the intelligent lad, who even at that early age, gave promise of a successful career.

From Arbroath he proceeded to Glasgow for the purpose of entering on his engineering apprenticeship in the Vulcan Foundry. No better selection of a training school in marine engineering could have been made, and here he became a deft workman. From Glasgow he migrated to London, entering the service there of Maudslay, Sons, & Field, the eminent marine engineers, where he rapidly rose step by step till he occupied the position of chief draughtsman, no mean post for one so young. Leaving the Thames, he was appointed managing engineer at the Paraffin Works of Young & Co., Bathgate, where he introduced important improvements in the manufacture and refining of paraffin oil, many of which were adopted in the new works which he designed, and which, under his supervision, were built for the firm at West Calder. While in their employment, he initiated other improvements in the conduct of their business. Not the least important of these was the invention of a freezing machine, to be used for separating the solid paraffin, which is held in solution in the oil up to a certain stage. This invention, which was introduced to the scientific world in a paper read before the Institute of Civil Engineers in 1864, was pronounced as "the embodiment of one of the happiest combinations of physical and mechanical principles worked out during the present generation." This freezing machine was also applied to the manufacture of ice in hot climates, and, as such, was one of the most successful, especially in its later form, which he brought out in 1870. His next appointment was that of manager at the Engineering Works of James Aitken & Co., at Cranstonhill, which he retained for five or six years. He then entered the service of John Elder & Co., as managing engineer of the famed Fairfield Engine Works, in which he remained for some years, the while taking a distinguished place in his profession. It was while there that he carried into effect the idea of the triple expansion type of engine, the discovery of which he claimed, and for which he obtained a patent, although he afterwards relinquished the rights he had thus secured. The economical advantages of the triple expansion system were very considerable. In the case of the "Aberdeen," for example, on a single voyage to Australia, a saving of five hundred tons of coal was effected, and a consequent increase of cargo space.

In 1877, after the death of Robert Napier, he severed his connection with Elder & Co., and became a partner in the firm of Robert Napier & Son. Under his supervision they continued to hold the high place among the leading engineering establishments of the world for which the firm had so long been famed. After joining the Napiers' firm, besides introducing the triple expansion system into the merchant service, Dr Kirk succeeded in inducing the Admiralty to adopt it in the cruisers, "Australia" and "Galatea," which his firm built and engined.

The high-class warships and merchant steamers built by Napier & Son during his connection with the firm is sufficient proof of the ability with which the business was conducted. It has been acknowledged that few men stood higher in the profession than did Alexander Carnegie Kirk. He was looked upon as one of the most all-round and most accomplished mechanical engineers in this country. To his inventive genius we owe many valuable inventions and improvements in naval engineering, besides those to which special reference has been made.

In 1884, at the request of the Institute of Engineers of Scotland he delivered one of a special course of lectures to the members of that body on the general subject of Heat in its mechanical applications, the title of his lecture being "Compressed Air and other Refractory Machinery," a lecture which was highly spoken of by his professional brethren.

The last of his papers read to the Institute was entitled "A Graphical form of Froude's law." What adds a special interest to this paper was the fact that it was received by the secretary on the day of Dr. Kirk's death, and was read to the members of the Institute, after the grave had closed on its author.

In 1888 the University of Glasgow conferred on him the degree of LL.D. He was also a Fellow of the Royal Society of Edinburgh and a member of other learned bodies. At various times he held office in the Institution of Engineers and Shipbuilders in Scotland, and was president during two sessions. He had also been a vice-president of the Institute of Naval Architects of London. Shortly before his death he was appointed a member of the Advisory Council on Marine Engineering for the Chicago Exhibition, and the night before his death he was engaged in writing a paper on the Triple Expansion Engine to be read at one of the meetings at Chicago which he had hoped to attend. Outside his own profession he took little or no part in public affairs.

He was a silent man, and very absent minded. While he spoke sparingly at the meetings of the Institute over which he presided, or at the other scientific societies of which he was a member, yet when he did speak it was always to the point, and his utterances were ever listened to with interest and respect. How Carlyle would have magnified that trait of his character — a strong, silent man, who, while others were discussing with infinity of talk the whys and why nots, went solemnly and steadily on with his labour, till, one morning, the talkers opened their eyes to find that their old problem had ceased to exist; that, at anyrate, it had become a new and strange one, because, while they were talking and theorising there was a man working who treated their pet problem as a thing which he, like Diogenes, must settle out of hand.

Notwithstanding his apparently reserved demeanour, he was noted for his kindness and generosity to any earnest worker, and he spared neither time nor trouble in helping forward young and struggling beginners, or indeed any others who sought his advice.

Dr Kirk's fame as a naval engineer was not confined to his native country, and the announcement of his sudden death from heart disease, which took place in Glasgow early on the morning of the 5th October, 1892, was received with universal regret.

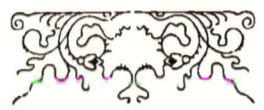

ALEXANDER BROWN LL.D.

ALEXANDER BROWN, LL.D.,
The Arbroath Astronomer.

IN the midst of a snow storm, the like of which had not been witnessed in this country for forty years before, nor surpassed since, was the subject of this sketch ushered into the world. In turning over the register of births and baptisms of the parish of St Vigeans, we find it there recorded that on the "8th February, 1814, Alexander Brown and Margaret Buick, at Grange of Conon, had a son named Alexander."

The hamlet of Grange of Conon is situated on the side of an old road, which, two centuries ago, was the highway between the ancient towns of Forfar and Arbroath. It consisted of a number of small crofts, the occupants of which, in addition to tilling their little bit of land, were employed in such handicrafts as those of smiths, wrights, tailors, and weavers. Up till a hundred years or so ago, there was also a brewery at the Grange, the well that supplied the water for it being still in use there. The house in which Alexander Brown was born, and in which four generations of the Browns resided, was near the centre of the hamlet. It consisted of a but and a ben, with a weaving shop and barn and byre attached. The little biggin', which disappeared some years ago, was beautifully situated. Standing on its site, and looking down the valley, the spectator is charmed with the lovely view which meets his eye as he gazes on the variegated hues of the sloping banks which lie between him and "the Scarborough of Scotland "—Lunan Bay, bits of which can be seen in the distance with the golden rays of the midday sun playing on its sparkling waters.

The name of Brown has long been connected with this locality. So far back as 1485 we find John Brown, tenant of Wardmill, founding the altar of St Sebastian, and endowing the same "for the salvation of his soul and those of his three successive wives," and Alexander Brown, his cousin, was then appointed chaplain of that altar. Whether these Browns were the forebears of the subject of this sketch we know not, but this we know—that Alexander Brown could trace his direct line of descent for nearly two centuries.

For generations the Browns were crofters and tailors at the Grange of Conon. Alexander's father was the first to break the family line of tailors, choosing, instead, the trade of weaver.

"The bapteesment o' the bairn"—taking place as it did during a snow storm, the like of which was only remembered by "the oldest inhabitant"—was a serious matter, the puny little thing—for he was but a weary bairn—having to be carried from the Grange of Conon to Tarry House, which then did duty for the manse of St Vigeans. The roads were all but impassable, and a consultation took place as to whether the bearers of the babe should first go into Arbroath, and then get round to St Vigeans by way of Warddykes, or whether the direct route from the Grange to St Vigeans should be attempted. The former, though the longest was the best, and the father pleaded that it, as being the safest, should be chosen, but the women folk insisted on the latter being taken, and so it was, and a stiff job they found it. Often, exhausted and weary with their tiny burden, they stuck in a snow wreath, from which, with difficulty, they managed to extricate themselves, and glad they were when Mr Aitken's house was reached and the ceremony performed.

Brown was early sent to school, at which he was kept till he reached the age of thirteen. In those days it was not customary for country boys in the humble position of Brown to be kept at school till they attained such an age, but this gave him educational advantages which were very serviceable to him in the scientific pursuits of his after life. On leaving school, he was sent to learn his father's occupation of handloom weaver, and while so engaged he continued the study of mathematics, some knowledge of which he had gained at school. His father's library, as might be expected from his position in life, was not a large one, but the few books he had were carefully selected. Among others, there was one of five volumes, which he had taken out in monthly parts. It was a serial published in Glasgow, and treated of history, geography, and various scientific subjects, and of this Alexander made good use. He began the study of astronomy when quite a young lad. On the 2nd September, 1830, when he was in his seventeenth year, there occurred a total eclipse of the moon. His father called him out from his loom to witness the phenomenon. This sent him in to consult the Glasgow book, and from it he was able to ascertain the nature of eclipses, and thus he laid the foundation of his astronomical studies. The pleasure which this initiatory sip of scientific knowledge gave him only served to increase his thirst for still deeper draughts. On one of his visits to town he saw a handbill intimating that George Carey was to commence a class for instruction in navigation, astronomy, and kindred sciences. Carey, a native of Arbirlot, was a man of considerable literary attainments, besides being the author of several scientific works. Brown attended Carey, and was largely benefited by the instruction he received from that gentleman. Among other books which Carey advised Brown to avail himself of was a small treatise by David Thomson, another scientific Arbroathian, and from this book he gained a considerable amount of astronomical information. Thus did the country lad plod on, adding bit by bit to his stock of knowledge. In 1833 he came to reside in Arbroath, and while working at his trade of handloom weaver, he continued his scientific studies under somewhat more favourable circumstances than he was able to secure in the country. About this time Robert Naughty, an old man-of-war's-man, who, when in the navy, had managed to pick up a smattering of knowledge of navigation, and of plain and spherical trigonometry, opened an adventure school, and drawn thither by his thirst for information, Alexander Brown became a pupil, but within three weeks of his joining the classes, Naughty told him that he knew as much of these subjects as he did himself. Not long thereafter, Robert was fain to come to his former pupil for instruction in the same branches which he had formerly professed to teach him.

In 1835, a literary and scientific society was formed in Arbroath for the purpose chiefly of arranging for lectures on scientific subjects. Among the lecturers was the late William Allan, the minister of St Paul's U.P. (then the "Relief") Church, a gentleman who for many years rendered valuable services to Arbroath in this and other ways. One of his lectures was on Comets, and with special reference to Halley's Comet, expected to be visible about the month of October of that year. Shortly before this, Brown had constructed a diagram of the orbit of the comet, showing the computed places along its path. This diagram he gave to Mr M'Ash, a teacher in the Arbroath Academy (afterwards known as the High School), who took an interest in this and kindred subjects. Mr M'Ash, appreciating its value, handed it to Mr Allan, who made use of it as illustrative of his lecture, mentioning at the same time that it was the production of a young weaver belonging to the town. It soon became known who this weaver lad was, and from that day Alexander Brown came to be a widely-known name. About this time he also calculated and projected the different elements and phases of the remarkable annular eclipse of the sun which occurred on Sunday, the 15th May, of the following year (1836), an eclipse which was long remembered in Arbroath, and which Alexander Brown, writing fifty years after the event, described as being one of the most interesting spectacles which his fellow-townsmen ever witnessed.

These astronomical labours were the means of his introduction to Professor Nichol, of Glasgow, who then occasionally lectured at Arbroath under the auspices of the Scientific and Literary Society already referred to.

Meteorology also formed a branch of study in which Brown became deeply interested. He began to take meteorological observations with a thermometer as his only instrument in 1842. Some years before this he had formed an intimacy with John Muir, of St Vigeans, who was his minister before he came into town, and after he came to reside in Arbroath he was a frequent visitor at the manse, scarcely a week passing without finding him wending his way towards St Vigeans.

Mr Muir had a considerable knowledge of scientific subjects, and, among the rest, of meteorology. To him Brown was indebted, not only for adding to his stock of information on this and kindred subjects, but also for his help in making and repairing his scientific tools, for Mr Muir had also a good knowledge of mechanics, which, in his workshop at the manse, he put to practical use.

Besides having the run of the minister's library, which contained a fine collection of scientific works, he had also the privilege of meeting at the manse men, his seniors in years and his superiors in position and education, all of which contributed largely to his intellectual advancement. In short, to Mr Muir, more than to any other man, was Brown indebted for a large amount of his early scientific training. His superior education pointed him out as one fitted to fill a more important sphere than that of a hand-loom weaver, so in 1840 he was offered and accepted an appointment as clerk in the law office of Lyon & Andson, in which position he remained till the dissolution of that firm in 1857. He then found employment in the Town Clerk's office, in which he assiduously discharged his duties for well nigh a quarter of a century, but from which, through failing health, he was obliged to retire in 1880.

Three years after leaving the loom, Alexander Brown was married to Betty Bowman. They had no family.

In 1841, he became acquainted with Hugh Miller, the geologist, and several contributions from his pen appeared in the "Witness." About the same time he obtained—what he for some years longed for—an introduction to Sir David Brewster, of St Andrews, through Dr John Kyd, of Spynie, in Morayshire. Dr Kyd was an Arbroath man, and was a favourite student of Brewster's. The acquaintance thus formed with Sir David gradually ripened into a friendship, which only ended with the death of the distinguished principal.

In 1843 an extraordinarily high tide had been observed all along the coast, and Brown wrote a paper on the subject, which he sent to Sir David Brewster for communication to the St. Andrews Literary and Philosophical Society. Instead of using it there, Sir David took it with him to Cork, and there read it before a meeting of the British Association, which sat in that city in September, 1843. After this, various contributions from Brown's pen were read at the meetings of that learned body. At the first and only meeting of the British Association, held in the county (at Dundee), the only scientific contribution by a resident in the county to that meeting was a descriptive paper on the rainfall at Arbroath, prepared by Alexander Brown.

His knowledge of meteorology has been of considerable public value. In 1852 he began to contribute observations to the Meteorological Department of Greenwich Observatory. His services, as one of the best observers, were recognised, and the result thereof may be found in a published report on the meteorology of London, which was laid before both Houses of Parliament in 1854. He continued his services to the department until the establishment of the Meteorological Society of Scotland in 1855, and for many years thereafter he was a constant contributor to that society. These papers were ranked amongst the most important contributions made by any single observer to Scottish meteorology. Not only in this country have his services to science been acknowledged, but his papers have also been reprinted for, and reviewed by, the Meteorological Society of Austria and the Imperial Institute of France.

For forty years he acted as meteorological observer at Arbroath, and it was at his suggestion, and under his superintendence, that the Meteorological Station connected with the Natural History Society was erected at the New Cemetery, when failing health caused him to cease from the active duties of local observer. Since then the meteorological station has been removed to Dishland Hill.

Besides his communications to learned societies and scientific journals, he was a frequent contributor to the local newspapers, his articles being chiefly on his favourite topics, and possessing much local and general interest. He also occasionally delivered lectures in Arbroath and elsewhere on scientific subjects.

Excepting a small volume of twenty-five pages, entitled "Remarkable Seventeeth and Nineteenth Century Eclipses of the Sun," of which only one hundred copies were printed, and these for private circulation, his numerous and valuable contributions to scientific research have not appeared in collected form, but are scattered over the pages of newspapers and scientific journals.

His valuable services to science were not allowed to pass unnoticed nor unrewarded. Although a self-taught man, the Senatus of the University of St Andrews, in recognition of his scholarship and proficiency in science, in 1870 conferred on him the degree of Doctor of Laws. More recently he was presented with his portrait, and the painting thereafter became public property, and now hangs on the walls of the Arbroath Picture Gallery. In 1879, a memorial, signed by the leading scientific men of the kingdom, was presented, praying that the Prime Minister would confer on Alexander Brown a grant from the Royal Bounty. The prayer of the petitioners was not granted, but this expression of opinion, on the part of so many learned men, in time bore ample fruit.

In the latter end of 1883 it was felt, not only among his own townsmen, but also among his admirers at a distance, that it would be a graceful act to present him with a tangible expression of the esteem in which his important scientific services were held. A committee was formed, whose public appeal in an incredibly short space of time produced the sum of four hundred and fifty odd pounds. With part of this money a Government annuity bond of fifty pounds a-year was purchased and at a meeting held in the Town Hall of Arbroath on the 21st of March, 1884, in the presence of a large concourse of spectators, he was presented with this annuity bond, together with a purse of sovereigns.

Although deeply devoted to science, Dr Brown did not fail to perceive that he had other duties to discharge, so in early life he began to take an active hand in Christian work. After coming to reside in Arbroath he became a member of Inverbrothock Church, or St Vigeans Chapel, as it was at first called, and in connection with it he became a Sabbath School teacher and librarian of the church library. During the Ten-Years' Conflict, he manifested a keen and intelligent interest in the controversy then being carried on, and of many of the discussions he retained a lively recollection. At the Disruption he joined the Free Church, and in October, 1843, was elected a deacon of Free Inverbrothock. In 1849 he became an elder of that congregation, an office which he worthily filled till the day of his death, which event took place on the 27th July, 1893. In perpetuation of his name, he left a legacy of two hundred pounds, the interest of which is to be expended on the poor of Free Inverbrothock congregation, the residue of his estate to be applied for the establishment of a bursary for boys belonging to, and resident in the town of Arbroath, who may be studying the physical sciences at the University of St Andrews or the University College, Dundee.

INDEX.

ABBACY OF ARBROATH sold (1642) to Sir Patrick Maule (Earl of Panmure), 123.
Abbey of Arbroath or Aberbrothock, 12-20, 23·7, 33-9, 41, 46, 59, 60, 85, 102, 104, 106, 110, 157, 203, 272, 379-81, 384, 393-4.
... Its Site, 12.
... Founded by William the Lion (1178), 13, 109, 393.
... Dedicated to St. Thomas (à Becket) of Canterbury, 12, 393.
... Completed (1233), 13.
... Dr Johnson's Visit to, 13.
... Royal Visitors, 13, 36.
... Kings of Scotland kept Court at, 13.
... Meeting of Convention of Estates at, when Declaration of Independence framed, and sent to the Pope (1320), 14-18.
... At the Reformation, 19.
... John Barbour and Alexander Mylne, first President of Court of Session, educated at, 23·4.
... The "St. Ruth's Priory" of the "Antiquary," 24.
... The Abbey lands in various Counties, 37-9, 76, 85, 206.
... Walter Myln of Lunan probably a Monk, 46.
... "Staines, Tymmer," &c., of, used in building Parish Church (1580), 59.
... Petition to discharge Tithes of (1574), 60
... Tradition of Burning of, by Ouchterlony of Kelly, 104.
... Despoiled by the people of Arbroath, 110.
... Its Importance, 33, 393.
... Sir Walter Scott's Visits to, 25.

Abbey of Arbroath or Aberbrothock, Abbots of. (See "Abbots.")
... Chartulary of, (See "Chartulary.")
... Duke of Lennox, Commendator of, 59.
... John Pierson, Monk of, 157.
... Alexander Lindsay, Master of Crawford, appointed Justiciar of, 203.
... Almshouse Chapel, 92
... Barn and Byre. (See "Hospitalfield.")
... Churchyard of, 102, 175, 243, 250, 384.
... Convent Gardens, 85.
... High Altar (where William the Lion was buried), 13. Litigation as to Burial Place in, 106.
... Hospital of. (See "Hospitalfield.")
... St. John the Baptist's Chapel. (See "Hospitalfield.")
... St. Thomas Chapel, despoiled by Monks, 110.
... "Yairds" of, 85.
... History of, by James Thomson, 104.
... Miller's History. (See "Arbroath and its Abbey.")
Abbey (Abbot's) House, 193-4, 393; let by Town Council for Thread Factory (1744), 193.
Abbey Parish Church, Arbroath, 297, 317, 319-22, 332.
Abbots of Arbroath or Aberbrothock, 13-21, 25, 27, 33-4, 46-7, 122, 136, 157, 203, 381, 394-5.
... Bernard de Linton, 14-16, 33, 394.
... John Gedy, 18, 33.
... William Bonkil, 18.
... Walter Panter, 203

INDEX.

Abbots of Arbroath—*Continued.*
... Richard Guthrie, 18.
... George Hepburn, 27, 156.
... James Beaton, 35.
... David Beaton, 19, 33-44, 46-7, 122, 157, 395.
A'Becket, St. Thomas, of Canterbury, Arbroath Abbey dedicated to, 12, 393.
Aberbrothock. (See "Arbroath.")
Abercrombie, Giles, wife of Richard Melville (1) of Baldovy, 55.
Abercrombie, Margaret, wife of Sir Thomas Maule, 120.
... Sir Thomas, of that Ilk, 120.
... Thomas, 55.
Aberdeen Burghs, 184, 273.
... Grammar School, 256-8.
... Free Church College, 343-4.
... Marischal College, 256-8, 263, 289.
... University, 263, 289.
"Account of the Shyre" (Forfarshire). (See "Ouchterlony, John.")
Academy, Arbroath. (See "Schools, Arbroath.")
Adamson, Patrick, Archbishop of St Andrews, 61, 68. Excommunicated by the Synod of Fife (1586), 61.
Adhesive Postage Stamp. (See "Chalmers, James.")
Africa, East, Sir John Kirk's work in, 29-30.
... West, William Wallace's work in, 30-1.
Agriculture in Scotland in beginning of 17th Century, 78.
... Grain Purchases in 18th Century, 192-3.
... The Reaping Machine. (See "Bell, Patrick," and "Reaping Machine.")
Agricultural Implements in 17th Century, 78.
Aikmans of Lordburn and Cairnie, 98, 171-82.
... Progenitors of the family with Macduff's Army, 171; origin of the name "Oakman" or "Aikman," 171; Arms, 171; Progenitors settle in Forfarshire, Lanarkshire, and Kirkcudbright, 172; Tomb of "Ten John Aikmans" in Abbey Burying Ground, 175.

Aikman, Alysandre de, swears fealty to Edward I. (1296), 172.
... Alexander threatened with Banishment, 172.
... George, of Lordburn (1560-1625), Bailie of Regality of Aberbrothock, 173.
... Captain George Robertson, of Ross, 174.
.. George Robertson, of Ross, 174-5.
... Hugh H. Robertson, of Ross, 174.
... James, Dingwall Pursuivant (1460-88), 172.
... John, held land in Lordburn (1505), 172.
Aikman, John, Lynar, Bailyie and Quartermaster of Arbroath, 172.
... John (Akman), Decane and Elimosinar of Arbroath, 173.
... John, the "Gude Laird" of Cairnie (1613-93), 171; 173 5; acquires Cairnie, 171; marries (1) Margaret, sister of Sir T. Hamilton of Preston and Rossaven, 173; (2) Euphemia Ouchterlony, who scolds the Magistrates, 173.
... John. (See "Hekman, John.")
... John, of Ross, 174.
... John Forbes, of Ross, 174.
... Margaret, marries Hugh Forbes, 174.
... Thomas, of Broomhilton and Ross, Keeper of the Records, 174.
... Major Thomas S. G. H. Robertson, of Ross and Broomhilton, 175.
... William, of Cairnie, Advocate (d. 1699), 174, 176; married Margaret Clerk, 174; Sheriff Depute of Forfarshire, 174.
... William, the Painter, (1682-1731), 98, 171-82; Student under Sir John Medina, 176; Foreign Residence, 177; settles in Edinburgh, 177; Friend of Allan Ramsay, 177, 179, 181, and James Thomson, 177, 181; marries (1723) Marion Lawson, 178; settles in London, 178; Allan Ramsay's Poem on his Departure, 178; Aikman's Portraits of Ramsay, 179, 181; his Portraits of many Celebrated Men, 180-1; His Works in Scottish National Portrait Gallery, 181; Death and Burial in Edinburgh, 182; Epitaph by Mallet, 182.
... William, of Ross, 174.
Airlie, Earl of (1846), 220.

INDEX.   427

Albert Victor, Prince, (Duke of Clarence), 149.
Ale, Act for laying Duty on, in Arbroath (1738), 186.
Alexander II., kept Court at Arbroath Abbey, 13; borrows from Abbot and Monks, 14; Progress of Scotland under him, 14.
... III., holds Court at Arbroath, 13; Prosperity of Scotland during his Reign, 14; National Dangers follow his Death, 14.
Allan, Alexander and James, Arbroath, 195.
Allan, Patrick (Allan-Fraser), of Hospitalfield, (See "Fraser").
Allan, Rev. William, Arbroath, 418.
Allan, Robert (father of P. Allan-Fraser), Stocking Weaver, Arbroath, 195, 396-7.
Almerieclose, 81, 87-102, 229-30.
... Almshouse Chapel at, 92.
... Mansion House, 92, 102, 229.
Almory, ly, Arbroath, 156.
Almshouse Chapel. (See "Almerieclose.")
Altars of Abbey—St. Duthacus, 37; St. Sebastian, 416.
Angus, County of (see "Forfarshire").
... or Forfarshire, Warden's. (See "Warden.")
... Countess of, 205.
... Earl of (1528), 36.
... Fencibles at Burns' Funeral, 396.
Anna of Denmark, James VI.'s Queen, 76.
Anderson, Joseph, LL.D., Archæologist, 29.
Ansold, Lord of Maule (1015) (See "Maule.")
"Antiquary, The" (Sir Walter Scott's), Scene laid in Arbroath and Neighbourhood, 23, 25, 38, 40, 231, 394, 396. Fairport Post Office Scene in real life, 231.
Applegate, Arbroath, 86.
Arbikie, 71.
Arbirlot, 205, 287, 291-300, 336, 356, 407, 410, 417.
... Lands of Balinhard in, 205.
... Library and Savings Bank, 296.
... Ministers of, Richard Watson (see "Watson"); Thomas Guthrie (see "Guthrie"); John Kirk (see "Kirk").
... Popular Election of Elders, 296.
... Free Church, 356, 410.

Arbroath, Aberbrothock, or Aberbrothwick, 11-31, 36-7, 40, 81-2, 84-96, 101, 107, 109-111, 145-60, 171-7, 183-201, 212-20, 227-34, 244-5, 251-4, 266-8, 379-81, 384, 393, 395, 398, 401-2, 404-5.
... In History, 11-31; existed prior to Foundation of the Abbey, 33, 379; Cromwell's attempt to land Troops frustrated, 21, 183; but borrowed Cannon taken and consequent Litigation, 22; Bombarded by Captain Fall (1781), 20-1, 208, 396: Town's indebtedness to Sir Walter Scott, 23; first represented in Scots Parliament (1579), 158; Convention of Royal Burghs held in A. (1612), 159; A Royal Burgh, 160, 184. Representatives in Scots Parliament:—David Pierson of Barngreen (1579), 158-9; John Auchterlony (1644), 105; Provost John Ouchterlony, 105. Representatives in British Parliament (see "Aberdeen Burghs" and "Montrose Burghs"); Slezer's View of A. (1692), 93; Ouchterlony's Description of the Town (1684-85), 183; John Barbour, the Poet, probably a Native, 22; The "Fairport" of Sir Walter Scott's "Antiquary," 23, 40, 231, 394, 397; Dr Johnson's Visit to, 13; Presentations of Freedom of the Burgh, 145, 216, 402.
... Men in Jacobite Rebellions (1715 and 1745), 24, 130, 185.
... Places or Streets in or near — Abbey Yairds, 85; Almerieclose, 81, 87-102, 229-30; ly Almory, 156; Applegate, 86; Barber's Croft, 37; Barngreen, 157-9; Cairnie, 171, 173-6, 272; Cobis Croft, 86; Convent Gardens, 85; Copgait, 93, 254; Dern Yett, 37; Dishland, 86; Dishland Hill, 421; Dog Hillocks, 86; Elemosinarie Croft, 87, 91; Elemosinary Street, 92; Grimsby, 93; Guest Meadow, 87, 91; Guthrieshill, 85; High Street, 85, 92-3, 244, 252-4; Hill Street, 244; Horner's Wynd (Commerce Street), 93; Keptie, 85-6, 90, 157, 159; Kirklands, 62; Lamblaw Croft, 157; Lochlands, 157,

Arbroath—*Continued.*
   Lochlands *(Continued)*, 159, 160, 161; Loch Schede, 86; Lordburn, 82, 93, 171, 175, 194; Millgate, 93; Millgate Loan, 93; Newgate, 107, 111, 252; North West Port, 90; Old Marketgate, 86; Rotton Raw, 85; School Wynd, 59; The Shuilbreeds, 90; Smithy Croft, 157; Wareslap Sched, 86.
... Cliffs and Caves near, 23, 111, 272.
... Trade in, 186, 188-97, 212-3, 231, 251, 266-8, 276-7, 396-7. Linen Trade, 188, 193-5; Importation of Flax, 188; Trade with Riga, 189; Manufacture of Osnaburgs, 189; Shipping, 186, 188; Duty on Ale, 186; Timber Trade (1737), 191; Grain Trade, 192, 231; Thread-making, 194; Stocking-making, 195, 396-7; Herring Fishing, 197; Commercial Depression early in Nineteenth Century, 212-3; Railway Enterprise, 213-8; Bakers' Corporation, 251; Printing, 266, 268; Government Contracts for Canvas, 267; Handloom Weaving, 276-7.
... Battle of (1445), 20, 203-4.
... Burgh Records, 84, 94-5, 99, 253, 380.
... Canal from A. to Forfar proposed, 213.
... Dean of Guild of, 184, 185, 252.
.. *Herald*, 281.
... *Magazine* (1799-1800), 268.
... Magistracy composed of Wallaces, 185.
... Magistrates raise Company in "the Fifteen," 130.
... Meteorological Station, 421.
... Town Hall, 214, 220, 229.
... Town House and Prison, rebuilding of, 186.
... Water Supply, 402, 405.
... Abbacy. (See "Abbacy.") Abbey. (See "Abbey.") Abbots of A. (See "Abbots") Academy. (See "Schools.") Artists. (See "Artists.")
... Churches. (See "Churches.")
... Free Church Presbytery. (See "Presbytery.")

Arbroath—*Continued.*
... Free Public Library. (See "Library: Arbroath Public.")
... Grammar School. (See "Schools.")
... Harbour. (See "Harbour.")
... Infirmary. (See "Infirmary.")
... Literary and Scientific Association and Literary Club. (See "Literary Societies.")
... Museum Society. (See "Museum.")
.. Parish Ministers. (See "Parish Ministers.")
... Picture Gallery. (See "Picture Gallery.")
... Poets. (See "Poets.")
... Presbytery. (See "Presbytery.")
... Provosts. (See "Provosts.")
... Public Library. (See "Public Library.")
... Schools. (See "Schools.")
.. Town Clerks. (See "Town Clerks.")
... Town Council. (See "Town Council.")
... Volunteers. (See "Volunteers.")
Arbroath and Forfar Railway, 213-8; early Schemes, 213; W. F. Lindsay Carnegie, the first Promoter, 214; Rejoicings at Cutting of first sod, 216-7.
"Arbroath and its Abbey," (1860), by D. Miller, 37, 379-81; First Popular History of Burgh, 379; Light thrown on Early History of Abbey, 380; Old Burgh Records, 380; Scope of Book.
Arbuthnot, Alexander, 62.
... Lord (1749)—Grain transactions with Arbroath Merchants, 193.
... Lords of, 224.
Argyle, Duke of, the friend of William Aikman of Cairnie, 180.
... Earl of, possesses lands of Boysack, 206.
Arnat, Captain, 73.
Arnott, Family of, 251-64; in Arbroath, 251-5.
... Alexander, Merchant, Arbroath, 254-6; Father of Neil Arnott, 254; marries Ann Maclean, daughter of Maclean of Borreray, 254; a Runaway Match, 254; Tenant of Over Dysart, 254; an unsuccessful Farmer, 255; removes to Blairs, near Aberdeen, 255; trys Shopkeeping in Aberdeen, 256.

Arnott—*Continued.*
... Ann Maclean, Wife of William A., and Mother of Neil A. (See "Maclean.")
... James, Merchant, Arbroath, 252.
... Neil (1788-1874), M.D., LL.D., F.R.S., Physician Extra ordinary to the Queen, 27, 249, 251-64; Friendship with Dr Sharpey, 249, 263; Born in High Street, Arbroath, 254; Error as to Birthplace, 254-5; his Parents, 254-6; Extract from Register of Births, 255; spends early years at Upper Dysart, 255; removed to Blairs, Aberdeenshire, 255; at School at Lunan and Maryculter, 255-6; his Mother's Influence, 256; removes to Aberdeen, 256; Family Straits, 256-7; at Aberdeen Grammar School and Marischal College, 256; Apprentice to a Chemist, 257; a distinguished Student, 257; not Contemporary of Lord Byron at School, 257; at St George's Hospital, London, 258; favourite Pupil of Sir Everard Home, 258; Surgeon on East Indiaman, 259; Practises in London, 260; Physician to Foreign Embassies, 261; Lectures, 260-1; his Book "The Elements of Physics," 261; Rapid Sale and many Editions and Translations, 261-2; other Works, 262; Member of Senatus, London University, 262; Physician to the Queen, 262; Inventions, 262-4; marries Mrs Knight, 262; founds Scholarships, 263; his Death, 263.
... Thomas (1), Town Councillor and Burgh Treasurer, Arbroath (1729), 251-2.
... Thomas (2). Bailie of Arbroath (1752), 252-3.
... William, Grandfather of Neil Arnott, 252-4; holds Property in Arbroath, 252; Tenant of Over Dysart, 252-4.
Arrat. (See "Arrott.")
Arrat, Lands and Barony of, near Brechin, 223-4; part sold by David de Arroch to Thomas de Rate, 223; acquired by Lords of Arbuthnot, 224.
Arrath, Arroch. (See "Arrott.")

Arrott (Arrot, Arrat, Ariot, Arrade, Arroch, or Arrath), Family of, 223-43, 245; Antiquity, 223; Name derived from Estate of Arrat, 223.
... of Dumbarrow and Almerieclose, Family of, 223-43.
... Alexander, son of Dr William A., 232.
... Andrew, of Dumbarrow (1654), 224-5.
... ... (grandson) (d. 1760), 225-6; Minister of Dunnichen, 225; deposed (1745), 226; builds Church at Dumbarrow, and officiates as Secession Minister, 226.
... Andrew, Original Secession Minister of Wick, 226.
... Christian, wife of William Murray, Brechin (1606), 224.
... Catherine, daughter of William A. of Dumbarrow, 227.
... Colin, son of William A. of Dumbarrow, 227.
... David (de Arroch) (1378), 223.
... David, Bailie, Aberdeen (1531-38), 224
. David, son of William A., of Dumbarrow, 227.
... David (1807-76), M.D., Arbroath, son of Dr William A., 232-8; 250. Education, 232-3; at Berlin University, 233; in Practice with his Father at Arbroath, 233; a Linguist, 233; Literary taste, 234; a Poet, 234-5; Love affairs and Verses by, 234-6; Public Appointments and Offices, 237; Lines by David Carnegie on his Death, 238.
... Elizabeth (circa 1606), 224.
... ... wife of John Bell, minister of Logie Pert, 225
... Elizabeth, daughter of William A. of Dumbarrow, 227.
... Grant, daughter of William A. of Dumbarrow, 227.
... Jacobina (Mrs Martin), daughter of Dr William A., 230, 232.
... James, son of William A, of Dumbarrow, 227.
... Dr James, a relative of Arbroath Family, 228.

Arrott—*Continued.*
... James (1808-83), M.D., Dundee, son of Dr William A., 232, 239-43, 250; Education, 239; Travel and Studies on Continent, 239; settles in Dundee, 239; Public and Professional Life, 240; instrumental in erection of Dundee Infirmary, 240; the Inventor Laennec's Stethescope in his Possession, 240, 242; publicly presented with Portrait, 242; Abilities and Character, 242-3; Buried at Arbroath Abbey, 243; Bequests for Arbroath Poor, 243.
... John de Arrat, in Ragman Roll (1296), 223.
... John, of Baikie, Professor of Philosophy, St Andrews, 224-5.
... Julia, daughter of William A. of Dumbarrow, 227.
... Magdalene, daughter of William A. of Dumbarrow, 227.
... Margaret, wife of John Willison, minister of Dundee, 225.
... Mary, daughter of Dr William A., 232.
... Richard, of Arrath, 223.
... Robert, son of Wm. A., of Dumbarrow, 227.
... William, of Arrade or Arrath (1256), 222.
... William, of Dumbarrow (circa 1650), 224-6.
... William, of Dumbarrow (circa 1730), 225.
... William, of Dumbarrow, Minister of Montrose (d. 1730) 225-6.
... William, of Dumbarrow, (d. 1811), 226-8; sells Dumbarrow and removes to Arbroath, 227.
... Willam (b. 1774, d. 1862), M.A., M.D., Arbroath, 227-33, 239, 242, 245; born at Dumbarrow, 228; marries Mary Balfour, widow of Henry Sharpey, 228-9, 245; Education, 228; Classfellow of Joseph Hume, 228; practises in Forfar and in Arbroath, 229; acquires Almerieclose Mansion House, 229; his Death. 230.
... William Henry, son of Dr William A., 232.
Arrott's Mortification, Arbroath, 243.

Artists, Arbroath, William Aikman of Cairnie. (See " Aikman.")
... Patrick Allan-Fraser. (See " Fraser.")
... A. Bell Middleton. (See " Middleton.")
Arran, Earl of, defied by Andrew Melville, 61
Athole, Earl of (Walter Stewart), 118.
Auchmithie (the Musselcrag of Scott's " Antiquary "), 23-4, 38.
Auchterhouse, 125, 366.

BALDOVY, a Rendezvous of Reformers, 46, 55.
Balfour, in Fifeshire, 35.
... Alexander (1767-1829), Poet and Novelist, 23, 228, 265-74; born at Monikie, 265; early Writings, 266; Apprentice Weaver, 266; Teacher, 266; Clerk in Arbroath, Canvas Manufacturer, 267; formation of Arbroath Literary Club and Arbroath Public Library, 267; Contributor to " Arbroath Magazine," 268; Elegy on Burns, 269; Patriotic Songs, 269-70; leaves Arbroath, 270; Bankrupt and ill, 270; at Balgonie, 271; with Blackwood in Edinburgh, 271; confirmed Invalid, 271; Novels and Poems, 272-3; Grant from Treasury, 273; Death, 274.
... David, Provost and leading Merchant of Arbroath, 227-8.
... George, of Tarry, 70.
... James, cousin of James Melville, 57.
... James, Minister of " Edvie," 61
... Janet, daughter of Sir Michael B.. 34.
... Mary (d. 1836), marries (1) Henry Sharpey, 228, 244; (2) Dr William Arrott, 228, 245; assists Jameson with " Popular Ballads and Songs," 231; her Family, 232, 244.
... Sir Michael, of Balfour, 34.
... Patrick, Burgess of Arbroath (1605), 85.
Balfoure, David, de Guynd, 87.
... James, of North Tarry, 87.
Balinhard, Lands of, 205.
... John de, Ancestor of Carnegie Family, 205-6
Balnamoon, 223.

"Band," Protestant, of Gentlemen of Mearns (1556), 45.
... "Common or Godlie" (1557), 45.
Barber's Croft, Arbroath, 37.
Barbor, John. Croft near Dern Yett let to, 37.
Barclay of Mathers, a Mearn's Epicure, 54.
... Sir David, of Lindores, 118.
... Jean, marries Sir D. Fleming, 118.
... Margaret, wife of Sir D. B., acquires Brechin Estate, 118.
... Margaret, Countess of Athole, succeeds to Lordship of Brechin, 118.
... Robert, purchases Almerieclose, 101.
... Rev. Robert, of Lunan, 340-1.
Barngreen, Arbroath, 157-9.
Barrie, J. M., 25.
Barry, 22, 122, 294-5, 336-42, 410.
.. Free Church, 340-1.
... Links, 122, 295, 336; Golf and Football on (1497), 122; Horse-racing, 336.
... Ministers, John Kirk, (see "Kirk"); James Lumsden, (see "Lumsden.")
... Parish Church. 336, 340.
Bassendean, Berwickshire, 345-6.
Beaton, Beton, Bethune, family in Forfarshire and Fifeshire, 34, 107.
... David, of Ethiebeaton, Sheriff of Forfar (1290), 34.
... David (1494-1546), Abbot of Arbroath. 19, 26, 33-44, 46, 47, 122, 157, 395, 400; Rector of Campsie, 35; Abbot of Arbroath, 35; Hatred of Reformation Principles, 36; Lord Privy Seal, 36; Alienation of Abbey Lands, 37, 38; his Mistress Marion Ogilvie (see "Ogilvie"); resided at Ethie, 38; Legend of "Beaton's Leg," 38; gifts Hospitalfield to Marion Ogilvie, 40; his Autograph at Hospitalfield, 40, 400; his Character, Cruelty, Persecutions, 19, 40, 41; his Children, 39, 40, 122; made Cardinal, 41; Chancellor of Scotland, 41; murdered at St Andrews, 42-3; his Patriotism, 44; condemns Walter Myln and Petrie to Death, 47.

Beaton—*Continued*.
... David, son of Cardinal B., 39.
... James, Abbot of Arbroath, 35.
.. Margaret, daughter of Cardinal B., 40, 122.
... Mary. (See "Betune.")
Beatoun of Westhall, 107.
Bell, George, brother of Rev. Patrick B., 371-4.
... James, minister of Logie Pert, 225.
... Rev. Patrick, LL.D., Carmyllie (1801-69), Inventor of the Reaping Machine, 363-78, 399; Education, 366; Tutor to Charles Baillie (Lord Jerviswoode), 366; in Canada, 366; Presented to Carmyllie Parish (1843), 366; Mechanical Ingenuity, 366; Invention of the Reaping Machine, 367-71; a Successful Trial, 371; at British Association, 372; the Reaper in Practical use, 372; Bell's Reaper Publicly Proved Superior to all Others, 374-6; Public Testimonial, 377.
Bell Rock Lighthouse, 25-6*
Bennet, Lady Ida, Countess of Dalhousie. (See "Dalhousie.")
Bernard de Linton, Abbot of Arbroath, 14-16, 33, 394; Draws up Declaration of Scotland's Independence (1320), 15-17; Fights at Bannockburn, 17.
Berwick-on-Tweed, 303, 306.
Betune, Sir Alexander, 34.
... David, Comptroller to James IV., 34.
... John (1), of Balfour, 34-5.
... John (5), of Balfour, 34.
... (Beaton), Mary, one of the "Four Maries," 34.
... Robert of, 34
... Beza, Theodore, Sir Peter Young a Pupil of, 64, 74.
Blackcraig, Perthshire, 404.
Blackness, near Dundee, 156.
Blair, Dr (Cupar Angus), at Sheriffmuir, 133.
Blairs, near Aberdeen, 255-6.
Blawearie, Berwickshire, 345-6.
Blindloch, 159.
Blind Toll, 385.
"Boiled Sheriff," a Royal Recipe, 54.

Bolshan, 123.
Bonkil, William, Abbot of Aberbrothock, 18.
Border Quarries, 211.
Boysack, Lands of, 206; belonged to Arbroath Abbey, 206; Acquired by Alexander, Lord Spynie, 206; by Sir John Carnegie (Earl of Northesk), 206.
Boysackmuir, 385-6.
Bowar, George (Arbroath), "missays" George Crysty (1564), 158.
Bowman, Betty, wife of Alexander Brown, LL.D., 420.
Breach of Promise Case, in 16th century, 40, 122.
Brechin, 21, 117-8, 123, 129, 134, 223, 253, 287-91, 321-2, 324, 331.
... Castle Beseiged by English, 117.
... Castle, Chevalier de St George at, 134.
... East Free Church, 324, 331.
... Estate Gifted to Lady Margaret Barclay, 118.
... Lordship of, 118, 123.
... Parish Church of, 21, 253, 321-2.
... Presbytery, 322.
Brewster, Sir David, 420.
Briechen, David de, 16, 118; Marries sister of King Robert de Bruce, 118.
British Association at Dundee (1867), 247, 372, 421.
British Linen Company, 196.
Broomhilton, Lanarkshire, 174.
Brown, Alexander, Chaplain of Altar of St Sebastian, 416.
... Alexander, LL.D., the Arbroath Astronomer (1814-93), 27, 415-23; born at Grange of Conun, 415; his Parents, 415-6; baptised during Snow Storm, 416; a Handloom Weaver, 417; studies Astronomy, 417-8; Meteorological Work, 419, 421; leaves the loom and becomes a Clerk, 420; friendship with Sir David Brewster, 420; his Papers read at the British Association Meetings, 420-1; public recognition, 422-3; LL.D. of St Andrews, 422; public presentation of annuity, 422-3; Church Work, 423; founds University Bursary, 423

Bruce, King Robert. (See "Robert I.")
Brunton, of Ethie, 37, 46.
Buchan, William, Town Councillor, Arbroath (1624), 86.
Buchanan, George, Preceptor to James VI., 65, 66, 68, 70, 75-6; his treatment of the King, 65.
... Isabella, wife of Dr Robert Lee, 312.
... Rev. Dr Robert, 312.
Burns, Robert, 269, 396, 409; Angus Fencibles at his Funeral, 396; Portrait by Archibald Skirving, 409.
Byron, Lord, at Aberdeen Grammar School, 257.

CAIRNCONAN, 385.
Cairnie, 98, 171, 173-7, 218.
Caithness, Earl of (1320), 16.
Campbell, Jane, wife of Earl Panmure, 124.
Campsie, 35, 311-2, 334.
Carey, David, Arbroath, 266.
Carey, George, Arbroath, 417-8.
Carmichael, Alexander, Dundee. lends cannon to defend Arbroath against Cromwell, 22.
Carmyllie, 206, 295, 347-56, 366; non-intrusion conflict in, 347-50; the Disruption, 351-6.
.. Free Church, 351; battle of the sites, 352.
... Free Church, William Wilson, Minister, 1843-8. (See "Wilson.")
... Parish Church, 347-51, 356
... Parish Ministers, William Robertson, (d. 1836), 348; William Wilson—(1837-43.) (See "Wilson.") Patrick Bell—(1843-69.) (See "Bell.")
... School in 18th century, 359.
Carnegie, Family of, 27-8, 205-22; John de Balinhard, their ancestor, 205.
... Lands of, give name to family, 206.
... Alexander, Minister of Inverkeilor (1805-36), 408-9; marries daughter of Adam Skirving, author of "Johnnie Cope," 408; purchases Redhall, 409.
... Captain Alexander, of Redhall, 409.
.. George Fullarton, of Pitarrow and Charlton, 409.

Carnegie—*Continued.*
... Sir David, of Kinnaird, 201-2; a Town Councillor of Arbroath (1781), 201.
... David, an Arbroath Poet, 238.
... James, fourth Laird of Boysack, 206; Private Secretary to Prince Charles Edward, 206; flees to France, 207; obtains Prince Charles' wig and coat, 208; last male Carnegie of Boysack Branch, 208.
... Lady Jane, daughter of Earl of Northesk, 210.
... Lady Jane Christian, daughter of William, seventh Earl of Northesk, 210, 219, 221; marries William F. L. Carnegie (1820), 210.
... Janet, marries William Maule, 120.
... John, ancestor of Earls of Southesk, 120.
... John de Balinhard (1210), 205.
... John, of Carnegie, 205.
... John, second Laird of Boysack (1678), 206.
.. John, third Laird of Boysack, M.P. for Forfarshire and Solicitor-General, 206.
... John, of Boysack (1738), 188.
... John, of Kinnaird, 70.
... John, of that ilk and Seaton, 70.
... John (d. 1805), Minister of Inverkeilor, 408; his wife Catherine Walker, 408.
... John, of Redhall (d. 1879), 409.
... Sir John, Earl of Northesk. (See "Northesk.")
... Margaret, marries John Fullerton, 206.
... Stewart, marries William Fullerton, 208-9.
... Lindsay-, of Spynie and Boysack, family of, 202, 204, 206, 209-22.
... ... Henry Alexander Fullerton, of Spynie and Boysack, 221-2; at Siege of Delhi, 222.
... ... James Fullerton (1764-1805), 209; assumed name of C., 209.
... ... James (d. 1814), Commander R.N., 209; at Trafalgar, 209

Carnegie, Lindsay—*Continued.*
... ... William Fullerton (1788-1860), 20, 201-22, 398; his ancestors, 202-9; hereditary fowler to Scottish Kings, 209; succeeds his brother, 209; service in Peninsula, 209; marries Lady Jane C. Carnegie, 210; his Quarries, 211; interest in Arbroath affairs, 211, 219; railway enterprise, 213-8; Arbroath and Forfar Railway promotion and opposition, 214-6; freedom of Arbroath presented, 216; public offices, 220-1; portrait presented, 220, 398.
Carnegies, Earls of Northesk. (See "Northesk.")
... of Redhall and Inverkeilor, 409-10.
Carnegy, James and Patrick, Town Councillors, Arbroath (1624), 86.
... of Newgait, 107, 111.
Cay (Guthrie), Clementina, mother of Thomas Guthrie, 288.
Chalmers, James (1782-1853), Inventor of Adhesive Postage Stamp, 28, 275-84; born in Arbroath, 276; Bookseller in Dundee, 277; marries Barbara Dickson, relative of Baron Oscar Dickson 277; publications, 277; Town Councillor and Treasurer, Dundee, 278; invention of adhesive postage stamp, 28, 278-80; exhibits stamp (1834), 280; submits plan to Select Committee of Commons (1837), to Rowland Hill (1838), 281; adopted by Treasury (1839), 282; now admitted he was the inventor, 282; importance of invention. 283-4.
... Patrick, of Aldbar, 14, 18-9; M.P. (Montrose Burghs), 217.
... Rev. Thomas, D.D., 238, 285, 306, 319, 333; a member of St Vigeans Masonic Lodge, Arbroath, 238.
... William, father of James Chalmers, 276.
... William, Bookseller, Dundee, 277.
Chapelton, 160, 221.
Chaplin, of Colliston, 215.
Charles I., 106, 123.
... II., 108.

Charles Edward, Prince, 206-8; relics at Kinblethmont, 208.
Chartulary of the Abbey of Arbroath, 14, 18, 33, 37, 379-80.
Chevalier de St George. (See "Stuart, James.")
Chisholm, Catherine, wife of William Arrott of Dumbarrow, 226.
Church of Scotland, 26-7, 55-62, 82-4, 96, 145, 225-6, 253, 285-6, 290-8, 303-5. 308-16, 319-22, 334-8, 340-1, 345-52, 365-6, 382, 407-10; poverty of clergy (1565-76), 57-8; clergy as tavernkeepers, 57-8; grievances of the Kirk, 61; prelatical party in, (1606), 82; "Five Articles of Perth," 83; persecutions by Claverhouse, 96; restoration of patronage (1712), leads to secession, 26, 226; Disruption (1843)—See "Free Church;" voluntary controversy, 286, 294-5, 309-10; non-intrusion question (ten years' conflict), 26, 286, 297, 312, 322-3 340-1, 347-51; Church extension, 297, 300, 335; forms of public worship, 304, 309, 313-6.
Churches in Arbroath—"The Lady Chapel," 59; Parish Church, 59; Inverbrothock Parish (St Vigeans Chapel), 229, 308-11, 314-5, 333-6, 423; Abbey Parish, 297, 311, 317, 319-22, 332; Ladyloan Parish, 335; Glassite, 276; St Paul's U.P. (Relief), 217, 418; East Free, 342, 356; Free Inverbrothock, 423.
Clarendon, Earl, appoints James M'Cosh professor in Belfast, 325.
Claverhouse. (See "Grahame, John.")
Clement, Ninian, first Parish Minister of Arbroath, 53.
Clerk, John, of Penicuik, 174.
... Sir John, of Penicuik, 179.
... Margaret, marries William Aikman, 174.
Cliffs and Caves near Arbroath, 25, 111, 272.
Clow, Pearsons of. (See "Pearson.")
Cobis Croft, Arbroath, 86.
Collace, William, 1st Regent of St Leonards, St Andrews, 57.

Colliston, 91
Convention of Estates, held at Arbroath (1320), 15-8.
... of Royal Burghs, 59, 158-9, 184; assist building of Arbroath Parish Church, 59; held in Arbroath (1612), 159.
Copgait, Arbroath, 93, 254.
Corbit, Jean, wife of James Philip (3) of Almerieclose, 95, 99.
... John of Tollcrosse, 95.
... Peter, Maltman, Glasgow (1686), 95.
Crawford, Archibald de (1442), 104.
... Earl of, killed at Battle of Arbroath, 204.
... Earl of (10th), David, 204.
... Earl of (21st), John Lindsay, 202.
... Master of, Alexander Lindsay. (See "Lindsay.")
... Master of, David, 38, 40.
Cromwell attempts to land troops at Arbroath (1651), 21-2, 183.
Crysty Willyam, Brewer, Arbroath, (1564), 157-8.
Culdees settle in Arbroath district, 381.

DALHOUSIE, Countess, Sarah Frances, wife of 12th Earl, 147.
... Countess, Ida, wife of 13th Earl, 149-50, 153.
... Earl of, (5th), William, 141.
... Earl of, (6th), George, 141.
... Earl of, (9th), George, 143.
... Earl of, (11th), Fox Maule. See "Maule."
... Earl of, (12th), George (1805-1880), 146-9; succeeds to Earldom (1874), 146; born at Kelly, 147; services in Navy, 147.
.. Earl of (13th), John William (1847-1887), 148-54; in Navy, 148; Lord Ramsay, 148; with Royal Princes, 148-9; student at Oxford, 149; contests Liverpool in Liberal interest, 149; M.P., 150; succeeds to Earldom, 150; a model Landlord, 151-3; his death, 153; "the good Earl," 154.
... Earl of (14th), Arthur George Maule (b. 1878), 147, 153.

INDEX.

Davidson, Lily (Mrs R. Lee). (See "Lee.")
... Rev. Dr, 286, 310.
Dean of Guild, Arbroath, 184.
Declaration of Scottish Independence by Scottish Convention at Arbroath Abbey (1320), 15-8; drawn up by Abbot Bernard, 15, 17.
Dern Yett, Arbroath, 37.
Dickmont Law, 71, 76, 273.
Dickson, Bailie, Montrose, 277.
... Barbara, wife of James Chalmers, 277.
... Baron Oscar, 277.
Dishland, Arbroath, 86; Hill, 421.
Disruption, The (1843). (See "Free Church.")
Doghillocks, Keptie, 86.
Donald, Lord of the Isles, revolts (1411), 119.
Douglas, Lord James (1320), 16.
Douglas, John, of Tilquhilly, 68.
Douglases in Battle of Arbroath (1445), 203.
Dress in 1586, Sir P. Young's instructions to his retinue, 73.
Drummond of Hawthornden, 121, 161; a friend of David Pierson of Lochlands, 161, 163.
Dumbarrow, Lands of, 224-8; acquired by Arrotts, 224.
... Secession Kirk at, 226.
Dun, a Rendezvous of Reformers, 46, 55.
Duncan, David, of Greenbank, his public bequests, 382-3.
Duncanson, James, Minister of Alloway (1612), 85.
Dundee, 21, 22, 129, 134, 239-43, 277-84, 356-7, 360-2, 421, 423.
.. Viscount. (See "Grahame, John.")
Dunnichen, 103, 225-6.
Durie, Simon, Minister of Arbroath, 88.
Dysart House, 46.
Dysart, Over or Upper, Lunan, 253-5; tenanted by Arnotts, 253; not birthplace of Neil Arnott, 254; transferred to various parishes, 253.

EAST FREE CHURCH, Arbroath, 342, 356.
Edinburgh, 137, 177, 300-2.
... Ragged Schools, 301-2.
... University, 232, 239, 245, 263, 313, 319, 334, 346, 357, 410.
Educational Institute, Arbroath. (See "Schools.")
Edward I., 13, 15, 117; at Arbroath, 13.
... II., 15-7.
Edzell, 129.
Electric light in 1831, 361.
Electric communication with America proposed by Lindsay, 361.
Elemosinarie Croft, Arbroath, 87.
Elemosinary Street, Arbroath, 92.
Eliot, Andro, Town Councillor, Arbroath (1624), 86.
Engine, the triple expansion, 411-2.
Erskine, John, of Dun, 46, 55, 123.
... Margaret, wife of Patrick Maule (1), 123.
Established Church of Scotland (See "Church.")
Ethie, 37-8, 60; gifted by William the Lion to Arbroath Abbey, 37.
... House, 23, 38, 40; residence of Cardinal Beaton, 38.
... ... "Knockwinnock" of "The Antiquary," 23, 38, 40.
Ethiebeaton Estate, 34.

"FAIRPORT" in Scott's "Antiquary," Arbroath, 23, 40, 231, 394, 397.
Fall, Captain, bombards Arbroath (1781), 20, 208, 396.
Fethe, Elizabeth, wife of Adam Pierson (1529), 157.
Fethyn, Duncan de (1254), 157.
Fife, Earl of (1320), 16.
... An archæological map of, 382.
Findlay, John, printer, Arbroath, 268.
... John Ritchie, of *The Scotsman*, 29, 31, 181; an Arbroathian, 29, 131; donor of Scottish National Portrait Gallery, 29, 31, 181.

Flax Trade, Arbroath. (See "Arbroath Trade.")
Fleming, Sir David, 118.
... Marion, marries William Maule, 118, 123.
... Lady Mary, marries Harry Maule, 136.
Flodden, Battle of, 27, 121, 156; Abbot of Arbroath killed at, 156
Forbes, Hugh, of Pittencrieff, 174.
... John (Aikman), 174.
... Patrick, of Cors, 57.
Forfar, 53, 160, 213, 228.
Forfarshire and Jacobite Plots, 125-35.
... In "the Fifteen," 130-5.
... Old Pretender's progress through, 134-5.
.. Members of Parliament, 140, 142, 206, 217.
... Volunteers. See "Volunteers."
Fothringham, Thomas, of Powrie, 125.
Fraser of Hospitalfield, Family of, 28, 88, 111, 208, 393-406.
... Captain David, of Hospitalfield (1766), 396.
... Elizabeth, wife of Patrick Allan-Fraser, 396, 398, 400.
... James, Minister of Arbroath (1653-69), 88, 395-6; marries Isobel Philip, 88, 395; buys Hospitalfield, 88, 395.
... James (2) of Hospitalfield, 396.
... John (1) of do., 396.
... John (2) of do., 396, 400; Major Angus Fencibles, 396; at Burns' Funeral, 396.
... Patrick Allan- (1813-90), of Hospitalfield, H.R.S.A., 28, 195, 220, 393-406; portraits by, 220, 398-9; marries Elizabeth Fraser, 396, 398; his parents, 397; apprenticed housepainter, 397; studies art, 397; succeeds through marriage to estates, 398; reconstructs Hospitalfield, 398; his art collection, 398; W. P. Frith's reminiscences of, 399; collection of artists' portraits by themselves, 399-400; erects Mortuary Chapel, 400-1; literary works, 401-2; Arbroath water supply, 402, 405; public offices and honours, 402; provisions of his will, 403-6.
... Sir William, 38, 205.

Free Church of Scotland, 26-7, 144-6, 286-7, 297, 301-2, 311-3, 323-4, 340 4, 350-8, 382-4, 407, 410; the Disruption, 26-7, 144-5, 286-7, 301, 311-3, 323-4, 340-1, 350-6, 382, 407, 410, 423; moderators of, 302, 346-7, 357; battle of the sites, 340, 352-6.
... Presbytery of Arbroath. (See "Presbytery.")
Frith, W. P., R.A., 399-400; reminiscences of Patrick Allan-Fraser, 399.
Friockheim, 216.
Fullerton (Foulerton), of that ilk, 202, 206-9; hereditary Fowlers to Kings of Scotland, 209.
... John, marries Margaret Carnegie, 206.
... Jean, 206.
... Colonel William, of Fullerton. (See "Lindsay, W. Fullerton.")
Funerals on Sundays discountenanced, 336-7.
Fyff, David, "reader" at Kinnell (1574), 60.

GAIRDNER, John, Bailie of Arbroath (1760), 253.
Gallowden, 100.
Gardener, John, merchant, Arbroath (18th century), 190, 193-4.
Gardiner, Guy, teacher, Berwick, 305-6.
Gardyne, James, of Middleton, 189, 192, 194, 199.
Gardyne of Middleton, 215, 348.
Gardyne, widow, gives site for Carmyllie Free Church, and is ejected, 353-5.
Gedy, John, Abbot of Arbroath, builder of Harbour, 18, 33.
Gellatly sues Arbroath Town Council for malversation, 198.
Gemmels, Andrew, and Edie Ochiltree, 24.
George, Prince (Duke of York), 149.
Gib, Eliz., 1st wife of Sir P. Young, 68.
Gladstone, Sir John, 323-4.
... Right Hon. W. E., 323-4.
Glamis, Lord, 107, 205.
... Old Pretender at, 134.
Glasgow University, 263, 312, 319.

Glassite Church, Arbroath, 276.
Gleig, Rev. George, Minister of Arbroath (1787-1835), 292.
"Glenlusse, the last Abbot." 73.
Goodall, James, Provost of Arbroath, 217.
Grahame, John, of Claverhouse, Viscount Dundee, 24, 27, 95-6, 98-100.
... John, "The Grameid"—Poem descriptive of his campaign, 96.
... Margaret (Duntrune), wife of James Philip (2) (1653), 91, 93, 95, 99.
... Walter, of Duntrune, 91.
... Sir William, of Claverhouse, 91.
Grainger, John, Bailie of Arbroath (1624), 86, 91.
"Grameid, The," by James Philip, poem descriptive of Claverhouse's campaign, 27, 96-8; manuscript in Advocate's Library, 96.
Grammar School, Arbroath. (See "Schools.")
Grange of Conon, 415-6.
Gray, Sir Andrew, of Foulis, 119.
... Elizabeth, wife of Sir T. Maule, 119.
... Lord, 107.
... James, charged with spoliation of Ethie, 38.
Greenford, Lands of, 103, 118.
Greyfriars (Old) Church, Edinburgh, 297-300, 313, 321.
"Grievances of the Kirk, The," 61.
Guestmeadow, Arbroath, 87.
Guthrie, of Guthrie, 220.
... Dr Alexander, Brechin, 331.
... Sir David, of that ilk, Justice General, 120.
... David, grandfather of Thomas Guthrie, 129.
... David, Provost of Brechin, father of Thomas Guthrie, 288.
... Colonel David, 291.
... Harie, of Colistoun, 91.
... Isabella, wife of Principal M'Cosh, 331.
... James, Incumbent of Arbirlot, 90.
... Jane, his daughter, 90.
... John, brother of Thomas Guthrie, 291.
... Richard, Abbot of Aberbrothock, 18.

Guthrie—*Continued*.
... Rev. Thomas (1803-1873), D.D., Minister of Arbirlot, 26, 129, 285-302, 308-13, 321, 331, 335-6, 340, 345, 347, 407; opposes voluntaryism, 286-7, 309; his ancestors, 129, 288; education, 288; pupil of Dr M'Crie, 289; at Aberdeen University, 289; licensed to preach, 290; banker in Brechin, 291; presented to Arbirlot, 293; as a preacher and speaker, 293-5, 299; introduces popular election of elders, 296; advocates Church extension and abolition of patronage, 297, 300; recommended for Old Greyfriars, Edinburgh, 297, 321; unwillingly accepts, 298; work in Edinburgh, 300; out at the Disruption, 301; Free Church Manse Scheme, 301; "Plea for ragged schools," 300-2; Moderator of Free Assembly, 302; his death, 302; friendship with Robert Lee, 311
Guthrieshill, Lands of, 85, 91.
Guynd, 87, 104-7; acquired by Ouchterlonys, 104; described by Ouchterlony, 107. (See also "Ouchterlony" and "Pearson.")

HALES, Lord (2), 156.
Halley's Comet, Dr Brown's diagram, 418-9.
Hallyburton, Lord Douglas, M.P. for Forfarshire, 217.
Hamilton, Archibald, apprehends Walter Myln, 48.
... John, "Chalmerlain of Aberbrothock" (1624), 86.
... Margaret, wife of John Aikman, 173
... Patrick, the martyr, 36.
... Sir William, 319, 327.
Hamiltons in Battle of Arbroath, 203.
Harbour of Arbroath, 18, 33, 185-8, 191, 211-2; built by Abbot Gedy, 18, 33; special Act to levy money (1738), 186-8; affairs separated from those of the Burgh (1836), 212.
Harlaw, Battle of, 119.

Harris, Rev. David, Fearn, "a self important Presbyter," 322.
Harvesters before the reaping machine days, 363.
Hats, a large order for (18th century), 199.
Hawkesbury Hall, 396, 398.
Hay, of Letham Grange, 215.
... Gilbert de, Constable of Scotland (1320), 16.
Hekman, John, Bailie of Montrose (1490), 172.
Henderson, John, Arbroath (1643), 99.
Hepburn, George, Abbot of Arbroath, third son of Lord Hales, fell at Flodden, 27, 156.
Herring fishing in 18th century, 197.
High School, Arbroath. (See "Schools.")
High Street, Arbroath, 85, 92-3, 244, 252-4.
Highland and Agricultural Society, 365, 373-5, 377.
Hill School, Arbroath. (See "Schools.")
Hill Street, Arbroath, 244.
Hill, Sir Rowland, not the Inventor of the Adhesive Postage Stamp, 275-6, 281-3
Hislop, Rev. Alexander, Arbroath, 342.
Hodge, Dr Charles, Princeton, 327-8.
Home, Sir Everard, 258-9.
Hooke, Colonel, plan for Rebellion (1707), 125; visits Forfarshire, 125-6
Horner's Wynd (Commerce Street), Arbroath, 93
Horse-racing on Barry Links, 336.
Hospitalfield, 23, 25, 39-40, 88, 111, 208, 393-406; given by Cardinal Beaton to Marion Ogilvie, 39, 395; "Monkbarns" of "The Antiquary," 40, 394; Beaton's Autograph at, 40, 400; purchased by James Fraser, Minister of Arbroath, 88, 395; Ouchterlony's description, 111; the Hospital of the Abbey, 393-4; Abbey Barn and Byre at, 394; Paintings by P. Allan-Fraser at, 397-9; P. Allan-Fraser succeeds through marriage, 398; the Art Collection, 397 400, 406; Portraits of Artists by themselves at, 399-400; the Library, 400; Art Students to be educated at, 403-5.
"Howff, The," Dundee, 284.

Huddlestone, Robert (d. 1820), teacher, Lunan, 256.
Hume, John, of Cumeragane, 73.
... Joseph, M.P. for Montrose Burghs, 28, 228, 273, 282.
Hunter, James, Leysmill, invents stone-dressing machines, 211.
Huntingdon, David, Earl of, 118
Huntly, Marquis of, acquires Melgund, 39.

INCHCAPE ROCK, The, 25-6.
Inchmichael, reaping machine at, 372, 374.
Infirmary, Arbroath, 229, 402, 404.
Innes, Cosmo, 14, 18-9.
Inverbrothock Free Church, Arbroath, 423
... Parish Church, 229, 308-11, 314-5, 333-6, 423.
Inverkeilor, 47, 408-10.
Irvines, of Drum, 104.

JACOBITE PLOTS (1707), 125, (1715), 127.
... Poems, 96, 408-9.
... Relics at Kinblethmont, 208.
... Rebellion (1715), 24, 129-35; (1745), 24-5, 185, 206-8, 409; festivities in Arbroath, 24 5; Arbroath rebels, 24, 185.
James I., 15, 54; recipe for cooking a sheriff, 54.
... III., 13.
... IV., 13, 121.
... V., visits Arbroath, 13, 36, 40, 122; advice to one about to marry, 40, 122.
... VI., 65, 77, 79, 82, 123, 204-5; George Buchanan and Peter Young, his preceptors, 65; catalogue of his library, 66-8; his handwriting, 67-8; friendship with Alex. Lindsay, 204; aids in his wooing, 205; makes him Lord Spynie, 205.
... VII. and II., 124-5.
... VIII. (See "Stuart, James.")
Jameson's "Popular Ballads, &c.," 230.
Jervise, Andrew, F.S.A.Scot., 394, 399.
"Johnnie Cope," the author of, 408-9.
Johnson, Dr, visits Arbroath and Abbey, 13.
Johnstone, Arthur, the King's Physician, 161.

KEILLOR, Trial of Reaping Machines at, 374-6.
Keith, Lords Marischall, 16, 107.
Kelly, Arbirlot, 70, 103-4, 113, 139-40, 147, 407.
Kenny in Kingoldrum, 103.
Keptie (Arbroath), Lands in, 85-6, 90, 157, 159.
Kinblethmont, 71, 206-8; acquired by Carnegies, 206 ; Jacobite Relics at, 208.
Kincardineshire, Melvilles Hereditary Sheriffs of, 53-4.
Kings, Scottish, and Arbroath Abbey, 12-8, 36-7, 109, 111, 393.
Kinnell Church (1574), 60.
Kinnaird, the Old Pretender at, 134.
... Lord, 374.
Kippenross (Dunblane). (See " Pearson.")
Kirk, Alexander Carnegie (1830-92), LL.D., Engineer, 28, 299, 407-14; born at Barry, 407 ; the Carnegies, his mother's family, 408 ; descendant of author of "Johnnie Cope," 408; education, 410; professional training, 410 ; manages important works, 411-2; inventions, 411-2; the triple expansion engine, 411-2; joins firm of Napier, 412; lectures, &c., 412 ; his character, 413.
... Rev. John, minister of (1) Barry and (2) Arbirlot, 286, 299, 309, 336, 345, 407-8, 410 ; at Barry, 299, 336, 407 ; at Arbirlot, 299, 336, 407; out at the Disruption, 407
... Sir John, 29-30, 299, 408 ; in Crimean War, 29 ; travels with Livingstone, 29-30 ; British Consul at Zanzibar, 30 ; virtual ruler of Country, 30 ; Knighthood, 30.
Kirk lands of Arbroath, 62.
Kirkland, —, Rector of Hill School, Arbroath, 245.
Kirkton of St Vigeans. (See "St Vigeans.")
Knight, Mrs, marries Neil Arnott, 263.
"Knockwinnock" ("The Antiquary"), Ethie House, 23, 38.

Knox, John, 19, 26, 55, 75 ; at Baldovy and Dun, 55 ; personal appearance described by Sir P. Young, 75.
Kyd, Dr John, Spynie, 420.

LADY CHAPEL, The, Arbroath, 59.
Ladyloan Parish Church, Arbroath, 335.
Laennec, inventor of the stethoscope, 241-2.
Laird, Rev. John, D.D., Inverkeilor and Cupar, 286, 346-7.
Lamb, Andrew, Minister of Arbroath, afterwards Bishop of Brechin, 81.
... James, of South Tarrie, 89.
Lambert, Jane (Mrs G. Lee), mother of Robert Lee. (See " Lee.")
... Robert and Joanna, grand-parents of Robert Lee, 304.
Lauder, Robert Scott, R.S.A., 28, 397-8, 400.
Lauderdale, Earl of, 408.
"Law, The." (See " Marywell.")
Lawson, Marion, wife of William Aikman of Cairnie (the painter), 178.
Leases of Arbroath Abbey Lands, 37.
Lee, Rev. Anthony Pye, 305.
... George, Tweedmouth, father of Robert Lee, 303-6 ; as precentor improves psalmody, 303-4
... George, brother of Robert Lee, 306.
... George, son of Robert Lee, 315-6.
... Jane (Lambert), mother of Robert Lee, 303-4.
... Robert and Lilly (Davidson), grandparents of Robert Lee. 303
... Rev. Robert (1804-67), Minister of Inverbrothock Church, Arbroath, and Greyfriars, Edinburgh, 286-7, 297, 303-16, 333-4, 340, 345 ; born at Tweedmouth, 303 ; his parents, 303-4 ; his grandfather an innovating precentor, 304 ; bred a Presbyterian, 304-5 ; Anglican environment, 304 313-4 ; education, 305 ; learns boat building, 305 ; his brothers, 305 ; at St Andrews University, 305 8 ;

Lee—*Continued.*
 private tutor at Exeter, 306-7; tutor to Whyte Melville, the novelist, 307-8; Minister of St Vigeans Chapel of Ease, Arbroath (Inverbrothock), 308; practical preaching gives offence, 308-9; congregational and public work, 286, 309-11; called to Campsie, 311; Guthrie's letter of farewell, 311; a "Moderate," 312; marriage, 312; appointed to Old Greyfriars, 313; Professor of Biblical Criticism, Edinburgh, 313; troublous times and struggles in Church Courts, 313-6; "innovations" in Church service, 309, 313-15; doctrines called in question, 315; death, 316.
... Robert, "Life and Remains of," by Professor Story, 305-6, 309-14.
... William, brother of Robert Lee, transported to Siberia, 305.
Lennox, Duke of, commendator of Arbroath Abbey, 59.
... Earl of (1320), 16.
Leslie, John } kill Cardinal Beaton, 42-3.
... Norman }
Leven, Earl of, 408.
Leysmill Quarries, 211.
Library, Arbroath Public, 228, 265, 267-8, 310, 402,
... of James VI, 66-8.
... James Maule's designs for a, 137.
Limesay, Randolph de (see "Lindsay.")
Lindsay, family of, 202-4.
... of Pitscottie, 203.
... Alexander, Master of Crawford, 20, 203; appointed Justiciar of Monastery of Arbroath, 203; fights Ogilvies at Battle of Arbroath (144-5), 20, 203.
... Alexander, first Lord Spynie, 204-6, 209; a friend of James VI., 204-5; marries Dame Jean Lyon, 205; acquires Boysack, 206.
.. Colin, marries Lady Jane Carnegie, 210; Charles II. interested in match, 210.
... David, sells Edzell, 129.

Lindsay—*Continued.*
... James Bowman, (1799-1862), electrician and linguist, 27, 359-62; born at Carmyllie, 359; education, 359-60; a weaver, 360; at St Andrews University, 360; teacher in Dundee, 360; electric light, 361; proposes telegraph between Britain and America, 361; electric communication without wires, 361; "Pentecontaglossal Dictionary," 361; Government Pension, 362; death, 362.
... James Fullerton. (See "Carnegie, James F. Lindsay-.")
... Thomas, "reader," Arbroath (1570-4), 60, 173.
... Walter de, first Lindsay in Scotland, 203.
... William Fullerton, 208, 396; marries Stewart Carnegie, 208; assumes name of Lindsay, 208; at Fall's Bombardment of Arbroath, 280, 396.
Lindsay-Carnegie. (See "Carnegie.")
Linen trade in Arbroath. (See "Arbroath Trade.")
... British Linen Company, 196.
Linton, Bernard de. (See "Bernard.")
Literary and Scientific Societies, Arbroath, 219, 234, 267, 418-9.
Livingstone, David, Sir John Kirk's travels with, 29-30.
... Helen, spouse of James Duncanson, minister of Alloway, 85.
Lochlands, 157, 159, 161.
.. Piersons of. (See "Piersons.")
Loch Schede, Arbroath, 86.
London University, 262-3.
Lordburn, Arbroath, 82, 93, 172.
Loudon, Earl of, 124.
Lownie, Lands of, 103.
Lowsone, James (1574), 68, 75.
Lumgair, John, Provost of Arbroath, 229.
Lumsden, Rev. James (1810-1875), of Inverbrothock and Barry Churches, Principal of Free Church College, Aberdeen, 286-7, 333-45; born at Dysart, 333; education, 333; at St Andrews and Edinburgh,

Lumsden—*Continued.*
333-4; assistant to Dr Bonar at Larbert, 334; City Missionary, Dunfermline, 334; Minister of Inverbrothock, 334-5; presented to Barry, 336; attacks horse-racing and Sunday funerals, 336-7; comes out at Disruption, 340-1; joint editor of *The Presbyterian*, 341; charged with heresy, 342; relations with Sweden, 342; a Knight of Sweden, 342; Professor Aberdeen Free College, 343; Principal, 344; his death, 344.
Lunan, 36, 46, 52, 71, 88, 90, 253-6, 340-1, 416.
... Walter Myln, Priest of. (See "Myln.")
Lyell, ———, an Arbroath merchant (1764), 198.
... Catherine, spouse of Richard Watson, Arbroath (1605), 85.
... Sir Charles, 23.
... Captain Thomas, 130.
Lyndsay, Sir David, 35, 43.
Lyne, Robert, Town Councillor, Arbroath (1624), 86.
Lyon, Dame Jean, wife of Alexander, Lord Spynie, 205.
... Lord Glamis, 107.
... Patrick, of Auchterhouse, 125.

M'Ash, ———, teacher, Arbroath, 418.
M'Beth, Rev. James, Ladyloan Church, 334-5.
M'Cheyne, Rev. R. M., 334, 346-7.
M'Cosh, Rev. James (1811-94), Minister of Abbey Church, Arbroath, Principal of Princeton University, America, 26. 286-7, 295, 297-9, 317-32, 336, 340, 345 348; born in Ayrshire, 317; education, 319; Minister of Abbey Church (1835), 319; asked to become candidate for Old Greyfriars, 297, 321; recommends Guthrie, 297, 321; presented to Brechin, 321; Presbyterial objections, 322; Disruption, 323; Sir John Gladstone's tribute, 324; and W. E. Gladstone, 324; Minister East Free Church, Brechin, 324; philosophical

M'Cosh—*Continued.*
works bring him into prominence, 324-5; Professor Queen's College, Belfast, 325; Thackeray's ballad on the appointment, 325; President Princeton College (1868), 326; Princeton's importance increases under him, 328-9; his wife Isabella Guthrie, 331; visits early home, 331; interest in Arbroath, 332; death, 332.
... Jaspar (d. 1729), 332.
M'Crie, Rev. Dr, teaches in Brechin, 289.
M'Culloch, Rev. J. M., Arbroath and Greenock, 286, 308, 333.
Macdonald, Alexander, painter, Arbroath, 397.
... Flora, kinswoman of Neil Arnott, 254.
... Isabella, wife of Robert Allen, 397.
Mackay, Sir James L., K.C.I.E., 29.
Mackie, Alexander, Minister of Arbroath (d. 1787), 292.
MacLean, Ann (d. 1860), daughter of MacLean of Borrerary, wife of William and mother of Neil Arnott, 254.
Maisondieu Hospital, Brechin, 223.
Mallet, David, verses on William Aikman of Cairnie, 382.
Mann, Provost, Arbroath, 219, 398.
Mar, Earl of, at Battle of Harlaw, 119.
... Earl of, (1634), sells Lordship of Brechin, 123.
... Earl of, (Charles), 124.
... Earl of, (John), 24, 124, 127-34.
.. Earl of, (John), demands men and money from Arbroath, Montrose, &c., 130-2.
... Lady, and James VI., 65.
March, Earl of, (1320), 16.
"Maries, The Four," 34.
Marischal College, Aberdeen, 256, 261.
... Lord, 107.
Marketgate, Old (Arbroath), 86.
Martin, David, Dundee, 232; his wife, Jacobina Arrott, 220, 232.
Mary, Queen of Scots, 12, 34, 76.
Maryton Parish, 253.
Marywell, 189.
Martyrs, Scots, 26, 36, 45-52.

Maule, Family of, 26-7, 39-40, 107, 113-54, 160; French stock, 113-6, 135: came over with conqueror, 116; alliance with House of Brechin, 118; union with Ramsays of Dalhousie, 141
... Alexander, son of Sir Thomas (4), 120.
... Ansold (1), Lord of (1015), 114; (2) "The Rich Parisian," 114; (3), 115.
... Elizabeth, wife of Thomas Pierson, 160.
... Fox (1801-74), 2nd Baron Panmure, 11th Earl of Dalhousie, 26-7, 113, 142-7, 148-51; Succeeds to Barony, 143; in army and in Parliament, 143; Government offices and honours, 143; War Secretary during Crimean War, 144; succeeds to Earldom, 144; takes part in Disruption, 26, 145; freedom of Burgh of Arbroath, 145; Barony extinct at his death, 147.
... Gaurin, Lord of, 114.
... George, 2nd Earl Panmure, 124.
...   ...   3rd Earl Panmure, 124.
... Harry, of Kelly ("Earl Harie" of Panmure), 113-40; compiles "Registrum de Panmure," 113; a Jacobite, 124; distrust of his nephew, Earl of Mar, 128; joins Mar's Rebellion, 129; at Sheriffmuir, 133; rescues his brother, the Earl, 133; flees to Holland, 135; Jacobite correspondence, 135; valuable historical work, 136; death, 140.
... Sir Henry, 118.
... Janet, wife of Alexander of Ouchterlony (1394), 103, 118.
... Lady Jean, Countess of Northesk, 124.
... Jean (daughter of Harry Maule) marries George, Lord Ramsay, son of 5th Earl of Dalhousie, 141.
.. James, 4th Earl of Panmure (d. 1723), 113-4, 124-36; visits Panmore in France, 114, 135; a Jacobite, 125; distrusts Mar, his nephew, 128; raises Jacobite standard in Brechin (1715), 129; his regiment in "the Fifteen," 130, 132-3; wounded and taken prisoner at Sheriffmuir, 133; Mar's neglect, 134; entertains Old Pretender at

Maule—*Continued.*
Brechin, 134; in France, 135; attainted, and estates forfeited, 135; death, 135.
... James (d. 1729), son of Harry Maule, 114, 127, 135-40; visits Panmore in France, 114, 135-6; assists in compilation of "Registrum de Panmure," 136; designs for library in Edinburgh, 137; death, 140.
... John, of Inverkeilor (1738), 188.
... Mary, Countess of Mar, 124.
... Sir Patrick (1) (d. 1605), 123.
...   ...   (2) 1st Earl Panmure (1586-1661), 123-4; attends Charles I. at English Court, 123; purchases Lordship of Brechin and Abbacy of Arbroath, 123; created Earl, 123; writes History of Wallace, 124.
... Lord Peter (1), 114.
...   ...   (2), 115.
... Sir Peter (d. 1254), 116-7; marries heiress of Panmure, 116.
... Richard, 116.
... Robert (a Norman), comes to Scotland with David I., 116.
... Sir Robert, 120 a; besieged by English at Panmure, 121; prisoner in Tower of London, 121; embraces reformed religion, 122.
... Robert, Commissary of St Andrews, 122.
... Roger, 116.
... Sir Thomas (1) (d. 1303), is killed at siege of Brechin Castle, 117.
... Sir Thomas (2) (d. 1411), 118-9; killed at Harlaw, 119.
... Sir Thomas (3) (1411-50), 119.
... Sir Thomas (4), "the Blind Knight," 120.
... Sir Thomas (5) (d. 1573) fell at Flodden, 27, 121.
... Sir Thomas (6) (d. 1600), at siege of Panmure and battle of Pinkie, 122; James V. dissuades him from marrying Cardinal Beaton's daughter, 40, 122.
... Sir Walter (d. 1348), 118.

INDEX.

Maule—*Continued.*
... William, in Battle of the Standard (1138), 116.
.. William, of Panmure (1254), Sheriff of Forfarshire, 117.
... Sir William, of Panmure, 103, 118-9.
... William, grandson of Sir Thomas Maule (4), 120.
... William (d. 1782), Earl of Panmure (Irish Peerage), 140-1, 188, 199; M.P. for Forfarshire, 140; last of male line of Maules, 140.
... William Ramsay (d. 1852), 1st Baron Panmure, 141-3, 214, 293, 299, 351-6, 377, 400; succeeds to Panmure estates, 142; M.P. for Forfarshire, 142; created Peer, 142; prodigality and neglect of estates, 142, 147, 151; evicts non-intrusionists in Carmyllie, 351-2; refuses site for church, 352-6.
... Rev. Dr, Monikie, 266.
Mearns gentlemen's "Religious Band," 45.
Melbourne, 388-91; Ormond College, 390-1.
Melgund, 39, 103.
Melville, Andrew, the reformer, 54, 61, 68, 77, 83.
... George J. Whyte, the novelist, 307.
... James, at Beaton's murder, 43.
... James, second Protestant Minister of Arbroath, 26, 53-62, 69, 77; Minister of Tannadice. 53. 58; meets the leading reformers, 55; education, 55; stipend withheld, 57; Minister of Arbroath, 58; aids building of Parish Church, 59; stipend in Arbroath, 60; presents "grievances of the Kirk" to the King, 61; date of death uncertain, 62.
... James, the younger, 55-7, 61, 68; his diary, 57, 61, 68.
... John, of Dysart, 46.
... Richard (1), 46. 54-5: fell at Pinkie, 54; father of James and Andrew Melville, 54.
... Richard (2), of Baldovy (d. 1575), 54-5; 60.
... Sheriff of Kincardineshire, "sodden and supped in broo," 54.

Melville—*Continued.*
... Melvilles, Hereditary Sheriffs of Kincardine, 53-4.
Meteorological Station, Arbroath, 421.
Middleton, A. Bell, an Arbroath artist, 28, 230, 400.
Miller, David (1809-79), author of "Arbroath and its Abbey," 37, 379-84; scope of his work, 379-81; born in Strathmiglo, Fife, 381; constructs archæological map of Fife, 382; writer in Arbroath, 382; public work in Arbroath, 383; frames provisions of Duncan bequests, 383-4.
... Hugh, 23, 420.
Ministers of Arbroath. (See "Parish Ministers.")
Miln, David, reader at Ethie Church, 60.
Minto Family and Melgund, 39.
"Moderates, The." (See "Church of Scotland.")
Monastery of Arbroath. (See "Abbey.")
Monasticism, downfall of, in Scotland, 19.
Moncrieff, Rev. Sir Henry W. (8th Baronet), 285.
... Rev. Sir Henry (10th Baronet), 346, 358.
Monikie, 265
"Monkbarns" of "The Antiquary," Hospitalfield, 23, 40, 394.
Montrose, 129, 131-2, 135, 225, 269-70.
... Burghs, Members of Parliament for, Joseph Hume—(see "Hume"); Patrick Chalmers (1836), 14, 18-9, 217; John Morley, 28.
Moray, Earl of (1320), 16.
Morley, Right Hon. John, M.P., 28.
Mortimer, Peter, burgess, Cupar (1629), 88.
Mortuary Chapel, Arbroath Cemetery, 400-1.
Mowbray, Roger de (1320), 16.
Mudie, David, Town Clerk, Arbroath (1738) 188.
... John, Town Councillor, Arbroath (1624), 86.
... John, merchant, Riga, 189.
Mudies of Pitmuies, 189, 215.
Muir, Rev John, St Vigeans, 419-20.
Muirlands, 101.

Murdoch, Rev. Alexander D., editor of *The Grameid*, 96.
Murray, A. S., LL.D., British Museum, 29
... Lady Janet, of Torphichen, second wife of Sir P. Young, 69.
... William, Brechin (1606), 224.
Murrays of Melgund, tradition of, 39.
Museum Society, Arbroath, 219, 237.
"Musselcrag" of "The Antiquary," Auchmithie, 23, 24.
Mylne, Alexander, first President of Court of Session, educated at Arbroath, 23.
Myln, John and Robert, Brunton, Ethie (1510), 46.
... Thomas, Arbroath, (1653), 85.
... Walter (1476?-1558), of Lunan, the last of the Scots martyrs, 26, 36, 45-52; presented by Beaton to Lunan (1526), 46; condemned to death by Beaton, but flees to Continent, 47; returns to Scotland, 47; trial at St Andrews, 48-51; burned at stake, 51; influence of his death on Reformation principles, 51; obelisk at St Andrews, 52; tablet in Lunan Church, 52.

NAIRNE, Marjory, third wife of Sir Peter Young, 69.
Napier, R. & Son, shipbuilders, 412.
Natural History Society, Arbroath, 421.
Naughty, Robert, a teacher of navigation, 418.
New Testament, Tyndall's translation in Forfarshire, 47.
Newgate, Arbroath, 107, 111, 252.
Nicol, Professor, 419.
Nicolson, James, a Prelatic Minister (1606), 83.
Niger Company's Territories, Wm. Wallace administrator of, 30.
Nolt Loan Water Supply, Arbroath, 402, 405.
Northesk, Earl of (1st), Sir John Carnegie, 206.
.. Earl of (2nd), David, 124.
... Earl of (5th), David, 188.
... Earl of (7th), William, 28, 210; at Trafalgar, 28.

"OCHILTREE, EDIE," an Arbroath prototype of, 23, 24.
Ochterlony, John, Town Councillor, Arbroath (1624), 86.
Ogg, Sir William A., 29.
Ogilvie, Alexander, usurps Bailiary of Arbroath causing Battle of Arbroath, 203.
... Sir James, Lord Ogilvie of Airlie, 37.
... Marion or Mariote, mistress of Cardinal Beaton, 37-9, 395.
Ogilvie's (Lord) battalion in the '45, 24.
... (Lord) regiment in French service, 208.
Ogilvy, Agnes, spouse of Patrick Balfour, Arbroath (1605), 85.
... Sir John, of Inverquharity and Cairnie, 176, 240, 242.
... of Lintrathen, 107.
Oliphant, Andrew, priest, an accuser of Walter Myln, 48-9.
... Magdalene, wife of Rev. William Arrott of Dumbarrow, 225.
Orkney, Earl of (1320), 16.
Ormond College, Melbourne, 389-90.
... Francis, sen., 386-7; early life at Boysack Muir, 385-6; voyages to Australia, 386-7; emigrates to Australia, 387; hardships of pioneer life, 387.
... Francis, M.L.C. of Victoria, emigrates (1842), 387; sheep-farming, 387; a wealthy landowner, 388; interest in education, 388-91; his munificence, 390-1; the Ormond College, 389-90; member of Legislative Council, 391-2; his death, 392.
... James, Boysack Muir, 385-6; his sons, George, James, Robert, and Thomas, 386.
... Port, Australia, 386.
"Osnaburgs," manufactured in Arbroath, 189-90.
Oswald, Margaret (Lumsden), mother of Principal Lumsden, 333.
... Robert, Dysart, grandfather of Do., 333.
Over Dysart. (See "Lunan" and "Arnott, Neil.")
Ouchterlony (estate), William Young of, 63. (See also "Ouchterlony of that ilk.")

Ouchterlony—*Continued*.
... (Auchterlonie), Family of, 27, 103, 107, 160.
... of that ilk, 27, 103 4, 107, 118; appeal by Sir William Wallace to, 27, 104.
... of Kintrocket, 106, 107.
... of the Guynd, 27, 103-12, 127, 160, 188; burial place in High Altar, Arbroath, 106; tradition of burning Arbroath Abbey by, 104.
... Alexander (1394), 103, 118.
... Alexander, of Kelly (1409), 104
... Euphemia (1693). wife of John Aikman of Cairnie, 173; slanders the Magistrates, 173.
... Isobell, wife of (1) James Philip, (2) James Lamb, (3) Peter Young, 89-91.
... John, of the Guynd, marries Janet Pearson, 160.
... John, of the Guynd, author of "The Account of the Shire," 92, 94, 103-12, 160, 224; his account of his family, 107; his "Account of the Shire" (of Forfar) (1684-5), 92, 94, 107, 108, 224; plan of work, 108-9; description of Arbroath and neighbourhood, 109-12, 183.
... John, of the Guynd (1715), 127.
... John, of the Guynd (1738), 188.
... John, of the Guynd (d. 1843), 106.
... John, represents Arbroath in Parliament (1644), 105.
... John, Provost, Arbroath, represents town in Parliament, 105, 173.
... John, town-clerk, Arbroath, 94.
.. John, of Montrose, marries Ruperta Skinner, descendant of Prince Rupert, 106-7.
... Robert, of Kintrocket, 107.
... William, of Kintrocket, 103.
... William, laird of Kelly (1583), 70.
... William, laird of Wester Seaton (1583), 70.
... Major-General, of the Russian army, 106.
... a prying post-master of Arbroath, 231.

PALMER, Johnnie, an Arbroath Jacobite soldier and gaberlunzie, 245.
Panlathy, 122, 372.
Panmore, France, 114, 135.
Panmure, Baron (1), William Ramsay Maule. (See "Maule, William R.")
... Baron (2), Fox Maule. (See "Maule, Fox.")
... Baron, title extinct (1874), 147.
... Earl of, had election of 1st Bailie of Arbroath, 109.
... Earl of (1). (See "Maule, Sir Patrick.")
... Earl of (2). (See "Maule, George.")
... Earl of (3). (See "Maule, George.")
... Earl of (4). (See "Maule, James.")
... "Earl Harie" of. (See "Maule, Harry.")
... Estate, 139, 141-2, 147, 151.
... House besieged by English, 121-2.
... "Registrum de," 113-4.
... and Forth, Earl. (See "Maule, William.")
Panmure's regiment in "The Fifteen," 130, 132.
Parish Ministers of Arbroath after Reformation—Ninian Clement (-1573), 53; James Melville (1573-9—) (see "Melville, James"); Andrew Lamb (1596-1601), 81; Henry Philip (1601-27) (see "Philip, Henry"); Simon Durie (1628-53), 88; James Fraser (1653-69), 88, 395-6; Alexander Mackie (1776-87), 292; George Gleig (1787-1835), 292; William Stevenson (1835-44), 286-7, 309.
Parliament, Scottish, held in Arbroath. (See "Convention of Estates.")
Patna, Ayrshire, 318, 331.
Patronage, Church. (See "Church of Scotland.")
Pearson families, of Clow, 157, 170, 408; of Kippenross, 157, 170; of Pierson's Baithe, 157.
... Alexander, of Clow, 408.
... Sir Charles, Lord Pearson, 169.
... David R., M.D., Kensington, 170.
Peirson. (See "Pierson.")
"Pentecontaglossal Dictionary," 361.
Perison. (See "Pierson.")
Perrot, Elizabeth, daughter of Francis Perrot, of Hawkesbury Hall, marries Major John Fraser, 396.

INDEX.

"Pest, The," precautions against, in Arbroath (1566), 172.
Peter, Alexander, Councillor, Arbroath (1624), 86.
Petersone, Isabella, wife of Dr Henry Philip, 85, 87, 91, 102.
.. Robert, "Bailly of Cowper" (1629), 88.
Petrie, John, Priest of Inverkeilor, 47.
Philip, Philp, Philpe, Philipe, or Phillip, Family of, Almerieclose, 78, 81-102, 182, 229, 395.
... (Philpe), David, Lordburn (1587), 82.
... (Philp), David, in Pittilly (1629), 88.
... Henry, D.D., Minister of Arbroath, 26, 78, 81-8, 90-1, 395; his origin, 81; Minister of Arbroath (1601), 82; a prelatist, 82; church business, 83-4; property in Arbroath, 84-5; his house in Rotton Raw, 85; Town Councillor (extra-ordinary) Arbroath, 86; tomb, 102
... Isobel, wife of Rev. James Fraser of Hospitalfield (1654), 87, 88, 395.
... (Philipe) James (1587), 82.
... (Philpe) James (1614), schoolmaster, Arbroath, 90.
... James (1629), Minister of Lunan, 88, 90.
... James (1) of Almerieclose (d. 1634), Bailie of Arbroath, 87-91.
... James (2) of Almerieclose, 89, 90-3, 95; marries (1653) Margaret Graham, Duntrune, 61; supposed to be builder of Almerieclose House, 92; bound over to "keep the peace," 99.
... James (3) of Almerieclose (b. 1654-5), author of *The Grameid*, 27, 93-101; at Arbroath Grammar School and St Andrews University, 93; his classfellows, 93; probably studied law in Edinburgh, 93; discovery of manuscript law notes supposed to be written by him, 94; marries Jean Corbit, 95; standard bearer to Graham of Claverhouse, 96; epitaph on Aikman, 98, 182; abuses the Magistrates, 99.
... James (4) of Almerieclose, 100-1.
... James (5) of Almerieclose, 101; merchant in Arbroath and governor of St Martin's, 101.

Philip—*Continued.*
... John, R. A., "Spanish Philip," 399-400.
... Margaret, wife of James Piersone, Town Clerk, Arbroath, 89.
... Marjory, daughter of Henry Philip, 87.
... Peter (Almerieclose), 92, 95.
... Susanna, wife of Alexander Wilson, sells Almerieclose to Robert Barclay (1753), 101
... Walter (Almerieclose), 92.
Picture Gallery, Arbroath, 230, 422.
Pierson (Person, Perisone, Peirson, Pearson. Piersonne), Family of, 23, 86, 89, 99, 106-7, 155-70, 188.
... Family of, Lochlands, 86, 99, 155-70.
... Adam, of Keptie (1529), 157.
... (Peirson), Alexander, Councillor, Arbroath (1624), 86.
... (Piersone) Alexander, Dumfries, (1369), 156.
... Archibald (1582), 159-60.
... Archibald, of Chapelton, Sheriff-Depute of Forfarshire, 160.
... Bernard, 157.
... (Perisone), "Mercator de Scotia" (1369), 155.
... (Piersone) David, North Berwick (1369), 156.
... David, Arbroath, ancestor of Pearsons of Pierson's Baithe, 157.
... David, of Barngreen, Bailie of Arbroath (1564), 157-60; first representative of Arbroath in Parliament (1579), 158.
... David, of Lochlands, author of "Pierson's Varieties," 23, 155-70; a friend of Drummond of Hawthornden, 161. 163; publishes (1635) "The Varieties," 161; oldest book by Arbroathian in existence, 161; the contents and curiosities of the book, 162-9.
... George. first Treasurer of Arbroath, 159-60.
... Henry (1396), 156.
... (Peirsone), Henry, Councillor, Arbroath (1524) 86.
... Isobel, wife of Archibald Pierson, 160.
... James, of Keptie, Lochlands, &c., 157.

Pierson—*Continued.*
... (Piersone) James, Town Clerk, Arbroath, 89.
... (Piersone) James, Arbroath (1643), 99.
... James Alexander, of the Guynd (d. 1873), 106, 169.
... Janet, wife of John Ouchterlony of the Guynd, 160.
... (Piersone) John, Haddington (1369), 156.
... (Perison), John de, Servitor to James I. (1425), 156.
... John, Monk of Arbroath, 157.
... James, of Balmadies (1738), 188.
... (Persoun), Mariota (1508), 156-7
... (Perison), Thomas, of Blackness (1450), 156-7.
... (Piersone) Thomas, of Keptie (d. 1524), 156 7.
... (Pearson), Thomas, Arbroath, ancestor of Pearsons of Clow, 157.
... Thomas, of Lochlands and Barngreen, 86, 159-60; president of Convention of Burghs at Arbroath (1612), 159; negotiates for Charter to Arbroath as Royal Burgh, 160.
... Thomas, Minister of Forfar, 160.
... Thomas, of Lochlands (1643), 99.
... (Piersonne) Wautier de, signs Ragman Roll, 155.
... (Pearson), Walter, Arbroath, ancestor of the Pearsons of Kippenross, 157.
Pierson's Baithe, Dunfermline, 157.
Port Ormond, Australia, 386.
Portrait Gallery, Scottish National, founded by John Ritchie Findlay, an Arbroathian, 29, 31, 181.
Postage Stamp, Adhesive, Invention of, (See "Chalmers, James.")
Postal System, Penny, 275-6, 278-84; Exorbitant Rates of Postage, 278-9; Rev. S. Roberts' scheme for uniform rate, 279; James Chalmers' and other plans for prepayment, 280-1; Hill's plans complicated, 281; Chalmers' scheme adopted, 282.
Powrie, Colonel Hooke at, 125.

Prain, David, Brechin, and the Adhesive Stamp, 280.
"Presbyterian, The," 341.
Presbytery, Arbroath Established, 285-7, 292, 297, 308, 310, 335, 337, 339-41, 345, 347, 349-50, 395, 410; longevity of members, 292; "never out of hot water," 339.
... Arbroath Free, 341, 356, 383-4; David Duncan's bequests, 383.
Preston, Battle of, 409.
Preyston, Ayrshire, 103-4.
Princeton College, New Jersey, 297, 321, 326-32.
"Princetoniana," by Rev. C. A. Salmond, 328.
Printing in Arbroath, 265, 268.
Provosts of Arbroath, 105, 183-5, 217, 219, 227, 229, 395, 398; John Ouchterlony (1653), 105; William Wallace (1724 and 1728), 184-5; John Wallace (1727-8); Patrick Wallace (1729), 185; John Wallace (1738-41), 183-5; David Balfour (1796-99), 227; James Goodall (1822-5), 217; Alexander Mann (1839-43), 219, 398; John Lumgair (1855-8 and 1861-7), 229.

QUAIN'S ANATOMY, Sharpey's edition, 249.
Queen's College, Belfast, 321, 325-6.

RAGGED SCHOOLS, Dr Guthrie's, 301-2.
"Ragman Roll, The," 155, 223.
Railway, Arbroath and Forfar. (See "Arbroath and Forfar Railway.")
... Dundee and Arbroath, 218.
... Station, Arbroath, 157.
Rait, Colonel, C. B., of Anniston, and the Ashantee War, 28.
Ramsay, Allan, 141, 177-9, 181; claimed kinship with Dalhousie family, 141; ode on union of houses of Maule and Ramsay, 141; a friend of Aikman of Cairnie, 177-9, 181; portraits by Aikman, 179, 181.

Ramsay—*Continued.*
.. Arthur George Maule, 14th Earl of Dalhousie. (See "Dalhousie.")
... George (Lord), marries Jean Maule (1726), 141.
... George, 6th Earl of Dalhousie. (See "Dalhousie.")
... George, 9th Earl of Dalhousie. (See "Dalhousie.")
... George, 12th Earl of Dalhousie. (See "Dalhousie.")
... John, father of 12th Earl of Dalhousie, 146.
... John William, 13th Earl of Dalhousie. (See "Dalhousie.")
... Lady. (See "Dalhousie, Countess Ida")
... Thomas, in Kirkton (1591), 62.
Rany, John, cordiner in Aberbrothock (1628), 78.
Rate, Thomas de (1378), 223.
Raysis Myl (Ethie), 46.
"Readers" in churches of Arbroath, &c , (1574), 60.
"Reading the Line," 303-4.
Reaping Machine, The, 363-77; Patrick Bell, the inventor of (See "Bell, Patrick"); harvesting before its invention, 363; unsuccessful machines, 364-5; public trials, 373-6; American machines modelled on Bell's, 373-4.
Rebellions of 1715 and 1745. (See "Jacobite Rebellions.")
"Rebels, List of" (1745), 185.
Redcastle, 111.
Redhall, Carnegies of, 409-10.
Redlintie, in Barrie's "Sentimental Tommy," Arbroath, 25.
Reformation in Scotland, 19, 45, 51-6, 122.
"Registrum de Panmure," 113, 136, 140.
"Registrum vetus de Aberbrothoc." (See "Chartulary.")
Relief Church, Arbroath. (See "St Pauls.")
Renny or Rany, Family of, in Arbroath for 300 years, 78.
Richardson, John, in Kirklands of Arbroath, 62.
Riga, Trade between Arbroath and, 189.
Ritchie, John, a founder of *The Scotsman*, 31.

Ritchie, Rev. Dr, of Potterrow, 286, 310.
Robert I. (Bruce), 13-18, 118; at convention of estates in Arbroath Abbey (1320), when declaration of independence issued, 15-18.
Roberts, Rev. Samuel, originator of uniform rate of postage, 279.
Robertson, Elizabeth, Perth, wife of William Arrott, 227.
... Sarah Frances, Countess Dalhousie. (See "Dalhousie.")
... William, Minister of Carmyllie (d. 1836), 348.
Robertson-Aikman. (See "Aikman.")
Rolt on the Lindsay pedigree, 202.
Ross, Earl of (1320) 16.
Ross and Broomhilton, Lanarkshire, 16.
Rotton Raw, Arbroath, 85.
Royal Society of London, Professor Sharpey and, 247.
Rupert, Prince, 106.
Rynd, Alexander, Town Councillor, Arbroath (1624), 86.

St Andrews, Archbishop of, 35, 61.
... University, 55-7, 83, 93, 209, 224-5, 228-9, 263, 305-8, 313, 333, 360, 366, 377, 422-3.
St Duthacus Altar, 37.
St Fort, Walkers of, 408.
St John's Church, Edinburgh, 300-1.
St Paul's U.P. Church, Arbroath (Relief), 217, 418.
"St Ruth's Priory" in "The Antiquary," Arbroath Abbey, 24.
St Thomas à Becket, Arbroath Abbey dedicated to, 12, 393.
St Vigean Lodge of Free Masons, Arbroath, 238.
St Vigeans, 38, 60-1, 70, 78-9, 111, 386, 415-6, 419
... Chapel. (See "Inverbrothock Church.")
... Church, 70, 78-9.
... Church of Aberbrothock or, 60.
... Kirkton of, 38, 62.

INDEX.   449

Salmon exportation in 18th century, 196-7.
"Sandpots, The," Arbroath, 38.
School Wynd, Arbroath, 59, 93.
Schools in Arbroath, 58, 85, 93, 239. 244-5, 310, 383, 397, 410, 418; Grammar School (established 1573), 58, 85, 93, 244-5; Academy (afterwards High School). 239, 245, 383, 397, 410, 418; Hill School, 245; Dames' Schools, 244-5; Infant School, 310; Educational Institute, 383.
Scientific and Literary Society, Arbroath. (See "Literary.")
Schort, Margareta, wife of Thomas Pierson, 157.
Scot, Robert, endows altar of St Duthacus, 37.
Scott, Sir Walter, 16, 23-6, 40, 231, 394; scenes in "The Antiquary" in Arbroath and neighbourhood, 23, 40, 231, 394, 397; visits to Arbroath and the Abbey, 25, 231.
... William, Bailie of Arbroath (1564), 157-8.
"Scotsman, The," 29, 31.
Scrimger of Dudope, 107.
Scrimgeour, Professor Henry, Genoa and Geneva, 63-5, 68; Uncle of Sir Peter Young, 63; his library bequeathed to Young, 64.
... Margaret (1510-78), mother of Sir P. Young, 63; her sister, wife of Richard Melville of Baldovy, 63.
Seaton, Easter, 70, 76, 80, 91, site of Sir P. Young's house at, 70.
... Wester, 70.
Secession from Church of Scotland (1733), 26, 226.
... Church at Dunnichen (1745), 226.
Shakespeare, First folio edition at Hospitalfield, 400.
Sharp, Archbishop, and the Arbroath Presbytery, 395.
Sharpey, Henry, Arbroath (d. 1801), 228, 232; marries Mary Balfour, 228.
... Professor William, M.D., LL.D., F.R.S. (1802-80), 27, 244-50, 263; Birthplace, 244; early education in Arbroath, 244-5; studies in Edinburgh, London, and Paris,

Sharpey—*Continued*.
245; practises in Arbroath, 245; travels on foot on the Continent, 246; studies in Berlin, 246; Extra-mural Medical Teacher in Edinburgh, 246; Professor of Anatomy, &c., University College, London, 246; with British Association at Dundee (1867), 247; entertained by Arbroath Magistrates, 247-8; resignation and Government pension, 248; as a teacher and author, 248-9; friend of Neil Arnott, 248, 263; Buried at Arbroath Abbey, 250.
Sheriffmuir, Battle of, Earl of Panmure and Harry Maule at, 133-4.
Shipping, Scottish in 1587, 73-4.
... Arbroath, 109, 186, 188.
"Shuil Breeds, The," Arbroath, 90.
Sibbald, Sir Robert, Physician to Charles II., 108.
Sinclair, Master of, "Memoirs of the Rebellion" (1715), 128.
Simpson, Rev. Robert, Kintore, Professor in Aberdeen, 289.
Skirving, Adam, author of "Johnnie Cope," 408-9.
... Archibald, painter of Burns' Portrait, 409.
Slezer's view of Arbroath (1693), 93, 109.
Southesk, Earl of, in the '15, 129-30, 133.
... Earl of (6th), 202.
Southey's "Inchcape Bell," 25-6.
Spence, John, town clerk, Montrose (1715), 131.
Spynie, Lord (1st), Alexander Lindsay. (See "Lindsay.")
.. Lord, title claimed by Wm. Fullerton Lindsay, 208.
Somervil, Alexander, judge at Walter Myln's trial, 51.
Stamp, Adhesive Postage. (See "Chalmers, James")
Stanhope, Sir Edward, of Grimstone, 124.
Stethoscope, the invention of, 241-2.
Stevenson, civil engineer (1817), 213.
... Rev. William, minister of Arbroath (1835-44), 286-7, 309.

Steward of Scotland, Walter, 16.
Stewart of Innermeath, 107.
... of Rosyth (Fife), 107.
Stewart, Jamie, Dr Guthrie's first teacher, 288.
... Walter, Earl of Athole, 118.
Stocking-making in Arbroath, 195.
Stone - planing machines invented by James Hunter, 211.
Story, Rev. Professor Herbert; "Life of Dr Robert Lee," 305, 309, 314.
Strachan, Alexander, of Tarry (1838), 188.
... James, of Thornton, 209.
... Mary Elizabeth, wife of J. F. Lindsay-Carnegie (1786), 209.
Straiton, Ayrshire, 318-9, 331-2.
Stratherne, Earl of, 16.
Strathmiglo (Fife), 381.
Strathmore, Earl of (1st), in the '15, 125-6, 129-30, 133.
Stuart, James (VIII.), Chevalier de St George, 126-35; Earl Panmure's Letter to, 126; Mar's Rebellion (the '15), 126-35; arrived in Scotland, 134; at Brechin Castle, 134; progress through Forfarshire, 134; embarks at Montrose for France, 135.
... Rebellions and Plots. (See "Jacobite.")
Sunday Funerals discountenanced, 336-7.
Sutherland, Earl of (1320), 16.
Sweden, Principal Lumsden and, 342.
Swedish Agricultural Students in Scotland, 342.
Sym, Rev. John, Old Greyfriars, Edinburgh, 299, 313.

Tankerville, Earl of (6th), 149.
Tannadice, 53, 58.
Tarry, North, 70, 87, 416.
... South, 89.
Telegraphing without wires, 361.
Ten Years' Conflict. (See "Church of Scotland" and "Free Church of Scotland.")
Thackeray's Ballad on Professor M'Cosh's appointment, 325.
Thomson, David, an Arbroath Scientist, 418.

Thomson, James, the Poet, a friend of Wm. Aikman, 177.
... James; "History of Abbey of Aberbrothock," 104.
Tithes of "Sybboes, leeks," &c., petition for discharge of (1574), 60.
Town Clerks, Arbroath: Jas. Pierson, 89, 160; John Ouchterlony, 94; David Mudie, 188.
... Council, Magistrates, and Councillors of Arbroath, 20-1, 59, 86-9, 91, 99, 109, 157-8, 172-3, 184-8, 191, 193, 197-8, 201, 214, 216-7, 227, 245, 248, 251-3, 292, 384, 401, 405; members (1624-7), 86-7; the Magistrates abused (1692), 99; Earl of Panmure had election of first Bailie, 109; Magistrates raise Jacobite Company in the '15, 130; precautions against the pest (1566), 172; a lady scolds the Magistrates (1693), 173; power to elect Dean of Guild (1724), 184; Council largely composed of Wallaces, 184-5; power to levy duty on Ale (1738), 186-7; an impecunious Council, 188; feuing of lands to members of Council, 191; sub-let Abbey House for thread factory, 193; action against Council for misapplying revenues (1766), 197-8; Sir David Carnegie a Councillor (1781), 201; Magistrates entertain Professor Sharpey (1867), 247-8.
... House, Arbroath, rebuilding of, 186.
Tweedmouth, 303-6.
Tyndall's New Testament in Forfarshire, 47.

Union, The (1707), Effect of, on Scottish Trade, 190.
University College, London, 246-8, 250.
Upper Dysart. (See "Lunan.")

Valoniis, Christian de, marries (1224) Sir Peter Mauie, 116.
... Philip, acquires Panmure, 116.
... Sir William, 116.
Vans, Sir Patrick, of Barnbarroch, 71-4.

INDEX.

Wilson—*Continued.*
education, 346-7; alter, 16.
work in Glasgow, 07.
settlement in Carmyllie
appoint him minister, 3; e's first teacher,
351; evictions of non-
site for Church refused,
in open air, in barns, 95-
354-6; called to Dundee, 35 by James
of Free Church Assembly,
of Assembly, 358. e of Dr
Wood trade in Arbroath (1737), 19 188.

YONG, Wylliame, of Ouchterlony (1392),
Young, Alexander, usher to James VI., 63.
... Sir James, son of Sir Peter Young, 69, 89.
... John, Dundee (d. 1583), father of Sir Peter Young, 63.
... John, brother of Sir Peter Young, 63.
... Sir Peter, of Seaton (1544-1628), 27, 63-80, 89, 107; his mother, Margaret Scrimgeour, 63; his uncle, Professor Henry Scrimgeour, 63-5: studies in

Thomson, James, the Poet, a friend of Wm. Aikman, 177.
... James; "History of Abbey of Aberbrothock," 104.
Tithes of "Sybboes, leeks," &c., petition for discharge of (1574), 60.
Town Clerks, Arbroath : Jas. Pierson, 89, 160; John Ouchterlony, 94; David Mudie, 188.
... Council, Magistrates, and Councillors of Arbroath, 20-1, 59, 86-9, 91, 99, 109, 157-8, 172-3, 184-8, 191, 193, 197-8, 201, 214, 216-7, 227, 245, 248, 251-3, 292, 384, 401, 405; members (1624-7), 86-7; the Magistrates abused (1692), 99; Earl of Panmure had election of first bailie 109; Magistrates raise Jacobite there, 79. the '15, 130; precautions
... Peter, grandson of 1566), 172; a lady 90. 3), 173; power
... Robert, of Auldbar, 96, 99, 100, 184;

ZANZIBAR, Sir John Kirk, British Consul at, 30.

..., 29, 86,
... er in Arbroath (1738), 185.
... eth, wife of Bailie David Arnott, Arbroath, 252.
James, 1st Dean of Guild, Arbroath (circa 1724), 184, 252.
John, Town Councillor, Arbroath (1624), 86.
John, of Wallace Craigie (1715), 131.
John, Provost of Arbroath (1727-8), 184-5.
John, Shipmaster, Town Councillor, Arbroath (1738), 185.
John, Provost of Arbroath (1738-41), 183-200, 252; public offices held by him, 184-5; engaged in flax trade, linen manufacture, and shipping, 188-90; trade with Riga, 189; first manufacture of Osnaburgs, 189-90; in timber trade, 191-2; gets feu for windmill near harbour, 191; consequent litigation, 191, 197; exports grain, 192; leases Abbey House for thread factory, 193; stocking making, 195; exports herring and salmon, 196-7; his house in High Street, 199; first drawing-room in Arbroath, 199; his son in the army, 199; a large order for hats, 199.

and

Arbroat...
... Arbroath, 18...
... broath in ...
... ower of Lond...
... of Bailie Patri...
... er of London, 18...
27, 105, History ...
... anmure, 124.
Provost of Arbroath
... 9), 184-5.
... m, C.M.G., F.R.G.S., Ad...
Royal Niger Company, 29-31.
"War-wolf, The," an engine of ...
117.
Warden's Angus or Forfarshire, 22...
Wardmill, 416.
Wareslap Schede, Arbroath, 86.
Watson, Hugh, of Keillor, 374-6.
... Janet, wife of Thomas Arnott,
... Richard, Arbroath (1605), 85.
... Richard (d. 1829), minister o...
291-3; assistant minister of ...
(1773-90), 292; his pulpit bi...
... Thomas, an Arbroath Poet, 23...
... Rev. ——, Embleton, pr...
Carmyllie, 349.
Waverley Novels, 23, 40, 231, ...
illustrated by P. Allan-Fraser, ...
Whitelaw, William, Chalmers' appr...
Whitworth, ——, C.E. (1788), 21...
William the Lion, King of Scotl...
37, 109, 111, 116, 118, 393...
of Arbroath Abbey, 12, 109, ...
Court at Abbey, 13; buried ...
13; gifts Ethie to the Abbey ...
Willison, John, minister of Dunde...
Wilson, Alexander, husband of Susa...
101.
... Patrick, bookseller, Arbroath, 2...
... Rev. William, D.D. (1808-88) ...
of Carmyllie, 286, 341, 345...
Joint Editor of "The Presbyter...
born at Blawearie, Berwicksh...

www.ingramcontent.com/pod-product-compliance
Lightning Source LLC
Chambersburg PA
CBHW021424300426
44114CB00010B/635